# TOWARDS A SOCIAL ARCHITECTURE

Stirrat Johnson-Marshall (1912–81), the architectural inspirer, enabler and eminence of English post-war school-building. A portrait photograph of 1952.

# TOWARDS A SOCIAL ARCHITECTURE

## THE ROLE OF SCHOOL-BUILDING IN POST-WAR ENGLAND

Andrew Saint

Yale University Press
New Haven and London 1987

In memory of Stirrat Johnson-Marshall, Dan Lacey and Hugh Morris, three architects who believed in social purposes for their profession.

Designed by Mary Carruthers
Set in Linotron Bembo, printed and bound by
The Bath Press, Avon

**Library of Congress Cataloguing-in-Publication Data**

Saint, Andrew
  Towards a Social Architecture.
  Includes index.
  1. School buildings—Great Britain.  2. Great
Britain—Social conditions—1945–    I. Title.
LB3219.G7S25  1987    690′.7′0941    86-28179
ISBN 0-300-03830-5

# PREFACE AND ACKNOWLEDGEMENTS

This book began in the following way. After the death of Stirrat Johnson-Marshall in December 1981 friends and colleagues, spurred on by Hugh Morris, considered whether some fitting tribute to his career might not be written. They agreed that an orthodox biography would be wrong for a man who shunned publicity for himself and was in everything he did a collaborator. They felt also that a straightforward account of the English★ post-war school-building movement, in which he had been the architectural protagonist, would not be the right aim. They resolved instead that the book should set out the architectural ideals, principles and methods which informed public-sector building in Britain after the Second World War, explain how and why these enjoyed special success in school-building, and indicate in what ways they still mattered and required restating for the future good of architecture. Hence the title, slant and structure of the book.

In due course a committee formed itself, consisting of Colin Boyne, Sir Anthony Cox, (Sir) Andrew Derbyshire, Percy Johnson-Marshall, John Kay, Dan Lacey, David Medd, Hugh Morris and Henry Swain. (Two members of this group, Dan Lacey and Hugh Morris, have since died; their names are linked with Stirrat Johnson-Marshall's in this book's dedication.) Some preparatory discussion and work ensued, co-ordinated by Colin Boyne. In 1983 I was invited to take on research and writing for the project. Through the generosity and broad vision of my late-lamented employer, the Greater London Council, I was permitted leave of absence from my work for its Historic Buildings Division for the first six months of 1984 in order to concentrate full-time on the commission. During this period and sporadically thereafter the shape and contents of the book were thrashed out in frequent collaboration with the committee, collectively and singly. I should like to put on record the enthusiasm and *rapport* generated in these discussions. I had not worked seriously before on the history of post-war architecture in Britain. It was necessary for me to learn. That process was one of the happiest and most illuminating periods of learning that I can recall.

This book therefore, like the buildings which it discusses, is the fruit of collaboration. Some gloss on this statement may be helpful. The committee indicated principles and a broad interpretation to which I was able to assent wholeheartedly. But I was left free to follow my own bent, pursue the subject in whatever direction I chose, structure the book as I wished and impose my own judgement upon any set of events. Drafts were widely circulated and a major revision of the text took place in 1985–6. Often I heeded criticisms but sometimes I did not. Responsibility for all views and errors must be deemed to be mine.

I would like to draw attention to two particular points. Firstly, this book seeks neither to cover the whole history of post-war school-building in Britain nor to constitute any sort of official record. For a fuller educational and national picture, the reader may wish to consult Stuart Maclure's *Educational Development and School Building* (1984). Maclure's book was conceived as a memorial to the educationist John Newsom, just as this book memorializes the architect Stirrat Johnson-Marshall; it may be hoped that the two books complement each other. Secondly, all the buildings discussed and illustrated in the following pages are the work of co-operation. Where it seems pertinent and informative, 'job architects'

★ The words 'English' and 'England' are used throughout the text as a shorthand for 'English and Welsh', 'England and Wales', for which I pray Welsh readers may forgive me. Since educational arrangements in Scotland are different, there is little reference to that country in this book. Where post-war building in general (as opposed to school-building in particular) is referred to, the words 'British' and 'Britain' are used.

are identified in captions or in the text, in order to pierce the shroud of anonymity which envelops public-sector architecture. But it is worth emphasizing that teamwork of this kind has no clear boundaries. The educationists, engineers, building workers and other technicians who helped to shape the buildings discussed are as much their creators as the architects. It has been feasible to mention only a few even of the architects involved in each project. I have striven to be fair and accurate, but apologies are offered in advance for inevitable omissions.

The nature and subject of the book have left me with many and deep obligations. First and foremost thanks must go to Colin Boyne and Gill Collymore, who have wrestled with the administrative complexities of the project for five years and given unremitting support and friendship. Over and above those on the 'committee', I interviewed many people and discussed the book's progress and drafts with many others. Special thanks are due to Joan and Jeremy Johnson-Marshall for their tolerance and sensitivity, and to Cleeve Barr, Oliver Cox, Lister Heathcote, Mary Medd and Guy Oddie for particular help and encouragement. Those who kindly provided recollections and views included Alan and Bryan Adams, William Allen, Sydney Bell, Kenneth Campbell, Elizabeth Chesterton, Denis Clarke Hall, Geoffrey Fardell, Sir Donald Gibson, William Glare, Ernö Goldfinger, Michael Hacker, Sir Alan Harris, Birkin Haward, the late Gerald Holtom, Ralph Hopkinson, Lord James of Rusholme, Maurice Lee, Max Lock, Cyril Mardall, Len Marsh, Bruce Martin, Alan Meikle, Edith Moorhouse, Henry C. Morris, Vasco de Moura, Peter Newnham, James Nisbet, Patrick Nuttgens, John Onslow, Sir Antony Part, Sir William Pile, Jack Platt, Fred Pooley, Harry Rée, Pat Tindale and John West-Taylor. Others who have helped at various stages of the project include John Carter, Freddie Charles, Dennis Claude, Ray Eisenstark, Rosemary Ellis, James Gardner, Robert Gardner-Medwin, Colin Giffard, David Gregory-Jones, Tim Holtom, Quentin Hughes, Douglas Jones, Judy Millett, John Morton, Graham Parker, Colin Penn, Jack Pritchard, Trevor Prosser and Joseph Rykwert. Among those of a younger generation I had invaluable advice in the early stages from Steven Groak and Patrick Hannay. Michael Keath was generous in allowing me to plunder freely his researches on the technical side of the Hertfordshire schools, while I have had helpful discussions or correspondence with Dan Cruickshank, Peter Davey, Charlotte Ellis, Ellen Leopold, Jules Lubbock, Rodney Mace, Martha Matzke, Ruth Owens, Steve Parsons, Patricia Potts, Alan Powers, Denise Riley, Barry Russell, Gavin Stamp, Hetty Startup, Deborah Thom, Robert Thorne and Deborah Weiner. Some of the photographs were specially taken by Martin Charles, while the drawings and diagrams were contributed by Alan Fagan and David Medd. Jane Fulton did some invaluable typing at a crucial stage, while Mary Carruthers, Gillian Malpass and John Nicoll at Yale University Press have been efficient and fun to work with.

I am greatly indebted to the Architectural Press, which for a period undertook the role of host and 'banker' to the project, and to Maritz Vandenberg for his considerable efforts on our behalf. The book would not have happened without generous financial aid from a number of institutions and individuals: Andrews-Weatherfoil Ltd.; British Gypsum Ltd.; Nottinghamshire County Council; the CLASP Development Group; Robert Matthew, Johnson-Marshall and Partners (London and Edinburgh offices); the Norwich Union Group; Richard Rogers Partnership; Shapland and Petter; and Cecil Elsom. Both the *Architects' Journal* and the *Architectural Review* have contributed bountifully to the project, while special grants from Peter Palumbo and the Radcliffe Trust have helped to make its publication more economic. Over and above these, Hertfordshire and Nottinghamshire County Councils and the Department of Education and Science's Architects and Buildings Branch were invariably responsive to my repeated requests for help, particularly in connection with plans and photographs. Others who have helped in this respect include Cambridgeshire County Council, the Consortium for Method Building, and CLASP International.

I must finally thank teachers and children in all the schools I visited for letting me watch them in action and learn about school-building in the best possible way – by observation.

Andrew Saint
September 1986

# CONTENTS

# INTRODUCTION

The adventure of the 'Modern Movement', the coherence of architectural expression and belief which lasted from the 1920s to the 1970s, is over. No chapter in the long history of building has been so pored over, so much acclaimed, debated or, latterly, reviled as this, its most recent one. But as the passions of the period cool and the circumstances that engendered them recede, we still comprehend little about this sea change in the making and shaping of buildings. Up till now, architects and their orthodox chroniclers have told us chiefly about stars and styles, about the landmarks upon the map of modernism and the transmission of images. From a harsher, longer standpoint we see architecture pressed in the cities of the post-war world into a multitude of institutional services, until its progress and reputation have become so bound up with wider social forces and issues as almost to lose independent identity or history. About the connections between these processes and therefore about the real successes and failures of the twentieth century's new ways of building, we still have only the crudest notions.

Somewhere between the blinkered tradition of judging buildings by appearance alone and a perspective of such social breadth as to allow no focus at all, a fuller, richer history of modern architecture will, with the benefit of study and hindsight, emerge. But those in the best position to learn from that history cannot afford to wait for it. It is in the belief that there are practical, positive lessons yet to be learnt from the annals of modernism that this book is written, at perhaps its subject's lowest ebb of reputation. It aims to provide a record, before memories fail and participants die, of one remarkable attempt to put the fullest possible interpretation of the Modern Movement into effect, and to point some morals from that effort.

At the heart of the book is a field of endeavour which made no great architectural reputations and produced no masterpieces in the conventional sense: English school-building of the post-war years. Some readers will find this puzzling. But the book's real subject is not school-building itself but a particular attitude of mind, an approach towards architecture which bore most fruit in educational building. It was able to do so because of the coming-together of many things: the Modern Movement, a puritan strain in British philosophy and design, the needs, constraints, opportunities and organization of post-war reconstruction, and the triumph of fresh thought about childhood, teaching and learning. How this came about and who were the men and women responsible for it make up the matter of the book's central chapters. Yet the school-builders stand for more than the schools they built. Because their practical work grew out of a radical enquiry into the ends of architecture, it has implications not so much for the future school-builder (since chances rarely recur) as for any architect, policy-maker, manufacturer or layman brave enough to take up the most ambitious architectural challenge of all—the making of buildings of real benefit to society.

One of the great ambitions of the twentieth century has been to find ways of sharing the proceeds of material, technical and cultural development equitably among all. In architecture, this was the driving social dynamic behind the Modern Movement, at constant odds with issues of style, meaning and appearance. This book traces the history of one such quest. It is about a small group of people who sought fair shares for all in building, and made it their business to get themselves into positions where they could work effectively to that end. At present we are going through a reaction against such a scale of social ambition—a reaction felt nowhere more strongly than in architecture and planning because of shortcomings in the post-war building record. It is this which has driven so much architectural ambition and discussion back upon surface, personality and the individual project. But the circumstances in which most building takes place, the world over, belie these preoccupations. Pressures of population and politics and the limited resources of every country, developed and developing, make the search for a just way of building more urgent than ever.

We have therefore to try and understand the achievements and the errors of the best previous efforts to build imaginatively and responsibly for all, not just for a few. That is why English school-building or, more precisely, the work of those who dominated this field for the three post-war decades, is important. It was the fullest expression of the movement for a social architecture in Britain which gathered pace in the 1930s and found its outlet in the service of the post-war welfare state. No more ambitious, disciplined, self-conscious or far-reaching application of the concept of architecture as social service can be found in any western country. More than any other modern programme of building, the English schools fulfilled Walter Gropius's ideals about an architecture which should be simple, practical, universal and imaginative. The programme faced problems of policy, cost, technology, education, organization, production and style. Each of these issues was addressed by recourse to a set of priorities and principles. On slender resources, a new school was finished every day in England and Wales between 1950 and 1970. Yet practically none was built to a uniform pattern, and most enjoyed space, facilities and a quality of environment unimagined before the war. Reservations can be—and are in the course of the following pages—expressed about this achievement. But a plain claim may at the outset be ventured. Good was done and opportunities were brought to the lives of the post-war generations of English teachers and children as an outcome of the continuous round of co-operation which informed the school-building programme.

This book, it has been said, is concerned with an approach to architecture, with certain principles about the making of buildings. It is about how designers may work justly and creatively with others, whether fellow-designers, manufacturers, builders, administrators, clients or users; how technology in building may be controlled and directed to advantage; and how buildings may be conceived not as individual, sufficient entities but as items in a concerted programme of production which allows fair shares for all while also leaving room for continuity, development, improvement and variety. In sum, it is about ideas for making architecture more responsible and more effective in modern life.

As yet we have only the haziest of historical notions about how these ideas entered architectural currency in Britain during the 1930s and '40s. For this reason, the early chapters focus upon the consciousness of young British architects in the years before the Second World War and upon the impact of their experiences in the war. These sections amount only to a sketch, enough to give outline to the spirit in which socially minded architects grasped the opportunity of post-war reconstruction. From here the book moves on the school-building, its circumstances, concepts and record from the 1930s to the 1970s. Again, these chapters are not intended to be complete; for a general account of post-war school-building the reader may turn to Stuart Maclure's estimable *Educational Development and School Building* (1984). Instead they look discursively and with a degree of technical detail at the centres (chiefly Hertfordshire, Nottinghamshire and the Ministry of Education) where the critical ideas were most strenuously explored, and at the people who did most to explore them, above all Stirrat Johnson-Marshall. The final section reverts to issues of principle. It enquires why school-building proved a more fertile ground for these methods than other spheres of architecture, particularly housing; and it hazards directions which the methods may take in the future, following the collapse of the British public-building programmes and of the consensus in architectural direction.

I have opted to write the book, for the most part, in narrative and personal form. There are several reasons for this choice. In the absence of any comprehensive, analytic history of British post-war architecture, I felt it important to proffer an outline of what happened and in what order. In addition, since many of the protagonists in the movement for a social architecture in Britain are still living, the opportunity for vivid, oral testimony presented itself and I have seized upon it gratefully. It might have been subordinated to a more objective mode of writing, dominated by the plethoric documentation available. But in the end policies, programmes and buildings alike remain the responsibility of individuals. Economic and political pressures are far from ignored in what follows, but they appear as forces which individual architects and others strove to comprehend, control or take advantages from, rather than as inexorable determinants. Furthermore, the public sector in British architectural practice has been too often and easily portrayed as faceless and lifeless. In school-building, at any rate, the reality was quite otherwise; no other sphere of post-war architectural endeavour could boast figures of such determination and conviction. Some contributions may have been overemphasized, and others have certainly been underplayed. But by dwelling on the experience and recollections of those who took part in the school-building programmes, I have tried to break through the veil of anonymity which shrouds most discussion of 'public architecture' in Britain.

Perhaps this approach may in some small measure help to bridge the gap between the facile kind of talk which treats buildings as the intellectual and artistic property of individual architects working in isolation, and the cold social science which has sterilized so much writing on the post-war environment in Britain. The vast experiment in post-war public building, we are slowly coming to realize, was the biggest and most radical adventure ever undertaken in the history of British architecture. It has to be made lively and accessible if it is to be understood and learnt from. And learnt from it must be. How the advances of civilization and technology may fairly be shared among all remains on the agenda for all those genuinely concerned with architecture and building, as it does for all nations and political systems.

# PART I

# IDEALS AND ANTECEDENTS

# CHAPTER 1

# BEFORE THE WAR

'We were born in the war.' So opens the first, radical issue of *Focus*, the short-lived magazine which burst upon British architecture in the summer of 1938 (Fig. 1.1). It was to turn out to be a more poignant declaration than its youthful authors could then appreciate. A generation of aspiring architects and students, born before, during and after the crass and bloody conflict of 1914–18, found their ambitions defined, their attitudes deepened and their tasks made manifest by the subtler struggle of 1939–45.

Of this the editors of *Focus*, standing close to the abyss, had some presentiment:

> We were born in the war ... We were born into a civilisation whose leaders, whose ideals, whose culture had failed. They are still in power to-day. But we, the generation who follow, cannot accept their domination. They lead us always deeper into reaction that we are convinced can only end in disaster. We have set out to produce a journal where we can develop our still chaotic ideas on the foundations of those built by certain older men (in age, not spirit) who early in this century had realised contemporary problems.

## STIRRINGS IN THE SCHOOLS

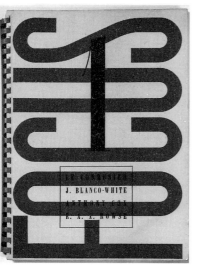

1.1. *Focus:* the first number, 1938. A laminated cover (designed by Oliver Cox), an up-to-the-minute spiral binding, and a name redolent of purpose and intensity after the manner of *Scrutiny*.

Most of the students who founded *Focus* hailed from the Architectural Association, then the smartest and liveliest of Britain's schools of architecture. Here it was that the intellectual iconoclasm of the 1930s, heightened by the decay of European politics and culture, penetrated furthest into British architectural thought, transforming the designer's traditional alertness to changes of fashion and function into something deeper. Together with the Liverpool School of Architecture, where a similar transition took place almost by stealth, the AA trained most of the leaders of post-war architectural practice, private and public. The two schools offer a fit starting point from which to survey the birth and growth of the post-war movement for a 'social architecture' in Britain.

The AA had started in 1849 as a gathering-place for students dissatisfied with the deficiencies of architectural pupillage, and matured by slow degrees. It grew in status from the Edwardian period, after architectural training in general was better organized and recognized. Following the First World War, the AA entered upon a golden phase which lasted some forty years. It never offered so systematic or elegant a training as some of the newer university schools of architecture. But its constitution and atmosphere were consistently informal, its debates animated, its teachers young and fashionable, its students privileged and self-confident. Until the 1950s few pupils came from anything but private schools; before then, the interview was chiefly 'to determine whether your father's wallet was full enough'. The AA was strategically located too in a handsome Georgian square in the heart of London, where architects, students and others met on terms of equality. It was, in fact, a club as well as a school of architecture: 'one felt one was joining the profession, not a school,' recalls an alumnus.

As successive Directors of Education, Robert Atkinson and Howard Robertson did much to build up the AA in the 1920s and early '30s. They were undogmatic architects and devoted teachers who believed in a watered-down version of the French approach to architectural instruction. Students were given their heads, so long as they got a grasp of construction, classical proportion and drawing technique. In style, Atkinson and Robertson applauded the sundry Scandinavian, Dutch and American successes in breaking out of the Beaux-Arts strait-jacket. They cared less for contemporary German architecture or Le Corbusier's early work, but they were broad-minded in comparison with teachers at most other British schools.

Methods of teaching at the AA remained conservative until the mid 1930s. Students were taught in self-contained years, worked little with their seniors and juniors, and cut their teeth individually on 'ideal' projects set by their year-masters. 'An Admiral's House on a Rocky Promontory' was a notorious, perhaps mythical, design programme. If most subjects were less ludicrous, few trespassed upon the greyer or grimmer tracts of an increasingly complex world, as it appeared to the more percipient students after the Crash of 1929. The world of British architectural training was still an isolated one. Robertson was a gentleman who expected to preside over 'gentlemen': with sufferance too over 'ladies', as they started to filter into Bedford Square. The products of the school, it was assumed, would in due course advance to become principals in the small private practices and partnerships which helped themselves to the icing on the cake of British construction: individual houses, large civic and commercial buildings, churches, and the more prestigious schemes for schools and housing.

All this started to change from the time of Hitler's rise to power in 1933. There ensued a period, in John Summerson's words, of 'much experiment, some uncertainty, and a renewed stirring of dry bones'. A trickle of refugee architects, mostly Germans, began arriving in London. A few had known the Bauhaus during its vibrant Dessau years, more had taken a hand in the brief flowering of German reconstruction during the later 1920s, and almost all had some inkling of what Walter Gropius christened 'total architecture'—a phrase encompassing functionalism, social purpose and co-operative endeavour. Many had suffered to the point of exile for this commitment. For them the new architecture stood not for a pleasant professional pursuit but for a cause and a way of life, applicable to everything and available to all.

It took time for these views to percolate. Architects, even budding ones, do not read a lot; they prefer designs and images to kindle their enthusiasm. Before the mid 1930s little that was explicit or coherent had been set down on these subjects—and what had been written, like the later writings of Lethaby, was out of vogue. Le Corbusier's rash manifestos, memorably *Vers une architecture* (translated in 1927), provided the brand to light the fire. But the exiles, not at first through writing but through word of mouth, friendship and teaching, did much to pile on the slow-burning fuel which in due course was to burst out into flame.

At the AA, the first sign of a shift came when E. A. A. Rowse arrived from Edinburgh to become Assistant Director of Education in 1933. An enthusiast and communicator more than an architect, Rowse (Fig. 1.2) was an internationalist in outlook and a believer in planning, in social theory, in research, science and 'Taylorist' managerial efficiency. At the time these attributes were practically unheard of in a British architectural school. One of the 'certain older men' alluded to in *Focus*, Patrick Geddes, the numinous Scots philosopher of planning, had influenced Rowse profoundly. The perception of groups, institutions and cities as 'biological' organisms which had to be broken down to an optimum size; the 'diagnostic' habit of understanding pattern, behaviour and movement, whether in a room, a building or an urban agglomeration, before offering a design solution; in sum, the ideal of reintegrating art and science in architecture through a proper study of human nature: these were all Geddesian doctrines which Rowse zealously relayed to his students. At first the novelty baffled them, but the lessons found their mark in the end:

> The thing he used to talk about was what he called the 'action sequence', which was trying to analyse what people did when they entered a room, or when they worked in a kitchen or made a bed. And he made some of us anyway always think in these terms—whether things in the kitchen were in reach, whether two people could go through

1.2.  E. A. A. Rowse at arms: a wartime photograph.

a door together, whether that was important. It all sounds terribly simple and obvious, but it wasn't then. People weren't thinking in those terms, not as students at all.

Besides being a sympathizing and energizing spirit who raised our sights from the building to the community, Rowse rubbed into us, in a way we are unlikely ever to forget, the fact that design is based on the activities of man—man with a certain length of stride and a certain amount of reach, whose actions and comfort (rather than abstractions like circulation, symmetry and unresolved duality) could be the generator of architectural dispositions.

He argued that the optimum human group was of the order of ten or twelve. He instanced the Roman army, where an officer commanded ten men, and then each man commanded ten and so on, and also the twelve apostles. He also held that until we knew the proper grouping of human beings all the way up the scale, you couldn't design a cowhouse. So the first job was to understand how humans work together and how their groupings are arranged.

## REBELLION

When Howard Robertson resigned from the AA in 1935, an administrative reshuffle took place. Rowse became Principal, and also persuaded the AA Council to let him start a graduate school of planning nearby, the School for Planning and Research for National Development. Thereafter most of his energies were devoted to this, the precursor of the Association for Planning and Regional Reconstruction. As a counter-weight, H. S. Goodhart-Rendel became part-time Director of Education. This turned out to be a disastrous pairing. Rowse, for all his enthusiasm about organization, lacked administrative *savoir faire* and levity. Goodhart-Rendel was acutely individualistic, a practically able architect in the gentlemanly tradition, a snob, a mordant wit, and a profound respecter of history. Though broad-minded about style, he despised the newer ideas about collaborative teaching and practice. His stubbornness was to prove inflammatory: 'He was too clever for the students—they did not appreciate his sarcasm and wit. He spoke in paradoxes and they thought they were being got at.'

Between 1936 and 1939 the AA underwent polarization, as Goodhart-Rendel strove to stem the results of changes unleashed by Rowse. These were symptoms of a wider mood of excitement, restlessness and anger which spread further as the international situation deteriorated. This tension was far from unproductive. On taking control, Rowse reorganized the school's five years into fifteen units of a size which, in the Geddesian manner, he decided was best for teaching. Educationally, the 'unit system' proved stimulating. The different years, which were scattered throughout the units, began exchanging ideas and older students were able to help younger ones. The units also started to work collectively, to take on bigger, more serious projects for longer periods, and to build up experience of research instead of accepting an unquestioned brief. In this arrangement of 'group working' lay the germ of the 'development group', a key concept in post-war British architecture.

By 1938–9 the stronger units were working in some independence on an unprecedented range of 'social' projects. One team spent two years on a new-town study, first made in the abstract, then applied to a site at Farringdon and christened 'Tomorrow Town' by Rowse, 'rather to the group's disgust'. Personal links with the Mass Observation study, then at its height, drew others into techniques of social recording. One unit studied farming and village communities in the Wantage area; another teamed up with a Mass Observation enquiry into suburban London, surveying.working-class houses in a set of streets in Fulham and detailing not only the buildings but also occupancy, patterns of movement, diet and so on. Under Max Lock, a young Quaker architect who had drunk deep of the Geddesian spring, one group even secured from the London County Council an East End 'clearance area', Ocean Street in Stepney, for semi-official study and reconstruction. There were street meetings in Stepney, tenants were ferried up to the AA by car to discuss the proposals, and the scheme might have gone further had it not been for the war. Today these experiments seem slight and commonplace, perhaps also naive and presumptuous. At the time they were revolutionary within a British school of architecture.

The new spirit went well beyond dabbling in socially or politically alluring projects. One current was the urge to improve technical knowledge so as to meet the challenges of the new European architecture. Here the better teachers could help. Douglas Jones, later successively head of the architectural schools at Birmingham and Bristol, got a group of students to build a traditional cottage—a simple expedient, but one hardly tried since Arts and Crafts days. Reginald Cottrell Butler, who was to desert architecture for sculpture, gave illuminating lectures on plastics. Cyril Sjöström (afterwards Cyril Mardall) shared his expertise in prefabricated timber housing, at a time when the capabilities of 'industrial' or 'light and dry' buildings were starting dimly to excite young architects. Others were available for occasional advice and inspiration. Memorable lectures by Aalto and a series of talks on colour by Ozenfant stimulated minds and opened eyes. Ove Arup and Felix Samuely, who between them shook the stagnant British structural engineering profession to new life in the 1930s and '40s, visited the AA now and again. The revered Lubetkin also came in on occasions to help with 'crits'. Once he picked out three students, Bruce Martin, John Madge and David Medd. They were to find out how well Tecton's drawings for the Finsbury Health Centre, then being built, served the needs of the specialized sub-contractors. Medd, who took the heating, acquired from this an invaluable practical grounding in ventilation, warming, ducting and, most important, in how men work on site. 'We got to know every bucket on that job, every scantling, every detail,' he recalls.

But there were drawbacks. By bringing in the unit system in one fell swoop rather than staggering it over several years, the tactless Rowse disrupted teaching relationships and administration. For Goodhart-Rendel and the older staff, there were other difficulties. The methods which Rowse fostered could result in a report, a model, or even a series of rough pencil sketches of the type then coming into vogue. How could they judge individual progress or instill the basic drawing skills which they deemed vital for an architect? No longer were they able to drift from drawing board to drawing board 'sketching in their urns and axes', as one student of the time put it. And all the time there were political undercurrents which bothered the AA Council.

Political activity never consumed more than a small group at the AA. But most students connected the collapse of the European democracies, the outbreak of a new architecture and the internal troubles of the school sufficiently to see some justification for a generally renewed order of things. Radicalism or at the least 'scientific humanism' therefore found broad support which the left wing ably harnessed. Their mentor was Richard Llewelyn-Davies. Aloof and a little formidable even in youth, Llewelyn-Davies (Fig. 1.3) had the edge in maturity over his contemporaries. In those days few AA students had been to university, but he had studied engineering at Cambridge and there joined the Communist Party. He soon evangelized others, notably Anthony Cox, a courteous but determined young man who became Goodhart-Rendel's frankest opponent. Llewelyn-Davies, Cox and some others took themselves off to the Marx Memorial Library in Clerkenwell for instruction, Cox remembers.

> We didn't much like the party discipline, with these awful study groups reading beastly little pamphlets almost like Jehovah's Witnesses. So (I think it was probably Richard's influence) our policy became that it was no good just going around preaching the revolution because nobody would listen to us. What we had to do was to be very good at our jobs, then people would listen. So, partly to escape the rigours of these damned political study groups, we said 'We'll work in architecture, we'll work in the school'. It was all muddled up with the potential of modern architecture not as a style (although one couldn't avoid being excited by Corb and that sort of thing) but as a social instrument—schools, housing and so forth.

The influence of this group was great and continued after they had left the school. But the socialists and communists did no more than articulate a spirit which was everywhere at work in the AA.

1.3. Richard Llewelyn-Davies at the time of the building of the wartime hostels under Holford at Swynnerton, 1942 (see page 18); Birkin Haward behind.

1.4. Ferment in Bedford Square. A drawing by Oliver Cox from *Plan*, 1948, capturing the spirit of student dissent at the immediate pre-war and post-war AA.

In 1938 the conflict came to a head, when with the AA Council's connivance Goodhart-Rendel sought to 'stamp out as far as possible the political and sociological tendencies in the school'. Fernand Billerey, a Frenchman who had built his best work before the First World War, was appointed as temporary principal in place of Rowse, who resigned or was dismissed (though he retained office for a while at his planning school). Open revolt, then practically unheard of, broke out among the students (Fig. 1.4); *Focus* was founded in part to give expression to their views. In the event Goodhart-Rendel proved so obdurate about reverting to a full Beaux-Arts curriculum that he and Billerey had also to go. The school was settling down under Geoffrey Jellicoe with a modified unit system when war supervened, consigning the issues to the sidelines.

## LIVERPOOL

No open strife like that at the AA took place in any other British school of architecture. In most, up to and indeed beyond the Second World War, teaching clung to its traditional course unruffled by deeper currents. There was much superficial modernization of style, but the students overwhelmingly stuck to their drawing boards, their professional horizons no higher than successful, conventional private practice.

The exception was the Liverpool University School of Architecture. There the transition from old-fashioned attitudes to a social and collaborative philosophy of design was so gradual that Liverpool-trained architects were apt in retrospect to put down the row at the AA to mere disorganization and amateurism. At the roots of Liverpool's success lay the personality and shrewd theatrics of Charles Reilly, head of the school from 1904 to 1933. Reilly was no profound teacher or designer, but he was one of the few British architectural educators of his day with any intellectual breadth. Through his influence Liverpool had acquired the country's first chair of town planning in 1908, and the links built up there between architecture and planning had become increasingly strong. By the 1930s it was the one architectural school where the course-structure induced students to relate issues of social policy and geography to their essays in design. A succession of gifted teachers encouraged this. Stanley Adshead was the first; then came Patrick Abercrombie, then William Holford—a figure at the centre of much post-war thinking on planning policy—and his ally Gordon Stephenson. During the decade, as the tempo of social change quickened, graduates from Liverpool started getting jobs in the nascent public sector in architecture because they had thought about these things, however primitively, when others had not.

There was nothing *avant garde* about the typical 'Liverpool school' building of the 1930s. Indeed a certain Beaux-Arts idiom persisted in many of its students' architectural and

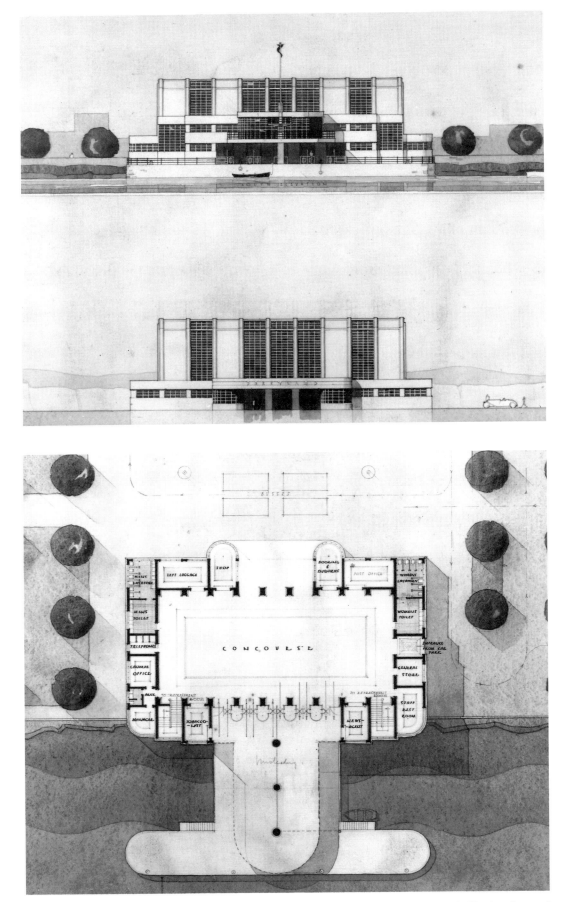

1.5. A Liverpool School of Architecture student project of the 1930s: Stirrat Johnson-Marshall's elevations and plan for a lakeside ferry station, 1933.

planning projects (Fig. 1.5). But their work, or at any rate the work of those who had ears to hear, was informed by an awakening conception of how architecture might serve society, reinforced by daily sight of a noble city scarred—then as now—by depression and by moral and social evils. A procession of celebrities bearing news of what had been tried in Europe, only to be expunged, quickened hearts and minds: Mendelsohn, Chermayeff and, in 1934, Walter Gropius. For two young architect-brothers, Stirrat and Percy Johnson-Marshall, Gropius's visit was a turning point:

> Gropius gave us what we thought was the clue to the problem that had been eluding us, and the secret lay perhaps in two areas of thought. One was the fallacy of the styles continued from the battles of the previous century, which had muddled first Le Corbusier and then his less gifted followers ever since; and the second was the need to come to terms with the Industrial Revolution and learn the secrets of its methods and techniques. With this was coupled the idea that architecture was for everyone, and that architects should focus their attention not on the rich, with their mansions and banks and clubs, but on the poor, and the large-scale housing, schools and community building which flowed from that human objective. The problem which Gropius elucidated so clearly was the absolute necessity to think in entirely different terms if one were to turn from the concept of architecture for the few to that of the many. This had already happened in the nineteenth century, from pins to machines, and the secret lay in the industrial approach to manufacture and the methods and techniques employed . . .

> The immediate impact of Gropius faded away, but his thought was indelibly implanted in our minds. Here was the real and deep solution to the problem of creating 'modern' architecture. No instant new style was possible, although in a hundred years architectural historians might identify it. Instead, there was the steady step-by-step approach in changing building basically from a craft to an industrial process, with the objective of the total scope of architecture before us. It was a blenching process, especially for members of a profession who had had a new personal style as a desirable fulfilment . . .

## SCIENCE

The charisma of teachers like Gropius and Rowse, the sharpening of wits as a by-product of faction, the trauma of national slump and international foreboding: all these left their mark on an impressionable youth in the two leading British schools of architecture. War, the psychology and organization of war, and the pledges made in war, were to release some of the tension built up in this period and open up possibilities barely glimpsed at that time. But before we see how this happened, it is helpful to glance at the context of the new British architectural dreams of the late 1930s and trace how a few key ideas were filtering into the slow-moving consciousness of architecture and building.

The 1930s in Britain witnessed an explosion in the popular advocacy of scientific thought. This sprang most immediately from scientists themselves. An exceptional group of Cambridge-trained scientists, mostly socialists or 'humanists' and including J. D. Bernal, Joseph Needham, J. B. S. Haldane, Julian Huxley, Hyman Levy and Lancelot Hogben, clamoured for a better understanding of science, wider application of its methods and a just use of its social powers. These ideas were far from new. They had been current in thought since the time of Comte and Spencer; within the academies there was no lack of debate about the limitations of scientific method, the irresponsibility of scientific power and the sterility of scientific 'reductionism'. But the popular impact of science was at its height during the 1930s and '40s. Among intellectuals it affected the whole basis of discourse.

The implications of 'scientific method' were as wide as anyone wished them to be. It could mean that all problems and propositions—in building, for instance, briefs, materials and techniques—had to be re-examined from first principles. More broadly, it could imply a shift in the values assigned to the different procedures followed in physical planning and building. Identification of the problem, research, analysis and organization had to precede design, which previously had been the first stage to meet with most architects' conscious consideration. Beyond this again, science was able to set out more sharply than ever before the vision of a planned society: not just one which was equitable and efficient, the goals of the Fabian gradualists, but a society in which planning and building would be key elements in the reasoned distribution and use of resources. The thought is now commonplace. But fifty years ago it had only begun to percolate beyond the academies and government departments.

To account for this spurt in consciousness of scientific ideology in Britain would need a book in itself. Here a brief sketch must suffice to set the scene for the conscious application of scientific ideas to architecture and building. Science itself had matured and grown throughout the nineteenth century, and with it scientists had increased in number and education. The improvements in statistics and information-gathering, the contraction of the world through international trade and travel, and the growing use and abuse of technology had all played their part. Above all, the First World War had proved to scientists and governments that they needed each other. It drew many articulate British scientists into regular collaboration with researchers, manufacturers, users and paymasters. Afterwards many of these programmes were dismantled and academic science, traditionally disdainful of the applied branches, regained its hegemony within the universities. But the links were far from completely severed. There were too many areas of modern life in which the government needed science. Also, some few scientists had acquired a taste for broader power and responsibilities.

Until 1929 the notion of a scientific, planned society still seemed to most people in Britain speculative and cranky—the province of a few utopians, a small and suspect band of eugenicists, or the odd socialist who had read Marx and had an inkling that the vast and distant experiment in the Soviet Union, if ever it should settle down, might have lessons to teach. With the onset of economic depression, thoughts began to stir. During the early 1930s Russia assumed, briefly, a more benign and hopeful countenance and attracted admirers. A powerful delegation under Bukharin in 1931 at a London scientific conference first impressed Desmond Bernal, for instance, with the status and opportunities of Soviet science and the prevarications of western democracies in all matters of planning. The rise of Hitler and the renewed threat of war only confirmed this. From then until the outbreak of war the Cambridge scientists found themselves heading a band of socialist professionals calling for a planned economy which could emulate the Soviet Union and stand up to Germany.

H. G. Wells was the author who articulated this type of radicalism first and best. His series of crystal-gazings, starting with *Anticipations* (1902) and stretching forward to *The Shape of Things To Come* (1935) diffused and romanticized the idea of scientific planning and influenced the younger, socially-minded scientists more than they cared to admit. *The Social Function of Science*, for example, Bernal's own call for the planned use of science to transform the world, assumes an unmistakeably Wellsian tone of vaticination. At stages in their career, both writers took more than a passing interest in planning and construction. While the essays gathered in *Anticipations* were in the making, Wells was having a house built for himself to Voysey's designs. The frustrations of this experience called forth a long, restless footnote demanding 'a sweeping revolution in the methods of building during the next century' and adumbrating developments in prefabrication then still far off. Another essay in the same book on the diffusion of cities may be set alongside Ebenezer Howard's theories of town-planning, while in later works Wells throws out sundry rash, provocative hints about the nature and appearance of buildings.

Bernal's thoughts have special value because he himself (Fig. 1.6) was a crystallographer who, through his knowledge of building materials and their properties, became more involved with construction after 1945 than any other of the radical scientists. *The Social Function of Science* appeared in 1939 on the eve of war, but it brings together many of the arguments of the decade and in four pregnant pages suggests how science may revolutionize the whole of architecture and building.

> The main principles of architecture are just beginning to feel the effect of the revolution introduced by new materials and new processes. It will soon be possible to break altogether with conventional architecture, with its tradition of putting stone on stone or brick on brick unchanged since the time of the Pharaohs, and move in the direction of rational fabrication. The physical functions of architecture are principally insulation and support,

1.6. J. D. Bernal at work: a post-war study.

8

but these are perfectly separable factors. Thick walls and heavy girders are a most inconvenient way of providing both together.

*New Materials.* Of the new materials, some, such as the light metals, can be used exclusively for support, others, as yet but imperfectly developed, for insulation. What we require at the moment is a material as light as, if not lighter than, cork, strong enough to withstand wind-pressure, fireproof, and offering good insulation against heat and sound. These are not impossible requirements. Indeed, materials satisfying nearly all of them have been already prepared and it is almost certain that, with the development of aerogels, the problem can be satisfactorily resolved. As such material will not be built up but furnished in large slabs attached to the framework, building will come to resemble more and more the assembly stage of machine production, the preparation of the materials corresponding to the fabrication stage.

*Internal Climate.* The services attached to buildings have in the past only too often been afterthoughts: in rational architecture they will become essential parts. Given good insulating walls, the problem of heating houses entirely disappears . . . But it is beginning to be realized that with the appropriate use of properly shaped channels it is possible to maintain an opening secure against wind without the interposition of any material . . . In this way it might be possible to be able to have open windows summer and winter alike, guarded either by the wind itself or by jets of air forming part of the general ventilating system. The ultimate development would be the weather-proof room without walls or roof . . . As in many other cases, the solution to domestic problems may well be found where the conditions which have to be fulfilled are rigorously limited, as, for instance, in the motor-house or caravan-trailer, and we may expect from these developments a much greater flexibility and compactness in internal arrangements and a complete breakaway from the restriction of traditional methods.

*The City of the Future.* Great as are the changes which science can introduce in the details of dwelling accommodation, far more could be done in the construction of large dwellings or houses. With the use of strong and light materials it should be possible to enclose spaces much larger than those dreamt of by past or present architects. The totally enclosed spacious air-conditioned town is rapidly becoming a practical proposition. It would be undesirable to attempt to concentrate all human activities in one such enclosure; probably several would be needed for different kinds of productive work and for recreation, each with its appropriate climate . . .

*Planning.* The problem of housing, however, is far more an organizational than a technical one. Urban and regional planning are as necessary as the building of the houses themselves, and planning requires the development of applied human geography which is only beginning. The various degrees of centralized or decentralized building, the position of factories and of means of transport all require to be thought out in relation to the development of economic life with the aim of providing for the well-being of the whole community rather than producing the biggest private profit. The difference between the position of town planning in Britain and in the Soviet Union shows effectively enough the disadvantages of private ownership, particularly in exaggerated ground values amounting to obstructive blackmail.

Few of these thoughts, as they appeared in 1939, were original to Bernal. But they were set out with a richness of technical and social detail absent from previous, purely architectural manifestos. They were imbued with the apparent authority of science and they emanated from a man of magnetism and breadth who numbered young artists and architects among his friends. Among a generation under the stress of impending war, they had the capacity to spread fast.

The pitfalls of such technological romanticism need no stressing today. Even at the time and among those drawn to scientific planning, they were far from uncritically received. The Cambridge scientists were not a single group but a medley of brilliant, argumentative individuals. Broadly speaking, the Marxists like Bernal stood for a utopian, root-and-branch approach to physical planning and assumed high levels of material production and consumption; in other words, they hoped to combine Soviet centralism with American consumerism and efficiency. But others less vocal and more cautious—'humanists', Fabians, Quakers and reformers of all kinds—opted for a more gradualist version of a planned future. They had read the Victorian socialists, and they shared these authors' distrust of unfettered technology, consumerism and the great city. Among them was the prickly but perceptive Lancelot Hogben:

> The distribution of purchasing power to increase the volume of effective demand is esssentially different from the view held by the pioneers of Socialism fifty or a hundred years ago, and it would have been regarded by them as a capitulation to the prevailing doctrine of *laisser-faire*, against which they revolted. Men like Owen and Morris were far less taken in by the glamour of capitalism than ourselves. They were not content to criticize it because it distributes its products unjustly, or because it was incapable of producing as large a quantity of goods as a planned economy could deliver. They also, and more especially, attacked it because it was not producing the kind of goods which are good for people to want and to strive for, and they were not hypnotized by the liberal delusion that things people have been educated to demand by capitalist advertisement are necessarily the things they *need* most.
>
> Today we are apt to dismiss their lament on the ugliness which capitalist enterprise has bequeathed us as mere aestheticism with no significance for a realistic political programme. In this context realism implies a servile acceptance of the three cardinal errors of early capitalist ideology. The first is the assumption that the greatest good of the greatest number is achieved by the greatest number of saleable goods and ensuring that the greatest number of people can take their choice. The second is that the large community is a necessary condition of high productive capacity. The third is that peace between nations can only be ensured by maximum division of labour with free trade. I believe that each of these postulates is biologically false, and that the results of acting as if they were true will be biologically disastrous.

The 'neo-technic' era of electric power and light industry, prophesied Hogben (echoing Geddes and Mumford), would allow greater self-sufficiency, less international rivalry and a cleaner and purer style of life in smaller conglomerations; things to come would be shaped by the vision of Morris, not of Wells. 'It is not far from the truth,' he argued, 'to say that the much-despised aestheticism of the Utopians is being vindicated by events.'

These arguments were to inform the whole post-war movement for a social architecture. The homespun, slow, moralistic, Arts-and-Crafts utopian humanism of Ruskin, Morris and Lethaby adapted itself slowly to the so-called machine age, only to find itself playing counterpoint to a more radical view of building as an exercise in technological production made necessary by economic and political urgencies. During the 1930s the older tradition could not match the out-and-out modernism of the Bernalists in freshness, and the books of its founding fathers gathered dust in the libraries of British schools of architecture. But its stock was to prove more pliant and vigorous than it then appeared. Today, the next generation's judgement has gone decisively against those on the Left who set too much store by the possibilities of planning and technology. 'I was doing the kind of architecture my left-wing friends ought to have been doing,' blurted out one upholder of 'architectural humanism' in a burst of unguarded candour. Yet for much of the post-war period in British architecture these traditions co-existed and regulated each other. One way of looking at the school-building movement which occupies the centre of this book is as the area where the tension between these traditions was most thoughtfully resolved.

## RESEARCH

So much for the scientific ideas themselves. But how and in what form were they communicated? For a start, several of the leading scientists were friendly with architects and painters and were keen to help reinvigorate the sciences and the arts by exploring the links between them—a common preoccupation of the period. Architects too were eager to assert their scientific pedigree. C. H. Waddington, a geneticist in this circle, was to write a Penguin which touched on this subject, *The Scientific Attitude* (1941) and married Justin Blanco White, one of the politically active young architects of the 1930s. Bernal, a colossus of all-embracing interests, knew Henry Moore, Barbara Hepworth and the so-called 'Belsize Park Group' of artists, and he contributed to *Circle*, a short-lived magazine edited by Leslie Martin, Ben Nicholson and Naum Gabo with pieces by many of the *avant garde* in art and architecture. The closest of Bernal's friends in architecture was E. J. (Bobby) Carter, librarian and editor at the Royal Institute of British Architects but always something of a rebel inside that citadel of the establishment. Carter sedulously advanced and defended new ideas about science and architecture not only to his conservative employers but also among mandarins elsewhere in the British establishment.

The most popular and widespread manifestation of scientific thinking in architecture became the ideal of 'research'. Such was the millstone of amateurism and individualism still hanging around architecture in Britain, that organized investigation into architectural problems could appear as new in the 1930s, a century or so after the practice had become ingrained in the natural sciences and medicine and fifty years after it had spread to the social sciences. In fact an appreciable amount of research was going on into matters of construction. But it took time for even the better-informed architects to wake up to this. As a self-conscious activity, architectural research in Britain goes back no further than 1932, when Berthold Lubetkin set up the Tecton group practice. This team, which included six ex-AA students, must have studied the manifesto-like diagrams on methodology emanating from the Dessau Bauhaus and other European strongholds of the 'new objectivity' between 1926 and 1930. But they also knew and tried to emulate British scientists. The Tecton member with the best contacts was Godfrey Samuel, through whose friendship with the zoologist Solly Zuckerman the group acquired their first proper commission, the Gorilla House at the London Zoo. To perfect the brief, Zuckerman was 'bombarded with endless questions which I could answer only by reference to the literature, about the temperature and humidity preferred by gorillas, about their agility, about the food they ate, and so on'. In Tecton, this technique developed by degrees into 'a valuable habit of exhaustive research ... Each man inevitably found his special aptitude and devoted a major portion of his time to it. The result was a powerful concentration of technical knowledge, extremely usable because all were bent on achieving the same end.'

The ideal of research was taken up in the very title of the MARS (Modern Architecture Research) Group, founded in 1933. But it was never really tested by that loose-knit, loud-mouthed organization. The more that research was talked about, the emptier it could become. At the AA it became a vogue word meaning anything from a miniscule 'voyage of social discovery' along the route taken by Priestley and Orwell, to an investigation of joints, bolts and ducts. Sometimes it was an excuse for the innocent researcher to start from first principles, uncluttered by precedent or previous design. Or sometimes it amounted to simple information-gathering: identifying, building up or plundering some body of knowledge through libraries, journals or links with experts. Usually there was a bit of both. That was how Denis Clarke Hall, fresh out of the AA, set about his winning entry for the *News Chronicle* schools competition in 1937:

> I didn't know anything about school building. I'd never thought about it before. So I went and just did investigation, you could call it research, into the basic requirements. I started off with what children needed in the way of health and light and air and found out all sorts of fantastic things I'd never thought of before. Somebody told me that there was a good library in the National Institute of Industrial Psychology which had been doing some work on this and I worked a lot there. I didn't really look at an existing school or any report or anything like that at all. I did it purely from 'What is a school?' I had seen one or two French schools outside Paris which set me up to thinking 'I'm going to go back to first principles'. I know that I spent far more time doing the research than doing the design. We had about three months to do it in, and I think I spent nearly two on the research.

At this time the openings for research of this kind were very limited. So 'researchers' were drawn to make their own presumptuous observations and decisions. Few British universities or other institutions offered structured help to any outsider seeking social or technical information. Much had to be done by ingenuity or word of mouth. The inter-war period, and particularly the 1930s, saw an expansion in research organizations, but the network was still rudimentary. Housing, education and health, all fields of 'official' investigation, were those in which most expertise was available and research could offer tangible results. For instance at Kensal House, an experimental block of London flats, Maxwell Fry and a group of fellow architects procured the housing expert Elizabeth Denby to help compose the brief and determine the plan form. A similar process of enquiry took place before plans were drawn up for the Pioneer Health Centre in Peckham. Here was good co-operative research put to practical action.

The one concerted programme of research to bring architects and scientists together in the 1930s was the 'ARP' campaign, for extended air-raid protection and deep-level shelters. This was sparked off principally by J. B. S. Haldane, who had witnessed the effects of bombing in Spain. Fearful that saturation bombing in London would cause near-annihilation, Haldane and his friends strove to stir up a sluggish government to prompter action. On the architects' side, the burden of initial propagandizing fell to the Architects' and Technicians' Organization (ATO), a little group of 'activists' built up around Freddie Skinner, Lubetkin's right-hand man in the Tecton office. The ATO had broken away from the MARS Group out of impatience at its lack of social conviction. It concentrated at first upon giving technical help to tenants in the London area suffering from housing problems. But as war approached, it switched its attention to ARP agitation. This brought together architects, engineers and scientists: Bernal, Haldane, Hyman Levy, Ove Arup, Felix Samuely, Skinner, Lubetkin and others less well-known. In due course it became a joint campaign of the Association of Architects, Surveyors and Technical Assistants (AASTA) and the Association of Scientific Workers (AScW). These bodies had parallel histories. Both had been founded at the end of the First World War as white-collar unions to organize underpaid and undervalued architects and scientists in government and local government. Having fallen into respectable doldrums by the early 1930s, both were energized and politicized by radical new secretaries, W. A. Wooster of the AScW and A. W. C. Barr, a young architect who took over the reins at the AASTA in 1936. From this time until the late 1940s the AASTA (known after 1942 as the Association of Building Technicians or ABT) enjoyed growing membership and influence, mainly among architects in public service. Though its name is all but forgotten today, it was the most important of the various architectural pressure-groups of the 1930s and '40s in Britain and was greatly feared by the RIBA. Under joint AScW and AASTA leadership, the campaign for more and better shelters achieved a measure of grudging government recognition in 1939. This led at the outset of war to the first collaboration between Bernal, Zuckerman and other well-known scientists with the one established arm of architectural research in Britain—the Building Research Station.

## THE BUILDING RESEARCH STATION

Building research and building science are as old as construction itself. The difficulty is to pinpoint a moment when private enquiry and occasional publication give way first to the ideal, and then a system, of regularly accumulating and disseminating technical know-how.

In Britain, Edwin Sachs ought justly to be recognized as the father of the building-research ideal. Between 1895 and 1910 this remarkable Anglo-German architect wore himself out promoting the disinterested, scientific testing of building materials. Sachs worked without government support and, as so often, only under the stress of wartime needs and with government intervention could further progress be made. In 1915–16 the Department of Scientific and Industrial Research came into being. This quickly spawned a Building Materials Research Committee chaired by Raymond Unwin, the first modern British architect of

1.7. The welded-steel Mopin system erecting for the Quarry Hill flats, Leeds, 1936. In its day, Quarry Hill seemed the spearhead of a technological assault upon the social problems of building. In the event, the technical faults which it generated suggested dangers which were heeded too late. Quarry Hill has now been demolished.

reputation to enter the civil service. Unwin was then working towards a better understanding of the technical needs which he anticipated housing would have after the end of the First World War.

In 1920, with the first national housing programme under way, this committee turned into the Building Research Board, and a temporary 'station' for experiments was established at East Acton outside London soon afterwards. With the dwindling of the housing programme in 1923 its future came in question. But in 1924–5 an energetic engineer, Reginald Stradling, took over its direction. A larger site at Garston, some twenty miles north of London, was acquired, and the BRS was set up there on an expanded footing.

BRS, therefore, was a government agency, charged initially with investigating the properties of materials for the first great national housing programme. This shaped its character and early influence in several ways. It started out as a passive body, geared to the needs of big building programmes of potentially many units, not of one-off structures. It tested materials and 'systems' for houses, mainly concrete types of construction devised by engineers and builders; and it reported on its findings only to itself and to government departments. It established links with a few enterprising contractors and engineers, and rather fewer architects in government employ. But with the architectural profession as a whole, with architectural education or the architectural press, its contacts were poor. Before 1933 BRS employed hardly more than a single architect (not counting consultants). Most of the staff were engineers and physicists, who concentrated on the sound, scientific analysis of materials and their properties. Application came second, if at all, to this.

Prodded along perhaps by the new enthusiasm for research, BRS began by degrees to adopt a more outward-looking attitude, especially after the arrival of the far-sighted Robert Fitzmaurice in 1933. An enquiry service commenced, offering free expert investigation of recalcitrant problems anywhere in the country for those who knew about it. Links were also built up with the more scientifically minded architects. Rowse of the AA, for instance, persuaded BRS to evaluate Eugène Mopin's structural system, then scheduled for use on the ill-fated Quarry Hill flats at Leeds (Fig. 1.7); about this the experts were commendably cautious. Fitzmaurice also instituted a campaign to get building regulation changed from a footing of prohibition and restriction to one of 'performance'—an idea with far-reaching implications, many still unrealized today. He also tried to get the lessons learnt at BRS in the process of monitoring and research out into architects' and builders' practice, and hence to work towards a 'modern vernacular' in building technique. In 1938 the first volume of Fitzmaurice's *Principles of Modern Building* appeared, to the benefit of outsiders but the chagrin of some of the BRS staff. William Allen, a young Canadian architect who joined BRS in 1937, remembers:

> It was a sort of bible of a certain group of modern architects at the time. F. R. S. Yorke and Wells Coates I met through Fitz at the station. These young chaps said that they saw BRS and the Bauhaus as two branches of the same idea.
>
> Fitzmaurice incidentally in writing *Principles of Modern Building* was heartily disliked by every major scientist at BRS. They thought he was popularizing what they were creating as a new branch of science. He was very popular among builders, and becoming influential among architects. Although his book is scientifically very good, it was essentially applied science. The other boys had some confused ideas about science and publication in archival journals and things of that sort. Even the people who didn't read *Principles* were influenced by it, if you know what I mean.

Here then was another strand in the argument: a national centre for the assessment and dissemination of building techniques. By the outbreak of war architects were beginning to hear about BRS, learn from it and exploit it. But the mechanisms for making its services and influence known were still far from effective.

## CITY–PLANNING, PROGRAMMES AND PUBLIC PRACTICE

Like science and research, planning was a powerful and as yet untarnished ideal among the British professions of the 1930s. It pervaded every strategy and every advanced theory about industry and society: demography, economics, health-care, housing and so on. Not until the 1930s were the foot-dragging, bodge-loving British at last bullied into embracing the idea's most palpable expression—physical planning or, to use the apter but narrower term, urbanism. A little must be said here of how pre-war city planning shaped the post-war possibilities for a social architecture.

To echo a common observation, urbanism as a public discipline was slow off the mark in Britain. Great squares were built, parks laid out, estates created, slums razed, sewage disposed of and traffic accelerated without any integrated theory or practice. Victorian munici-palities intervened more to prohibit and contain than to direct or initiate. The celebrated exemplars of English planning, from Blaise Hamlet and Saltaire to Letchworth, Hampstead Garden Suburb and even Welwyn Garden City proceeded from private initiative. The profes-sional 'planner' was a term without meaning until the 1930s. Landlords, engineers, surveyors, valuers and contractors all poured their talents into this void, but architects, accustomed to command and co-ordinate, gradually became dominant in the process. The first Englishman to whom the title 'planner' can be plausibly ascribed was Raymond Unwin; he himself preferred the definition 'interpreter'. Whichever word is chosen, Unwin himself earned the title less as the chief architect of Letchworth and the Hampstead Garden Suburb than as the first person to grasp the fact that to improve the standard of environment for the mass of the population, national policies and nationally supported expertise were necessary.

The earliest British town-planning act, ambitious in intention but hopelessly mutilated in the legislative womb, passed into law in 1909, soon followed by an influential conference on the subject at the RIBA. Then came the war and its sequel, the post-war housing pro-gramme of 1919–23. These events revolutionized physical planning. The clear-sighted now saw that planning in small pockets was trifling without some sense of the overall shape of things: the movement of population and industry, the availability of labour and materials, and so forth. The teaching of planning in such few places as addressed the subject, like Liverpool, matured from the simplicities of geometry to embrace the thinking of Unwin and other pioneers like Camillo Sitte and Patrick Geddes. Without national or municipal direction, further progress could hardly be made. This was what induced Unwin to embark upon his second career as a government planner and adviser, the forefather of a powerful line of men like Patrick Abercrombie and William Holford whose plans were to transform the nation's cities almost by stealth.

It was at this time too that city-planning became bound up with another consideration, that of a national building programme. Certain nationally specified building-types, initially housing and (to a lesser extent) schools, were by law to feature in British towns and suburbs. It became the task of the municipal architect-planner to carry out these programmes in whatever quantity national and local politics might prescribe, and to ensure their good design, setting and variability. By this means ideas about 'production' and 'quality control', borrowed from the language and thinking of industry, trickled into architectural consciousness alongside that of the 'city beautiful'—and in the emergent public sector of activity, not the larger private one.

Public and municipal architectural activity had long pre-dated the First World War. In its modern form, British local-authority architecture came into being around the end of the last century, as a tributary to the deep, slow-moving current of municipal enterprise and pragmatism which did so much to tame British cities between 1890 and 1940. The London County Council, for instance, had employed architects of its own to design its housing since 1893; its predecessor, the Metropolitan Board of Works, had used in-house architects well before then, and the London School Board enjoyed similar arrangements. The example of London and a few other cities like Liverpool and Glasgow was slowly taken up by smaller towns and districts. The 1902 Education Act, which transferred the onus of building and maintaining schools to the elected local authorities, was a further inducement to employing salaried architects. But in few places did the pre-war demand for new schools or housing mount up far enough to be labelled a 'programme'.

So, across the breadth of the country, the demands of the Addison Housing Act of 1919 smote upon hundreds of little local authorities unequipped to cope. Previously a borough engineer or surveyor with a clerk or two and perhaps a drudging, unqualified architect had sufficed to vet submitted plans for approval and put up the occasional omnibus shelter, possibly even a school or two. Now these people were beset with unfamiliar tasks: preparing a housing plan, grappling with laws and ministerial directives and seeing schemes through to completion. Some places still fobbed the design responsibilities off on to private architects. But experience with changes in the law and in rules for housing finance showed continuity and co-operation with officials in other departments to be vital. So the larger authorities began, as far as politics and staffing permitted, to design as much work as they could 'in-house'.

The depression after 1930 fed this trend. As workloads fell, the security of municipal employment for architects began to outweigh its lowly, underpaid status. Subordination to a borough surveyor or engineer was preferable to no work at all and occasionally allowed a young architect to enjoy big responsibilities and freedom from interference and administrative tasks. After 1935, the building programmes of local authorities and other collective bodies which employed their own architects steadily increased, at any rate in the cities. Changes in housing policy led to a renewal of slum-clearance programmes and a reversion to building municipal flats, for which architects were nearly always employed. Education saw a short-lived boom in school-building. A smattering of proto-Keynesian organizations which not only built for themselves but built handsomely, like the Miners Welfare Commission and the Scottish Department of Health, also enriched the new pattern of practice.

Above all, a new political will to build and plan municipally emerged in the 1930s. Often the decade is looked upon as one of setback for the Labour Party, a period of dressing the wounds caused by Ramsay MacDonald's betrayal, while the intellectual left ran headlong towards communism. That is to pass over some potent municipal successes enjoyed by Labour. Leeds (for instance) fell to Labour in 1933, the London County Council in 1934, Coventry in 1938; the last two were to remain in Labour control for years to follow. In each of these cities the incoming councillors were determined to show that Labour could not only govern competently and cleanly, but could also inspire social renewal and reconstruction through programmes of housing and civic works, somewhat on Viennese and German models. At Leeds, the Labour group had its programme for modern flats ready long before the election; almost their first action on coming to power was to appoint the architect R. A. H. Livett from Manchester to set up a new department and start research for the Quarry Hill flats. In Coventry, the new council likewise established a city architect's department and appointed Donald Gibson to the job. Though it was no part of his brief and poached upon the city engineer's territory, Gibson and his young staff responded by devising a plan for the city centre—then a seemingly impractical proposition, but one to have profound implications after Coventry was devastated in 1940. In Finsbury, a small London borough with a tiny professional staff, a lively council tackled its problems in another way, by teaming up with the firm of Tecton and commissioning a comprehensive plan for health, housing and, as war approached, shelter.

In the county, borough and city councils of Britain, irrespective of political affiliation, separate architects' departments now began to proliferate and attract graduates from the architectural schools. Even the engineers' and surveyors' departments of unreformed authorities could get able staff, where they had the programmes. Willesden and West Ham, to name two on the fringes of London, employed young architects and engineers who were to be among the leading lights of post-war reconstruction, while the bigger Middlesex County Council had a concerted programme of school-building on stream by 1937. The experience of working in these offices offered chances for continuity and development unobtainable from the normal private architect. All this encouraged a few younger, idealistic architects to opt for local-authority work, to the bafflement of older teachers. Goodhart-Rendel's taunt, alluding perhaps more to the past than the present, that 'departmental architecture' was so much 'stale chocolate', angered these few younger men and women very much. Meanwhile the AASTA orchestrated a fervent campaign to ginger up the RIBA and get proper pay and recognition for municipal and other salaried architects. Municipal and co-operative employees formed the backbone of the AASTA membership and gave it a growing influence in these years, despite the enmity of the RIBA and the more old-fashioned private architects.

By the time of the war, therefore, public practice in British architecture had, in a manner, grown up. Its strength should not be overestimated. 'Official' architects, to use the name then current, were still disdained by most members of the profession. Many continued to work in obscurity, without high aspiration or hope of promotion. In terms of architectural quality, 'stale chocolate' was not so inaccurate a charge. Seen in the national context, Leeds, Coventry and Finsbury were 'drops in an ocean of indifference'; at the LCC, for instance, dull repetitive flats were being churned out by the score in the later 1930s. Yet despite these shortcomings the public offices were beginning, here and there, to offer the kind of varied, continuous, collaborative programmes of building for which private architectural practice was totally unequipped. In such, at a time of great prospective sobriety, the future seemed to lie. Writing for *Horizon* in 1942, John Summerson put the situation thus:

> One does not have to be particularly 'Left', or indeed politically minded at all, to appreciate that the architectural opportunities of the future are more likely to lie in the hands of administrative authorities or commercial corporations (whether publicly or privately controlled) than in the hands of any private individuals whatever; or to appreciate the many excellent reasons for such bodies having permanent architects' departments of their own . . . It is competence and quality we need most at the moment, not the vanity of trying to fly level with the poet-innovator, Le Corbusier, or the stupidity (as it seems to me) of being more interested in getting a few exciting, immaculate, individual results than in getting the roots of architecture untangled and properly planted in the soil where they belong . . . The next thing to be done is to render architecture *effective* in English life.

# CHAPTER 2

# WAR

It is tempting to look upon the world wars as barriers in social history, full stops at which one set of values ends abruptly and gives place after the duration of hostilities to another. With civil architecture between 1939 and 1945, that seems specially plausible. People had still to be fed, clothed and taught, but wartime brought normal building programmes to a halt. The workforce, manual and professional, dispersed to military units or dwindled to next to nothing; occasion was curtailed for personal and printed debate.

Under closer scrutiny, the war appears as a violent emetic administered to British architecture and building. The patient is prostrated by the dose, his system is shaken up, much ancient and obsolete matter is purged. But he recovers cleansed and revitalized, with tone, energy and appetite for the tasks which have been piling up during his confinement.

Consider first the personal experiences of young and potential architects. Most of those called up, and pre-eminently the graduates of the more privileged schools of architecture, were classified as 'officer material'. Recruitment policy handled such people more delicately than in the First World War. This time there was no chaotic stampede to the colours, no unselective dispatch to the front and, in consequence, no 'lost generation of leaders'. Able men died, and everyone mourned the loss of friends. But among middle-class Britons as a whole the slaughter was not so great.

For those who underwent a long span of service life these years rang the spasmodic changes, so well conveyed in the wartime novels of Evelyn Waugh and Anthony Powell, upon boredom, discomfort, routine and inaction interspersed with bouts of frenetic activity. The few compensations of such an existence need not be unduly romanticized. But during the doldrums many people read and reflected, and built up a head of steam about what they would do with their lives once this necessary interlude was over. They also worked and mixed more broadly and continuously than most of them had done in peacetime. Collaboration and group activity became a habit of mind, where previously it had been at best an ideal for a few. People learnt to tend some small part of a very complex, theoretically flexible, administrative machinery, and to see their individual tasks in subordination to a larger whole. As a result, not only military terminology and metaphor but also habits of strategic organization persisted into the post-war world.

## UNDERSTANDING INDUSTRY

Such was the bare minimum of experience. Luckier or cleverer men and women both inside and outside the services found their careers opened up in illuminating, unpredictable ways.

To take one simple, purely architectural instance, at the outset of war a great programme of military construction in Britain was entrusted to a favoured 'hundred contractors'. A run of ordnance factories fell to the lot of Sir Alexander Gibb and Partners, a firm of Liverpool civil engineers under the direction of Hugh Beaver. Beaver called in William Holford, the

2.1. Hall and community buildings at one of the hostels for munitions workers at Swynnerton, Staffordshire, designed by a cadre of architects under William Holford, 1942–3. Few of the hostels were ever used by factory workers; most eventually billeted American troops.

young planning professor at the Liverpool School of Architecture who had already collaborated with him on the Team Valley Industrial Plan for revitalizing a depressed area close to Newcastle. This gave British architects a first taste of the massive, American-style method of group-working on industrial projects at speed, of the kind over which Albert Kahn had presided in Detroit. Holford, a born organizer, gathered round him a multi-disciplinary team of hundreds which included a strong presence of radical young architects: F. R. S. Yorke, Hannes Schreiner, Birkin Haward, Gordon Stephenson, Anthony Cox, Colin Penn, Nares Craig, Graeme Shankland, Richard Llewelyn-Davies, Myles Wright, Terence Kennedy and others. Augmented and reshuffled, the group went on to build hostels for munitions workers, one set near Warrington and another in Staffordshire. Here took place some early, fumbling experiments in the standardization of parts and in mural decoration, as the team strove for the first time to master the disciplines of industrial production and temper its harshness with some show of spirit and art (Figs. 2.1, 2).

2.2. Mural in one of the Swynnerton hostels, designed and carried out by Birkin Haward.

This example shows merely how architectural practice could be prolonged and redirected by the war, with the added ingredients of speed, shortage of materials and a 'production mentality'. Many architects, however, were taken right away from their immediate specialism and forced to learn new skills. This brought them face to face with the needs and conditions of research, design and production in time of war. It was a profound, unpalatable but very influential lesson. Bruce Martin, a clever, still-callow AA graduate, was drafted in on the basis of some slender engineering experience to work in the aeronautical design office of Short Brothers, who were then laying out the Stirling bomber:

I was given the drawings of the undercarriage and I could make neither head nor tail of it. I spent three whole weeks trying to understand those drawings. I eventually made a model of the thing and taught myself how it worked. At the end of those three weeks I had learnt it, I could do engineering drawings.

The people were nice, but the experience was appalling. I couldn't stand the routine. It was a real factory, I really understood what factory labour was. We had communists in the drawing office, and equally we had theologians; this was fascinating because they were all trying to convert you. The important thing about these people was that it set me reading. I was ignorant and naive and unread, and they shook me intellectually, absolutely devastated me.

The whole organization of design I learnt there, and still maintain it's the only way to do it. Even their organization of the drawing office is sound. The organization of the drawings itself is a hierarchical one and this is really the best way of looking at an organized thing and, therefore, also at building.

This forcible accommodation, this shotgun marriage with industry, was the great new ingredient to enter architectural thinking as a result of war. Group-working, scientific method, research, social idealism, prefabrication, the concept of the programme rather than one-off design: all these ideas were conscious and present by 1939. What architects lacked was intimacy with the shape, methods and problems of industry, of a kind which would allow them to conceive of researchers, designers, makers and users putting their heads together regularly to arrange an evolving, improving programme of work. All this was first revealed by the wartime practice of 'operational research'.

Echoes of a kind there certainly were. The call to reintegrate hand and brain, design and production, was a familiar one to those still responsive to the Arts-and-Crafts message: 'We are always in these days trying to separate the two; we want one man to be always thinking, and another to be always working, and we call one a gentleman, and the other the operative; whereas the workman ought often to be thinking, and the thinker often to be working.' But Ruskin's successors had got bogged down in the elusive debate about craftsmanship and 'the machine'. For those reared upon the technological Corbusian or Bernalist *soufflé*, rescrambled Arts-and-Crafts omelette tasted stale and old. Lethaby in his later writings had made the wisest synthesis between the older and newer radicalism about architecture and building. But Lethaby and Morris were not much read by the young in the 1930s; only after the war and in the light of ideas thrown up by war did they become intellectual mentors for a fresh generation of students. Only a newly technical, roving, fast-moving war, which penetrated every corner of the world, all arms of military service, each aspect of productive life, which persistently demanded of its experts quick solutions, repairs, alterations, replacements and up-datings, which called for 'making-do' and 'mucking-in'; only this convulsion proved capable of tearing down the near-impenetrable barriers of British class and culture and pointing a way to the remarriage of hand and brain.

Rightly or wrongly, some came to feel that this was a major cause of allied victory. One such was Andrew Derbyshire, then a young naval physicist fixing and repairing direction-finding equipment on warships:

The Germans never got their scientists into action, and they never got their fighting men into labs. They were always kept separate, whereas R. V. Jones and the other proponents of operational research insisted that users and inventors and designers had to get together so that they could understand the stresses and strains of actual use. It was discovering faults in design in practice that was the other part of this work. That was fascinating. Operational research taught people a hell of a lot about the user-designer relationship.

## SCIENCE AND RESEARCH IN WAR

For some short time up to the outbreak of hostilities, the Building Research Station had been stepping up its war-work. At a secret compound at Garston, cooped-up government scientists toiled away unseen on scale models of explosions and their effects. Then after September 1939 came a maelstrom of reorganization. Reginald Stradling, the director, rose to eminence in the new Ministry of Home Security. Extra space was commandeered at the Forest Products Research Laboratory, Princes Risborough, where Desmond Bernal, pressed from above upon a reluctant Stradling, came in with J. F. Baker, Solly Zuckerman and others including a pair of ex-AA young architects, Leo de Syllas and John Madge, to test the resistance of structures to explosions. Bernal's *The Social Function of Science* had just been published and his work at Princes Risborough followed on logically from the battle over ARP. Despite the gag on publicity, BRS was no longer a backwater.

But beneath the bustle of activity lay malaise. Scientists everywhere felt ignored and undervalued by government and military. Many believed that no proper planned use of their talents was being made at a moment of dire national emergency. One expression of this came out of the Tots and Quots, an élite dining-club-*cum*-ginger-group of the scientists and their establishment contacts which had been founded by Zuckerman and others in 1931. After long slumber, the Tots and Quots were reactivated in November 1939. Their chance came at a dinner just after Dunkirk in June 1940 when Allen Lane, hearing the scientists' lament, agreed to publish their arguments as soon as they could get them together. By dint of hectic collaboration, the typescript of *Science in War* took eleven days to deliver; the book itself was out about a month after the dinner. Uniquely for a Penguin, it was issued anonymously so that those engaged in war-work could savage officialdom with impunity. Arm-twisting secured favourable publicity (20,000 copies were sold) and a strong impact on Churchill's administration, already alive to the inadequacies of links between science and government. From about this time, official attitudes to science and technology in war started to alter.

*Science in War* now looks scrappy, a mere hasty reworking of Bernalist homilies to fit the urgencies of prospective defeat:

> A fundamental scientific discovery may take anything from twenty to one hundred years before it influences the lives of the majority of people. A particular scientific study of some aspect of a manufacturing process may, on the other hand, be effective in production in as many days ... The usual materials are not to be found. Men, particularly skilled men, are few. The ordinary institutions of business are working in an unfamiliar war economy. Not to use science under these conditions is not just obstinate stupidity, which at worst could lead to stagnation; it is a sure way to confusion and defeat. Only scientific methods can deal with the problems brought about by new conditions.

Nevertheless it hit the right note at the right time, and succinctly. It also incorporated a short section on building written by Bernal himself with Alec Skempton and William Allen, all then BRS employees. This section upheld BRS as the only organized nucleus of building science, called for the more rational use of materials and space on lines indicated by its work, and demanded that architects be used for wartime research, not 'as executives to apply in their own special field other men's second-rate reasoning'.

After the Soviet Union entered the war, some of the Tots and Quots scientists went on to enjoy much military trust and influence, best exemplified by Bernal and Zuckerman's bizarre exploits in Combined Operations under Lord Louis Mountbatten during 1941–2. As a result it is easy to over-rate the impact of *Science in War*. In building, for instance, work at BRS on designing mass-producible factories with a reduced steel content and a frame able to resist collapse was merely stepped up, as Britain began to recover after the fall of France. The important point is that these ideas now appeared in a climate of acceptance. Thereafter institutions like BRS were able to operate in increasingly unfettered and influential ways. All the time, military urgency was promoting quicker feedback and closer relations between scientists, makers, designers and users. The concept of operational research began to percolate. It was to refine everyone's understanding of technical collaboration and organization. Bernal, for instance, apologizing in 1946 to the RIBA for the facility of his earlier views on the relation between science and architecture and explaining how they had changed, put the transformation thus:

> In the early days of the war, the whole emphasis of science in war was science in relation to scientific gadgets ... But as the war progressed, it became noticed that it was not so much the scientific gadgeteering side which was important; it was the scientific approach to the problems raised by military situations generally; problems raised in the factory, production problems, planning problems in the general preparation of war weapons, and finally, towards the middle and end of the war, the problems of actual operations. While this was going on, organisation was drawing the scientists more and more closely in with the practical people. It was an experience which was common, I think, to all branches of science and led to an entirely new and wider view of the relations of science and practical things.

## THE CAMOUFLAGE TEAM

Of the many instances of wartime research of this kind, the one most pregnant for post-war architecture took place in 1943–4 at the Camouflage Development and Training Centre. It may be singled out not for what it achieved immediately, nor even for its eccentricity, though elements of flamboyance, artistry and sheer farce set it apart from certain greater and grittier tasks. But here two of the most influential architects of the post-war years, Stirrat Johnson-Marshall and David Medd, first met and worked together. From this collaboration under Major James Gardner (himself to gain fame as an exhibition designer) sprang, quite consciously, methods of designing and making which later bore fruit in the Hertfordshire schools.

Camouflage and deception units were well established by this time. They had since the start of the war sheltered sundry architects, designers, artists and other misfits from the tribulations of ordinary service life. Johnson-Marshall arrived at CDTC in 1943, having previously been posted to camouflage in Delhi after an audacious escape from Singapore at the time of its surrender.★ The centre was then split between the venerable Farnham Castle and the ampler grounds and mock-timberwork of Pierrepont, one of Norman Shaw's coarser country houses a few miles away. David Medd:

> Deception was our business really. 'Camouflage' was a word associated with conspicuously funny shapes painted on buildings which (wrongly) we regarded as a somewhat dilettante pursuit. If we were to deceive the enemy—whether it was to suggest that a landing had to be at 'a' rather than at 'b'; a bridge was being built at 'c' rather than at 'd'; a large convoy was going towards 'e' rather than a small convoy towards 'f' and so on—it was necessary for designers and makers to have advance information about strategy, tactics, theatre of operations and the degree of fidelity for example. Hence one or two officers were sent to the centre (War Office) whence strategic information and briefs could be made available and thus design and manufacture could proceed sensibly. Designing and making prototypes of all manner of devices, and organising their manufacture in larger quantities was only part of the job ... We had responsibility for demonstrating their use and for training troops in their deployment. Neither was this all, for of paramount importance was the experience of the use of the devices in the field. This, with ever-changing briefs from the centre (War Office) meant that we, as designers, were part of a chain in a complete cycle which didn't repeat but evolved as it went round: policy, thinking, designing, making, using, new policy, rethinking and so on. The designer was a link in a complete chain, not a detached component.

---

★ For a biographical account of Stirrat Johnson-Marshall, see Appendix I.

2.3.  (*above*) Lumbering about with dummy tanks at the Camouflage Development and Training Centre, Pierrepont, Surrey, 1944. A half-timbered house by Norman Shaw furnishes the aptly incongruous backdrop.

2.4.  A CDTC tank made of 'pneumatic slab' fraudulently menaces an English country lane.

.5. A bogus Bailey bridge, the work of
ːDTC, 1944.

It was not surprising that after a year or more of this the penny dropped in Stirrat's mind (and not long after in mine, I like to think) as to how an architect should function after 1945. In short, not detached from those who determine policy nor from those who use the designer's products—to identify two separated links in the chain.

What specifically jolted Stirrat Johnson-Marshall into fresh thought about architecture and production was the task of turning out quantities of dummy tanks, landing craft, lorries and so on for the run-up to D-Day, to confuse German intelligence about where invasion forces were massing and, later, where thrusts would occur in France. Dummies of course had been used before. The Germans, naive perfectionists, went in for meticulously crafted carpentry, exact down to the last rivet and tank-track though the details might be indiscernible at a hundred yards. The British failing was the opposite. They had started to mass-produce lightweight, pack-away inflatables. But even after improvements had been made with new synthetic materials in the CDTC workshops, these were still too crude and balloon-like. James Gardner:

These dummies tended to have a rather busty appearance when inflated. As soon as he arrived J-M, who had lived in a ninety-degree-angled world, said he was sure he could make them inflate rectangular. I was sure this was not possible as air pressure tries to convert any soft container into a sphere, but one trouble with J-M was that he exhibited inflated enthusiasms and talked rather much (for the army, that is). So I said 'Right, you do just that', and got on with other work.
Velvet is produced by weaving two layers of fabric together on one machine with a multitude of threads connecting them. Cut through the finished sandwich and you have two pieces of cut velvet.
Johnson-Marshall talked the makers (who were not selling much velvet at that time) into an experiment. First he got them to weaving the textile layers $4\frac{1}{2}$ inches apart. That successfully accomplished he asked them to torture their machine again so that the connecting threads would be located in bunches at 5-inch centres. We rubberized the surface, sealed the edges, pumped in air and produced a stiff slab rather like a giant breakfast biscuit. So, I was wrong. J-M could produce rectangular balloons at a toss of a hat (Figs. 2.3–4).
J-M and I had similar motivations and we both had the habit of working hard, but we had different outlooks. I am a troglodyte, only at home within the confines of my own mind and a drawing board. J-M actually enjoyed people, talking to them and selling enthusiasm and ideas. In this way he helped to sort out production problems, and ultimately the logistics of our part in the invasion-deception plan, for which he needed to contact and convince prejudiced experts in the art of doing what had already been done.

In itself, the CDTC work on 'pneumatic slab', as it was called, was just one example of a rediscovery made time and again during the war, in every conceivable realm of production, about the use of collaborative means towards urgent, extemporary ends. Architects played no more than a tiny, walk-on part in this drama. But the enthusiasm and concentration and confidence built up by experiences such as these were to prove seminal when they came to the tasks of what is known as 'post-war reconstruction'.

## THE ROAD TO RIGHTEOUS RECONSTRUCTION

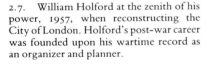

2.6. Lord Reith, man of righteous purposes, and as much as Butler or Beveridge a force in the shaping and psychology of post-war Britain.

2.7. William Holford at the zenith of his power, 1957, when reconstructing the City of London. Holford's post-war career was founded upon his wartime record as an organizer and planner.

It is hard and perhaps mistaken to pinpoint a precise moment when the switch to reconstruction began. The ideas long preceded active planning, just as replanning preceded by so many painful years much meaningful activity on the ground. The key originating figure appears to have been the much-abused Lord Reith, Minister-Designate of Works between 1940 and 1942. Reith had been brought into the Cabinet by a reluctant Churchill, who acknowledged the man's administrative reputation but disliked him. The loathing was reciprocated. Reith knew he had been shoved into a side-alley away from the war effort, and confided to his diary his contempt for the publicity-conscious antics and directives of Churchill and Beaverbrook, the 'war lord' and the 'press lord'. He never attended Cabinet if he could avoid it. But he was determined to make something of his job, to reshape his department so that it in turn could reshape Britain. In his inimitable words, 'I wished there might be an inspiration, a design, a plan towards the righteousness that alone exalteth, towards the truth that makes men free'.

During his term of office Reith struggled inwardly with himself and outwardly with others. He proffered daffodils from the lunch table at Claridge's to the blitzed burghers of Coventry and bade them replan their city as boldly as they wanted. He commissioned the seminal Uthwatt and Scott reports on betterment and land use. Finally, in early 1942, he secured a proper Ministry of Works from Parliament, with responsibility for post-war reconstruction. Ten days later he was sacked by Churchill, an irrelevant scapegoat for the fall of Singapore; the real reason seems to have been that he was going too far and too fast for the Conservatives in the coalition. 'And you'd just got things going too,' sympathized George VI. Reith never held high office again, though he was to play a crucial role in shaping the legislation for the New Towns programme. His name, unlike those of Butler and Beveridge, is rarely coupled with the creation of post-war Britain. Yet his legacy was deep-rooted; the austere outlook of the next decade stemmed from the austerity of Reith as much as of Cripps. When Reith left, the civil engineer Hugh Beaver was already in position in charge of the Ministry's Directorate of Post-War Building along with his friend and ally William Holford, who was to wield Unwinian powers and more; and Holford's Liverpool-trained architect-planners, Gordon Stephenson, Terence Kennedy, Peter Shepheard and Myles Wright, along with Hugh Casson, William Tatton-Brown and others were soon crowding in, proliferating into the Ministry of Town and Country Planning when that was established and took over reconstruction in 1943, and working towards the potent town-planning acts of 1944 and 1947. The foundations for post-war building in Britain were beginning to be laid.

The war dragged on (it is sometimes forgotten) beyond expectation. As it did so the vision of reconstruction, fanned by belated social legislation, fed by the Ministry of Information's graphic newsreels, and fuelled not a little by the legitimation of left-wing thinking through the alliance with the suffering Soviet people, increasingly obsessed the British. Servicemen and women alike longed for it, school-leavers chose their careers in the expectation of it. 'We won the war together, now let's work together in peacetime': such official platitudes, easy now to dismiss as cant, struck deep. Collaboration and co-operation, once painfully achieved, ought surely not to be lightly given up? Methods learnt in war could now be applied in peace. Bobby Carter, answering on American wireless a question about plans for Britain's cities after the war, caught an authentic tone:

At the present time architects are engaged on planning and building camps, defence housing and health and ARP services, factories and military buildings, and it's in this tough daily work that we are making the best scientific and imaginative contribution to the building of Britain. That field of work is the ground where the solutions to many of our post-war architectural problems will germinate and I can assure you that, in their present activities, architects are promoting radical changes.

In token of this, even the previously backward RIBA joined the enthusiasm for reconstruction, getting down to forming an influential Architectural Science Group (later Board) in 1941 to liaise with BRS and other organizations, and to promoting a *Rebuilding Britain* exhibition in 1943.

The preamble to reconstruction consisted of a plethora of government plans, committees, regulations and reports, hard to disentangle at the time, well nigh impossible now. They make 'righteous' but far from enchanting reading. Two in the field of building stand out for their influence: *Post-War Building Studies Nos. 1 and 2*, on housing and schools, both of 1944. The former derived from the lucubrations of Sir George Burt's Inter-Departmental Committee on House Construction, guided by Judith Ledeboer; the latter was the upshot of Sir Robert Wood's Committee on School Construction. In these documents and in the long run of *Post-War Building Studies* which followed, the advice of the Building Research Station was crucial. BRS now entered into its own as the dominating technical force upon how people built in Britain. In 1943 the throttle at Garston had been opened; the whole institution was now careering down the road towards reconstruction. New blood came in, experimental houses were built, the Burt, Wood and other committees were served upon, cajoled and sometimes confronted. BRS's destiny, as Robert Fitzmaurice had seen it, of influencing the whole national practice of building had arrived. Ivor Evans, acting director until 1946 during Stradling's absence, even talked of starting a post-graduate school of architecture there, but was moved on before anything could be planned. In the event a kind of anonymous, informal little finishing school for socially and technically minded architects did operate at Garston after 1945. Among those prominent or quietly influential in post-war British architecture, William Allen, Anthony Pott, Cecil Handisyde, Guy Oddie, John Bickerdike, George Atkinson, Andrew Derbyshire, H. L. Gloag, John Eastwick Field, Nares Craig and John Kay all did stints at BRS; Stirrat Johnson-Marshall was offered a job there in 1945 but went to Hertfordshire instead. It was 'the most impressive learning experience I've had,' says Oddie.

In the newly created Architectural Physics Division of BRS, the architects worked alongside a bevy of scientists who had been tried in the furnace of wartime operational research and believed in getting results into practice fast. One group, including Alan Pickles (the physicist who headed the division), Peter Parkin the acoustician, James Dick and John Weston had been together in the Admiralty's research team at Rosyth. It was through this division that BRS got to grips with a new field of study, that of subjective response in the environmental sciences, heating and ventilation, lighting and acoustics. Ralph Hopkinson, for instance, came into the field of lighting from wartime work on the visual-display aspects of radar, in which he had made a 'particular study of relating people's responses to what we were providing for them'. Aloof from users, the engineers had at first tended to design radar sets on physical principles alone. Then it became clear that users couldn't operate them for long because the physiological and psychological conditions for their use hadn't been understood. It had been Hopkinson's job to get the design of the sets altered accordingly. Now the same principles of 'psychophysics' and 'ergonomics' (a term coined in 1947) were to be applied to the field of lighting buildings.

This is to anticipate. The post-war investigations in environmental science at BRS are mentioned here to show how principles of operational research in war translated into the direction of building research in peacetime. In chronology and significance, they came after the vexed questions of structure and materials. And here in 1944 the Burt and Wood committees were receiving a clear message from BRS, not as an ideal but as the only possible resort in the conditions likely to obtain after the end of hostilities: 'prefabricate'.

# PREFABRICATION

The complicated subject of prefabrication still provokes high passions, attracting single-minded adherents and repelling single-minded opponents alike. In the mountains of modern literature on prefabrication there has been a tendency to push its history back, to recall that the brick is a prefabricated unit, that ancient timber dwellings were regularly built to a common scantling, and that the traditional Japanese house draws its dimensions from the Tatami mat. In the nineteenth century, we have rediscovered, British contractors exported iron churches, hospitals and barracks to the colonies, while at home conservatories, kiosks, public urinals, arcades, markets and small railway stations could to differing degrees be assembled from a 'kit of parts'. Even major one-off buildings like London's Royal Opera House or its Coal Exchange could embody hidden portions of both iron and timber not only fabricated but more or less finished off-site, to secure speed and economy of construction.

Yet British architects were only selectively aware of all this. Prefabrication did not impinge as much or as regularly upon their activities as it did, for example, in timber-building countries like the Soviet Union, the United States, and those of Scandinavia. This was why, purely as an architectural ideal, prefabrication came so late to maturity in Britain. The great Victorian exemplars of iron prefabrication belong to the worlds of engineering and industrial production, and these were never central to architectural discourse, however enviously the profession might look upon a Brunel or a Paxton. There were dabblers in these waters, but Ruskin and his followers warned off several generations of designers from getting their feet wetter. Practical collaboration, technical know-how, dirtying one's hands, were endorsed in early Arts-and-Crafts theory: factory production was not, or not until it was too late.

By the time of the First World War the climate had thawed a little. The merely reactive phase of hostility to 'the machine' had passed, and the two clearest thinkers of the British Arts and Crafts Movement, Ashbee and Lethaby, were striving for a *rapprochement*. They were cognizant of the saner attitudes which prevailed in Europe and America and of the prospects for a cleaner, humaner, co-operative, suburbanized, electrically powered, 'garden-city' model of industry in the future. Ashbee wrestled with the issues of 'the machine' and of 'standardization' for several years, almost wrote a book about it, then boiled down his thoughts to a set of axioms, three of which bear repeating in the context of prefabrication's later history.

1. Modern civilization rests on machinery, and no system for the encouragement, or the endowment, or the teaching of the arts can be sound that does not recognize this.
6. The distinction between what should and what should not be produced by machinery has in many trades and crafts now been made. This has been the discovery of the last twenty-five years.
8. Man's control of mechanical power has yet to be made effective. The making it effective is not only a matter of inventing or exploiting new processes, it is the discovering of means whereby mechanical power shall be best used in the public service—in other words, how it shall be 'socialized', and not merely used to enable men to exploit each other.

The Arts-and-Crafts legacy on this problem, therefore, was far from negative. As elsewhere in the history of modern British architecture, a half-conscious continuity with seemingly outmoded traditions of thought turns out to be as meaningful as any radical break with the past.

Only in the 1920s, when government for the first time called for and co-ordinated a national programme of house-building, did prefabrication in Britain take on its present-day connotations. As has been said, the structural experimentation of these years took place without much involvement on the part of architects. In a situation of shortages to be repeated after 1945, prototypical designs for houses were solicited and then, if found promising, tested by the infant Building Research Station. The prototypes emanated overwhelmingly from builders and engineers, not from architects, who for the most part were neither involved in the provision of everyday housing nor geared to 'production' thinking'. The experiment was instructive but discouraging. Some 50,000 'non-traditional' houses had been built by 1928, almost all in the public sector, and they were not conspicuously disliked by their occupants. But they had proved themselves in neither economic nor structural terms, let alone in appearance. After 1925 house-builders reverted with relief to brickwork. In so far as BRS arrived at a concerted attitude towards structural prefabrication in these years, it was a very cautious one. Nevertheless standardized fittings of one kind or another, like steel window-units and plasterboard partitions, were finding their way slowly into commercial acceptance, somewhat after the same process had started to gather speed in most other industrialized countries.

Meanwhile in Germany, Walter Gropius had been thinking hard about prefabricated housing for mass production as far back as 1910. Like other Modern-Movement architects, Gropius designed some short-lived prototypes for factory production as part of the German housing drive after 1925, in particular a copper-clad house-type for the firm of Hirsch-Kupfer. But it is not for his practical work of this period, nor for his later collaboration in the United States with Konrad Wachsmann on the ill-fated General Panel house (1947–9), nor even for his early appreciation of the broad possibilities for factory production in architecture, that the founder of the Bauhaus deserves his special place in the saga of prefabrication. The contribution of Gropius was that he was the first architect to shun the easy rhetoric of comparing the prefabrication of buildings with the making of identical technological products—principally cars—for the mass market. Gropius saw, as Ashbee had dimly glimpsed, that prefabrication and standardization would become a crushing burden unless they were controlled by the designer and user, not the manufacturer or engineer. Progress in the production of prefabricated building on any scale, he believed, could only come about by continuous interchange between design, research, manufacture and policy; and the technology of prefabrication had to be harnessed so as to combine standardized, dimensionally co-ordinated components in a variety of ways, not by producing complete buildings or parts of buildings. This is the philosophy which has since lain behind all responsible attempts to design permanent prefabricated buildings, and it was gratefully embraced by the pioneering architects of the British post-war school-building movement. 'Gropius had the ideas. We had the opportunities', says one of them.

Some of this rational all-round thinking about prefabrication Gropius must have tried to instill in his English colleagues during his exile of 1934–7. Certainly the subject was at last beginning to stir among young architects. The concept of prefabrication tied in with the utopian science of Wells and Bernal and the renewed romanticizing of industrial production. But in technical terms it still remained vague in architecture. The early Modern-Movement buildings admired in the schools were one-off jobs; occasionally they pushed building technology forward but they scarcely standardized at all. Gropius's writings on prefabrication were never translated; similarly, the mechanization of portions of the German and Soviet housing programmes was not fully reported or understood in Britain. More accessible were the Swedish systems of timber-framed housing, which caught on in Stockholm in the late 1920s and were starting to take hold in Britain a decade later. Cyril Sjöström, who taught at the AA, had worked on one such system in both Sweden and Scotland and so had a rare practical experience in structural prefabrication just when the students were starting to take an interest. On a larger scale, there were increasing examples of the use of standardized structural components in British flats and commercial buildings. The privately sponsored Council for Research on Housing Construction, calling in 1934 for a programme of flat-building to clear the inner-city slums, commended the large-scale standardization of components but added an almost Gropian note of caution: 'Sound standardization is no bed of Procrustes to which sites must be forcibly adjusted, nor is it by any means the enemy of significant variety'. This was the kind of approach adopted in the much-publicized Quarry Hill flats at Leeds (Fig. 1.7). Meanwhile private concerns which dealt in more than one-off buildings were rapidly coming to similar conclusions. The chain of Odeon cinemas designed by Harry Weedon in the 1930s often put the same elements together in different ways, while Marks and Spencers were toying with a modular approach to the design of their High Street stores.

2.8. *(left)* The 'Radiation House', Coventry, prototype in course of construction, 1945, during the third day's work on the superstructure. This light-steel, concrete-clad prototype was designed in 1942–3 by Edric Neel working unofficially with Donald Gibson and Coventry's city architects, but not built till 1945. It never went into production but may have had some influence on the early Hertfordshire schools.

2.9. *(right)* The 'Radiation House' complete, 1945. It took its name from Radiation Limited, the Birmingham firm which sponsored its production and used it to demonstrate gadgets for heating and cooking.

In 1936 the Crystal Palace, that enticing, beckoning vision of prefabrication's past and future, shimmering atop a ridge overlooking South London, burnt down. The fire was visible for miles and widely reported. Illogically, the event unleashed a wave of enthusiasm for prefabrication. Robert Furneaux Jordan at the AA represented it as a tragedy. In New York, Henry-Russell Hitchcock's catalogue for an exhibition on British modern architecture gave over the frontispiece to a photograph of the ruins. The ideological ancestor of modernism, the Parthenon of prefabrication, had been destroyed. All this whetted impatient, youthful appetites. But they did not think in terms of the stodgy utility housing of the 1920s. The new, architect-conceived, prefabricated structure was to be quickly built for limited life, to be easily extended, altered or scrapped, and to be 'light, loosely grouped and "flexible"'—qualities specially suited to schools, in which a major building programme was then anticipated.

With the war came the added elements of urgency and shortage to buoy up an already existing enthusiasm. During these years the belief in prefabricated housing in particular was rekindled and blazed up to unrealistic heights. Denis Clarke Hall started a private study of the subject in 1939. His work was subsumed into that of a Committee for the Industrial and Scientific Provision of Housing, set up in 1941. The committee included names of post-war significance: Ove Arup, Clarke Hall himself, Donald Gibson, Edric Neel, Joan Robinson, Felix Samuely and Lewis Silkin. Its activity was limited and it reported only once, in 1943. But its report has a certain cautionary significance. Forgetting Gropius, it pressed the seductive analogy between the prefabricated dwelling and the motor car, popular since Le Corbusier and Henry Ford, further than it had ever gone before. Since the committee was financed by industry, not government, it reflected the anxiety of steel and aluminium producers to find new outlets for their products once wartime production should drop off. The report also drew on evidence and views coming from Coventry, a car-producing city with special wartime problems. Here Gibson, the City Architect, built several prototypes of prefabricated housing which, though never taken into extended production, had some influence on post-war developments, in schools as well as housing (Figs. 2.8–9; 6.2–3).

Wiser architects and technologists, it must be stressed, fast retreated from this peak of theoretical enthusiasm for complete units of prefabrication. Nor did the reports of the Reithian Ministry of Works or the *Post-War Building Studies* indulge in facile industrial analogy. As a government agency, BRS had no commercial reasons for promoting prefabrication and it was aware of some of the drawbacks. But in the aftermath of war they all accepted that prefabrication was an inevitability—at least for a time.

Many embraced that destiny as a necessary outcome of war and an essential concomitant of industrial democracy. The sorry state of the building industry lent powerful support to this view. Up till then, conditions of work in construction had been backward in comparison with other industries. On site, workmen put up with wet, cold, dangerous and unpredictable conditions; they smeared and bodged in odd corners, they carried back-breaking loads, they were hectically busy for a few hours, they hung about for another few, and they were hired and fired with little or no notice. Building was, as it has generally remained, a rough job. Many people had been lured into factory production during the war. Would they ever return from the warm factory to the windswept site? Why should they do so? Prefabrication, coupled with organized management, seemed to offer an answer. More of the work could be done under shelter off site, while on the site simple, dry tasks of assembly, familiar from continuities in the building programme, would occupy less men less time. The ideal was a fine one and a clear one.

Over and above this, there was the practical influence of wartime production. Factories, hospitals, huts of all kinds, Bailey bridges, temporary houses had, like dummy tanks, been produced in numbers and at speed by co-operation with industry and techniques of standardization. The cruder objects had been made by reduplicating standard designs, the subtler ones by using component parts in a variety of ways. The important battle for designers was to ensure that subtlety would triumph over crudity. That there was any alternative to employing prefabrication in post-war building on a hitherto unattempted scale, hardly anyone believed. The same sharp shortage of labour and materials that had obtained after the First World War was accurately anticipated, and also a similar inflation in building prices. Because of bombing and the promised social programmes, the backlog in building was even greater than in 1918; and this war had lasted longer. The new education act promised secondary schooling for all. The population was starting to shoot up after the sag of the inter-war years. Housing was in chronic arrears, with nothing to speak of built since 1939 and thousands of homes damaged or destroyed. Prefabrication seemed to offer the structural key.

Acquiescing therefore in prefabrication, whether as a way of coping with the temporary emergency, a supplement to traditional techniques, or a faith which promised the purification and rebirth of building, the small band of architects privileged to be drawn into the beginnings of reconstruction sallied forth to their tasks in the latter stages of the war. They advised committees; they visited the United States for hints on the efficient production and better servicing of buildings; and they sat down with manufacturers to design (with very varying degrees of involvement and control) an assortment of prefabricated house-types: the aluminium AIROH house (Fig. 2.10), the steel BISF house, the more completely architectural Arcon bungalow (Fig. 2.11), and many others long forgotten. Bernal, asked by the Ministry

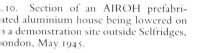

10. Section of an AIROH prefabricated aluminium house being lowered on to a demonstration site outside Selfridges, London, May 1945.

2.11. Some of the 711 Arcon houses on the Shrublands Estate, Great Yarmouth, c. 1947. The official caption claims it as the 'largest temporary pre-fabricated house site in the country. . . . Gardens are encouraged and all roads will eventually be planted with the trees and shrubs whose names they already bear.'

of Works in 1945 to examine the qualities of these prototypes and narrow their number down, found himself faced with literally hundreds of methods of construction—mostly in concrete, the one certainly available material. The difficulty of controlling manufacturers, of getting them to respond flexibly to what was needed rather than to supply what they wanted, was already looming, but the problem was at least perceived. Compared to the situation after 1918, lasting links seemed to have been forged between architecture and industry and only awaited consolidation. The issues of prefabrication had been thought through this time. This time, they would get it right.

## BACK TO SCHOOL

As the war neared its end, therefore, the few architects committed to the success of reconstruction and intimate with its issues had some inkling of what they needed to do and how they might do it. They wanted to build for the many, not for the few, and to do so co-operatively, modestly, justly, efficiently. Through a blend of national and local initiative and through the coming-together of architecture, science and industry, there was a glimmer of hope for this ambition in Britain. But they scarcely felt in charge or control. Within their profession they were still beleaguered, a tiny group of idealists outnumbered by those in private practice who continued to control the RIBA and expected to revert to their usual business of getting a living and mongering styles—the chief thing that the architectural profession and press, then as now, cared about. They were conscious too that in a nation nearly destitute of labour, materials and plain hard cash, their lofty aims left scant room for personal pleasures or recognition. Like the war itself, the future promised years of toil, experiment and persuasion. The prospect of prolonging self-sacrifice into the peace could be welcome only to a few puritan temperaments.

Yet the immediate future lay with these few. Labour's victory in 1945 was no panacea, but it ensured that the sights of reconstruction would not be lowered, that there would be no rapid deregulation, no craven return to pre-war policies on building. Reinforcement was on the way, too: as the troops returned, the schools of architecture resumed their rhythm and began disgorging young men and women infected by the fresh mood.

Most of the schools gradually woke up to this sense of a new start, but the AA (followed by Birmingham) was the first to do so and is a sufficient example. During the war the AA had been evacuated to the London suburb of Barnet, where a dwindling student body got on as best they could with their studies, distracted, curtailed and overshadowed by larger events. In 1945 the school regrouped back in Bedford Square. Pre-war grievances soon bubbled up anew as the Principal, an ex-parachute major named Gordon Brown, sought to contain student demands on curricular and other matters. Those ex-students who had seen war service and now returned to complete their training were overwhelmed by a sense of *déjà vu*. Again the unit system and group-working had to be fought for, again the vision of a social architecture had to be upheld. But there were potent differences. The older students exuded the confidence of victory; they sensed, in the celebrated phrase of the time, that they were the masters. They had commanded tanks, constructed bridges, organized operations and worked in a way they had merely dreamt of before the war. They came back to the AA with the marks and bearing of an officer class. Many were maturer in experience, and some in years, than their teachers. The younger students acknowledged this and reacted to it.

More of the staff too were sympathetic, in particular Robert Furneaux Jordan. Before the war Jordan had been second only to Rowse as a catalyst at the AA. His arresting history lectures, then and later, were the first in a British school of architecture to bring social, economic and technological concepts to bear upon the understanding of style. 'Familiar buildings suddenly took on a new life for us, bristling with social and technical significance,' remembers Oliver Cox. Brown's resignation in 1949 and his replacement by Jordan seemed to confirm that social architecture as an ideal, public practice as a career, were at last legitimated in architectural education.

Intellectually, politically and pragmatically, the post-war students were more sophisticated than before. Lethaby, Morris, Geddes, Mumford, even D'Arcy Thompson the biologist on growth and form—all these authors were devoured. A few students were drawn to Marxism, some others to a constructive type of anarchism, many more to a simple socialism which endorsed the ideals of reconstruction. The pages of *Plan*, the student magazine which succeeded *Focus*, are imbued not with rebelliousness but with a sense of jobs to be done and problems to be solved. A symposium on the various methods of group-working, fully reported in 1948, exemplifies the intense practicality of outlook.

Above all, the students were impatient to go about the task of rebuilding Britain, so long held out as a hope, so tantalizingly deferred during the first few years after 1945. Starved of new buildings, they were avid in their pursuit wherever there was any real intimation of building activity—Hertfordshire's new schools, plans for a big factory in Wales by the young Architects' Co-operative Partnership, or designs for the Royal Festival Hall. If the reconstruction programme was indeed to realize the potential of the new approach to building released by war, the psychology of war and the pledges made in war, it was high time to be up and at it.

# PART II

# THE SCHOOLS

# CHAPTER 3

# BUILDING UP TO BUTLER

How was it possible for fresh, imaginative and practical schools to be built in Britain after the Second World War not just for a few but for many? The familiar answer is the guarantee of secondary education for all under the Butler Education Act of 1944, coupled with the spurt in population which overtook Britain in the latter phase of the war and continued into the 1950s. Schools had to be supplied and funds found to put 'roofs over heads'. Educationalists, architects and technicians were therefore in positions of strength and had to be heeded if there was to be any hope of keeping the absolute pledges made to the war-weary parents of the nation.

Were this the whole picture, school-building should have fared neither worse nor better than public housing, which also enjoyed a fresh start in the post-war years under circumstances of similar urgency. Some of the impediments to a fair and humane system of public housing for all must be touched upon in due course (pp. 226–9). Here, before we see how a small group of architects whose growth was shaped by ideals and experiences outlined in the previous chapters altered the complexion of British schools, we have first to comprehend the advantages which they enjoyed and the conditions which furnished them with the opportunities to seize. What follows in this chapter, therefore, is a sketch of those previous developments in educational thought, administration and architecture most pertinent to the position of the post-war school-builders. It is far from being a survey of all British school-building, let alone British education, before the Butler Act.

Like most major social legislation, the 1944 Act rationalized and epitomized developments which had gone before, stretching back to the Forster Act of 1870. That original law, undertaking to provide elementary education of a kind to every English child which might come forward to receive it, offered a unique contract between the state and the citizen. However tenuous and lowly the nature of its original provision, this contract was not to be duplicated in other spheres of social policy for years to come and its writ runs to this day. If children are born, the state promises (up to a certain age) to educate them. The confidence generated by that guarantee permeates the whole of educational provision. The 1944 Act, after delay and compromise, extended the guarantee by creating, within a framework which was understood and broadly (albeit loosely) accepted, a national pattern of secondary education. Health and housing did not enjoy this long-standing tradition of political acquiescence in the concept of provision for all.

## SCHOOL-BUILDING IN THE 1930S

Over the half-century that preceded the passing of the 1944 Act two themes had dominated British governments' response to state education: the health of the population, and the ampler provision of secondary schools. Both were symptoms of concern about national performance and competitiveness, and both affected the nature of school-building.

The dearth of secondary schools had been troubling prescient politicians and educators since well before the turn of the century. The 1902 and 1903 Balfour Acts, which transferred control of state schools from school boards to county and borough councils, also began the process of regularizing arrangements previously made by some boards, especially in cities, to go beyond 'elementary' education. A higher level of skills, notably technical ones, was vital if Britain were to sustain her industrial edge. Yet despite further acts of 1918 and 1921, the provision of secondary schools remained haphazard and inadequate. To remedy this, Labour's first President of the Board of Education, Charles Trevelyan, put the problem before the Board's standing consultative committee in 1924. In due course the committee, chaired first by Sir Henry Hadow, later by Sir William Spens, took on the task of reviewing the whole structure of English schooling. Their investigations and reports, published in 1926, 1931, 1933 and 1938, shaped the Board's attitudes, informed the spirit of the Butler Act and so determined the direction of post-war education.

The first and most influential Hadow Report (1926) advised that after the age of eleven all children who did not go on to a grammar or a technical school should transfer to a separate 'modern' school rather than linger on at elementary school till they left at fourteen (or fifteen, the leaving age which was then first urged upon the government). This became the Board of Education's policy; and 'Hadow reorganization', which in all but name had been sluggishly lumbering along since 1918, became the official watchword of the period 1926 to 1939. But the policy never became mandatory. The poorer education authorities dallied; others reshuffled their existing elementary schools by dividing them administratively but building little; others again strove whenever possible to build new 'senior' or 'central' or 'modern' schools. The Board had various pecuniary powers of stick and carrot, wherewith to persuade and coerce. But as always where legislation is permissive, there must be local political will and national economic means if anything is to be achieved. And much of the inter-war struggle for better schools was played out against a backdrop of economic recession and the expectation of a stable, even falling, population.

In the late 1920s some progress was made in school-building. Then came the depression and a period of retrenchment, from which the Board did not emerge until 1936. In January of that year it announced that the school-leaving age would at last be raised to fifteen in, of all months, September 1939. In an attempt to complete 'Hadow reorganization' and reduce class-sizes, school-building grants from central government, which had been cut back in 1931, were increased. Between 1936 and 1939 a short-lived fever of school-building broke out. The *News Chronicle*, prompted by Gerald Barry and Paul Reilly, promoted an open competition for the 'ideal' school. The RIBA put on an exhibition which showed all the latest international schools. The *Architects' Journal* brought out a forward-looking series of articles by two young Liverpool-trained architects, Myles Wright and Robert Gardner-Medwin, on school layout, design and equipment, which were quickly republished in book form. The last of the great consultative committee's lucubrations, the Spens Report of 1938 on grammar and technical schools, elicited an enthusiasm among architects which its predecessors had failed to find.

Many of the schools then envisaged were never built. Selective cuts in funding occurred late in 1938 so that resources could be diverted into rearmament; and then a year later came the war and virtual standstill. Nevertheless, this little spurt set the scene for the pattern of post-war building. Predominantly, the schools then planned lay not in the cities but in the suburbs which had spread unchecked beyond their boundaries. So they fell to the lot not of cities or county boroughs but of the then less encumbered county councils. At the time, schools were much the greatest item of responsibility for county councils. In many counties there had been precious little school-building since they had first taken over education from the school boards in 1903 and therefore little cause to organize any continuous programme of building, let alone to consider how those who taught and their representatives might work together with those who designed for teaching. But now the prospect of a prolonged school-building campaign encouraged county councils to take on architectural staff and, in some cases, to create independent architects' departments for the first time. These embryonic county-council departments were to be there, fresh and undistracted by the exigencies of housing and planning when the real explosion of school-building took place after 1945—again in the suburban districts. It was in the unfashionable counties, not in the great cities, that local initiatives in English post-war school-building took shape.

Nearly all the secondary and elementary schools built in the later 1930s were conventional. They were designed for the most part by local-authority architects working to written briefs and undiluted by contact with the teaching profession. In accordance with the Board of Education's mixed bag of rules and 'suggestions', the briefs detailed the accommodation to be provided and thus perpetuated the nature of existing teaching practice. Classrooms, whether they were strung out in long, airy pavilions or jammed together more densely, would be grouped together in runs off corridors; each would be strictly orientated towards a blackboard and equipped with rows of rigid, uncomfortable locker-desks (Fig. 3.1). Besides these there would be a large, generally central hall, perhaps a separate dining hall, a few specialized teaching rooms for grammar or technical schools, some administrative rooms, and serried ranks of WCs.

Nevertheless, there was some loosening-up, owing mainly to the first stirrings of joint medical and architectural research. Classical, symmetrical arrangements were gradually giving place to plans which allowed better environmental provision. The worst of the fresh-air fetish was dying out, as the appreciation dawned that small brains function feebly in chilly rooms. But the 'pavilion' arrangement lingered on, more now on grounds of lighting than of ventilation. Nothing did more to destroy the formally planned school during this period than the movement for improved natural lighting. By the best post-war standards, the

3.1. Classroom at Priestmead School, Harrow, Middlesex. Conventional interior arrangement for classes of all ages, with locker-desks facing a big blackboard and light flooding in from the left, supplemented by clerestory lighting from the right.

3.2. Cray Valley Technical School, Sidcup, Kent (now Kemnal Manor Upper School, London Borough of Bexley). One of the smartest inter-war British schools, designed in the 'Liverpool-modern' idiom for Kent County Council, 1934–8, and characterized by the fashionable over-glazing.

schools of the late 1930s tend to be over-glazed (Fig. 3.2). This is no accident, no result of a mere architectural craze for Modern-Movement detailing and metal windows; 'traditional' as well as 'modern' schools suffer from the same fault. It stemmed from a joint investigation by the Medical Research Council and the Building Research Station, which suggested that children's eyesight was being harmed by poor school lighting; larger areas of glazing (it was then thought) might rectify this. The impact of these findings on heating and ventilation was considerable, and the questions together were the subject of effort at many levels, from research institutes to architects' offices. Denis Clarke Hall's winning submission for the *News Chronicle* competition laid much stress on environmental matters, especially lighting, while Donald Gibson, during his short spell as deputy county architect to the Isle of Ely went so far as to organize an evening class for his staff on school lighting.

Despite these incipient enthusiasms, few schools of this period were in any way revolutionary. The rush of the programmes, the procedures of the Board of Education, and the conservatism of councillors and chief officers alike, all led to stereotypes and sounded a warning note which the younger public architects became determined to heed after the war. The larger the municipal department, the more this seemed to occur. It happened to the London County Council's great programme of flats in the 1930s and to its closest educational counterpart, the Middlesex County Council's school-building programme of the same period. These no doubt were the 'stale chocolate' which Goodhart-Rendel cast in the teeth of public architecture. In the decade before the war, London spilt over into Middlesex's few remaining green fields. The county was enduring the largest national growth and correspondingly had the biggest schools programme on hand. In 1931 the County Council's architects came up with a compact, cheap, and 'aggressively utilitarian' type of school design, which avoided the extravagance of pavilion planning and made use of a steel frame, clad customarily in a faintly Dutch garb of brick with ample fenestration and flat roofs (Fig. 3.3). This solution

3.3. Lady Margaret School, Southall, Middlesex. Another stylish brick school of the inter-war years, built by Middlesex County Council, 1937, and more alive to appearance than to educational need.

then stuck for the rest of the decade, despite a growing programme and an able complement of staff in the department. Shortly after graduating from the Liverpool school, Percy Johnson-Marshall arrived at Middlesex in 1937, 'as keen as mustard'. But he could stick the 'plan factory' for only a few months:

> Curtis was the Chief Architect and Burchett was the schools architect. They had a very big programme, and Burchett was running a staff of forty; he had a large number of schools all over Middlesex. It was all done in a totally mechanical way. Burchett came up to me on the very first day, and he said: 'Well, well now, you're the first of these fancy school of architecture men. We've been waiting for your type now for quite a long time and so we're happy to see you. What's more we want your design abilities and we'll give you a school to design. I'll go and get the drawings.' So he went and produced a complete set of plans. I said, 'But it's already been designed.' So he said, 'I don't want you to design them, I want you to do some elevations.' He came round the next week and put his hand round my shoulder, he was an avuncular chap. 'My God,' he said, 'My God! Oh! We don't hold with all this French and German stuff, we don't oh, no, no, no! We like the Dutch you know, it's much more human. Just go over there and have a look at that school, but in the meantime I'm going to ask you to work with Mr X who was one of Lutyens' staff.' So I worked with Mr X doing half-inch details of a Lutyens-type elevation. After that I thought I could get better experience elsewhere.

For most architects in public service, such were still the realities of work at the end of the 1930s, despite all the idealism and the arguments of that decade. In the circumstances, the standard of the average state school of the 'mini-boom' of 1936–9 was tolerably high.

## CHILDREN AND BUILDINGS

Throughout the era of 'Hadow reorganization', intellectual ferment was going on in the background. Latent in the minds of a few state teachers of the 1920s, shivering in their pavilion classrooms or drilling their PT squads, lay ideas as yet unhallowed by official blessing. Of these, 'child-centred education' was the profoundest in influence. The phrase, so conventional, broad and acceptable now, can easily appear empty of meaning. Volumes have been devoted to tracing it back via Froebel, Montessori, Dewey and a hundred other teachers and philosophers to Rousseau and beyond. It is almost best defined negatively. Child-centred education denies that the needs of the state, the church or the economy ought to shape the development of a child's expanding consciousness. Even the call for improved physical health, which so much abetted this movement's growth and first made it acceptable, should not exert too lopsided an influence upon educational development. These are 'protestant' or 'dissenting' views in the proper meaning of those terms, and they have long held special value for people who put their trust in the individual conscience: Quakers, Theosophists, and politico-religious radicals of one persuasion or another. Anyone who studies the history of modern English education and its expression in building is bound to be struck by the recurrence of this strand in belief and thought.

For these reasons, child-centred education has always been an uneasy bedfellow of authority. It found its first upholders, as it continues to find its extreme ones, outside state education altogether. It could only penetrate this realm once the state felt reasonably secure, prosperous and confident of its own continuity. And it could only establish itself there strongly among younger age-groups, where the clash between a child's development and the nation's requirements is muted. Since 1945, English primary education has seen the successful incursion of child-centred thinking upon territory once dominated by the state but now at least in part and for a time voluntarily ceded. But our secondary schools too often resemble a battleground over which educational idealism and economic contingency march and countermarch, in dispute over the souls of our adolescents.

Between the wars, child-centred ideas of education grew greatly in articulacy and influence.

3.4. Outdoor classroom at King Alfred School, Golders Green, London, Eugene Kaufmann, architect, 1936. A private school with a proud 'progressive' tradition.

Two strands in it have special strength: the movement for nursery education, and the movement to teach older children in a civilized, humane and 'progressive' atmosphere. Both recognize the child as autonomous, as an object for attention, care, even veneration. Both have champions inside state education, but operate (with exceptions) more imaginatively and radically outside its bounds. Though they overlap, there are unresolved tensions between them. Nursery education tries to cut off the younger child from the pressures of later schooling, to allow infancy its own room for manoeuvre, while progressive secondary education seeks to tear down the barriers between childhood and adulthood and to conceive the school as the microcosm of a wider community.

Common to the movements for nursery education and progressive schooling is the belief that buildings must be at the service of the child, must not overawe or inhibit or distract for the sake of some ideal of authority or proportion. 'Monumentality', decree Myles Wright and Gardner-Medwin in 1938, 'should have no place in the school today where education, its monumental E struck down by child psychology, is no longer stern but smiling'. Beyond that, the two paths diverge. Nursery and infant education, it will be seen, threw up some radical briefs which could be translated into new plans and structures. But it proved harder to give memorable, built expression to the idea that older children should be treated more like adults and better integrated in the community.

This may partly have been because progressive secondary education was confined in this period almost wholly to private schools. A network of such schools were founded or reformed around the time of the First World War. Some were frankly experimental, others no more than traditional English 'public schools' where the grim discipline had been loosened up, the curriculum broadened, and a liberal note sounded. By the 1930s they were beginning to find a concerted voice through magazines like *New Era* and the forum of the New Education Fellowship. But few of them built buildings of genuine educational interest (Fig. 3.4). One exception, Bedales, with its handsome timber buildings in the Arts-and-Crafts tradition by Lupton and Gimson, came too early to exert much influence. Later, in 1933, Dorothy and Leonard Elmhirst hired the 'advanced' Swiss-American architect, William Lescaze, to add to their set of schools at Dartington Hall. On examination, Lescaze's buildings purvey a superficial air of modernism and progressiveness but little evidence that he had thought much about teaching or learning. Justifiably, many progressive educators thought 'architecture' as such was to be avoided for schoolchildren. 'Your gangster age ought to be in dirty hovels, moving gradually up to the swagger rooms all people now have,' A. S. Neill told Headmaster Curry of Dartington.

The prime effect of these progressive schools upon state education came through their products. By 1939 their pupils were seeping into the professions and dragging their educational baggage along with them. From Bedales, Bryanston, Dartington, Frensham Heights, Gresham's School Holt, and other such establishments proceeded not a few of the middle-class teachers, architects and others who were to set the tone for a shift in post-war attitudes in the state system. At the least, their experiences came as a shock and a contrast to contemporaries. Here is the conventional reaction of one AA student of the 1930s to his Tom Brown-ish schooldays:

> At my prep school there was a vast, dark-green classroom with high cills and a monkey tree outside, and a master who hit me very hard on the head with a Latin grammar; the dark corridors smelt of food, and somewhere in their gloom were doors through which fussy, black figures came and went like bats.

Such reminiscences, whether of the public or of the board-school system, recur time after time in manifestos for progressive education. But they can do so only after there is the glimpse of a real alternative to 'chalk and talk' and to Dotheboys Hall. Henry Swain, another AA student, has this to say about Bryanston in the 1930s and what he learnt from it:

> It was an adventure, a bit like one of our new state schools here in Nottinghamshire. It was what was called the Dalton system of education where you didn't go to classes all the time, you worked on assignments, like the AA, like life, with a time-limit and reference books and people to talk to and great spaces to work in. It wasn't just the first fifteen, it was a good school for music, a good school for art. It was as progressive then as our best comprehensive schools are now. I refer constantly to my education. I went to a school where education was done well and I got interested in the process. We had the best teachers and they treated you as a civilized person. It was political as hell. They sold the *Daily Worker* in the main hall and collected milk for Spain.

From such fastnesses of progressive education Swain and others like him were to don the armour of modern architecture or modern teaching methods and sally forth, as they saw it, to extend the privileges of their own schooling to all English children. But just as the enlightened private schools which they had attended could never extend naturally into the wider community because of their distance from the ordinary British culture of their time, so also the progressive public schoolboys could not conceal their origins when they strove to sustain, extend and liberate the state educational system. About Stirrat Johnson-Marshall and his closest comrades, for instance, there was always a Tennysonian air of chivalry, of Arthurian knights in shining armour galloping to the aid of their oppressed brethren.

## THE VILLAGE COLLEGES

By reason of social isolation, therefore, the progressive private schools of the 1930s could never create a convincing identity for the civilized, community-based model of secondary school. In the state sector, there was little encouragement between the wars for so doing. But against powerful odds, one man did manage to suggest what might be possible. Had it not been for this single pioneer, Henry Morris, post-war architects would have lacked almost any home-grown guidance when state secondary schools at length reached the age of maturity in the 1960s.

Henry Morris's celebrated series of village colleges in Cambridgeshire were the most prophetic expression of what a 'community school' might mean. They began by offering an educational example, and went on to give an architectural one as well. Morris himself was a tragic figure. The odds against which he floated his network of schools combined with community centres were overwhelming. In a great city his vision might have met with proper fulfilment, but Morris served as education officer to a rural area of conservative

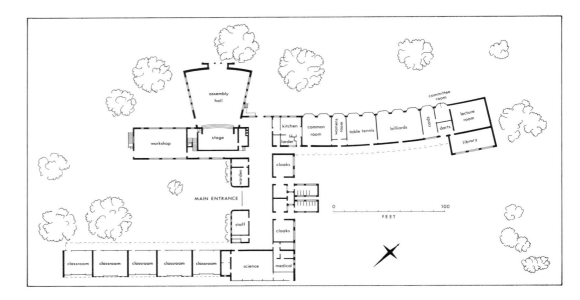

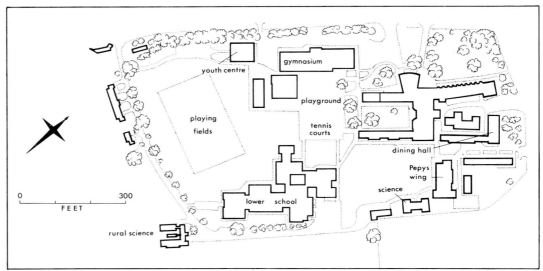

3.5. Impington Village College, Cambridgeshire, plans. Above: original building, Walter Gropius and Maxwell Fry, architects, 1938–40. Below: site plan showing growth to a full community college by means of gradual post-war additions.

political loyalties and scattered populations. He was at his zenith at a time when few public educators grasped what he stood for, and his touchy temperament and anti-urban prejudices isolated him further. Perhaps his chief support, besides his own idealism and determination, was the liberal and aesthetic atmosphere of inter-war Cambridge.

Like the pioneering post-war schools, the village colleges do not at first glance amount to much. As his biographer Harry Rée tells us, Morris was by personal taste a 'classical humanist', having fallen under the spell of that shallow Cambridge aesthete Geoffrey Scott. So the first college at Sawston (1927–30) is conservative, academic and quadrangular in plan. Its successors had to await the 'little boom' of 1936–9. Bottisham (1937) and Linton (1938) are plainer and looser than Sawston. But no one would look at any of the actual buildings at all, had not the last of the pre-war series, Impington Village College (1938–40), been designed by Maxwell Fry and Walter Gropius. Even here, what matters is not a precise solution to any educational or architectural problem, but the sense of congruity between form and social intention: the relaxed grouping of classrooms, community space and shared hall (Figs. 3.5–7). This ideal Morris had always envisaged. Unusually for an educator, he took pains to spread it among architects, in his first manifesto for village colleges in 1924, in talks at the AA (1939) and RIBA (1945 and 1956) and elsewhere. Here is the original formulation:

3.6. Boys striding out to the allotments, Impington Village College: a wartime photograph. The agency caption reads: 'Boys and girls do useful gardening work on the allotments. An area of steadily growing extent is "ploughed up" and mixed vegetables are grown. These provide free-of-charge additions to the midday luncheons at the College.'

3.7. 'Folk dancing under the trees during the girls' gym class': another dew-spangled photograph of wartime activity at Impington.

Let us say to the architect: 'Education is one of our greatest public services and one of the most widely diffused. Every year we spend on it some 80 millions. Every town and every village must have its educational buildings. Education touches every citizen. We have a conception of a new institution for the countryside, an institution that will touch every side of the life of the inhabitants of the district in which it is placed. Will you think out a design for such a building, a village college? ... If this can be done simply and effectually, and the varying needs which the village college will serve realised as an entity and epitomised in a building, a standard may be set and a great tradition may be begun; in such a synthesis architecture will find a fresh and widespread means of expression. If the village college is a true and workable conception, the institution will, with various modifications, spread over rural England; and in course of time a new series of worthy public buildings will stand side by side with the parish churches of the countryside.'

It took forty years and many isolated, exclusive secondary schools before these thoughts percolated very far. In the aftermath of war, Impington was admired for the sake of its architecture, but the village-college idea itself was shunned and Morris once more became a lonely, somewhat tiresome voice upon the sidelines. But he never ceased to preach and enthuse, to designers as well as to teachers. So the seed eventually grew. The origins and shape of the integrated community comprehensive schools of the 1960s and '70s as well as the colleges at the University of York, both owe much to Morris's refusal to accept the conventional barriers, stronger then than now, between learning and living, and to his insistence that architects and educators should collaborate in pursuit of the same civilized ideals.

## LESSONS FROM THE NURSERY

At the other end of the spectrum, the 1930s saw strides made in the movement to bring freshness, life and autonomy to the teaching of the youngest children. It was in this decade that English nursery and infant schools came to maturity and began after long neglect to gain admirers. Having emerged in alliance, however fitful and uneasy, with the state system of education, this movement furnished a channel through which 'child-centred' thinking could filter into local-authority teaching. And because its ideas implied radical changes in the form of schools, it was to have tremendous impact upon future school-building.

The tangled history of provision for the very young in English schools must be briefly summarized. Public and voluntary initiatives, educational and sanitary motivations, each played a part in its development. Among the voluntary infant and dame schools in existence before 1870 were some few Froebel-influenced kindergartens, and over the thirty years after the Forster Act it was the Froebelians who made the most progress, establishing themselves in middle-class pockets here and there, setting up a training college, and trying to procure better infant teaching in the board schools. Five was the theoretical age of entry to the board schools under the 1870 Act. But it was not rigorously enforced until the Edwardian period. Until then, many urban schools were filled with 'babies' who were 'dumped' there so that their mothers could work. They distracted the rigidly disciplined infant classes and rarely received proper provision of their own. The better authorities strove to set up municipal or charitable crèches to cope with them, but the conditions for them were rarely better than makeshift.

As under-age children began to be purged from elementary schools after 1900 the way became clear for a separate campaign for state-aided nursery schools, devoted to health and development rather than instruction. The first proper examples appeared in the years after 1914, through the pioneering efforts of the saintly McMillan sisters—Margaret the 'seer' and Rachel the 'doer', as Norman Lowndes dubs them—in Deptford. Their struggle, begun in Bradford in the 1890s and still not won today, was to wrest from the state benefits equal to those it receives from the employment of working mothers. As so often, war convinced the government to concede what it would never have proffered in peacetime, and the principle of permissive funding for nursery schools was acknowledged in 1918. Despite setbacks there were forty-five recognized nursery schools by 1931, many of them paid for by voluntary bodies but run by local authorities. By 1938, through the zeal of the Nursery School Association, this number had more than doubled.

During the war of 1939–45, nursery classes and non-educational day nurseries proliferated out of all proportion to previous efforts, until in 1944 they were caring for over 250,000 children. When peace came, many supposed that state nurseries attached to primary schools would be available to all. Such a provision was forseen under the Butler Act. In the event, pressures of population, a lack of political will, the search for economies and the recrudescence of the belief that young children ought to stay at home with their mothers cast nurseries down again to the bottom of educational priorities, until the Plowden Report of 1967 set things in train once more. For decades, sites earmarked for nurseries next to the new post-war primary schools lingered on uncovered. But the form of the schools themselves and the teaching which was carried on in them drew increasingly upon the example of their disregarded would-be neighbours.

The early years of the nursery-school movement were directed explicitly to the relief of the poor and to achieving some kind of recognition from the state and local authorities. Margaret McMillan, for instance, identified herself with the medical strand in national education policy, and saw her task as that of creating a healthier population by creating healthier schools. Yet she and her successors in the Nursery School Association were chary of state education's more authoritarian aims and impatient of its progress. Even in the poorer areas, many of the early nursery schools were privately provided and directed. Between the wars, as the physical health of the population improved and English educational thinking became less insular, the psychology of the pre-school child began to loom larger. The more interesting experiments of this period tended to be in the private nurseries, like Susan Isaacs' work at the Malting House School. By 1930 the emphasis in such private establishments was definitely shifting away from physical welfare towards activity, choice, freedom of expression and movement, and the graduated stages of learning. These changes brought the nursery-school movement into line with the Froebelians and Montessorians and encouraged a general campaign for extending informality up into the first years of official schooling through the creation of 'nursery-infant' schools. It was in the small private schools of the 1930s that the new progressive consensus on the care and teaching of younger children made its clearest mark through, for instance, the use of 'Froebel-Dewey' methods of group work or of the child-sized, movable furniture advocated by the Montessorians.

It took years for these ideas to penetrate fully into the state sector, but during the 1930s the process got under way. Already the infant departments in most state elementary schools were practically independent, allowing a special 'infant ethos' to make itself felt. Administratively, the turning points were the Hadow Reports of 1931 on primary schools and of 1933 on nursery and infant schools. The 1933 report gave official blessing to the concept of 'development' as the focus of nursery and infant education and looked forward to universal nursery provision. From this time on, women teachers trained in the principles of Froebel, Montessori and the McMillans were spilling into the profession in increasing numbers, especially in the cities. Well before the war, many of these younger teachers were struggling (usually in isolation) to impart warmth and breadth into infant classes in local-authority schools: through art, through activity, through the promotion of choices, sometimes through something as simple as the making of a garden in some corner of a tarmacadamed playground. For these teachers, no symptom of the past was more palpable and inhibiting than the rigid, unfriendly and overpowering buildings in which, against which, they struggled. The McMillan tradition and the new private nursery-infant schools suggested something utterly different for the future, if ever public funds should be available for building such schools. In the 1930s it never was, as the birthrate was low and almost all money for school-building went towards secondary schools and 'Hadow reorganization'. After the war, their chance would come.

One instance of this pent-up sense of potential is enough: that of Christian Schiller, a young inspector of elementary schools before the war, later staff inspector at the Ministry of Education and a great influence on the course of junior education and school-building in the 1950s. It was upon inspectors like Schiller as much as upon the teachers themselves that the spread of ideas and enthusiasm in the state sector depended. Schiller himself had been educated at a progressive private school, Gresham's School Holt, and taught at another private school before being thrown into the inspectorate at the deep end in Liverpool during the depression. There he observed the gradual decanting of children out of the slums into rigid new schools on the outskirts, with their 'string of classrooms connected by a long corridor, like horseboxes all in a row. They were filled with heavy desks and fifty or more children, which left little space to move'. For Schiller, the new schools themselves were no especial improvement. But the space around them in the playground, the hall and the corridor, was. It was to the better use of that space and the broader choice of activities within it that Schiller dedicated his post-war career.

By 1939, then, a scattered band of nursery and infant teachers in the local authorities, allied to a small number of inspectors, had an inkling of what could be achieved in primary schools if progress might prevail and new facilities, preferably new kinds of buildings, could be provided for them. When the next generation of teachers, matured and socialized (like the young architects described in the previous chapters) by the school of war and hastily thrust through the emergency training colleges of the post-war years came to their aid, the force for change in the form and organization of the primary school became stronger still. It was in partnership with the best of these teachers, inspectors and education officers that the pioneering schools of the Butler era took shape.

## THE FORM OF THE NURSERY–INFANT SCHOOL

From the start of the English nursery-school movement some quite specific architectural ideas took shape, based on the previous building traditions not of schools but of hospitals. Consciously or unconsciously, the nursery school owed most to the isolation hospital. Victorian isolation and fever hospitals were often built in a hurry, in response to some sudden scare; indeed it could be argued that they grew out of the tradition of temporary military hospitals, like the well-known example designed by Brunel and packed off in pieces to the Crimea for Florence Nightingale. For reasons of economy and health alike they tended to be disposed in simple timber huts, completely separated from one another. After the Boer War, when the national call for fitness reached fever pitch, open-air camps began to be run up in the suburban countryside in the hope of transforming tubercular, slum-bred weaklings into healthy lads and lasses with a good dose of fresh air. Half-clinics, half-schools, these colonies were the brainchildren of medical officers of health and so followed the lead of the isolation hospitals; again, hygiene and economy seemed to be mutually reinforcing. Even where an establishment was supposed to be permanent, like the London County Council's Bostall Wood, Britain's first 'open-air school' (1907), the same pattern of 'temporary' timber buildings was adopted.

Partly for lack of money, partly because the early pioneers of nursery schooling placed so much emphasis on health, the first such schools were in the same mould. This had the advantage of allowing improvisation, openness, informality and simplicity. The original McMillan school at Deptford grew out of open-air camps, and the first buildings were known as shelters. Margaret McMillan, we are told, as a matter of principle 'utilized what was to hand . . . she made equipment out of canvas, gas piping, sacks, and trestles'. Here are some of her pronouncements on the shape of such schools:

> The form of the open-air nursery school is not one large building, but many small shelters: a collection of small townships; of small classes, each one self-contained. Each has its own bathrooms and offices and is an open-air place which can be turned into a nursery or dormitory at will . . . There must, of course, be shelter and heating and common sense. But men must learn to build for the open air as they have learned to build for the deep sea. The idea at the back of the builder of yesterday, was shelter—shelter from animals, foes, weather. But the child's worst foes today are germs. All the rest is as nothing in view of that danger.

3.8. and 9.  Nursery school of the 1930s on the outskirts of Zurich. Hans Leuzinger, architect. A simple, orderly arrangement with wooden toys in place on made-to-measure tables.

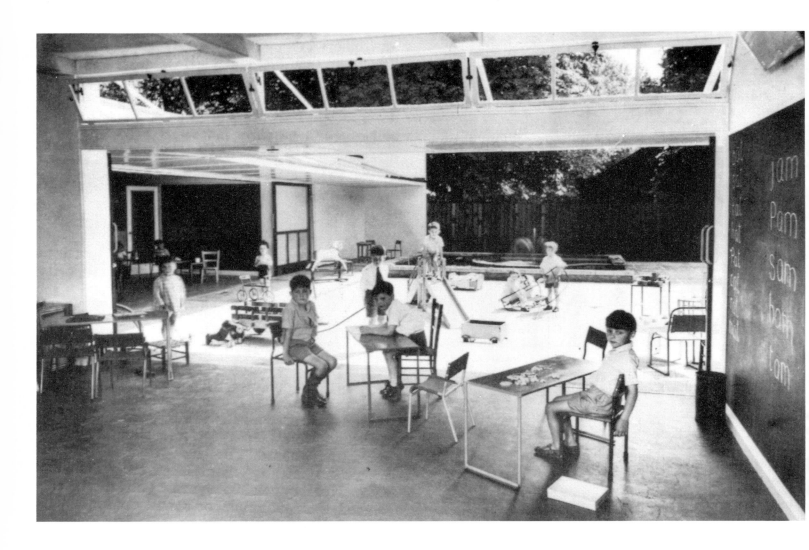

I think they spend too much on buildings, on administration, and there's nothing left for real things. Clothes, and music, and colour, and small group nurture, and they think it's the climate, God help 'em. They can ventilate submarines, but they build fortresses for the poor little things.

The old style of buildings, however handsome, will not do. Nursery school buildings are cheap and they must consist of self-contained shelters, built of asbestos, and costing a third of the usual price for buildings.

And on the organization of the Deptford school:

On entering they [the children] go, not all into one big house, but separate shelters or light buildings scattered all over a big garden. In each shelter there are baths and every child is made physically happy and sits down, warm and clean and glowing, at nine o'clock to a breakfast of oatmeal porridge, milk, and brown bread, etc. They thus begin the long day of adventure and life that we think they ought to have. For they need experience now, just as they need food. Colour and light and music, animals and the sight of birds a-wing, or tame in the garden and pigeon cotes. Apparatus too, gay and varied in its place, but above all free movement and experience—this is their life in the garden and shelters. Everything is planned for life. The shelters are oblong in shape. The air is moving there always, and nearly always the southern end is away! Healing light falls through lowered gable and open walls. This world, too, is full of colour and movement. Colour on the

3.11. (*left*) Timber pavilions at the Busch House Open Air School for Delicate Children, Isleworth, Middlesex, built by the Engineer's Department of the Borough of Heston and Isleworth, 1938. The resemblance to Burleigh Infants School, Cheshunt (Fig. 4.9) is striking.

3.12. (*right*) Looking out from one of the sleeping pavilions, Busch House School, Isleworth.

walls. Colour on the dinner table, colour in pinafore as well as in the garden. In short, the children just emerging from the long sleep of pre-natal life and fitful dream of the first year waken at last to a kind of Paradise.

Margaret McMillan died in 1931. Up till then, nursery schools' needs had been met mainly through drab sheds and shelters, not all perhaps quite as ramshackle as the original at Deptford. As the movement gained confidence, its buildings assumed greater permanence. Then in the 1930s the new architecture coming out of Europe offered a heaven-sent alternative which the 'progressive' wing of the Nursery School Association was delighted to embrace. Simplicity, lightness, openness and informality were advocated by both architects and educators, so the marriage was a natural one. There were some European examples of the genre: the Ecoles Maternelles of Switzerland (Figs. 3.8, 9), the kindergartens attached to the massive municipal housing estates of Vienna, and the crèches which accompanied a sprinkling of modern-style schools in the Paris suburbs, notably one at Suresnes designed by Beaudouin and Lods.

All these were brisk, healthy, fresh buildings of some size, but they look stale and formal beside the few little Modern-Movement nursery schools built in England in the later 1930s. Shortly after leaving the Tecton Partnership, Valentine Harding and Godfrey Samuel designed a delightful example for a private client in Dulwich. It has a couple of 'playrooms' clustered round a pool, a fully opening wall, and equipment and toys scattered casually about, both inside and outside (Fig. 3.10). Kensal House, the well-known experimental flats in North Kensington built on 'Viennese' lines in 1934–6 by a co-operative team under Maxwell Fry and Elizabeth Denby, has another nursery school, this time forming a handsome semi-circle. In schools such as these there might be pets in abundance, a jungle gym (a word just coming in), and a vegetable plot to grow 'cheap spinach and greens for the children'. Meals, if provided, could be served informally in the playroom. Year by year the older medical habits, the 'breathing and nose-blowing exercises' and the hefty sessions of outdoor sleeping, were ebbing away. From such uninhibiting bases, relaxed teaching practices were able to grow in strength and start to percolate into the infants' departments of primary schools.

Both these nursery schools were 'one-offs' in a consciously modern manner. More strictly consonant with Margaret McMillan's thinking were some quiet developments in the timber-framing of nursery schools. By the inter-war period, building structurally in wood had become almost a lost art in Britain, something restricted by regulation to makeshift huts and garages. All this began to change in the later 1930s, because of architectural interest in Scandinavia, because schools were exempt from normal building bye-laws, and because the nursery-school movement welcomed anything 'temporary' in preference to the leaden permanence of most schools. Some of these new timber nursery schools were just reduced, lightly built versions of the three-sided, symmetrical plan then in vogue for 'junior elemen-

3.13. Timber nursery school, Hartford, near Northwich, Cheshire. Leslie Martin and Sadie Speight, architects, 1937–8.

tary' schools. Others still clung to the healthful simplicity of separate, plain, breezy sheds, grouped more deliberately than before (Figs. 3.11, 12). One, a little nursery school at Hartford near Northwich, Cheshire, designed in 1938 by the young Leslie Martin and Sadie Speight for a Quaker benefactress, felt its way towards using timber with an easy elegance which English architects had long forgotten (Fig. 3.13).

More prophetic than any of these were a pair of experiments which, by the nature of their briefs and construction, led further along the road towards the 'prefabricated' school. Both involved young designers who were to have much to do with school-building after the war. In 1934 the Nursery School Association asked Ernö Goldfinger to design a cheap, standard nursery classroom in timber. With the help of Mary Crowley (the future mainstay of school-planning in Hertfordshire), he revised the design in 1937 so that it could be multiplied into any number of desired 'units', bolted together and weather-boarded. The woodworking firm of Boulton and Paul developed this to some degree but never marketed it. A small thing in itself, it was the first inkling in English school design that standard elements might with advantage be put together in different ways on different sites. The other experiment, the little Hilary Haworth Nursery School on the Lache Estate, Chester (1935), was the earliest building carried out by Donald Gibson, later to be one of the key architects in post-war reconstruction. It was pure, bald, engineer's architecture, done without regard for style (Figs. 3.14, 15). It had two playrooms under a pitched roof divided by a folding screen, with service rooms to the side; the whole was timber-framed and asbestos-clad, exactly as Margaret McMillan had suggested. If, as seems to have been hoped, the Lache experiment was meant to be a potential prototype for a government programme of nursery schools, that expectation was not realized. But in this plain nursery, at odds with the hefty, brick-built elementary school erected at the same time by Chester City Council nearby, the English movement for light and dry, prefabricated, architect-designed schools found a first, tentative realization.

## PREFABRICATING SCHOOLS IN THE 1930S

In these small and obscure nursery schools lay the germ of new attitudes to school-building. By their surrender of style, even 'modern' style, to the needs of children and teachers, they admitted service rather than expression as a sufficient goal for the whole future practice of school architecture. At the same time they suggested that techniques of prefabrication, then first coming into fashion among English architects, had something special and educationally worthwhile to offer schools—especially nursery-infant schools, with their single-storey layouts, flexible schedules, low budgets and short working hours.

14 and 15. Hilary Haworth Nursery School, Lache, Chester. Donald Gibson and C. W. Lemmon, architects, 1935. Asbestos-cement sheeting, steel windows and asbestos rainwater goods on a timber frame. The interior could be divided into separate playrooms for twenty children each, and had floors and dadoes of 'jointless magnesium oxychloride'.

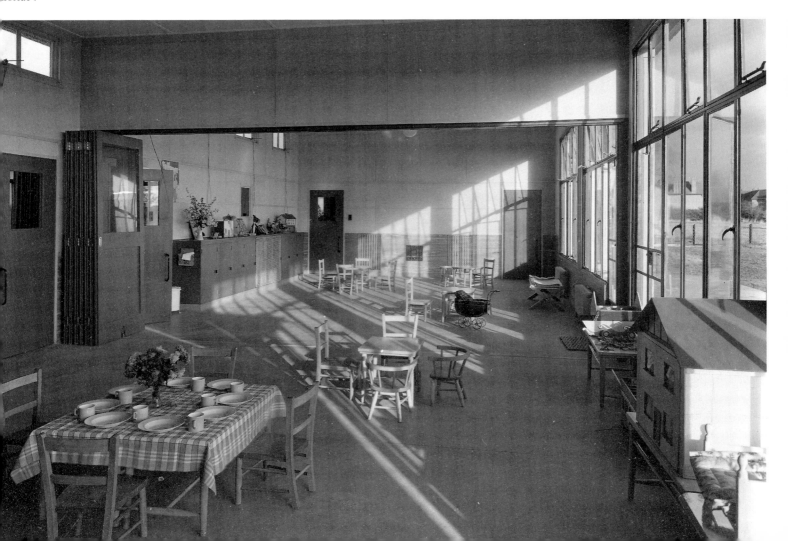

3.16. Richmond High School for Girls, Richmond, Yorkshire. Denis Clarke Hall, architect, 1938–40. The classrooms are pulled away from the school's general circulation, as in Clarke Hall's *News Chronicle* submission, but the planning is in other respects more cautious.

Prefabricating British schools was not quite a new idea in the 1930s. Up to this point, however, it had been looked upon as an occasional, cheap or stop-gap measure. Education had never submitted to the scale of structural experiment endured by public housing in the 1920s, perhaps because so little school-building took place then. But as early as 1911 the significantly named Departmental Committee on the Cost of School Buildings had told the Board of Education that local authorities ought to be looking at new methods and materials like timber, steel and reinforced concrete. This refrain was repeated on and off throughout the inter-war period, usually with an eye to cutting costs by sanctioning huts or other semi-permanent buildings. A new enquiry of 1925–7 into school-building costs had confirmed traditional brick building as generally cheapest. Then came the Hadow Reports of 1931 and 1933. Thereafter, the Board persistently prodded authorities to try building lighter types of schools with looser plans and shorter life-expectancy. These hints were enshrined in 1936, at the start of the pre-war school-building 'boomlet', in the *Suggestions for the Planning of Buildings for Public Elementary Schools*, a substitute for the Board's long-withdrawn school-building regulations. The ultimate motive for encouraging 'alternative methods of construction' in 1936 remained the same as it had been in 1911: economy. But now advanced educators and architects were also asking for the same thing.

By the time that war broke out, there can have been few local authorities who had not heard something about 'alternative methods of construction' for schools. But equally there were few who had actually tried them out. In this context it is worth glancing at the *News Chronicle* schools competitition of 1937 and its results. This competition did much to concentrate architects' attention upon schools. Coming at a peak of school-building activity and of enthusiasm for architectural research, its prizes drew in a big entry including the Tecton Group, Goldfinger and the Johnson-Marshall brothers. The competition was in two parts; ideal schools were solicited, the brief was broad, and the solutions varied greatly. Harry Durell (then a Tecton assistant), Colin Penn and Felix Walter jointly carried off the prize for rural schools with a timber-framed, Scandinavian design. Denis Clarke Hall, not long out of the AA, won the main section for larger schools. His entry, with paired classrooms cut off from the noise of the main corridor, lit from two sides and equipped with individual gardens and terraces, was to be influential, though perhaps less so than the radical report which accompanied the submission. On the strength of his success an enterprising county education officer, Frank Barraclough of North Yorkshire, gave Clarke Hall the chance of trying out his ideas in a new girls' school at Richmond (1938–40). This school (Fig. 3.16), together with Clarke Hall's competition entry and report, earned him a voice in the various official wartime and post-war deliberations on school construction. But though he was obsessed at the time with lightweight concrete construction and planned the *News Chronicle* entry for a forty-year life, when it actually came to building at Richmond the idea fell by the wayside. For the competition, he says,

> I tried to use light, quick building, really based on a very light steel frame, with reinforcement and expanded metal and pretty well spraying on concrete till you got up to the right thickness; so that you didn't have any shuttering or anything at all, you sprayed on a dry mix and just built it up to whatever you wanted.

Then came the challenge of Richmond:

> To start with I had to build in a town like Richmond, and my goodness, the opposition there would have been to a modern school, putting it through the planning people! To put a modern school there was asking for trouble, and of course we ran into it . . . Then when I went up and saw Richmond and its lovely stone buildings I got very excited about that, so that I mixed the two up. Wherever something had to be stressed I used *in situ* concrete, and wherever something had to be solid and load-bearing I used the stone in the traditional manner. I got it out of the local quarry. I got hold of Arup to help me out on the structural side. He was still working for Keirs, he hadn't then started out on his own.

Because of problems like this, few concrete or timber or prefabricated schools were actually built in Britain before the onset of war. Young architects were obliged to cast envious glances at photographs now appearing in the press of light-weight schools designed by Richard Neutra and one or two others in the milder climate and easier economic atmosphere of California, where architectural and educational ideas were coming together in somewhat the same way.

The one architect who enjoyed any sustained, practical success in prefabricating schools during this period was C. G. Stillman, then county architect of West Sussex. Stillman is a transitional figure in English school-building. His career as a local-authority architect spans the wars. After he became county architect for Middlesex in 1945, his ideas were opposed and in due course cast aside by the younger innovators of Hertfordshire and the Ministry of Education. By their standards, Stillman's structural initiatives were primitive and his educational ideals outdated. This is a post-war assessment. In the context of the 1930s Stillman stood alone among county architects in his alertness to the hints of the Board's *Suggestions*, his desire to fit school-building to educational need and his ability to conceive a programme of schools, however brief in scope and banal in character, based upon elements of a prefabricated steel structure. To Stillman more than any other individual was due the shift in the search for 'alternative methods of construction' from timber to steel, which was to be the dominant type of framework in the post-war prefabricated school.

The story of Stillman's Sussex schools is better known than that of the other experiments of this period and need not be unduly laboured here. The important thing is to convey the context of urgency. The Land Settlement Association had placed unemployed workers in the local countryside near the Sussex coast to work on farms, and this coupled with a sudden rise in the seaside population put pressure on a number of schools. *Faute de mieux*, for speed and cheapness, Stillman turned to prefabrication. He persuaded a local caravan manufacturer to make some light steel uprights and girders for flat roofs at centres of 8 feet 3 inches, choosing the measurements to allow a conventional classroom of twenty-four feet in length. This apparently was the origin of the 8 feet 3 inches dimension which affected so much post-war school-planning. In this way, Stillman secured a classroom unit which, with a corridor tacked alongside, could be lengthened to any extent wanted and finished off at either end with brick walls. The prototype extension at Sidlesham (1936) was followed in 1937–40 by new schools in the technique at Selsey, Rustington, North Lancing, Shoreham (Figs. 3.17, 18) and Littlehampton. They are neatly done and still possess, in Barry Russell's words, a certain 'faded panache'. They also closely followed the Board of Education's ideas about planning schools. This put Stillman in a position of trust in the Board's eyes and

3.17 (right) Staircase and side corridor to classrooms at the Shoreham school, showing the sparse finishes to the interior.

3.18. (below) Classrooms at Shoreham, Sussex. C. G. Stillman, architect, for West Sussex County Council, c. 1938. Brick end walls buttress a construction of steel uprights set at 8 foot 3 inch centres; three bays make up a classroom. The plan conforms to the pavilion arrangement, with lower corridors at the back so as to allow natural lighting from both sides.

earned him an authority on 'alternative methods of construction' which was to be crucial when, in a situation of greater urgency and shortage, the new Ministry of Education had to decide what should be done about post-war schools. But to start with, the Sussex schools were meant as no more than makeshifts. They had none of the educational interest of the prefabricated nursery schools or of Clarke Hall's design for Richmond. 'The architecture was novel, but the organization of the school was not,' pronounce the historians of school-building, Seaborne and Lowe.

## PREFABRICATING SCHOOLS, 1939–45

Though the war, when it came, spelt collapse for the short-lived boom of 1936–9, there was never any absolute hiatus in educational building activity or thought. In due course planning for future schools took shape until, once the Ministry of Education supplanted the Board in 1944, it became all-consuming. Both the humble buildings built during hostilities and the grand plans then laid for the future lent support in different ways to the claims of urgency and thus to the cause of the prefabricators.

Evacuation was the first great educational-building issue of the war. From one perspective, evacuation represented a late triumph for the old Victorian reformers' urge to decant children out of the slums into the clean, country air. As such, it fascinated middle-class reformers and 'progressives'. Little building was conceded to the evacuation programme and its corollary, the temporary war nurseries, but some felt that there ought to have been, and that with better facilities in the 'reception areas' there might have been no drift back to the cities. The AASTA in particular, convinced by Haldane's reports from Spain that mass-bombing would annihilate the urban population, savaged the threadbare official plans for the operation. Its Evacuation Committee poured forth a stream of suggestions in 1939–40 for cheap practical action that could be taken if the government would only release a modicum of money: evacuation camps in loose, disconnected units which could be converted back to holiday camps in peacetime; hostels for mothers and babies; and residential nursery schools to accommodate some of the burgeoning war nurseries (Fig. 3.19). The example of the pre-war nursery-infant school was strong throughout, while for building method the committee uniformly recommended prefabrication by structural unit—usually in concrete, the only material readily to hand. Though this campaign had no tangible results, it did further the cause of informality and dispersal in school-planning. In general, the conditions and psychology of war induced architects to disperse and decentralize their buildings, not to group them coherently. Stillman, for instance, had begun by 1942 to think of planning schools in loosely connected units disposed fluidly about an open site, just like an evacuation camp. It was to be another decade before the compact, homogeneous school returned to favour in England.

Meanwhile, the reality of most wartime building was the standard, prefabricated hut. Wartime school-building was no exception. To supplement bombed schools and educate children on the emergency housing estates for war-workers, the Ministry of Works erected hutted classrooms. Then in 1943 the Government decided to double the school-meals service. This meant building hutted canteens all over the country, many at schools of authorities which had never offered meals before. Once the Butler Act was law, there came the question of how to provide a great deal of extra secondary-school accommodation in a hurry. Again, huts were the only immediate answer. So in 1945 HORSA, the Hutting Operation for Raising the School-Leaving Age, swung into action. Even today, HORSA huts can still be found soldiering on at the backs of schools after forty years of despised, unromantic, solid service (Fig. 3.20).

It would be idle to propose that these cramped, cold and inflexible huts were popular. They came to be much resented, especially in the secondary schools. But like the whole experience of war, the huts altered expectations in favour of improvisation, simplicity, cheapness and impermanence, exactly the priorities emerging in pre-war educational ideals. In terms of future planning, the stark economic plight of the nation made it impossible to escape the hutted tradition entirely; educational progressives even seemed to be saying that in sympathetic hands it might have some advantages, particularly for primary children. The task for the planners of post-war school-building, therefore, was to get beyond huts,

3.19. Residential nursery school for twenty children, designed by Birkin Haward for the Evaluation Committee of the AASTA, 1940. Made with rigid regard to economy and availability of materials, the design was based on a 'self-centering block arch' principle and envisaged precast concrete or plaster units running from crosswall to crosswall.

NOTE ROOF FORMS SUITABLE FOR CAMOUFLAGE

3.20. A HORSA hut in full function as a science classroom, Mundella Road Grammar School, Nottingham, 1951.

to build as cheaply, simply and quickly as huts without building huts themselves. If they failed, if permanent schools cost too much money or could not be built rapidly enough or in enough numbers, the spectre which loomed was plain in shape—yet more huts.

All this pointed to some means of sharing and sparing materials, of building in the simplest and quickest way compatible with educational progress—in a word, to standardization and prefabrication. But standardization of what kind? This was the great question which presented itself to the second Wood Committee, the body set up jointly in 1943 by the Directorate of Post-War Building and the Board of Education to recommend means of construction for future school-building. The origins, conflicts and compromises of the Wood Committee have been carefully discussed by Stuart Maclure in his *Educational Development and School Building* and need not long detain us. The main architectural force in its deliberations was Stillman, a voice of authority by virtue of being the only architect with practical experience of prefabricating more than a single school. It was on the basis of Stillman's experiments in West Sussex that the Committee's exemplarily brief report, published in 1944 as *Post-War Building Studies No. 2*, rejected standardized plans, endorsed a modular dimension of 8 feet 3 inches and suggested a structural framework of light steel as the best hope for future schools (Fig. 3.21). On the technical issue of whether the selected dimension should be applied in one or more than one direction—the 'grid v. bay' debate as it came to be called— Stillman could not carry his colleagues in favour of 'bay planning' and both alternatives were put forward, somewhat lamely, in the report. In the event it was Stillman's bay planning, applied not (as he hoped) to randomly disposed, loosely connected classrooms of

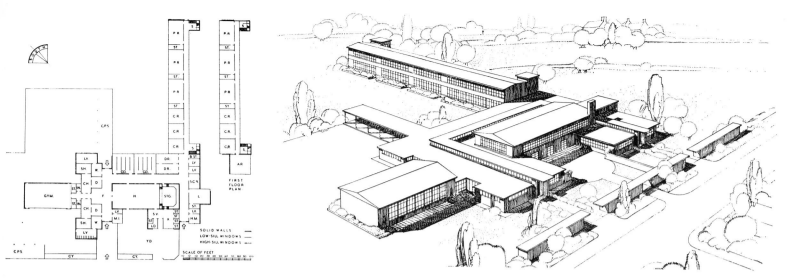

3.21 Official suggestions for prefabricating schools: plan and perspective of a model secondary school from the Wood Report, 1944. A steel-framed structure with a bay-plan arrangement of classrooms with side corridors is shown, but the complexities of roofs and junctions are unresolved. The report notes that this method of standardization cannot be carried up beyond two storeys.

the 'holiday camp' kind but to the old pre-war 'finger plan' type of arrangement with long corridors and classrooms leading off, which prevailed in most new schools until the coming of cost limits in 1950. Still, the Wood Committee offered a helpful lead when schools at last began to be built. For short-handed authorities, the rightness or wrongness of its exact recommendations mattered less than the fact that it offered a framework of advice from which to start.

## HOW THINGS STOOD

At this point, it is worth pausing and reflecting on how things really stood for school-building in 1945. By stressing those previous developments which were to be taken forward, this chapter may have seemed to suggest that a tide of educational and architectural energy was waiting to be unleashed upon a clear new programme of school-building. In fact, the situation was precarious. Those few young men and women who were zealous to make better schools were scattered about the country, dissipated and distracted by the war, and even fewer of them held posts of influence. At the centre was a new ministry with a small staff. Before it loomed a task 'unprecedentedly great', according to the Wood Report; how 'unprecedentedly' so was just beginning to emerge, as the birth statistics started to nudge upwards. The Ministry of Education had more powers than its predecessor, the Board, but constitutionally it was far from being able to coerce the local authorities who had to build the schools. In both their educational and their architectural departments these authorities were pitifully weak in trained staff and were mostly commanded by old men with pre-war ideas who yearned to revert to 'business as usual'. Money, labour and materials were all in short supply. How could the meagre resources of a near-bankrupt nation be prevented from condemning its children to chicken coops? As a 'sacrifice' to the 'realities of the situation', the Wood Report had come up with some structural expedients, but they were only expedients and they hardly touched on the educational side of the question. How anyway were the kinds of schools recommended by Wood to be built? Was it to be left to manufacturers to devise complete structural systems which the subservient local-authority architects would gratefully adopt? If so, how could the systems be controlled? Hardly by the tiny, overworked architectural staff at the Ministry. What then of the teaching which would take place in the schools? Was there to be a repetition of pre-war practice, with architects working from standard briefs at one end of county offices and educationalists moaning about the results at the other? How could new educational thinking find an outlet in the standardized planning which was threatening?

All told, the omens were far from good. It can hardly have seemed likely that an answer to many of these difficulties and, by implication, an escape from impending sterility and uniformity in school-building, should have first come from the obscure offices of a Tory county council—Hertfordshire.

# CHAPTER 4

# HERTS

## THE COUNTY

That the earliest advances in British post-war school-building happened in Hertfordshire was no accident. Lest too much weight be put upon individuals, the Herts story may begin with a glance at the county as it was in 1945.

Hertfordshire has never ranked among the most memorable of English counties. It is rarely singled out even among the 'home counties' around London. In the nineteenth century prosperous early commuters preferred to head south, to the wooded heathlands of Surrey or the orchards of Kent. Middlesex, Hertfordshire and Essex were never so alluring. They had their quiet comeliness, but they were still in the main flattish, fertile, agricultural counties. When at length ploughed land and market garden gave way to the metropolitan onslaught, they attracted less large houses but more small ones. Middlesex by its configuration sheltered Herts from the worst of inter-war development but had itself succumbed almost completely by 1939, leaving Herts and Essex prey to further spoliation. By the outbreak of war Hertfordshire's population too was starting to soar, with southern towns like Barnet, Watford and Cheshunt becoming overrun with under-serviced sprawl. But the county as a whole was still a backwater.

The resumption of building after 1945 coincided with an era of stricter and saner planning controls. By means of Herbert Morrison's green-belt policy, argued for throughout the 1930s, confirmed by law in 1938 and strengthened after the war, the flotsam of London was to be tightly contained. This did not mean that development was going to stop. Instead pristine, circumscribed, self-sufficient, 'satellite' new towns were to arise, located over-whelmingly in the more tractable counties to the north and east: Harlow and Basildon in Essex, Stevenage, Hatfield, Hemel Hempstead and Welwyn Garden City in Herts. On top of these, the London County Council was about to begin the wholesale decanting of Londoners into massive 'out-county' estates, really lower-grade new towns without new-town privileges, like South Oxhey and Borehamwood in Herts and Harold Hill in Essex. Schools for all these developments were to be built not by the new-town authorities or the LCC but by the local county councils. Meanwhile the existing towns—Hertford, Hitchin, Letchworth, St Albans and Watford in Herts, Romford and Chelmsford in Essex—were also girding themselves for faster growth. The troops were returning from the war just as their wives were cast out of the war factories, and the result was babies. Most of those lured to the new towns and the out-county estates were newly-weds or people with young families. The Butler Education Act had decreed secondary schools for all, and the school-leaving age was to rise to fifteen in April 1947. No wonder that Hertfordshire and Essex had a special problem.

Demography aside, something subtler sets Hertfordshire apart from its sister counties. By a quirk of fate, it seems to have inherited some portion of the puritan tradition in English culture. Topography may have a hand in this. History allots this role customarily to the neighbouring flat counties of Cambridgeshire, Bedfordshire and Huntingdonshire, regions akin to the Low Countries and centres of dissent since the seventeenth century. Bunyan came from Bedford, Cromwell from Huntingdon; Cambridge opposed the King and nurtured Newton. These reforming traditions were not dead by the twentieth century. The austere, scientific radicalism of the 1930s has deeper roots in Cambridge than anywhere else. Henry Morris played on the sober, farming consciences of his Cambridgeshire county councillors to pay for his village colleges.

It would be rash to make much of this. Though Hertfordshire trails off to the north into the drabber Cambridgeshire scenery, it is a warmer, more smiling county. Essex too has its flat lands and its libertarian traditions. Yet Hertfordshire alone since the turn of the century has been the cradle for continuous experiment in the making of cities—an experiment in which the reforming and dissenting strains have been constant. It was Herts which played host to the world's first garden cities, Letchworth, commenced in 1903, and the larger Welwyn Garden City, which followed on from 1919. These foundations came to Herts because it could offer the right landscape, the right facilities, the right price and the right ambience, near London yet not too near. They were planned and peopled (at least initially) by idealists. Letchworth was the butt of early amusement for its high-minded tone and its devotion to the simple life, for its spiritualists, vegetarians and anarchists. Welwyn Garden City was a bigger, maturer, more relaxed conception whose architect, Louis de Soissons, has yet to receive his fair due. Its creators and residents were never as obtrusive as the Letchworth pioneers, but they included a scatter of co-operators, self-helpers, Quakers, teetotallers and the like. Radical or revolutionary politics was not the style of these towns, set as they were in a sea of rural conservatism. Rather, they attracted gradualists, diligent small businessmen and earnest professionals possessed of liberal values and social consciences, who cared about matters like health and education. What C. B. Purdom says of Letchworth's early population could with equal truth be applied to either garden city: 'they were in the main ordinary people, who wanted, as far as they could get it, a free life; they were extraordinary only in taking some trouble to realize their wishes'. Hertfordshire County Council, as the 'receiving authority' for the sundry new developments foisted upon it after 1945, was familiar from the experience of the garden cities with the strains imposed by the arrival in its bosom of citizens with alien traditions and independent points of view.

One other accident of geography puts Herts on its own, and has a material part to play in the unfolding of the schools programme. For whatever reasons, several of the institutions which contributed technically to post-war reconstruction had their research headquarters in the county. Much the most important example was the Building Research Station (now Establishment) at Garston outside Watford, half an hour's drive from County Hall at Hertford in a Ford Popular. The comings and goings between Garston and Hertford are an integral part of the saga. There are other instances. The Fire Research Station was at Borehamwood, and the Furniture Industry Research Association in due course moved to Stevenage. Until the railways were nationalized in 1948, Watford housed the engineering and planning division of the LMS Railway, where the earliest architectural 'development group' worked under the aegis of Leslie Martin and Richard Llewelyn-Davies; and a little later the British Standards Institution had a testing laboratory at Hemel Hempstead. Hertfordshire's industries also had their role in the schools programme, part practical, part ideological. The area enjoyed its quota of reliable, medium-sized builders, flexible enough to take on the new organization of work entailed by the schools programme. ESA at Stevenage supplied some furniture (not, it must be said, of special merit) to the early schools. And at Hatfield, adjacent to the county council's supplies depot, De Havillands were working on the Comet, the revolutionary jet airliner. This was to raise in some minds a recrudescence of the 'industrial analogy'. The Herts architects pilgrimaged to De Havillands' works on one occasion to gain inspiration, and Stirrat Johnson-Marshall was to tell the first world conference on building research in 1951:

We have much to learn about timing from the aircraft industry, and from the makers of the Comet in particular. Our first school was in use eighteen months after work started on the board. This seemed to be fairly good going until one discovered that the Comet flew within two years of the inception of the project and that the first production model flew exactly a year later.

To sum up, Hertfordshire in the late 1940s was a county with a tradition of settled, conservative control, agricultural still in much of its outlook and exceptional only in the pressures of population which it faced. But beneath the surface were special currents: an early familiarity with town-planning problems; the facilities for expert advice upon technical questions of building and making; and above all, a half-hidden strain of sober, social idealism. At Ayot St Lawrence in his poky house and pokier garden cabin, George Bernard Shaw eked out his declining years, rebarbative to the last and self-denying in all but words. At Welwyn Garden City, the Shredded Wheat Company was turning out the purest and austerest of breakfast cereals, while at King's Langley just beyond Watford the Ovaltine factory supplied the demand for a healthful nightcap. The atmosphere and circumstances of reconstruction offered a chance for that tradition to take a new turn. It did: in the county's schools.

## THE TEAM AND THE TASK

John Newsom became chief education officer for Hertfordshire County Council in 1940. At that date the council's various branches had been gathered together for only two years, in a new, perversely neo-Georgian county hall set amid manicured lawns on the outskirts of Hertford. Previously they had gone about their business separately, some in Hertford, some in Hatfield, some even in London. No sooner had they been thus united than war dispersed much of the staff. So when peace came, it offered old employees as well as new ones a fresh beginning, with novel opportunities for concerted action.

Before the war the county council had been a backwater, recollects Geoffrey Fardell:

> The chief officers were all minor country gents. The land agent was part-time, I think, until he retired. While he was doing the county job he was also agent for Lord Brocket of Brocket Hall. The county surveyor was chauffeur-driven in a Daimler about as big as the one Queen Mary had. Then there was an enormous gap. The chief officers didn't fraternize at all with the rest of the staff, they were a race apart. On the other hand they were always very civilized and fair. The chief officers then had an enormous amount of authority and power. I think council meetings were over in a few minutes, that kind of thing.

Some of this quiet, uncontroversial atmosphere carried through after the war. The Tory 'independent' councillors accepted without demurral almost every important proposal about school-building, however unusual, so long as it was accompanied by persuasive professional advice. The same indeed happened throughout British local government in the 1940s, especially where education was concerned. These were years of social hope, when the wolf was to dwell with the lamb. Rab Butler, the temperate Tory, ceded the education ministry without rancour to Ellen Wilkinson, the warm-blooded socialist, and their minions, successors, representatives and appointees were expected to get on.

Newsom was the first of a new mould of chief officer at Herts and, by general consent, the person to galvanize the county into educational action. It was he who convinced everyone with whom he had to do that there were great jobs to be done in the county's schools after the war, great reforms to be made and great examples to be set. Newsom's energies, abilities and achievements are handsomely commemorated in Stuart Maclure's study of British post-war school-building. A 'zestful charlatan' somebody once called him, meaning nothing more malicious than that he was an 'ideas man', a publicist and a communicator, an educator who had never taught. He knew and admired Henry Morris of Cambridgeshire, had been greatly struck by Impington Village College and brought with him to Herts some firm beliefs about school-building. 'No architect should design a school until he has sat in a school for at least a week and seen what happens', Newsom told the AA in a discussion of 1946. Guy Oddie's early article on the English school-building movement sums up Newsom's attitudes:

4.1. Classroom, St Audrey's Secondary Modern School, Hatfield, Herts, 1947. Howard Lobb, architect. Trumpeted as the first British post-war school to be completed, its rigid seating, high brick walls and crude lighting represent what the Herts architects were reacting against. The school was a voluntary one and not part of the county's own building programme.

The basis of his approach was that education was inseparable from environment . . . He wanted schools designed for new and continuous developments in teaching, not repetitive railway carriages in which children and teachers would have to adapt themselves as best they could. But he had no blue-print for the ideal school; he would be content to learn as he went along.

Newsom soon gathered around him the team of practical men and women without whom ideals and communicative powers alone are vanity. Sidney Broad was his right-hand administrator. To the meticulous Broad fell, for instance, the burden of sorting out the details of the quiet deals which Newsom's friendship with John Maud, the ebullient young permanent secretary at the post-war Ministry of Education and previously Newsom's tutor at Oxford, made feasible for Hertfordshire. Percy Muncey, another of Newsom's aides, took on the business of maintaining the regular liaison between teachers, administrators and architects which was to be the corner-stone of the Herts school-building philosophy.

When Newsom took the helm at Hertford the war was at its height, the Butler package had yet to reach the consultative stage, and post-war reconstruction was little more than a glint in the steely, calvinist eye of Lord Reith. Hertfordshire's immediate educational headache was that of coping with evacuees. In the absence of school-building, the depleted county surveyor's department struggled merely to keep war damage at bay. Then gradually things picked up. In 1943 began the big, national Ministry of Works programme of huts for school canteens in areas which had not hitherto offered a school-meals service. Herts was one of these. To supervise the huts, Newman hired Mary Crowley to join the Education Department. A dedicated, self-effacing Quaker architect, Mary Crowley (Fig. 4.2) already enjoyed a quiet reputation as a modernist with social interests and a Scandinavian bent. Her father had been the principal medical officer for schools at Bradford and then at the Board of Education, and among the pioneer residents first of Letchworth and then of Welwyn Garden City, so hers was a classic Herts 'progressive' pedigree. The huts did their job. But when in 1945 the new Ministry of Education pressed further huts upon local authorities as the only way of reconciling the promises of the Butler Act with the shambles of the post-war building industry, Newsom wriggled as much as he could. In fact Herts was not able to escape the HORSA programme, the Hutting Operation for the Raising of the School-leaving Age. Six hundred HORSA units of two classrooms each were put up at Hertfordshire's secondary schools between 1947 and 1950.

Huts would have gone further in Hertfordshire, had it not been for Newsom's sense of purpose and his powers of resistance. Since 1943 he and his lieutenants had been planning the county's educational future and had set up a range of wartime meetings which for the first time drew together a local authority's teachers, its small educational and technical staff, and outside experts to debate the relationships between teaching and building. With the Butler Act looming, the discussions centred at first upon secondary schools, on which Henry Morris of Cambridgeshire and C. G. Stillman of West Sussex were among those to propound views. Hence Newsom conceived a 'programme' of lightly constructed secondary schools which were to be farmed out among forward-looking private architects rather than designed by the county's own architectural staff, in whom as yet he felt little confidence. In the event, the advent of HORSA huts meant that most of these schools were postponed. But on primary schools Newsom was able to dig his toes in. In 1945, with the birth bulge now unmistakeable and new towns in the air, Herts shifted its attention increasingly towards thinking about what good primary education might be and how it could be made possible in building. It was in this field that the real innovations were to take place.

Meanwhile the Ministry was pressing local authorities to come up with school-building programmes instead of proceeding in a pre-war, hand-to-mouth manner. Herts worked out that it would need over ten new schools per year or, to quote the exact figures of 1946, 175 schools to be built over fifteen years. This was a great deal for a small authority. Newsom's first thoughts were to farm out half the programme to outside architects and keep no more than half 'in-house'. Under the expected constraints this was hardly realistic. The byzantine business of collaring scarce building materials, the need to economize on the procedures and relationships in design in order to save time, and the ideal of collaboration between architect and educator all pointed to a strong 'in-house' team of architects in charge of a developing programme.

Until 1945 Herts had no independent architect's department. It was one of the last county councils to acquire one. The long-awaited change had been delayed until the county surveyor's retirement, which fell neatly in that year. Before the war, a small architectural staff answering to the surveyor had designed the county's schools, fire stations and police stations; anything larger had been farmed out. Now, with a big school-building programme in prospect, things were to be different. A complete team of architectural 'new blood', uncontaminated by caution or preconception, would be created. First to be offered the new job of Hertfordshire county architect in 1945 was C. G. Stillman. He accepted, then suddenly turned it down in favour of appointment as county architect to more prestigious, populous Middlesex. In due course a rivalry over school-building was to develop between Middlesex and Hertfordshire. Instead of Stillman, C. H. Aslin, previously borough architect for Derby, was appointed to the post.

Herbert Aslin was a pragmatic Yorkshireman of whom people have varying memories. He was shrewd, quiet-spoken, tenacious, courageous, technically proficient, but not personally imaginative or creative. Though not unambitious, he seems rarely to have stretched himself. To use a phrase which came into circulation as post-war local-authority architecture developed, he was an 'umbrella man', willing to trust the young, not to interfere too much, to take sizeable risks, to give an idea a run for its money, and—up to a point—to share credit. Conservative by instinct, he was skilled on the human level, good over a drink with the lads in 'The Salisbury' or in more refined surroundings with the councillors, but not especially a committee man; indeed Newsom frequently did much of Aslin's talking for him at committees. In due course an antipathy arose between Aslin and the more idealistic architects on his staff. Then (as will be seen) the umbrella leaked. But between 1945 and 1949 Aslin presided over a harmonious office and smoothed many a path for the fulfilment of the county's school-building programme.

Abetted by his wife Ethel, always acknowledged as a power in the land, Aslin hired staff quickly to supplement the 'rump' from the county surveyor's office. The first arrivals included several Derbyshire and Yorkshire men known to him personally: Sam Morrison, an architect of solid, practical experience; Henry Sugden, who became chief quantity surveyor; and Ken Hicklin, later county architect of Cornwall. Then late in 1945 a young architect of thirty-three, Stirrat Johnson-Marshall, fresh from a 'good war' and drawn to Herts by John Newsom's growing reputation, took up the post as Aslin's deputy. Immediately he became the energizing force in the office.

How far were the ideas which took shape in the Herts schools already present in Johnson-Marshall's mind? It is easy to talk retrospectively of strategy, when people are feeling their way. But certainly Johnson-Marshall arrived at Herts with some fixed intentions. He had experience of school-building from before the war, from three years at the Isle of Ely County Council. He had learnt from his wartime job in camouflage and deception (p. 21–3) the 'operational' way of getting an idea into quick production with the help of industry and then using feedback to improve on the original. He was attuned to the notion that it would be necessary to prefabricate in order to build schools in large numbers. He may have read the Wood Report of 1944 on school construction, with its recommendation of the 8 feet 3 inches planning module and a light steel frame. He knew from his friend Donald Gibson about the various prototype houses of steel with concrete cladding erected at Coventry during and just after the war. He knew too that he could get help from BRS nearby, where he actually turned down a job in order to go to Hertford. Technicalities apart, Johnson-Marshall had above all become convinced that architects, if they were ever to be of any real service in the post-war world, would have to forge some sort of new, proper, integral relationship both with those who decided what buildings should be built—the policy-makers—and with those who had to carry out and live with the consequences of those decisions—the makers and users of buildings. That is why he chose again after the war to work for a local authority, not for a research agency, and why Newsom's Herts in particular attracted him.

The idea of a programme of prefabricated schools preceded by a prototype was by no means Johnson-Marshall's own. Stillman had come to the same conclusions, had designed a prototype school in 1945 even before he left West Sussex, and hatched a school-building programme for Middlesex a little before things got going at Herts. There had been building programmes too, of a kind, in pre-war 'official' architecture: flats at the LCC, schools in Middlesex, the Miners Welfare pithead baths, incorporating standardized details, fittings and plan types and using a common architectural idiom. But it was the nature of Hertfordshire's 'rolling programme' which rendered it revolutionary in British architecture. The Herts schools programme would be dynamic, not static, in character, unlike the fitful, unco-ordinated progress which was all that Stillman managed in Middlesex. A continuous, organized cycle of design, production, feedback and development was to be linked to a means of construction which would be simple, fast, economic and unifying, yet flexible enough to permit regular revision and some variety of expression. From an industrial perspective this may sound commonplace. In the cumbersome, antiquated traditions of the British building industry it was then quite new. It needed special circumstances to be realized: the combination of a fresh start with big demands and dramatic difficulties, eliciting thought from first principles; an acquaintance with industrial methodology and a willingness to submit individualism to a common discipline; a strong team of public architects working for an authority which not only provided the opportunity for continuous work on a particular building-type but also fostered regular contact between the team and the users, or the users' representatives; and a building-type like a primary school which was self-contained and could be 'turned round' fast enough for the production cycle to be completed in time for the designers to remember and learn from their mistakes. Above all, the Herts programme in the first instance needed a leader who could convey the alluring prospect that, with the 'appropriate technology', sufficient humility, concentration and hard work it might be possible in due course to create a new type of humane, responsible, universal post-war architecture. It was this leadership, this vision of moral adventure, which Stirrat Johnson-Marshall brought to Herts.

4.2. David and Mary Medd (Mary Crowley) on holiday in Italy in the year of their marriage, 1949.

Johnson-Marshall can hardly have grasped all this when he first appeared at Hertford. But his purpose was resolute enough for him rapidly to establish himself with Newsom and to set about a plan of research. The first quest was for a prefabricated prototype, in line with the Wood Report's suggestions. Almost everything was still up in the air. What form of construction should the prototype adopt? Who would make it? What should be its lifespan? How could it release rather than constrain the teachers' energies? Was there time to evolve, design, erect, assess and test a prototype before the primary-school population was condemned to huts? How was the production team to be organized? How could Aslin, the county council and the ministry be convinced?

The answers to these questions sprang out of two years' fevered activity at the Hertford offices, between the arrival of Johnson-Marshall late in 1945 and the time that the first schools were all safely on site late in 1947. In the interim the school-building group had smartly picked up young staff, mostly in their twenties still: the first were David Medd (Fig. 4.2), Johnson-Marshall's crony from camouflage days, then Bruce Martin (a friend of Medd's from the pre-war AA), Bill Henderson, Dan Lacey, Oliver Carey, Anthony Garrod and (briefly) Anthony Cox. Mary Crowley crossed over from the education department, helping to cement the links between architects and teachers; her unique background and talents were to make her, over the years, the greatest single influence on the planning of the post-war schools. Veterans look back to this time as one of camaraderie and dedication intermixed with acute discomfort. John Newsom leading the combined architects and education staff in shovelling snow off the forecourt at County Hall during the gruelling winter of 1946–7; Johnson-Marshall descending from his private office after the day's work to enthuse into the night about the mission before them, architectural, educational and social; freezing railway-journeys to visit far-flung makers of components, followed by nights on camp beds in unheated railway hotels: such were the rewards and punishments of reconstruction. It was all akin to the army, and indeed a certain military style and argot, acronyms and catchphrases, pervaded the office. 'Herts were the happiest days of my life,' says Cleeve Barr (one of the architects who joined the team in 1947) and the confession is echoed by others. For these young men, eager to get on at last with their careers after the frustration of war, to create instead of destroying, these years set an abiding ideal of what architecture should be all about. The emotion of the period was tremendous. They were, in a manner of speaking, patriots fulfilled.

## THE MAKING OF A SYSTEM

The reasons for the frenzy of 1945–7 were simple. Because of the Damoclean danger of huts, Herts decided that it must do without a proper prototype. There could be no small 'development group' (to use the coming term), no team to be taken away from ordinary office routine, working drawings and site supervision to play with mock-ups. Pat Tindale, the first of several students brought in to aid the overstretched architects, went down from the AA for the summer vacation of 1946, when the working drawings for the earliest job, Cheshunt Infants School, were in the making. She describes the mood thus:

> Cheshunt was not a prototype, Cheshunt was the first-off. A prototype is something you do, you evaluate, and if it doesn't work you can do another prototype. We couldn't afford to have that kind of delay or that possibility of failure. Cheshunt had to be right, to show how the programme went. That was the kind of confidence and commitment.

This urgency meant that the Herts architects were unable to start from scratch, as by professional instinct they would have preferred. They knew that any system left to the creation of a manufacturer would leave them with scant control over its design and performance. That road led back to the old 'proprietary' systems, which had given prefabricated housing so bad a name in the 1920s and were to do so again in the 1960s. They were in the business of designing not buildings but a method of building, to be controlled, developed and altered by the authority itself. They wanted to compose not an essay or a book but a language and vocabulary, and to write the first literature in it all at the same time. The metaphor may seem too strong; prefabrication, after all, was not radically new, and there were engineers and manufacturers enough to supply a rudimentary, structural grammar. But the difficulty was to identify these people, get to them, cajole them, convince them of the opportunities, and lay before them a new ideal of collaboration based upon the philosophic triangle of design, manufacture and use. That done, the key suppliers had to be shocked out of routine, inflexible standardization by classroom or by bay into something far more revolutionary and harder to achieve, something never hitherto tried in Britain—the Gropian concept of a 'kit of parts', of prefabrication not by unit of structure but by components. By this means it might be possible to create an up-to-date, responsive, living 'language' of building. On top of all this, the war had sorely damaged the normal links between architects, contractors and suppliers. There were no glossy manufacturers' catalogues, few standard ranges of components around which a designer could fit his thinking. Everything had to be discovered or rediscovered.

For these reasons the first Hertfordshire schools, at Cheshunt and Essendon, relied abnormally on a single manufacturer, Hills and Company of West Bromwich. Indeed the celebrated Herts 8 feet 3 inches system owed more to Ernest Hinchliffe, the presiding and inventive genius at Hills, than to any other single individual. Hinchliffe was characteristic of certain British industrialists of the 1940s, infected by the period's idealism yet alive to its commercial opportunities. By nature he was a 'tinkerer', keen on ideas and on getting things going, not so good on matters of efficiency, profit and loss. He had founded Hills as a patent glazing company in 1932, since when it had rapidly expanded. It had divisions making steel window-frames, rooflights, and structural light-steel sections. During the war the firm had shared in the supply of welded sections for Bailey bridges, a *locus classicus* for the wartime revolution in design and mass-production of engineering structures. Like other sharp industrialists dependent on war production, Hinchliffe started to plan quite early for converting his capacity to peacetime reconstruction. By 1944 the first of the 'Hills Presweld' houses, with steel frame and concrete cladding, had been built. Hinchliffe had gone on to look into the possibilities of school-building. When Herts, apparently through the Ministry of Education, first got in touch with Hills, he already had an experimental 8 feet 3 inches classroom unit up at the West Bromwich works, and was setting up the plant to manufacture cladding slabs, roof blocks and floors for this and for his prefabricated houses.

Herts, therefore, 'bought' an existing prototype 'off the peg' from Hills in order to build the three original classrooms of Cheshunt Infants School. To quote from Michael Keath's definitive technical study of the Herts systems,

> The design of the components required to construct the shells of these three simple, repeating structures was thus completely the responsibility of the manufacturer. The architects' contribution was to sense their potential for development and to harness them to the purposes of the programme; they did not create the embryonic system themselves but acted rather as a midwife to the birth of the system.

In other words, they were from the first unwilling to leave Hinchliffe's system as they found it. The biggest technical development took place in 1947 after Cheshunt Infants had been built, when David Medd went up to West Bromwich for several months to loosen up and virtually recreate the system, in fact to rewrite the 'grammar' of the Hills prototype and inject sufficient flexibility and coherence for it successfully to be applied to the proper programme of schools due to start that autumn, beginning with Cheshunt Junior School. Every year hereafter, the system's structure and components were rescrutinized and updated for the annual programme of schools (Fig. 4.3). This routine became a feature of Herts methodology, and passed on unchanged to the schools consortia. The to-ing and fro-ing between Hertford and West Bromwich in the late 1940s did a great deal for establishing in school-building practice the concept of a cycle involving designer, manufacturer and user. The educationalists told the architects how the system so far developed failed to meet their needs; the architects took this on board while simultaneously stretching the system

4.3. Trial sections of the 8 feet 3 inches system at the Hills works, West Bromwich. These were used for experimenting with claddings, junctions, windows, etc. The Hills system here is at a mature stage in its development, *c.* 1953.

to cope with more complicated sites and technical briefs; and then the manufacturers strained to respond.

Throughout this process Hinchliffe, ever the inventor more than the businessman, committed funds and expertise beyond hope of immediate profit and entered into the spirit of what Herts was trying to do. So if Herts had no development group it had the next best thing, a band of engineers and tracers in the Hills draughting office who were as wedded to the experiment as the architects themselves. Unquestionably this was done with an eye to improving Hills' own 'proprietary' 8 feet 3 inches system for schools, a version which, though the Herts architects thought it inferior to their own, was in due course widely marketed to less demanding local authorities—the London County Council for one (Fig. 4.25). But Hinchliffe seems always to have cared less about selling than about building up an ingenious structural vocabulary for anything that the architects wanted to say. When prefabricated school-building became more competitive, his firm overstretched itself and foundered, but not before it had contributed remarkably to the whole movement.

Why did the Herts architects choose Hinchliffe's original prototype? The simple answer is that they did so because, in a situation of urgency, it already existed as a working tool and it conformed to advice then coming from central government. The planning module of 8 feet 3 inches, recommended by government in order to allow square classrooms of 24-foot sides, had not yet been much tried in practice. Modular theorists already feared that it would prove inflexible (and the Herts team even played around in the very early days with an alternative six-foot grid), but at least it offered a nationally approved point of departure. Greater modular sophistication, it was felt, could come later. For the moment, any dimensional discipline would save time on the drawing board and on site and would economize on materials. Given too was the desirability of a light-steel frame, also commended by the Wood Report. Structural prefabrication in concrete was still in a rudimentary phase of development. *In situ* concrete required extensive plant and site-labour and meant much heavy, wet work which it was part of the new 'light and dry' philosophy to minimize. The same was true of traditional construction, 'brick and bodge', as the Herts men loved contemptuously to label it. The materials situation, it must be emphasized, seemed desperate. 'The supply of steel was meagre, timber was almost unobtainable, and while bricks could be obtained there were no bricklayers to lay them'. Even when materials and labour were to be had, their use might delay a vital housing development elsewhere, especially in hard-

4.4. Steel frame of the early 8 feet 3 inches system in course of erection by Gee, Walker and Slater at Burleigh Junior School, Cheshunt, 1947. The early lattice girders have a delicate, artistic appearance.

pressed Herts. It was a conscious part of Johnson-Marshall's strategic philosophy that his team must, if necessary, be self-denying in the wider national interest. So the means of construction had to be 'alternative', sparing, and made up of components light enough to be borne by two or three men at a time, like the wartime Bailey bridge. All this pointed to light steel with a cladding of light concrete (Figs 4.4, 5).

Aesthetically too, the architects were most comfortable with this combination—the 'meccano' system, as it was dubbed. They had all played with meccano as boys; David Medd, who spearheaded the technical development of the 8 feet 3 inches system, had even won prizes for his models in the medium. With its simple concrete pad and array of steel uprights punched with holes, it appealed to their boyish hankering for something neat, flexible, mechanical and toylike, something to which bits could be rapidly screwed or bolted, added or taken away, which would last neither too long nor too short a time, which could be left out in the rain for a while as it had been left out on the nursery table, and then might be superseded by something cleverer. Bruce Martin, the most theoretically inclined of the early Herts architects, summed up this Bernalist philosophy of building materials thus:

The so-called building materials, the bricks and stones, the tiles and concrete . . . are ma-

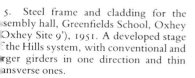

4.5. Steel frame and cladding for the assembly hall, Greenfields School, Oxhey (Oxhey Site 9'), 1951. A developed stage of the Hills system, with conventional and larger girders in one direction and thin transverse ones.

4.6. Four methods of school planning using standardized construction with a dimensional discipline, showing their advantages and disadvantages.
A. The 'bay' plan, with spans of 8 feet 3 inches in accordance with the recommendations of the Wood Report of 1944. Widely used in proprietary schools systems of the 1940s and early '50s, it offered limitless extension in one direction but caused problems when changes of level and direction were required. It inevitably produced plans with straight corridors and rows of rectangular classrooms.
B. The square grid, to a module of 8 feet 3 inches running in either direction. The system adopted in the early Herts schools. It permitted suppler planning with easy changes of direction, and was combined with a range of column-heights on a vertical module, allowing changes of ceiling and floor level. The structural and planning grids in these buildings coincided. Where columns and partitions met, it could look messy. The dimension also proved too big for optimum flexibility and economy.
C. The square grid to a module of 3 feet 4 inches, as recommended by the Cleary Working Party in 1948. This grid offered smaller planning increments, allowed the greater flexibility needed in secondary-school design and helped with the tighter planning required by cost limits after 1950. Adopted by the Ministry of Education, CLASP and many school-building authorities in the 1950s.
D. The 'tartan grid', again to a module of 3 feet 4 inches. In this variant, first championed by the architects of the wartime London Midland and Scottish Railway's Development Group, the columns are not on the same grid lines as the walls and partitions, but are arranged on a separate grid of their own. Beloved of structural purists for the clean and aesthetic separation it offered between supports and divisions. Used experimentally for Herts schools from 1949 onwards but never generally adopted because of the complexities involved in its design.

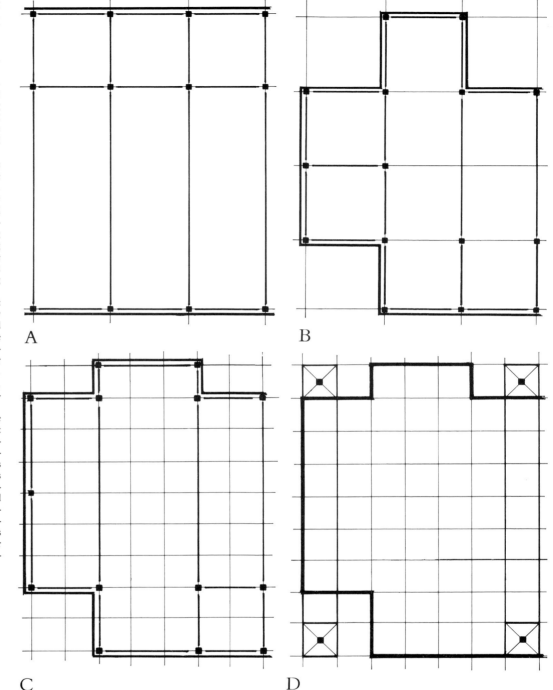

A

B

C

D

4.7. (facing page) Diagrammatic plans of Herts primary schools, 1947–50, showing grouping, siting and contours. The shading indicates the north side; classrooms are shown by numbers. H = Hall; D = Dining; K = Kitchen. 1, Monkfrith Infants School, East Barnet. 2, Cowley Hill School, Borehamwood. 3, Belswains School, Hemel Hempstead. 4, Morgans Walk School, Hertford. 5, Aboyne Lodge Infants School, St Albans. 6, Spencer School, St Albans. 7, Warren Dell School, Watford. 8, Templewood School, Welwyn Garden City.

terials for defence against a hostile world; pyramids and temples, castles and palaces, moats and dungeons, forts and air-raid shelters, dams and tombs. But they are not the new materials for the shelter of man in his brief life of seventy years. We must build lightly for a life of free and changing activity, for families with the space in which to grow as needs and ideas change.

In addition, the light-steel system followed the structural pattern of the latest and most approved experiments in housing. For the cladding, plain concrete was adopted for the stark reason that nothing else was then cheaply available, but the architects at first were confident that this too could be enhanced and developed further along the path which Le Corbusier had started to hew.

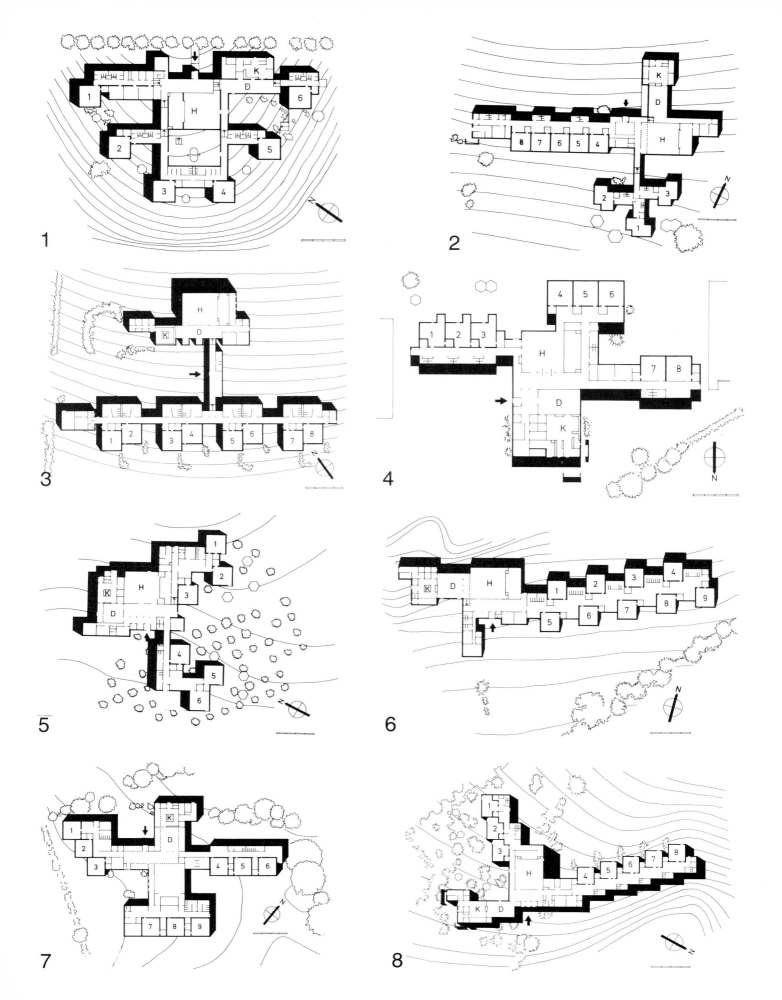

1

2

3

4

5

6

7

8

4.8. Burleigh School, Cheshunt, in 1947. Mary Crowley, David Medd and Bruce Martin, job architects. The three infant classrooms (right) are in use, while the junior school and assembly hall (foreshortened, left), near completion.

The most momentous decision taken by the Herts architects during the original development of their 8 feet 3 inches system during 1947 was to cast aside the 'bay' arrangement of prefabricated planning and to substitute a 'grid'. Hinchliffe's prototype, employed with few alterations in the Cheshunt Infants School, was a classroom unit. It had been devised to allow classrooms in long ranks with lower corridors to the side in accordance with pre-war ideas or to fit Stillman's newer notion of randomly dispersed classrooms connected by *in situ* work of one kind or another. Either arrangement implied a good deal of rigidity. But with a grid expressed structurally, it became possible to shift the plan in either direction and to turn corners and change levels more elegantly, so securing practical and aesthetic advantages (Fig. 4.6). This was the opening blow in the 'grid *v.* bay' war which was fought long and hard between 1947 and about 1952, with Stillman of Middlesex heading one team and Johnson-Marshall, first at Herts and then at the Ministry of Education, the other. Grid systems were more complex and cost more to develop, their opponents alleged, than bays. But they opened up school planning to flexibility and rearrangement on a scale only dimly at first perceived. 'With a grid you could build a whole school, not just the classroom bits', says David Medd. 'We had to break the view that a school was no more than the sum of its classrooms'.

Grids turned prefabricated school-building from a *pis aller*, to borrow Marian Bowley's

4.9. Burleigh Infants School, Cheshunt, 1946–7, showing the three staggered, sloping-roofed classrooms, separated by planted courts for use by the children. To the left, the hall of the junior school.

o and 11.   Court entrance to an infant
sroom, Burleigh School, Cheshunt,
ing erection and complete. Note the
pended flooring, a costly feature of the
y Hills package.

phrase, from a necessity arising out of shortages and urgencies, into a rival to traditional modes of construction. Thus a procedure which started as a stop-gap began to be seen as offering better chances for education, better value for money and therefore a tool specially applicable to a national programme of public building. With the Hertfordshire grid, its architects could have a first stab at the aims which Newsom and his educators had spoken of. They could vary the scale and layout of the primary school, break the long, drab, institutional corridors and stagger classrooms—known in progressive 'Herts-speak' as 'teaching spaces' (Fig. 4.7). Applying the 'modular discipline' to the third dimension as the Herts architects did, they could change heights and floor levels, step up, step down, and set schools on sloping sites in a way which was impossible for any 'bay' system (Fig. 4.16). They could offer teachers the options of privacy and intimacy, by decentralizing lavatories and cloakrooms, or of community and integration, by staggering the corridors and opening them up to the classes. In due course, the grid would make it possible—for better or worse— to cast out primary-school corridors altogether.

## CHESHUNT AND ESSENDON

Burleigh School at Cheshunt and the small village school at Essendon were the first schools built in the Herts 8 feet 3 inches system. Tentative though they are in technique, they still merit a visit, for they preserve a crisp, pioneering, Swedish quality which few later schools captured again once the big programmes got going in 1948. The Cheshunt school (Figs 4.4, 8–11), started late in 1946, built in two stages and finished in May 1948, has the handicap of an average suburban site, of a flatness all too typical. Like most primary schools of those early post-war days, when constraints upon space were few, it straggles. The single-storey scale and the scattered blocks conspire against overall architectural effect. That, its architects might have argued, was intentional. These were not to be propaganda buildings for the journals, angled to satisfy the photographer standing on the far side of the playing field, but working buildings for the sole benefit of the children and teachers.

For all that, Burleigh Infants, designed mainly by Mary Crowley on the basis of the

4.12. Essendon School. Bill Henderson and Dan Lacey, job architects, 1947–8. Infants' classroom to left, junior classroom in centre, hall to right.

Hills prototype, turns out on close quarters to be a strong enough statement. It shows the team struggling from the very start towards the grid. Three square, separate classrooms stand in a staggered row off a staggered corridor, each with its single-pitched roof, its eaves and hoods over a pair of entrances front and back, its lavatories and cloakroom, and its generous terrace and landscaped area for outdoor teaching. These quaint, self-contained little concoctions take up directly from where the pre-war, open-air nursery and infants' school movement had left off. The inspiration behind them is a Scandinavian one mediated by the experience of evacuation and the 'holiday camp'; the thought is of small, scattered outposts in field or forest, linked at most by a walk-way. Among the suburban lots of Cheshunt it takes a little imagination to smell the sap of pine trees, but the tang is clearly there. The veteran critic Trystan Edwards caught enough of it to ask gently: 'Do these scattered sheds in between the trees represent the right expression for a school or do they perhaps too closely resemble a colony for consumptives placed in separate hutments for the benefit of their health?'

Nothing quite like Burleigh Infants was built again. Burleigh Junior School, which followed on under the direction of David Medd and Bruce Martin, is in the revised Hills vocabulary, on a proper grid and with the first rationalizations. Here, for instance, only the assembly hall has a pitched roof. Since pitched roofs turned out to need too many 'specials' and involved complications at joints and angles, all the schools after Cheshunt and Essendon until about 1951 had flat roofs throughout, somewhat to the designers' regret. This at once was the discipline and the bane of prefabrication: an architect had to limit the range of his expression on any one building for the good of the whole programme. In practice, the schools always included more 'specials' and site-decisions about awkward corners than its proponents cared to admit. A good architect would chafe against the system's restrictions and occasionally overstep them, but to go too far caused delays and difficulties for others. Only some temperaments could work within this discipline. As early as Essendon, the second school, Bill Henderson 'distorted the system' in his sketch plans to make the building more characterful and artistic, says Oliver Cox. Dan Lacey then had to make the design work, a position equally honourable in Herts philosophy and a great deal more taxing. A simple truth about designing for a prefabricated system of building soon became apparent. So long as the system was thoroughly and intelligently worked out it assured a minimum level of competence in what was produced, but it was hard to attain any exalted level of architecture. High-flyers might chafe against this, but in post-war circumstances

4.13. Essendon School, hall, with class-rooms to left and covered playspace beneath. The Scandinavian aura is strong, but the Hills patent cladding appears crudely fixed.

it was the raising of average standards which was most needed. It is a moot point for architects to consider whether this may not still be the case.

Essendon today (Figs 4.12–15) is the easiest of the early Herts schools to admire. Most secrete themselves upon anonymous, suburban backlands. But here is that rare post-war event, a genuine village school, replacing one that had been bombed. It was built, ironically, with the help of unrepatriated prisoners of war. It is set handsomely against a hillock with a copse of oaks behind. For the sake of the children as much as the buildings the Herts architects took what care they could with their sites and their trees; in general, those that still look best are those best-favoured in these respects. Punchy, compact and clean, Essendon is quite different from Cheshunt, and a tribute to the flexibility of the early Hills vocabulary. Originally there were just two junior classrooms, an infants' room set back a little, and the higher assembly hall, doubling as a dining area and stuck up on stilts to permit a covered playspace beneath. In the brief compass of the school, the visitor can grasp the delicacy, intimacy and informality which its architects were trying to fashion out of the harsh materials and circumstances with which they were confronted: the changing scale of the building, the gradations in size of the fragile lattice girders (often within adult reach, and with the heating pipes threaded pragmatically through them), the tiny handbasins and so on. Much of the freshness and most of the bright, strong splashes of colour may have gone, but the original spirit of the place, 'forceful and also genial' as Edwards put it, can still be felt.

Cheshunt and Essendon were the earliest Herts schools to be completed by the best part of a year. In many ways they are fumbling first attempts. The junior classrooms are all self-contained, enclosed, square, conventionally lit boxes, with windows along one side and clerestory lighting from above the corridor opposite—which at Cheshunt stretches unfeelingly into the distance. They were equipped with locker-desks all facing the chalkboard (Fig. 4.15); as yet, revolutions in teaching method and school furniture had hardly begun. Today the two schools seem thoughtful, adaptable but hardly exceptional, and the disintegration of many of the original Hills cladding panels, which turned out faulty, is a definite discouragement. But for the students of the austerity years, starved of architectural novelty, these little schools were like manna from heaven. In 1948 they were practically the only objects yet built in impoverished, post-war Britain that could be called 'modern architecture'. The AA ran several trips to them which made a profound social and aesthetic impression on the participants. Henry Swain was one such:

4.14. Infants spilling out of their classroom at Essendon.

4.15 Junior classroom at Essendon. A traditional teaching arrangement still, with trappings of the old discipline: locker desks facing one way, light coming from the pupils' left, inkpots and bell. But the open view invites distraction.

One had modelled oneself on Tecton, High Point, all reinforced concrete and magnificent, and here was something quite different. I can't impress on you too much how different these buildings looked. Seen in the context of the Modern Movement, everything monstrous and big and reinforced, here was something light and delicate and hammered out of the process of studying the problem. It was totally new, it didn't seem to have roots in anything. Not a single concession to Banister Fletcher in proportion or materials even! It was simply the artefact to do the job, but that job included the care of children. Arthur Korn said: 'Henry, this is what Gropius would have liked to have seen'.

Things I now take for granted in design of infant schools then leapt at me—little chairs twelve inches high, low window sills for children to see out of, little child-sized lavatories and wash-basins. There was a total unity of architectural and technical thinking.

## PROPAGANDA AND COLLABORATION

The trips to Cheshunt and Essendon were a token of the skilful propaganda campaign waged by Stirrat Johnson–Marshall from the time of his arrival to put Herts 'on the map' and convince people that it and it alone had the right answer to the school-building question. This answer had three prongs. There was the bureaucratic prong, through which the formidable pair of persuaders, Newsom and Johnson–Marshall, got John Maud and Antony Part at the Ministry of Education to favour Herts. This worked in various subtle ways. Dan Lacey:

> The educationalists became very attached to us because we could get things done for them. We were able to benefit from the MoE, because all materials were rationed and you couldn't build anything without permits. The Ministry used to have a steel ration which they doled out to local authorities. Come the end of the quarter or the half year they used to find they'd got a bit left. They would ring up Sidney Broad and say 'Can you take some M-forms?', and Sidney always found that we could take these and that got him more schools. That helped to bind the two departments together; they found us utterly reliable. This was all possible because of our connections with Hills. We weren't engaged on building schools on a one-off basis, we were engaged on building programmes of schools, so therefore Hills were able to take the M-forms and bank 'em, and get the steel for the next half-dozen jobs.

This ability to cultivate people in the right place, to improvise, and to take sudden advantage of 'puffs of wind' was to be a key feature of school-building in the hands of Johnson–Marshall and his disciples.

Then there was the publicity prong. It did not take long for Johnson–Marshall and his men to build up a warm relationship with the Architectural Press. The editor of the *Architectural Review*, J. M. Richards, was sympathetic, but the person who came to be most committed to Johnson–Marshall's views about school-building and, in general, to improved ways of working in the public sector was Colin Boyne, a young AA-trained reporter on the *Architects' Journal*. This link became most important in the early 1950s; at the time of Cheshunt and Essendon it was just beginning to be established.

Finally there was the educational prong. Amid their other occupations, Johnson–Marshall and Medd found time for the occasional lecture or 'pep-talk' in the architectural schools, notably the AA and Birmingham (where Douglas Jones, one of Medd's former tutors, was now at the helm). These excursions helped make Herts a prime target for socially minded young architects. Johnson–Marshall would unabashedly woo the best students, even trying to persuade them to forget their exams. With over twenty new schools in the combined primary programme for 1948 and 1949 and with secondary schools soon coming up, the office was expanding fast. Oliver Cox, Cleeve Barr, Michael Smith, John Redpath, Donald Barron, Henry Swain, Edmund Tory, Ken Twist, Ken Evans and others joined during this period. All through 1948 and 1949, Herts was humming.

The basis of the team's success lay in group-working, the organizational method proposed both before and after the war at the AA but seldom, if ever, tried out properly. At first the schools architects were few enough to function as a single team; later they worked in sub-groups, the size of which was food for constant debate. But the optimum number within groups mattered little compared to the fact that through Aslin's good will and Johnson-Marshall's strategic skills young British architects were able for practically the first time to operate responsibly, independently, creatively and cohesively without feeling that their work was being subordinated to the ambitions of a private individual or that some bureaucratic hierarchy was inhibiting or misappropriating their talents. Aslin's name still appeared on all the drawings and in the publicity, and Aslin himself reaped sufficient reward from the efforts of his subalterns to become president of the RIBA in 1954–6. Yet the sense of the time was of freedoms and joint responsibilities hitherto unavailable in 'official' architecture. Later, teamwork in architecture spread so far that its novelty then seems hard to credit. But in the late 1940s the old hierarchies, whether of public or of private practice, were only just beginning to break down.

1948–9 was the period when the 8 feet 3 inches Herts system was refined into an art. The hasty groping of 1946–7, having been vindicated in the first ten schools and having staved off the threat of huts for good, now turned into a conscious, collaborative method of design with fixed principles. Nobody asserts that the best Herts schools were built in these early years. But the principles which emerged were so influential that it is worth looking at the process in detail.

One of the lessons of Cheshunt and Essendon had been that too many eggs should not be put into a single basket. Hills had not only designed, made and erected the steel skeleton for these schools, they had also supplied the windows, roof slabs, cladding and suspended floors. For much of the two schools, Hills therefore was a 'nominated sub-contractor' under the builders (Gee, Walker and Slater). In the event the quality of the concrete cladding turned out to be poor, the floors were expensive and there were delays and defects in connection with the steelwork for Essendon. Another firm had supplied fibrous plaster exclusively for all the linings, partitions, coat fittings and heating cabinets in the first ten schools. This too had led to complications, late deliveries and messy ways of working as John Redpath, a stickler for efficiency, found to his horror on arriving at Herts. Left to himself, Johnson-Marshall might have gone further down the road of a 'package' arrangement, whereby for reasons of simplicity and urgency one or two manufacturers went on handling much of the value of each building. But Aslin and the rest of the architects were adamant that the load must be spread among different specialists, to secure better quality among components and greater power and control over the product. Henceforward, Hills made the frame and the windows alone.

From this decision, taken in 1947, and from the Ministry's insistence that school-building authorities should split their tasks into clearly defined annual programmes, sprang an important division of labour among the Herts architects. In each year's programme the development of every separate main component, liaison with manufacturers, and its integration into the rest of the system would fall to the lot of a single architect. In addition, each architect had his or her own school to sort out with the educators, design, take through the working-drawing stage and put on site. Thus each member of the team enjoyed responsibility for a single job and was linked into the whole annual programme. Within this outline there was much 'give and take'. Not every architect developed a component; some worked on schools in pairs; some like David Medd and Oliver Cox with greater technical facility cornered whole hunks of the programme—plumbing, furniture and colour. And since there were too many schools to go round, a few each year were 'farmed out' to needy private architects, duly vetted for their willingness to subjugate individualism to the collective Herts ethic. Gollins and Melvin (friends of Aslin's) and Dex Harrison's firm of Harrison and Seel got the first ones (Fig. 4.16). From 1949 onwards the Architects' Co-operative Partnership (ACP) which Anthony Cox left Herts to help restart, built nine schools in the county. James Cubitt and Partners, Birkin Haward of Ipswich, and a few other firms also had a share in the booty. Normally they were required to use the 8 feet 3 inches system, and

4.16.    South Hill School, Hemel Hempstead. Harrison and Seel, private architects
(job architect, Roger Booth), 1949–50.

a hash they sometimes made of it, according to Herts veterans. So dominant was the public
sector in those days that the private architects sometimes merely made working drawings
from plans sketched out in the overpressed office. One or two firms were trusted and did
well. Oakland Infants School (1950–1) at East Barnet, for instance, designed by Leo de
Syllas of ACP, was reckoned as good as anything the regular staff ever did (Fig. 4.17).

The execution of these increasing programmes from 1948 onwards (Figs. 4.17–22) meant
that the office had to work to a timetable and with a precision which had been unheard
of in Britain before the war. Here, military experience came naturally to the team's aid.
The regular meetings, the progress charts on the walls, the careful coding and colouring
and filing of drawings according to their categories, the proper organization of office space

4.17.    Oakland Infants School, East Barnet (formerly Herts, now London Borough of Barnet), plan. An 8 feet 3 inches
school designed for Herts by a private
firm, the Architects Co-Operative Partnership (ACP), Leo de Syllas partner in
charge, 1950–1. Staggered classrooms
with movable partitions encroach into the
formerly sacrosanct corridor space. The
mural by Fred Millett illustrated in Plate I
on the west end of the assembly hall.

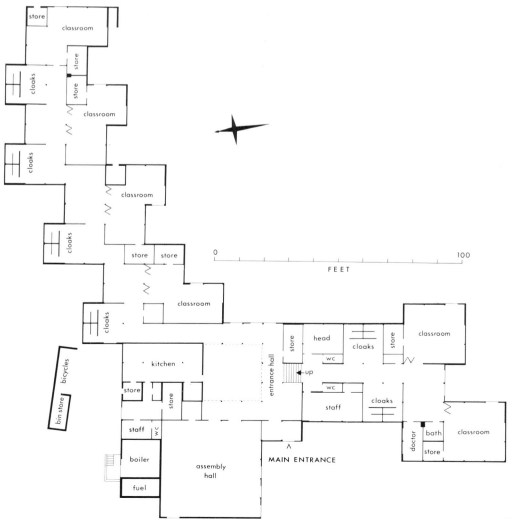

4.18. Preparatory drawings by Oliver Cox for St Meryl School, Carpenders Park, Watford, 1949. These are extracts from a set of drawings made by Cox to demonstrate the Herts methodology of design.

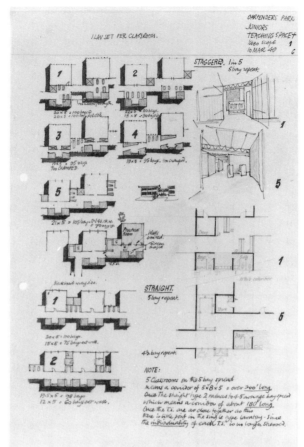

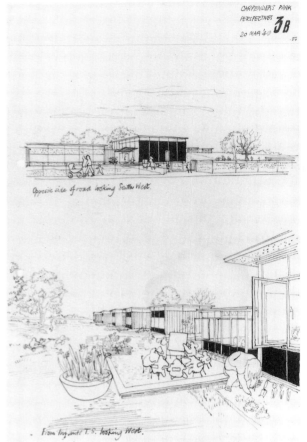

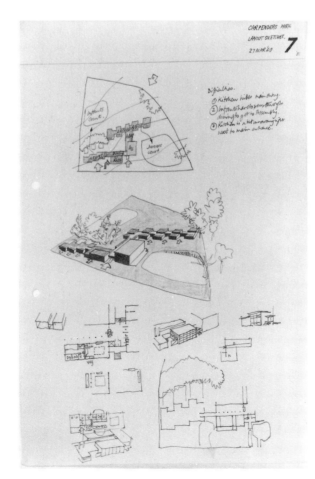

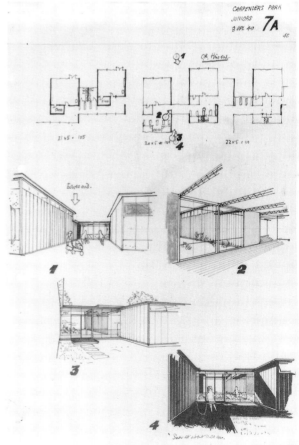

19. Maylands Infant School, Adeyfield, Hemel Hempstead, nearing completion. K. & E. Twist, job architects, 1949–51. The toplights, replacing previous clerestory lighting, can be clearly seen.

20. Gym in the hall, Hazelgrove School, Hatfield (Johns, Slater and Haward, private architects, 1954–5). The climbing ropes are hung from the girders of the steel frame. The patterned concrete panels seen on the outside wall were devised by Birkin Haward to cheer up the look of the Herts 8 feet 3 inches system but were not widely used.

4.21 and 22. Templewood School, Welwyn Garden City, frame and finished appearance of classrooms. A. W. Cleeve Barr, job architect, 1949–50.

in the basement at Hertford where they worked, were habits previously alien to even the largest British architectural offices. But to Johnson-Marshall and his lieutenants they were merely prolongations of the better aspects of discipline in the services—lessons which manufacturing and engineering had learnt long ago and which architecture had now to digest if it was not to slide back into purposeless amateurism.

Fundamental to Hertfordshire's successes at this stage was the consolidation of links between the architects and educationists at County Hall. Here the architects reaped the rewards of Newsom's wartime groundwork. Because he and his team had troubled to work out, in broad terms and with teachers, what the new schools ought to be like, they stood ready with ideas for the architects to translate when the time for action arrived. Newsom and Johnson-Marshall quickly came to an understanding about this. Along with a 'fairly objective set of requirements', the educationists tried to convey in a broad visual sense the environment which they felt the children needed, but they did not hem the architects in with constricting briefs or plan-types. At the outset they were told, for instance, that the schools should be broken up in bulk and not look institutional; that children should be able to see out of windows; and that the main entrance at each school should be used by children as well as adults. The original architectural responses to these demands were embodied in Cheshunt and Essendon, in particular through the efforts of Mary Crowley. Thereafter refinements, developments and corrections proceeded through exchanges between architects and education staff at every level, from the council chamber to the canteen. In a small authority like Herts where education was at the top of the agenda, they were constantly together and therefore able to respond to each other. Had the architects been in private practice, or had the authority been larger and more compartmentalized, such a rapport could never have developed.

At this early stage, the link between designers and users was almost exclusively through the education professionals, not directly through teachers. Nor was any dramatically 'progressive' mode of teaching being peddled in the new primary schools: that was to come later, if at all. For the moment the ethos of the schools was novelty enough, sufficient to offer teachers a sense of opportunity should they wish to take advantage of it. Elsewhere, go-ahead teachers were chafing at the frustrations of newly built, old-fangled schools. In Herts it was the other way round; to a degree, the county's advancement in architecture was 'design-led'.

## COMPONENT DEVELOPMENT

What was entailed by the development of a component? In the Herts philosophy, this was one of the most vital jobs. It meant having the freedom to identify a co-operative manufacturer, convincing him of the chances that a programme placed before him, urging upon him a continuous, collaborative approach to design and production, and superintending the results. The relationship with Hinchliffe of Hills provided the model, with its annual, meticulous, exhaustive revision of the steel frame and its scrutiny of every stanchion and girder. But it applied in equal measure to every item of structure and equipment in a year's primary programme: to the fibrous plaster partitions, the windows, the doors, the casings for the stanchions, the fixed and loose furniture, the drains, the blinds and so forth and so on. In the interests of the child, the humblest doorknob was handled with as much demonstrable, puritan seriousness as the very frame itself. A couple of examples will serve. Cleeve Barr:

> I remember one component I dealt with for a programme was the ground-floor tiling, the ordinary six-inch by six-inch quarry-tile. You've got the tile, its thickness, its bedding on something (which can vary), its angle round the edges, and its curvature. You've got its corrugation, if it's to be non-slip, and its colouring.
>
> I had a firm to get in touch with in Ruabon, J. C. Edwards. The directors had never been to London before! We set up a meeting to discuss these tiles, and then somebody died at their end and they never came. It looked like never happening, so I went up to Ruabon. One could do that sort of thing and just go. I went and told them the position, but there was no one man in the firm who could give me the answers. '*He* knows all about prices, *he* knows about corrugation, *he* knows about thicknesses or colours'; you had to get three or four people in the firm together. They hadn't got a single catalogue which gave all the facts about the tiles. So you virtually had to compose it for them, put down what you wanted and then they would see if it was possible and price it.
>
> They were producing tiles, particularly for Liverpool and Manchester, and even for export to the USA. They sold by the thousands of yards but had never fully worked out the co-ordination of their thicknesses, sizes and finishes. At Herts we wanted to exploit all components and materials to their maximum potential.

Somewhat later, Henry Swain helped develop the pitch-fibre drainpipe, an American innovation hitherto unused in Britain but suggested to the Herts architects by BRS when they were trying to cut down on messy site-work:

> When I got to the Herts office there were some examples of pitch-fibre drains lying about which Bruce Martin or someone was interested in, and nobody was manufacturing them. Then a firm [Key Engineering] started up. They had a great advantage, they saved a lot of labour and were more flexible. If you were building on the London clay you

23. Hughes Field School, Deptford, London. An example of the LCC Architect's Department's adaptation of the Hills 8 feet 3 inches system for urban primary schools, 1950–1.

4.24. Basins at Hunslet Moor School, Leeds, *c.* 1950: the type of institutional washroom-cum-locker-room against which Herts was reacting.

were likely to get less damage to the pipe. It was a flexible material, a plastic of a kind. I was called 'Pitch-fibre Swain' because I was so fascinated by the whole business. You could reduce the cost of drains. There was nothing particularly advanced about it. They were simply hammered together with a connecting ring. You could do a long line of drains on top of the ground and tip them in, so that you didn't have to go down into the dangerous trench. We now use the ordinary stoneware drains with flexible connections which didn't exist in those days. But we used them for several years.

The most powerful testimonial to the spirit of collaboration which informed 'component development' for the early Herts schools comes not from an architect but from a manufacturer. Alan Adams and his salesman cousin Bryan Adams were partners in the 'sanitary fireclay' firm of Adamsez Limited of Newcastle. Alone among the manifold sub-contractors for the schools programme, Adamsez had worked for Herts before the war, supplying water closets and washbasins for its schools. The firm was already well known among architects and had a distinctive crafts tradition. A Quaker, Alan Adams was as much a potter as a manufacturer, loved to shape prototypes with his own hands, and cared less for profit than for job-satisfaction and the contentment of his workforce. The Adams cousins had tried out profit-sharing in the 1930s and, during the stress of war, had (like other local firms) set up a works council. At that time, Alan Adams told his people:

I have been thinking about and reading about the new social order which it is hoped may result after the war. New and better international conditions; new and better industrial,

82

financial and social conditions with all of which I am in very full sympathy ... We are one of Britain's industries, only a small one, but still we can in our way each play a great and useful part, we produce useful things folk can ill do without and I wonder if we ever think about this and how the quality of our workmanship may increase this value to the community.

In other words, the ideals of Adamsez fitted precisely with the aspirations of the Hertfordshire architects.

Collaborating with Adamsez to make new, child-sized sanitary equipment for the decentralized water closets in primary schools was one of the few practical tasks which Stirrat Johnson-Marshall took passionately upon himself during his time at Herts. Aided and then superseded first by the industrious David Medd, later by Oliver Cox, he set up an early meeting at Hertford to outline a new form of handwashbasin. This had to be small enough for infants to use, hard to stuff with soap or make overflow on the floor; awkward angles—hitherto a feature of almost all basins—were to be eliminated and the tap tipped forwards, so that thirsty children would use the drinking fountains also provided. The result, fashioned over joint sessions in the Adamsez modelling shop, was the Bean basin, whimsically named after a little river that flows through Hertford. Ready in time for Cheshunt and Essendon, it was installed over the subsequent thirty years in great numbers of schools all over the country (Figs. 4.25,26). There followed a Bean drinking fountain and a Bean urinal, to accompany an adaptation of the 'rimless closet' which the Adamses had introduced for schools before the war. These designs, together with the Lotus range evolved on similar lines a little later for hospitals in partnership with Llewelyn-Davies, brought Adamsez several prizes, much repute and some prosperity during the 1950s and '60s when they became much the most successful suppliers of sanitary ware to British schools. But this mattered little to Alan Adams, compared to the poetic discovery of an equal, Ruskinian collaboration between designer and maker.

Imagine us, therefore the Architects and the sanitary fireclaymen in that holy of holies—the Architect's office, that sanctum whereunto the sanitary fireclayman can seldom penetrate but in fear and trembling, sprawled uncomfortably on the floor ... bent over large sheets of paper.

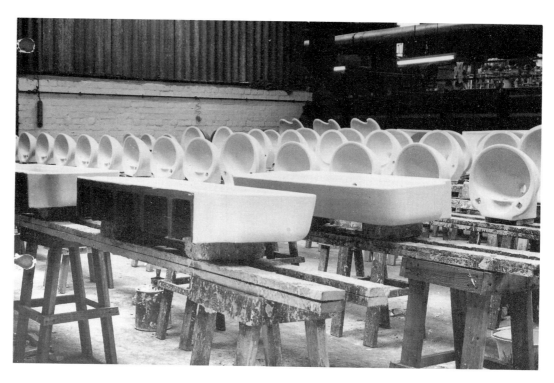

25. Lotus basins and other items at the Adamsez factory, Scotswood, Newcastle on Tyne.

4.26. 'Bean' basins in use, Little Green Lane School, Croxley Green, 1949.

Points under review were many—a reasonable size, combined with good bowl area, so that each child might have accommodation in a minimum of space. Clean and simple lines, with absence of needless rebates, corners and frills. Suitable positioning of tap or taps for accessibility and ready cleansing. Good accommodation for soap which must be kept dry by suitable drainage, and beauty of line and contour.

The general features being thus roughly planned, the next meeting was in our Moulding Shop in the North christened on the spot 'The Studio' where modellers, long skilled in clay craft, vetted the new design and brought outlines and contours into line with practical consideration of manufacture. It was a new and glorious sight for us to see Architects, building, shaping, and scraping away at the clay moulds, absorbed in the joys of creation and oblivious of the passing of time and the luncheon hour.

Here was a sight indeed to astonish the sanitary fireclayman. These high task masters, these Olympians, who for long sad years had scornfully declined our approach and firmly, but politely, returned our visiting cards, were here handling our base clay, indeed covered with dust, attired in old flannel bags with pipes in mouth, discussing the pleasures and pains of the craft and deferring to the superior skill and knowledge of the old modeller, who was pleased to demonstrate his skill and impart to them his knowledge, gained in over fifty years' work in the industry.

## SCIENCE AND ART IN THE SERVICE OF THE CHILD

All these were partnerships simple in scope, each entered into with a single manufacturer. A richer, further-reaching and more complex collaboration took place between Herts and the Building Research Station, so handily situated within the county and already established in 1946 as the technical force behind much work on post-war reconstruction. To a degree that pre-war scientists had only dreamed of, this liaison showed how building research could pass positively into architecture and be put to peacetime service. Some of this work was necessarily dry and technical, and merely helped supply the 'firmness' needed in the prefabricated schools to safeguard the 'commodity' for which its creators were striving. Such, for instance, was the advice given by Bill Ward of BRS's soil mechanics division on 'augered piles' beneath the light foundation slabs of the schools, to help them cope with the shrinkable London clays. But other aspects of the collaboration with BRS helped to transform the very nature of school-building.

Soon after Johnson-Marshall arrived at Herts, he took a group over to BRS to discuss everything that they were doing. 'We sat down for about three days and really sorted out ideas', recollects Bill Allen, then deputy head of the Architectural Physics Division there. From the start, Herts was looking to BRS for help mainly over questions of 'environmental science'. Over the simple, single-storey primary schools of the 8 feet 3 inches system, there were no structural problems with which Hinchliffe and his engineers could not cope. Nor did the Herts architects feel they needed aid over joints, cladding and roofs, the items which have since given systems-building a bad name. Within the limits of the available materials, these were designed according to traditional methods of building construction. As a result, few early Herts schools have given serious technical trouble. The commonest problems have been the roof-coverings which, with the optimism of cloud-cuckooland, were devised for a mere twenty-year life.

The environmental sciences—chiefly lighting, heating and ventilation, and acoustics—were the province of BRS's Architectural Physics Division. It was one of the station's liveliest units, peopled by scientists whose wartime service had given them insight into the aims of the Herts team. There the pre-war utopianism of Bernal, the easy idea that modern architecture ought in some hazy or intellectual sense to be 'scientific', was being steadily broken down into something more meaningful and attainable. Sphere by sphere, the division was starting to study and quantify human reaction and to translate it into limits and goals which were practicable for designers and technologists to introduce in the servicing of buildings. The division's staff was handling some big ventures in the late 1940s. In acoustics Peter Parkin, Hope Bagenal and Bill Allen were collaborating with LCC architects on the auditorium of the Royal Festival Hall. Acoustics on the whole were not deemed to be problematic in the Herts primary schools. There would always be background noise, but so long as the classrooms were planned with some of intervening baffle, usually storerooms, that was acceptable. Occasionally Bagenal, a lovable eccentric famous for the accuracy of his intuitive acoustical judgement, gave advice on assembly halls in secondary schools, but that was about all.

Heating was a profounder issue. On this subject there had been some experimentation between the wars, when the increased glazing made it wise to supplement the meagre, poor-law heating hitherto provided in state schools. Hot-water heating, the British norm, had proved inadequate and uneven in classrooms. Floor panels, ceiling panels and other types of radiant heat took time to warm classrooms up and were slow to respond to control. Because schools were occupied for quite few hours in the week and sunlight could suddenly heat classrooms up, it was better to have a system capable of quick warming and cooling. All this pointed to 'forced warm air', a traditional American method of heating. In the winter of 1944–5 Cecil Handisyde from BRS, Jack Pritchard and others returned from an investigation of domestic heating in the United States preaching the gospel of warm air. Here now was the chance to extend this to schools. Handisyde therefore put Herts in touch with John Fowler, a canny but open-minded heating engineer who was just setting up the firm of Weatherfoil.

Excepting Hinchliffe, Fowler contributed more to the technical success of the Herts schools than anyone outside the county council. Infected by Johnson-Marshall's enthusiasm, he took up the task with alacrity and devoted all his energies to it, spending whole nights in cold classrooms in the process of investigation. He quickly succeeded in cracking the problem. Hot water continued to be used in corridors and staff rooms, but from Cheshunt and Essendon onwards all the classrooms and halls sported Weatherfoil warm-air grilles fronting cabinets hidden behind. Considering that there was then no British tradition of warm-air heating, the Weatherfoil system was extraordinarily advanced. It was very sensitive to changes in ambient temperature and to the intermittent demands of school heating, and so saved fuel in a period of acute shortages. It was by no means perfect from the first. The cabinets were bulky, the fan motors noisy, and the apparatus needed regular cleaning if it was to function properly; later on, naughty children bent the bars on the fronts of the grilles. But Fowler continually refined and improved his system until it became not only one of the most popular means of heating schools but, effectively, the pioneer of all warm-air heating in British buildings with intermittent use.

There was a great heat loss from the first Herts schools, but this was no fault of the Weatherfoil system. In those early days of prefabrication, scant thought was paid to insulation. The post-war school-building regulations, based upon outdated theories of infection, still asked for no less than six complete air-changes in classrooms every hour, and half the window space had to be openable. The light-weight 'meccano' structure also shed heat through its walls and roof, so that by today's standards the schools were hot in summer and cold in winter. On this topic expectations have changed. In the knowledge that teachers and children alike would wear more clothes than they do today, the Weatherfoil system aimed to heat classrooms to only 60°F and corridors to 45° when the outside temperature was freezing.

Like all such endeavours, the investigation of school heating did not begin and end with the Weatherfoil system. When in the early 1950s the Ministry of Education persuaded BRS to look more systematically at the heating and ventilation of schools, it was to Herts that they naturally turned. The Hazelwood Infants School at Abbots Langley (1950–2) became after its completion the scene of a three-year series of heating trials of all kinds and in all weathers, the results of which were promulgated in a building bulletin published in 1955. The trials vindicated Weatherfoil but, more important, they allowed the principles affecting the comfort of teachers and pupils in schools to be much better understood and communicated. They formed the basis of the Ministry's advice to local authorities for years to follow.

Lighting was a larger question again. Since school lighting had already commanded much

4.27. Section of proposed classroom block for Essex County Council, 1947, showing the complexities involved in securing traditional, two-sided lighting for classrooms above a single storey.

4.29. (*facing page*) Infants' classroom at Monkfrith School, East Barnet. Mary Crowley and Oliver Cox, job architects, 1949–50. Daylighting from contiguous sides, dispersed seating round trapezoidal tables. On the right, Weatherfoil heating grilles.

28. Rooflight, Morgans Walk School, Hertford. The external frame is shown, but ~~t~~ the standard louvre fitted to filter light ~~ntly~~ into the classroom below.

attention, the task was to reconcile the requirements of the school-building regulations with a feeling for quality, sophistication and sensitivity. What the Herts architects did was to start from the perceptions of the child. They thought of lighting and colour together, as stimuli. In infant classes, the educationists and teachers told them, the child was learning how to see, how to interpret shapes and colours in two and three dimensions, how to make out letters, how to identify trees and birds and bushes outside the window. The architects solicited the aid of the technologists in easing these tasks and making them as exciting as possible. For their part, Ralph Hopkinson and his colleagues at BRS strove to acknowledge these subjective demands about quality in lighting and colour, treat them as seriously and scientifically as the objective, quantifiable facts about daylight, and reconcile the two.

So concerned about the poor vision of inter-war children had doctors and educators become, that the Ministry of Education's 1945 school-building regulations set out a minimum two per cent 'daylight factor' at 'all working positions' in classrooms—the daylight factor being 'the ratio of illumination at a given point inside a building to the general illumination outside a building, received from an unobstructed view of the sky'. An accompanying memorandum went beyond this by recommending that 'a higher figure of up to five per cent should be secured'. From the instant of their issue, school buildings were in trouble. The previous standard had been ½ per cent, so old classrooms came nowhere near this new demand. Even in schools of 1930s, with their sheet of glass on one wall and their clerestory lights opposite (Fig. 3.1), it was possible to find patches which dipped well below five per cent. Nor was the quality of lighting in these newer classrooms always very happy. With the usual orientation, children next to the big window would be baked in summer and blinded by the glare of low sunlight in winter. Furthermore, once classroom blocks

4.30. The school in the apple orchard: 'Wizard of Oz' setting for Aboyne Lodge Infants School, St Albans. Donald Barron, job architect, 1949–50; photograph by John Pantlin.

4.31. (*facing page, top*) Safely back to mother. Another of John Pantlin's stylized shots of Aboyne Lodge School, calculated to underline the 'nurturing' emphasis of new-style primary education.

4.32. (*facing page, bottom*) A corner at Aboyne Lodge School, showing the vertical cladding and broad eaves of the 1948 and 1949 Herts primary school-building programmes.

on this arrangement were built above a single storey, architects had to juggle expensively with the section so as to secure the desired five per cent lighting for the lower floors (Fig. 4.27). This could mean abandoning corridors on upper floors and building frequent stairs, or avoiding multi-storey classrooms altogether. Indeed the 1945 regulations on daylighting tipped the balance heavily in favour of single-storey school-building, with major consequences for the planning, massing and integration of schools.

The post-war lighting experts at BRS soon became aware of these failings. 'Daylight factor' and 'foot candles', the accepted measures of illumination, were crude tools. Nor did reflected daylight figure in the regulations; when this was taken into account, the recommended five per cent direct daylight appeared exaggerated. At about this time, the experts concluded that the onset of myopia in children had little to do with levels of school lighting. However, Hopkinson and his team also discovered from their researches in the Herts schools that better daylighting meant better performance, in reading particularly, and made teachers and pupils alike fresher and more buoyant, so long as they were not distracted by glare or heat. The result of their endeavours was to set a premium on the value and quality of direct daylight over and above its sheer quantity. These subtler, more responsive standards were embodied in revised regulations issued in 1951.

From 1947 onwards Hopkinson collaborated constantly with the Herts architects, using the earliest schools to try out new ideas about measuring light, colour and glare, and monitoring the reactions of pupils.

Work that I had done before and during the war had led to various techniques for the quantification of subjective judgements, and it was clear that these methods could be

used in studies of lighting which could 'put figures' on aspects of quality, such as the presence of glare, which Stirrat and his team had seen to be important, but which were beyond the bounds of lighting science at the time . . .

With hindsight, the most significant help we were able to give them was the scientific backing which they felt they needed for their reliance upon natural light in their school designs. I believe that they would have done what they did anyway, because their observation, architectural knowledge and instinct told them that they were right. We may have led them to refinements of their designs, especially relating to the reduction of glare, but they knew where they were going before we came on the scene. We had also shown them that the treatment of the interior surfaces of a building (walls, floor, ceiling) was of great significance, because the light-reflecting properties of these surfaces affected both the quantity of light and its quality, because the appraisement of the lighting was determined by the adapting characteristics of the whole visual environment.

What did this amount to in practical terms? Cheshunt, Essendon and the other 'first generation' schools built in 1947–9 are conventionally lit: that is to say, the classrooms are well-glazed along one wall and have clerestory lights opposite (Fig. 4.15). In the second generation (1949–51), rooflights (Fig. 4.30) supplant the clerestories, allowing ceilings in infants' rooms to be lowered to the more 'child-like' scale desired. And in some schools, depending upon contour and aspect, the classrooms are staggered so that each may have windows on contiguous sides (Figs. 4.7,22). With this more natural and even spread of light, children could comfortably take part in activities facing in different directions, rather than all be turned towards the chalkboard (Fig. 4.33). Throughout the primary programme, Herts believed emphatically in daylighting. Artificial lighting there certainly had to be, and for this a simple new incandescent fitting, the Percon light, was in due course devised. Like so many Herts innovations, it made its way very prosperously in the world of post-war building. But the architects thought of it as a makeshift, for teachers to fall back on only for those few hours of the school year when natural light was fading or dull. Fluorescent strip-lighting, then with its constant flicker and hum an imperfect proposition, was out of the question. For the alertness and performance of the child, daylight had an absolute value.

Colour, so closely allied to lighting, was an emotional topic for the Herts team. To a generation gorged upon multi-coloured packaging, clothing and plastics, the monotony of visible hue in wartime and post-war Britain, the endlessness of the olive greens and khaki browns sanctioned by economy, camouflage and uniformity are almost unimaginable. Today, a bold splash of colour is devoid of meaning. Forty years ago it could stand for hope and a half-forgotten gaiety. That is why panels of simple, primary colours, naive-looking today, feature so often in post-war schools and housing. In primary schools plain bright colour had extra connotations. It was a token of purity and of the learning from sensation championed by Froebel and Montessori. And it was a rejection of pre-war 'municipal mud', the pessimistic presumption that the dados of classrooms and corridors had to be muck-coloured because grazes and grease would always be laid on by rowdy, underwashed 'brats'.

For the first Herts schools, the paint salesmen turned up in hopes with their drab colour charts. They were promptly sent packing. Cheshunt was painted white, while David Medd, aided after a while by Oliver Cox, settled down to devise a new colour range with the technical help of H. L. Gloag of BRS and two paint manufacturers, R. Gay and Company and Docker Brothers. The pair spent several weekends mixing colours in the basement at Hertford County Hall. The new range was adopted in all the Herts schools. Duly extended, it was published in 1953 as the Archrome range and gained national recognition through a British Standard before being superseded in the 1960s. Here was another example of how public architecture in this period filled a want which private practice could never conceivably supply. Without charge, patent or restriction, the fruits of local experiment and experience were fed into the pattern of national building for others to take advantage from.

Some inspiration for the tonalities of the original Herts colour range came from Ozenfant, whose pre-war lectures on colour both Medd and Cox had attended at the AA. To specify and measure the colours they began with the old pre-war Ostwald system, but Gloag persuaded them to drop this in favour of the more rational Munsell system from America, with its scientifically determined intervals between tones. This allowed them to establish a direct link between colour and light, and so to use colour accurately to reflect light or diminish glare:

> It enabled one to define requirements, like chalkboards for example, by limits of chroma, limits of hue, and you could find the parameters and say these are the limits within which you should work on chalkboards for highest visibility, maximum comfort, etc. You could define the relationships, you could extend the monochromatic concept of flux computations for lighting to colours, because in fact you had also constant reflectivity through any value in the value system of Munsell.

In the schools, the colours were applied in large plain areas on the panels between the steel uprights according to consistent principles of function and use (Plates II, IV). Structural members were generally pale grey; classrooms were in light, undistracting colours; halls were bright and cheerful but dignified; and the strongest colours, rich reds and yellows and blues, were reserved for circulation spaces, entrance halls and occasional outside panels on which the eye would dwell for only a few moments. The principles were codified by Oliver Cox, who remembers their effect in the early schools: 'The impact of these schemes on the teachers was tremendous; few had ever seen such bold and striking use of colour in buildings before. Many dressed to match! The children took it completely for granted and carried on painting with a similar palette.' The bright, clean 'splodges' of colour in the schools were invariably what most struck early visitors, starved of visual sensation. Nearly all the schemes have been watered down now, and even if restored would hardly have the impact they made at the time.

These collaborations over lighting and colour amounted to more than a single, intense campaign. Here, as in structural matters, there was continuous development. The late 1940s saw the most exciting and fundamental work. But the refinements which would turn adequate schools into excellent ones could come only from a lengthy process of concentration and commitment. Thus the work on lighting with Hopkinson at BRS went on unbroken after Johnson-Marshall and Medd transferred to the Ministry of Education right up until 1960; the Archrome range was extended into housing when Oliver Cox moved to the LCC in 1950; while the habit of regularly refining the structural system made Herts unrivalled technically until the rise of the consortia in the 1960s.

School furniture (Fig. 4.33) is an example of how the fruits of this approach might be deferred. At the start of the Herts programme, Medd and Johnson-Marshall befriended

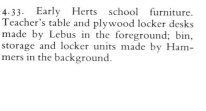

4.33. Early Herts school furniture. Teacher's table and plywood locker desks made by Lebus in the foreground; bin, storage and locker units made by Hammers in the background.

the county supplies officer. But they found little to hearten them in the equipment he was ordering from catalogues. Anthropometrically, most British school furniture was crude until the late 1940s when Bengt Åkerblom showed how scientific principles of posture could be applied in furniture design and Solly Zuckerman and E. M. B. Clements published the results of a survey measuring large numbers of children in Birmingham. Herts too carried out a modest dimensional survey of its schoolchildren. But before they could get any further, once again central government threatened, this time not with huts but with trestles. Via Gropius's ex-client and friend Jack Pritchard, soon to take charge of the new Furniture Development Council, the architects contacted Lebus Furniture. An exhibition of Dick Russell's new school designs for Lebus was put on in the county, and the junior school at Cheshunt was furnished with their locker-desk and trapezoidal table. Medd contributed a few designs, notably the first movable bins on castors for schools, and Oliver Cox added some more. But Lebus lost interest and the predominant part of furniture in the early Herts schools was bought in. It took time—and much further prodding from Medd and Pritchard—to convince manufacturers that school furniture needed to be educationally enlightened as well as scientifically based. Only after the second British Standard on school furniture had been published in 1955 did manufacturers sit up and take note, and not until the late 1960s did a range of loose school furniture equal in thoughtfulness and adaptability to the post-war schools themselves become readily available (see pp. 192–4). Once again, here was a story of continuous development from principles first laid down at Herts. The primary-school locker-unit for that range was to all intents the one that Medd had designed twenty years before for Cheshunt; everything else had grown from there.

Art, the most famous example of co-operative endeavour in the Herts schools, was in certain ways the exception to the two golden rules, that the schools were to contain nothing which could not be developed, and nothing which could not be shared around among all in equal measure. Indeed the policy of having professional art in the schools was a 'genuine Newsomism', not one that came from architects. They, though keen on the idea, were not always happy with the results.

Newsom may have taken the idea of having professional murals and sculpture in his schools from Henry Morris and the pre-war village colleges. 'Bringing art to the people' was in any case a popular, somewhat simplistic ideal of the post-war decade, and muralists flourished in Britain, decorating housing, schools and public buildings. Ever the persuader, Newsom convinced his benign county council that a nominal sum set aside for art, one-third of one per cent of the building budget, would confer prestige on Herts. So it did. The arrangement was always a casual one, like the comparable provision whereby promising landscape architects such as Sylvia Crowe and Brenda Colvin came in on a job-by-job basis to enhance the settings of schools, until Herts acquired 'in-house' strength enough to manage for themselves. Often there was no art; sometimes the figure was commuted into other uses. In practice two art policies were pursued simultaneously. Newsom liked to secure recognized artists to do their best, perhaps with some concessions to children's sensibilities. The most spectacular gainer from this policy was the Barclay School at Stevenage, the county's first post-war secondary school, which acquired a Henry Moore bronze outside and a Kenneth Rowntree mural in the entrance hall. In like manner, Julian Trevelyan painted a mural for Blackthorn School, Welwyn Garden City and Ceri Richards another at Mandeville School, St Albans. And in 1952 someone donated Barbara Hepworth pieces to a pair of grammar schools at St Albans.

Artists of this calibre tended to know their own minds and were not normally much interested in collaboration or in addressing themselves to children. After a while, the policy started to degenerate into a game of getting a famous name. For these reasons, the interested architects favoured a more anonymous, collective approach. They also felt that primary age children appreciated murals more than sculpture; they seemed to go best in dining halls, where children needed a little distraction to help them through their puddings. The Bath Academy of Art, a small and lively school run from Corsham by Clifford and Rosemary Ellis, was attracted by these ideas, and students and teachers from there co-operated in painting murals at the third Herts primary school to be finished, at Croxley Green. Oliver Cox:

The idea was to get the art students working in the schools so that quite large areas could be offered to them as part of their training. The idea fizzled out however, partly because of antagonism from some of the staff. I was championed by Rosemary and Clifford Ellis, but it didn't work out. I went to Corsham and had a flaming row with William Scott the painter who was then teaching there. He called it 'slave labour'. At the same time Don Barron organized a group of left-wing artists to carry out murals. One of them was Fred Millett, with whom I was to work later on murals for the Ministry of Education school at Wokingham. These artists were amenable workers in the concept of building a school in the way we saw it, serving a purpose. They were impressed with our approach to colour and were keen to fit their mostly representational work in with it.

The upshot of all this was a few murals by Corsham artists and a few by the left-wing group. The outstanding examples are the merry penguin mural painted by Clifford Ellis, with vague Froebelian overtones, at Maylands Infants School, Hemel Hempstead (Plate V), and a large one by Fred Millett at Oakland Infants School, East Barnet (Plate I). Early in the 1950s the policy began to fade away. Professional art in schools was sometimes taken up by other authorities, but it never received enough continuous attention to amount to more than a flash in the pan. The ethos of the early Herts schools was not really suited to the occasional artist who painted a mural over a few weeks in the holidays and then disappeared for ever.

In a related area, however, the policy achieved success and continuity. Gerald Holtom's series of curtains for halls and stages, started for the Batford Primary School at Harpenden in 1949, went on right through the Herts primary programme and the Ministry of Education's experimental schools up to 1962. Holtom began with simple, printed textiles and brought in Edward Bawden to discuss the range and produce a few designs. Later he was to move on to some dramatic experiments in textile appliqué work, notably a series of one-off stage curtains for secondary schools which explored the history and location of each school with audacity and wit. His curtains (Plates VI–VIII) constitute a unique record of accumulated thought and attention to applied art in British schools. And, as so often, the chance of working co-operatively on a developing programme gave Holtom a rational satisfaction which the isolated artist rarely enjoys: 'It was an inspiration which made possible and practical a way of life for me which gave me the conviction that I was doing something worthwhile in life and to the limits of my capabilities'.


## EARLY PROBLEMS

The aim, it has been stressed, of these sundry and strenuous liaisons between architects, manufacturers, artists and others was not to make a perfect object for one or even for ten or twenty schools. It was to realize a component or a piece of equipment which, after modification, refinement and standardization might find its way into the 'industrialized vernacular' of which architects then fondly spoke. 'We were creating a vocabulary of school design for nothing', says David Medd. Out of this, they hoped in their optimistic moments, would emerge a new, 'industrialized' language of architecture from which in the far-off future might be made buildings of equal originality and individuality to those fashioned in the old, hand-crafted vernacular materials: a refined discipline of construction which might eventually become a 'style', as Lethaby had envisaged in his later writings.

To a remarkable degree their short-term hopes were fulfilled. The Adamsez basins and urinals, Fowler's forced warm-air heating, the Percon light fittings, other innovations like the Econa all-in-one plumbing wastes or a unified system of electrical switchboxes, the lockers and bins and tables, all spread far and wide, mostly but not exclusively in the public sector. Over and above these 'firsts', Herts through its quantity surveyors, James Nisbet and Clifford Nott, also provided the spark for 'cost analysis', a new and far-reaching way of looking at building costs whose implications must be deferred to the next chapter (pp. 115–19).

But one dream never materialized, or at any rate not on any scale or for some time. This was the dream of freely interchangeable structural components, of an 'open' system of prefabricated building. The Herts 8 feet 3 inches system, like other post-war methods of standardized construction, was a 'closed' one; that is to say, the component parts for the frame, the linings and the cladding were made for the exclusive use of that system and that building programme. Annual improvements there certainly were, but with others using different modes of construction and the module of 8 feet 3 inches coming under increasing suspicion of inflexibility, the prospects of producing these components on a scale which could justify the intense development work they required became remoter.

At the same time, some of the snags of prefabrication were becoming manifest on site. The Herts architects prided themselves upon efficiency, a necessary quality in order to stay in favour with the Ministry and bag the needed resources. But if Herts was the smartest authority, what happened elsewhere must have been woeful. In reality none of the early schools, so urgently needed, was spectacularly quick to build. Small buildings though they were, most took over a year on site. For this there were many reasons. For a start, despite all the talk about factory production, at no stage in the Herts school-building programme did the value of components finished off-site amount to half the total value. Underlying the theory of 'light and dry' construction lay an inglorious amount of wet site-work, of digging, cutting, adjusting, plastering, sealing, revising and altering. Some errors in 'setting out' and many variations occurred in the early contracts. The neatly coded sheets for the joints and details of the whole annual programme were efficient and time-saving in theory, but in practice difficult choices had to be made in a hurry at working-drawing stage or even on site. Cleeve Barr:

> You've got a frame: all right, that's pre-programmed and the way in which the columns are bolted to the beams and so forth, that's pretty all right. So you don't bugger about with the frame on the whole; that goes up as programmed. When you come to clad it, your type of fibrous plaster lining (as it was early, it later became wood wool) is also fixed. But then you've got individual decisions. You can have it behind the face of the column, you can have it parallel to the face, you can have it in front of the face, and you can have it supported at the ends in various ways. All the meeting places of floors and ceilings with walls are by arrangement, and the same with your roofs. There's an awful lot of scope for *ad hoc* decisions.

On top of this there were always, as throughout the history of prefabricated school-building, many more 'specials' than the architects dared admit. On Cheshunt Infants School, records Michael Keath, 'out of a total of fifty of the 8′ 0″ high stanchions used in the prototype, thirty were different in some respect'. This was a first-off, and the whole bent of the annual process of revision was to reduce the 'specials', cut out *in situ* work and simplify the joints. But the battle proved to be a continuous one; the more complex the building brief, the more 'specials' started to creep back in.

Then again, there were difficulties over delivery. The employment of so many nominated sub-contractors lessened the builder's traditional responsibility on the site, and led to frequent argument over co-ordination when supplies were delayed. Since the builder's own contribution was smaller than in a normal contract, he was less able or inclined to supervise and speed up the work of sub-contractors. This confusion of loyalties and responsibilities led to poor communication and delay. Such were the problems posed by 'alternative methods of construction' even for simple, single-storey schools in a part of the country favoured with reliable builders and enterprising architects. When the scale of operations increased, as on urban housing sites, the managerial problems over the new manner of building would become almost insurmountable. For the time being, relationships with the main contractors of buildings and with the men on site remained traditional and unreformed. It was to be years before any of the schools architects came properly to grips with this nexus of problems, as part of the CLASP programme (pp. 177–83).

Finally came 'quality control'. Though the lure of a sizeable annual programme in theory gave the architects greater sanction against suppliers, this did not prevent defective batches.

Some of the early Hills steelwork was poor. Then there were the components which would never quite come right. Of these the most frustrating and visible was the cladding. Concrete was chosen for covering the steel frame because at first, in the aftermath of war, other materials like timber were simply unobtainable; later, after the coming of cost limits, it continued in use because it was practically the only thing that could be afforded. Despite ceaseless effort it would never come right, and it revealed one danger in the philosophy of 'component development' as applied to a rolling programme: if a fundamental choice in the programme proved unsatisfactory, it was far harder in the press of work to 'stop the train' and review the issue from the start than to make modest, tinkering, developmental changes. At Cheshunt and Essendon, Hills supplied the horizontal concrete slabs. They were tolerable in appearance but technically defective, with the reinforcement too close to the surface. For later schools, Aslin put out the cladding to other firms. The slabs were switched from horizontal to vertical, to allow greater flexibility in the positioning of windows, then in 1950 back to horizontal again. All the time, the architects were pressing to make the concrete more attractive by getting the makers to add cement or stone aggregates of one type or another. It cannot be said that they succeeded. For all Johnson-Marshall's stubborn rhetoric about spar-finished concrete 'sparkling in the rain', the concrete finishes of the Herts schools were never popular with teachers and administrators, leaving aside the children to whose sensibilities the buildings were otherwise so finely tuned. Then as now, for most people the schools were a miracle of refinement within but less than wholly prepossessing without. When Le Corbusier visited Cleeve Barr's handsome Templewood School at Welwyn Garden City (Figs. 4.21,22; Plates II,III) he was heard to concede, somewhat disparagingly perhaps: 'c'est très jolie'. But few even of his more fervent architectural disciples felt that his remark applied so fitly to the outsides as to the insides of the early Hertfordshire schools.

## REORGANIZATION

Stirrat Johnson-Marshall stayed at Hertfordshire less than three years, from late in 1945 till September 1948. During this period Cheshunt and Essendon were the only schools finished; the flood of completions did not come until 1949 and 1950. So although the programmes and policies described had been laid down in outline they were far from fully developed. Little had been the fruit of practical, architectural work on Johnson-Marshall's part, but nobody doubted that the inspiration, the tactics and the drive stemmed from his generalship. Aslin was a shrewd, benign ally; but that Herts after just two schools was able to appear as the national leader in school-building was due to Johnson-Marshall alone. In recognition of this, he was now off to be chief architect to the Ministry of Education, avowedly determined to apply the methods of Herts on a national scale. In April 1949 David Medd and Mary Crowley, now married, followed him to the Ministry. Thus were removed the high priest of Hertfordshire school-building and its principal architectural experts on technique and education.

The Herts office might have stumbled. There was indeed some disarray. But so firm was the ground laid in 1945–8, so strong the team built up, and so compelling the logic of the developing programme, that no severe crisis took place. With the building programmes mounting annually, primary schools had to be turned out at a rate of ten or twelve a year, while now that the birth-bulge was working its way through, the more exacting and time-consuming secondary schools were also coming into the picture. The danger was that initiative and innovation might founder beneath the sea of practical tasks.

William Tatton Brown replaced Johnson-Marshall as deputy county architect in charge of schools, pipping Llewelyn-Davies to the post. Tatton Brown had an impressive architectural pedigree. He had wits and charm, he had worked for Lurçat and for Tecton in the 1930s, and he interested himself in planning and research. But he lacked Johnson-Marshall's strain of 'commitment': 'He lived in Berkhamsted and he and his wife had a farm. He used to bring a trailer to the office at the back of his car every day. He had a contract for the pigswill from the Hertford County Hall kitchens which he took back to his farm every night.'

Tatton Brown's appointment presaged a shift of mood not just in Herts but in the nation. From about 1949 the long strain of social idealism began to tell. The Labour Government's popularity slid; people grew tired of Cripps's talk about sacrifice and thought about themselves instead; Communists came under increasing suspicion. Architecture, ever sensitive to the social mood, was affected by this change and Herts as much as anywhere. But first there was a brief flurry. For some time the more leftward-leaning architects had sought a measure of equalization among salaries in the office, partly out of idealism, partly because they feared that Herts might not continue to attract architects of calibre unless better salaries were on offer at the bottom of the scale. Higher pay for architectural assistants in the burgeoning local-authority offices in order to improve the quality of public architecture was a plank of the Association of Building Technicians' policy in these years. There was no formal ABT branch at Hertford, but many architects were members or supported its aims. Pressed on the subject, Aslin sensed encroachment on his prerogatives and political danger and became awkward. Briefly there was dissension. In 1950 four of the disaffected, Cleeve Barr, Oliver Cox, Anthony Garrod and 'Beak' Adams left together to join the LCC and work with Whitfield Lewis, who was setting up a development group there under Robert Matthew in order to raise the standard of inner London's housing. The group departed with some resolve to 'do a Herts in housing', so far as it might be possible, and they had some success in spreading the approach to component development which they had learned into the field of housing. They very soon found that housing was a harder nut to crack than the little primary schools with which they had been so happy. Meanwhile, Henry Swain and one or two other rebels remained at Hertford for a time. But after 1950 the pressure in the ideological barometer there dropped for good.

In itself, the 'row with Aslin' was not important. But it pointed to issues of purpose in the Herts endeavour, indeed in the whole of post-war public-sector building, which did not surface until after Johnson-Marshall had left. Few architects shared the special vision and commitment which he and his closest colleagues espoused. With architectural training mostly still narrow and a lessening of collective will throughout the nation, it was hard to maintain among new recruits the excitement, discipline and unanimity which had prevailed hitherto. For Johnson-Marshall, an un-political urge for fairness and for a simpler society impelled him towards a view of architecture as a social science, a pragmatic, reforming activity which could contribute to greater all-round equity. This strain continued strong at Herts, but after 1948 other, older conceptions gained ground. For some others, Bruce Martin in particular, architecture was at heart an intellectual and technical activity, and the great challenge of the post-war world was to invent a new manner of building possessing some sort of internal logic, artistry or perfection. Most Herts architects stood somewhere in between, happy to respect and work within the traditions set in 1945–8. But as time went on, as the educationalists grew fixed in their views and relationships with manufacturers became settled, they tended to narrow their sights to problems of technical development.

Under Tatton Brown, the schools architects divided into three groups. The primary group, under Dan Lacey, went on building schools on the established 8 feet 3 inches system, refining continuously upon what had been laid down. There was a secondary group under John Redpath, growing gradually in size and experience but with no agreed technical philosophy for some years. And there was a short-lived development group under Bruce Martin, whose experiments fed mainly into the secondary programme. All three groups aimed above the purely parochial level, and tried to contribute to the national debate about ways and means of building schools. There was some rivalry between them. When at one Christmas party the assembled primary group sang a taunting song (Alan Meikle remembers), John Redpath hastily convened the secondary architects in the lavatory to concoct an equally insulting response.

The primary group (or at least the ideologues among them, chiefly Lacey and Swain) consciously assumed the mantle of Johnson-Marshall. As the groundwork was established, theirs was the easier task. But they (Fig. 4.34) were not prepared to rest upon their reputation.

Plate I. (*facing page*) Oakland Infants School, East Barnet (formerly Herts, now London Borough of Barnet). Mural in the assembly hall by Fred Millett, 1951.

4.34. The Herts primary group poring over a model of Kenilworth School, Borehamwood, 1952. Left to right: C. H. Aslin (county architect); A. P. Tait, Dan Lacey, M. Wolicki, R. Haynes, Margaret Mason, A. Donnan, R. Brewerton, V. Lee, Henry Swain, Charles Cuthill. On the wall a Chianti flask and a poster in Serbo-Croat, symbols of hard-earned post-war foreign travel and 'progressive' sympathies.

The chance to show their mettle came when, after five years of generosity, the Ministry warned that cost limits would be imposed upon new schools after 1950 in order to build more of them. Already, the architects well knew, up to a third of the area in schools was underused and much money was being frittered away in circulation space. Every year they had been decreasing the amount of corridor space, but here was the opportunity to pursue a more formal initiative in 'user studies' and look more closely at the pattern of movement in schools. The impending cost limits, says Lacey,

> gave us a justification for saying to Percy Muncey and the other administrators, 'Look, we really ought to do a reassessment of primary school design'. So we developed the concept of the classroom unit, which was the teaching space and practical area, plus its own lavatory and cloakroom space. We started by analysing the timetable to see why we needed corridors, how much movement there was. What emerged was that apart from going to the hall or to get their lunch, when all the school moved at once, and apart from going to do music or PE which they didn't do every day, the amount of movement from the classrooms into other parts of the building was minimal.

Henry Swain:

> We used questionnaires, but we used interviews as well, along with the education officers,

and determined the idea that classrooms should be grouped in pairs, without any corridors at all, with a small lavatory unit for each, thus cutting out all circulation virtually. The magic was that you cut out the main circulation from classroom to lavatory, so the only circulation left (since primary education is fairly self-centred) was from classroom to assembly hall, or to outside, so the classrooms had outside doors. The minimum circulation, one class disrupting another going through, was felt to be worth it, for the enormous extra usable space they had.

By this means it proved possible to reduce the cost of new primary schools to the limits ordained by the Ministry, while also increasing the size of the classrooms. To prevent disruption from circulation, the group agreed to two rules: that classrooms on circulation routes should never be planned in more than pairs, and that children should move through the practical areas at the back of the rooms rather than through the main teaching space.

From this little revolution sprang a primary school compacter by far than the straggling plans of the 1940s, generally with a central hall and dining area off which at the corners, like spokes from a hub, ran tight little wings with blocks of two or four classrooms (Fig. 4.35). This type of jammed-up plan increased the school's intimacy and allowed landscaping to reach right up to the centre in semi-enclosed courts. The first of the new type was 'Oxhey Site 9', Greenfields School on the barren LCC overspill estate at South Oxhey, built in 1951–2 (Figs. 4.5,36). It impressed Johnson-Marshall and Antony Part, now together at the Ministry, and thus became a pacesetter for the nation as well as for Herts. That the Ministry's Development Group had come to similar conclusions in the one primary school they built at this time, Limbrick Wood at Coventry, only confirmed the solutions of 'Oxhey 9'. The difference was that the Herts primary group had developed the new type while 'in production' and could proceed to expand and refine upon the theme, whereas Limbrick Wood remained an isolated exemplar.

Up until a further reorganization of the Herts office in 1956, the primary group remained a cohesive team of about ten architects, turning out about one school each per year in the established Hills 8 feet 3 inches system. By now the structure was far less altered from year to year, and as alternatives became available was showing its limitations. With many schools completed, it was possible to establish a smooth-running routine and to take regular stock. Lacey again:

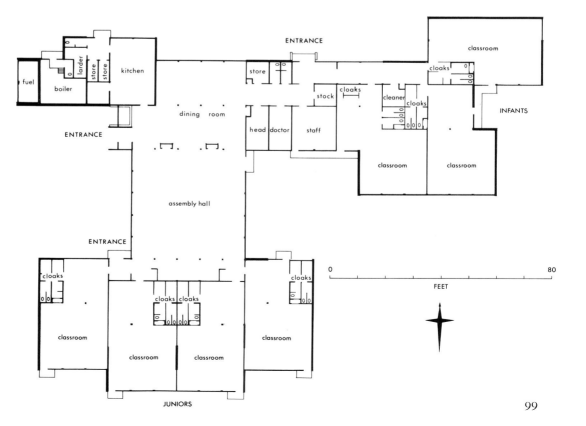

35. Kenilworth School, Kenilworth Drive, Borehamwood, plan. One of the last Herts 8 feet 3 inches primary schools planned after the coming of cost limits, 1951–2. Bunched groups of classrooms with limited circulation lead to a compact school.

Plate II.  Templewood Primary School, Welwyn Garden City, Herts, in its barely finished state, with staggered corridor showing early Herts colour scheme. A. W. Cleeve Barr, job architect, 1949–50.

Plate III.  Templewood Primary School, Welwyn Garden City, Herts. Mural in dining hall by Pat Tew, 1950.

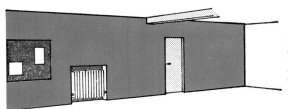

*Untidy arrangements of features
such as beams, notice boards,
radiators and doors are aggravated
by strong colour, whose use may
consequently be inhibited.*

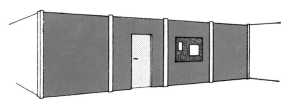

*Forms of construction in which the
stanchions "read" as pilasters make
tidy arrangements of doors, etc.,
more easy, and thus strong colours
are easier to use.*

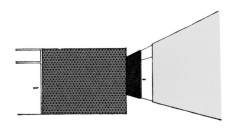

*Where there is no regular articula-
tion by stanchions or pilasters, door
frames carried to the ceiling simplify
wall shapes and may allow the colour
to be changed where required more
easily.*

*Diagram* 1.  COLOUR AND WALL PROPORTIONS

*B. Background surfaces to bright cloak fittings of less
saturated but still strong colour to reflect use of space
and express different directions of surfaces.*

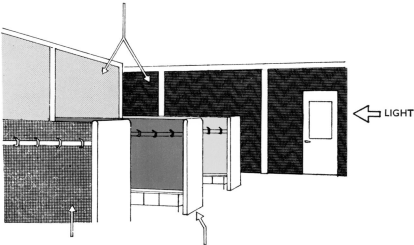

⇐ LIGHT

*A. Bright colours to contrast with full height walls
forming background to fittings. Added interest
by use of different hues but of similar chroma.*

*C. White ends to get full advantage of light source
opposite and to bring out full strength of bright
colours at right angles.*

*Diagram* 9.  CLOAKROOM AND CIRCULATION AREAS

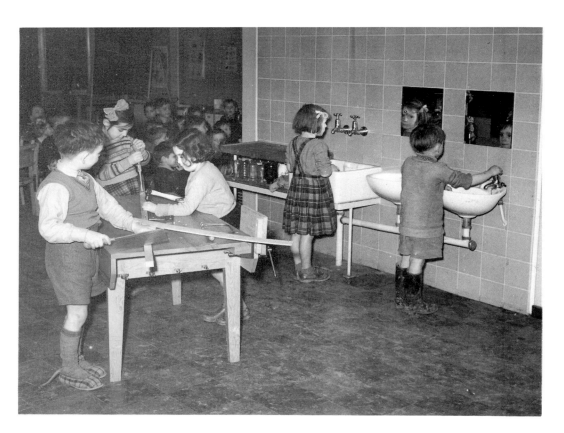

4.36. 'Messy area', infants' classroom,
Greenfields School, Oxhey, *c.* 1952.

As we went on and had some buildings to study, we made a regular practice of the whole group going to a completed building and having a very thorough session pulling it to pieces. We tended to get there about half-past three in the afternoon, so we saw it in operation and had the chance to talk to teachers. Then somebody was given the job of looking at the heating and lighting, somebody else was given the job of the architecture, somebody else was given the finishes. We had a complete structured discussion and we pulled the whole damned thing to pieces. That generated a lot of ideas, and the aesthetics was taken in as part of it. We worried as much about the details. Somebody used to say, 'Well, the architecture is the summation of all the details. We're not concerned about great concepts, what we're concerned about is having refinement everywhere in this building.' It's very much of a Scandinavian attitude, so that the impact comes from the total quality. This is why we fussed about the taps, the sanitary fittings, the light fittings and everything. No doubt now it looks very simple and plain, but that was the mood of the moment.

## SECONDARY SCHOOLS, 3 FEET 4 INCHES AND AFTER

Meanwhile the secondary group under the sturdy John Redpath, seconded by Ken Evans and Ken Twist, was growing in size and scope from year to year. From its inception the group laboured under difficulties which at root reflected the confusion surrounding the subject of secondary school-building in the early post-war years. Having decreed universal secondary education up to the age of fifteen, the government had left local authorities to settle its nature and structure. The only solidly established type of secondary school was the academic grammar school. Like most conservative counties, Herts looked to an expanded grammar-school programme to give coherence to its educational policies. In the absence of better models, the new secondary modern schools all too often looked merely like grammar schools with a few less formal classrooms, a few more workshops and practical areas. In Herts,

Newsom and Broad were distinctly cautious. They built up their grammar schools, securing some remarkable headteachers, and they insisted on keeping secondary schools manageable in size. But they were never able to be catalysts, to offer architects the lead which they had given over primary schools.

Hertfordshire's first county secondary school after the war was the Barclay School at Stevenage (1947–51), one of the few survivors from the crop which Newsom had 'farmed out' even before Johnson-Marshall arrived, in this case to F. R. S. Yorke's new firm of Yorke, Rosenberg and Mardall. It had a plan seemingly derived from Denis Clarke Hall's pre-war school at Richmond, was built in a bastard version of the Hills 8 feet 3 inches system and exhibited something of the Herts philosophy. But nobody was happy with it; it lacked the restraint and clarity of Cheshunt and Essendon. When Bill Henderson started on the first in-house secondary modern, Hampden School at Oxhey, he ran into the same trouble. The problem, some felt, lay in the crudity of the chosen dimension, 8 feet 3 inches, which was too large to cope with the niceties of room-size in specialized buildings. That had been the conclusion of the Ministry of Education's Cleary Working Party of 1948, set up to revise the technical advice on school-building given in the Wood Report. This new study leant heavily on the views of the RIBA's Architectural Science Board, which was then investigating dimensional co-ordination under the direction of Llewelyn-Davies. On the basis of various evidence, above all Leslie Martin and Llewelyn-Davies's development work for the London, Midland and Scottish Railway, the Cleary Report put forward the neater 3 feet 4 inches with its divisibility into units of four inches and its approximation to the metre, as a better dimensional basis for school-building than the 8 feet 3 inches recommended at Stillman's behest in 1944.

At Herts, Bruce Martin was the architect most expert in this sphere and most disgruntled with 8 feet 3 inches which, it was then feared, could never be amended to keep within the Ministry's impending cost limits. So with Tatton Brown's encouragement Martin and a fellow-enthusiast, Anthony Williams, came 'out of production' in 1948–9 to set up a small, short-lived development group which would experiment with a view to devising a new prefabricated system for secondary, multi-storey schools based on a module of 3 feet 4 inches.

At this time, following the first successes of prefabricated building by component rather than by unit, 'dimensional co-ordination' seemed to offer a real hope of knocking rationality into the sluggish and antiquated building industry. It commanded much enthusiasm among architects, and Martin was beginning to immerse himself in the subject as a member of the Architectural Science Board's study group, along with Llewelyn-Davies and Mark Hartland Thomas, the future founder of the Modular Society. If Herts could give a further lead here, its reputation as the aristocrat among school-building authorities would be assured for ever.

Martin therefore set out to devise for Herts a wholly new system of prefabricated school-building which would be aesthetically and proportionally superior to what had gone before, and at the same time fully flexible. Its creation was influenced by the elegant but ill-fated 3 feet 4 inches 'General Panel System' invented between 1943 and 1947 by Konrad Wachsmann and Gropius in the United States. It was agreed at the outset to work once again in light steel and with Hills, where Hinchliffe had already lured Llewelyn-Davies as his private architectural consultant to develop the possibilities of the new dimension. To Llewelyn-Davies and his colleague John Weeks was due the basic structure of the original Hills 3 feet 4 inches system, in particular the so-called 'tartan grid', whereby the structural frame of the building was arranged on a different grid from the planning and partitioning. This idea originated in the experimental railway stations designed by the LMS Development Group; it was supposed to save time in detailing and allow greater flexibility.

On Hertfordshire's behalf, Martin took much of this over, but imposed upon it a kind of classic, symmetrical grace; in his version there was even a column-and-capital arrangement, whereby each stanchion had its 'fully modular mushroom head', to which beams and plates were bolted or welded (Fig. 4.38). The dimensions were co-ordinated vertically as well as horizontally: in other words, the elevation rose in increments of 4 inches to fit with

Plate V. Penguin mural by Clifford Ellis at Maylands Infants School, Hemel Hempstead, Herts, 1950–1. The artist had been reading about Froebel blocks and picked a subject whose crystalline structure had, in his mind, Froebelian overtones. The scuffing is a reminder of the hard wear which works of art in schools must withstand.

Plate VI. Printed curtains by Gerald Holtom at an unidentified Herts school, Hemel Hempstead.

37. Clarendon Secondary Modern
School, Oxhey, first section, 1949–51.
Bruce Martin and R. de Yarborough-
Bateson, job architects, 1949–51. Hills 3
feet 4 inches proprietary system with
Holoplast cladding.

the 40-inch grid. The dour concrete cladding of the old system gave way to vertical panels of Holoplast, a layered composition of tough, light plastic and paper invented by a pair of clever Hungarian engineers. The Holoplast 'trays' could be pre-packed with insulating wool and clipped into position on the frame, thus eliminating hours of assembly and jointing and lining work on site. That at least was the theory of what was widely agreed to be a brilliant system.

The reality was different, and gave early notice to the school-builders that in prefabrication it was easy to go too far too fast. Llewelyn-Davies's version of the Hills 3 feet 4 inches system was tested out along with the Holoplast cladding at the first block (1949–50) of the Clarendon Secondary Modern School, Oxhey (Fig. 4.37). There then followed the only two schools to employ the full panoply of Martin's more developed system: Anthony Williams' Beechwood Day Nursery at Garston (1951) and Martin's own Summerswood Primary School at Borehamwood (1950–2), both single-storey buildings. Before a recent fire, Summerswood (Fig. 4.39) possessed an elegance of proportion and conception which other Herts architects almost fervently shunned. But the system did not prove itself. The joints leaked, sound carried through the partitions, the Holoplast discoloured and proved far too costly, and the teachers disliked the 'off-grid' arrangement whereby columns came down within rooms and sterilized space. Further development which might have ironed out the problems was ruled out by the urgencies of production, ever more pressing after 1950, and by the rapid collapse of the Holoplast company. Thereafter Martin worked with the secondary group, using Holoplast panels on one further school, Lyndhurst Secondary Modern at Borehamwood, before leaving Herts in 1953 to take up the topic of modular

38. Frame of Summerswood School,
Borehamwood, in course of erection,
1952. Herts 3 feet 4 inches system with
'mushroom head', devised by Bruce Martin and Anthony Williams.

4.39. Summerswood Primary School, Borehamwood. Bruce Martin, job architect, 1952–3. 'Tartan grid' system with stanchions off the perimeter, Holoplast cladding, and services contained in a roof zone.

co-ordination at the British Standards Institution. Alan Meikle sums up the reaction which most of the Herts architects had to these experiments:

> I found the Holoplast buildings very stimulating, because the concept of having a school that came in a furniture van (there were actually men in white coats who unloaded the Holoplast panels from furniture vans), of putting this upon a pristine slab, totally dry construction, that excited me particularly. There were no wet trades, no dirt, the whole thing was a totally clean civilized episode. But there were big problems. For example, the partitioning didn't work at all in lavatories and we had regular complaints about pee under the partitions. Little boys had missed the 'Bean' urinal and the urine had run under the partition into the classrooms.

This first stab at a 3 feet 4 inches system at Herts ran into difficulties, therefore, chiefly because technical and design issues became too far separated from those of educational purpose and practicality. But despite this distortion of the Herts ideal, the experiment had value. Martin's determination to pull together the outsides of the schools and give them a good, strong, clear horizontal character by gathering the services up into a proper 'roof zone' marked by a deep fascia seemed to offer a step towards the real future school 'architecture' which might one day lie ahead. During the heyday of the schools consortia in the 1960s this look was to become hackneyed and wearisome. But at the time of Summerswood it represented a fresh departure which made the 8 feet 3 inches schools suddenly look old and a little bit tired.

4.40. Eastbury Road Nursery School, Oxhey, 1952. One of the early Herts experiments in timber, with supports once again off the perimeter.

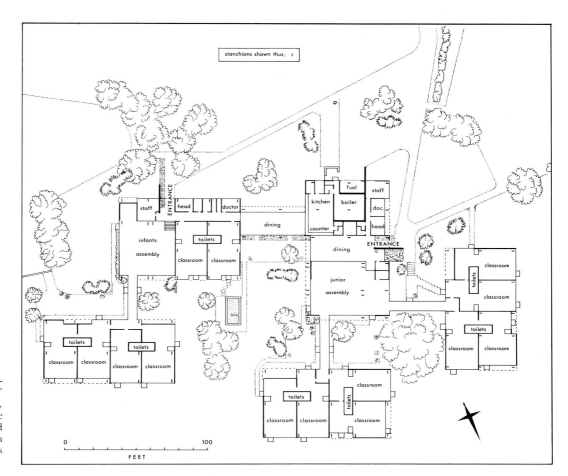

4.41. Roebuck Primary School, Broad-water, Stevenage, plan. An 'off-the-grid' design using the Elliott timber frame, 1953–4. To bring planting into the centre of the school, the classrooms are arranged in three separate blocks, with circulation permitted from one classroom through its neighbour.

Other trials with the 3 feet 4 inches grid followed Martin's experiments, as Herts in the early 1950s strove to diversify technically and avoid having all its eggs in the Hills basket (Fig. 4.40). 'There were a lot of things called prototypes. Sometimes the prototypes died then and there, on the drawing board sometimes, sometimes they got built and sometimes they became a mini-programme.' One remarkable little group was a handful of single-storey schools using a timber frame invented by the building firm Elliotts of Reading, and developed for Herts by Dick Paul and Alistair Tait. This group, built in 1952–4 (a time when timber had at last become more widely available again but steel was short because of the Korean War), consisted of two primary schools, Alban Wood at Watford (Fig. 4.41) and Roebuck at Stevenage (Fig. 4.42), and two secondary schools, Lyndhurst Secondary Modern (referred to above) at Borehamwood and Burleigh Secondary Modern at Hatfield (Fig. 4.43), a job farmed out to the Architects Co-Partnership. The most striking feature of these schools are the eccentric Y-shaped wooden columns of the Elliott frame, devised to carry broad spans. But they also carried on the logic of Bruce Martin's technical work by tidying up the different portions of the buildings into standardized zones, and by freeing the placing of partitions and walls further from the frame itself. 'Off-grid' systems of this kind proved harder to design in and for that reason were suspect to the loyalists of the primary group. In another experiment of these years, Dan Lacey tried out an alternative 3 feet 4 inches system in steel with walls and partitions on the grid and a cedar cladding, starting with a classroom unit at Brookmans Park jocularly known as 'Uncle Dan's Cabin'. The two secondary modern schools built in this system, Heronswood at Welwyn Garden City (1954–7) and Simon Balle at Hertford (1955–7), drew, as did many secondary schools of the period, upon the wealth of thought embodied in the Ministry of Education's first experimental school at Wokingham. They also provided technical experience for the system which Lacey and Swain were to develop when they moved to Nottinghamshire in 1955 and so can be numbered among the precursors of CLASP.

4.42.  Assembly hall, Alban Wood Infants School, Watford. R. C. N. Paul, job architect, 1953–4.    A 3 feet 4 inches school in timber with the distinctive V-shap[e] supports of the 'Elliott frame'.

4.43.  Woodworking, Burleigh Secondary Modern School, Hatfield. Architects Co-Partnership, private architects. 1953–4, using the timber Elliott frame. The suppo[rts] in this system sterilize some usable space.

None of these experiments was taken far 'into production'. So, for want of a proven alternative, Redpath's secondary group soldiered on with the old 8 feet 3 inches system (Fig. 4.44). Redpath himself appreciated that it was as important to implement and develop as to reinvent, and that is what he set his group to do. Despite prognostications, the Hills frame turned out to be remarkably resilient. First it was developed to go up to two storeys, and then at Ravenscroft Secondary Modern School, Barnet (1952–4) up to three. This school, Hertfordshire's hundredth to be completed since the war, was published in the *Architects' Journal* to show the smooth running of the county's programme, the extent to which technical development was still taking place, and how far problems in the system itself over junctions and eaves and windows had been overcome. Technical improvements became the main preoccupations of the secondary group; they were deliverers of goods now, not social innovators. But as in the primary group, there were still regular post-mortems, updatings of documents on 'user-requirements' and discussions with schools inspectors. The spontaneity of the 1940s had gone, but the schools were still improving year by year in all save perhaps appearance. There were still areas to be explored. Dennis White, a professional furniture designer who joined the staff in about 1950, was instrumental in putting secondary-school furniture on a par with the county's primary equipment. In particular he designed high-quality fittings in the hardwoods now once more available for the laboratories and technical areas of the secondary schools.

By the mid-1950s, Herts was very conscious of its primacy in school-building. Other counties might look to the Ministry of Education or to other authorities for help, but Herts in the main wanted to work out solutions for itself. The BRS was still consulted and Tatton Brown liaised with the Modular Society over dimensional problems, which Herts architects took more seriously than those elsewhere. But increasingly the county was known as one that went its own way. Unlike most other authorities, it kept up with its back-breaking burden of school-building; the 'rolling programmes', now reaching some fifteen or twenty educational projects per year, rolled onwards. Technically, Herts was as progressive as ever. In educational terms its schools were less remarkable, if only because of the councillors' cautious educational policies.

The 8 feet 3 inches system survived the end of building controls in 1954, the revitalization of traditional modes of construction, the merging of the primary and secondary groups in 1956, the respective retirements of Newsom and Aslin in 1957 and 1959, and even the sudden liquidation of Hills in 1962. The last school of the type, indeed, was built as late as 1963–4, and even then some regretted the demise of a faithful old friend. By then, however, Herts had long shifted to an alternative dimensional framework: not 3 feet 4 inches, which the rest of the country had dutifully adopted, but 2 feet 8 inches. Their few 3 feet 4 inches schools had convinced Geoffrey Fardell, now promoted as county architect, and Jack Platt, the strongest and stablest influence in these years, that it was the wrong dimension:

4.45 and 46. St Albans College of Further Education. R. J. A. Wakely, job architect, 1958–60. The first of Hertfordshire's higher-education colleges to be designed in a steel system to a module of 2 feet 8 inches.

mathematically inconvenient, too big for doors and lavatories, and irrelevant to manufacturers' sizes.

The new dimension was first tried out, as the 40-inch module had been, on a block at the Clarendon School at Oxhey (1958–9), but received its real baptism in a set of colleges of further education which the county wished to build quickly (Figs. 4.45, 46). As these colleges were quite complex and costly buildings, the range of the new system could be tested without the rigid cost restraints which would have operated in schools. After them, the system could be refined and brought down in cost for regular application in school-building.

The experiment triumphed, and after 1960 the county's whole educational building programme was shifted slowly on to a dimensional basis of 2 feet 8 inches. In early post-war days, the module would have been interpreted to fit one particular building system, but in the easier 1960s it was only sensible to fit the dimensional discipline to suit more than one structural material. So secondary schools were generally built with a light steel framework, primary schools with 'crosswall' construction (on a module of 1 foot 4 inches) and certain buildings with a heavier load were given a concrete frame. These were the school-building techniques in operation when Herts was reluctantly corralled up by the Ministry of Education and pressed with Kent and Essex in 1963 into SEAC, the South-Eastern Architects' Collaboration. Herts was much the most experienced partner in this consortium and the Herts systems, with emendations, provided the expertise for the various 'Marks' of SEAC which had to sustain the boom of the 1960s, when school-building was at its peak all over the south-east of England. But with the formation of SEAC, the story of Herts as an independent post-war authority in school-building comes effectively to an end.

## HERTFORDSHIRE'S ACHIEVEMENT

Hertfordshire's schools and colleges of the late 1950s and of the 1960s were more sophisticated buildings, more satisfactory educational entities, than the simple, somewhat awkward creations of the post-war years. Yet historical curiosity about Herts as a school-building authority is bound to centre upon that early period of struggling and searching, without which the pattern of later schools, not just in Herts but throughout Britain, would have been different.

Before leaving Herts, it is worth restating in outline what was so new in the history of British architecture and building about its early schools programmes.

1. Well before other local authorities, Herts seized the advantage of continuity of employment and investment offered in the post-war period by the public sector to develop a consistent set of architectural and educational objectives for both the short and the long term. This differed sharply from the hand-to-mouth way in which most private architects were obliged to operate and public architects had, as a matter of record, operated before the war.
2. The Herts architects created the groundwork for a new 'language of architecture': not a style, not a mode of construction, but something approaching a complete technology of building which was broadly applicable and tolerably flexible, something which designers could work in and develop. This transformed the possibilities of prefabricated building.
3. Herts laid down procedures for collaboration and interchange between users, designers, manufacturers, technologists and clients which were more ambitious, continuous and considered in scope than anything previously attempted in British architecture.
4. In a time of shortages and crises, Herts found the policies and the means to advance educational opportunity not just in the occasional school but equally throughout its building programmes. By so doing, it gave meaning to the old ideal that decent architecture should be available to all in fair shares, not just reserved for those who could afford it or were lucky enough to get it. Hertfordshire's post-war schools seemed at last to lift from public-sector building the shadow of the poor law and to give England its first taste of a democratic architecture.

But Herts was small and stood practically alone. How broadly could all this be spread? This was the question which Stirrat Johnson-Marshall set out quite consciously to answer, when he moved to the Ministry of Education in 1948.

# CHAPTER 5

# AT THE MINISTRY

From time beyond tracing, people have been employed directly by British governments for the design and construction of buildings. Palaces for the sovereign, stage-settings for the court, barracks, castles, churches, parks and street improvements all feature in the remoter history of this tradition. In the nineteenth century, the ramifications of democracy coupled with the ethic of private enterprise slowly curtailed all this. Few and poor were the opportunities available to architects, surveyors and engineers in full-time service with the Office of Works and other government departments apart from the army after 1850. By 1900, municipal architecture and engineering had gained a foothold in a few cities, but little civil construction fell to departments of state. Post offices, soon to be supplemented by telephone exchanges, were practically the only exception. Surveyors, sanitarians and a medley of other professionals laboured in the sundry offices and boards of government to vet building schemes of one kind or another submitted to them under act of Parliament by local authorities and 'statutory undertakers'. But they did so chiefly with an eye to regulation and economy. Their role was passive, and they were in almost everything junior servants to civil servants. Of wider accountability, initiative, imagination or responsibility to the public at large they exercised little, if ever they felt the need to do so.

The renaissance of government architecture—or, strictly, of government initiative in British architecture—followed from the formulation of national building programmes as a concept during and after the First World War. It was from the dogged, Fabian foresight and persistence of Raymond Unwin in particular, the first modern architect and planner of distinction to submit to salaried, regular employment in a British government department, that there developed in the Ministry of Health during the 1920s the principle of a team of professionals in central government encouraging and supporting local-authority building. Unwin and his cohorts went about this task by persuasion and information, by showing how good use could be made of limited funds, and by suggesting layouts and type-plans for the government-subsidised housing which began to be built after 1919. The importance of this innovation was immense. For the first time in the august history of 'the King's works', a group of technicians settled down to active, concerted work on the physical embodiment of a national, fairly shared programme of building, to be undertaken in partnership between central and local government.

To a degree, the Board of Education and other ministries involved in construction learnt from Unwin's example. But the learning depended upon continuous programmes of building. When these lapsed, as public housing did for a while in the 1930s, or merely trickled on, as did educational building during most of the inter-war years, the central body of experts tended to revert to mere passive regulation. There was a further flaw in the model of support evolved under Unwin. With the exception of the Office of Works, nobody at the centre actually designed and built. So the separation between national and local government easily degenerated into a gap between thinking and doing, the formulation of policy and its implementation.

Thus matters still stood after the Second World War. Despite the wartime spurt in direct building by government, despite the preparations for great public programmes of building when peace came, despite the establishment of a Ministry of Town and Country Planning to speed reconstruction, a gulf still yawned between government advice and directive on the one hand and local-authority action on the other. In the late 1940s the cities, counties, boroughs and districts of Britain were showered with exhortations to plan and build houses and schools as fast as they could. Yet most of them hardly knew where to turn, for lack of staff and expertise. Reconciliation between those who planned and those who built was crucial. With a worsening economy, the potential for a complete collapse of reconstruction could not be discounted. In education, that would have meant reversion everywhere to wartime-type huts, and the deferment yet again of all the hopes for better schools seemingly so near when the Butler Act was passed in 1944.

## 'A & B' BRANCH

Such was the situation in the summer of 1948, when Stirrat Johnson-Marshall left Hertford-shire after less than three years to become chief architect to the Ministry of Education. He was to hold the appointment for nearly eight years. Altogether Johnson-Marshall shaped the course of school-building as an 'official architect' for just over a decade—exactly the period of the public sector's undisputed dominance over British architecture. During his time at the Ministry, the revolution in attitudes of which he was the prime mover at Herts spread to the rest of the country. After he left in 1956 the school-building approach for which he stood went on developing and diversifying for at least another ten years, based on the conviction and consensus which had been built up during that arduous post-war decade.

In 1948 the new Ministry of Education, housed in makeshift offices in Curzon Street, was struggling to bear up under the strains imposed on it by the Butler Act, by shortages, and by the unexpected spurt in the birth-rate. George Tomlinson was the Minister, in succession to the lamented Ellen Wilkinson; but ministers, whether in the Attlee government or later, did not interfere a lot in the school-building process. John Maud was the permanent secretary, 'a very sparky, energetic and forward-looking man', young for the post at forty-two, his sails full with the educational afflatus of the Butler Act. A don drawn into government by the circumstances of war, he had no special respect for administrative proprieties. Three principal departments under him managed the national business of school-building. The Schools Branch, staffed by inspectors (HMIs) and others, vetted incoming plans from local authorities for conformity to educational standards; and the Architect's Branch, up till then under the experienced F. Jackman and his deputy P. B. R. ('Buster') Brown, also checked designs to see that they obeyed the Ministry's latest building regulations, issued in 1945. These were passive roles, carried over from the pre-war Board of Education. Real and active power lay with the Buildings and Priorities Branch, headed by Antony Part, another young mandarin who had been a staff officer under Montgomery and was thoroughly imbued with military methodology. This branch, like similar outfits in other ministries, had been a creation of war. It held the whip hand in decisions about building, because it had the vital power of rationing out materials. Part recalls how it functioned:

Each quarter a central government committee allocated, shall we say, steel to all departments for all purposes, and there was a great meeting which dealt with this handing-out of materials. All the principal priority officers sat on this committee and we battled for our own allocations. So I came away from the committee with an allocation of steel for the following quarter for all educational purposes. Then it was up to us at the Ministry what we did with that allocation. What normally happened was that when a school project came along it was issued with a permit of steel, a stated amount of steel for that project.

The national school-building picture had altered swiftly since the war ended. Materials, building labour and design staff alike had been so scarce in its immediate aftermath that

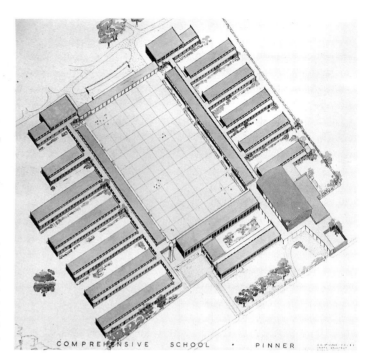

5.1. Headstone Lane Comprehensive School, Pinner, Middlesex, proposed layout, 1947. Middlesex County Council was among the first authorities to propose comprehensives. The type of plan first suggested by C. G. Stillman and his architects seemed authoritarian and unappealing to Stirrat Johnson-Marshall and his supporters.

the Ministry reluctantly promoted its HORSA programme—the Hutting Operation for the Raising of the School-Leaving Age. Gradually local authorities took on staff and shook themselves into shape for designing the mass of schools needed. But the material shortages showed no signs of abating; the allocations of softwood for schools, for instance, bordered on the derisory in the late 1940s. So at Part's insistence, the Ministry decreed that authorities must compile and submit in advance annual programmes for school-building. In this way overall planning, budgeting and allocations could be more rationally ordered. Once an authority had its programme for the year approved, materials for a given school could be guaranteed when the sketch plans were passed. This system came into effect in 1947, was soon refined and became a permanent arrangement even after rationing ended.

More than anything else, the introduction of annual programming led local authorities to think of school-building in terms of regular production and standardized techniques. Before Johnson-Marshall's arrival, the Ministry was encouraging architects to build schools in a standard system of bay construction based on the module of 8 feet 3 inches extended in a single direction (Fig. 5.1). But there was no compulsion and a good measure of experimentation. Already the heterodox 8 feet 3 inches grid taking shape at Herts had impressed Maud and Part, and there were many other ideas, cheap and costly. For the time being, control over costs did not matter much. Inflation and rationing were distorting the prices of materials. 'We thought it so important to get the quantity going that we really took a fairly loose look at the costs of the projects as they came in,' says Part.

At this stage, with few new schools actually on the ground but a rising number of 'starts' in prospect, Maud and Part turned their thoughts to restructuring the relevant branches within the Ministry. By mingling administrators, architects and HMIs, they hoped to offer a quicker, sharper response to the impending workload. The chance came when Jackman retired in 1948. Casting about for a successor, they hit upon Johnson-Marshall. For idealism, energy, compatibility and post-war experience there were no comparable candidates. Only Middlesex and Hertfordshire were forward with their school-building programmes, and of these two authorities Herts had the edge in persuasiveness and invention. Part had been greatly taken with Cheshunt and Essendon, and by the Herts architects' knack of planning their programme and using the allocations system to their advantage while others were only fumbling. Johnson-Marshall had two further advantages; Maud was friendly with John Newsom, with whom he had worked so well at Herts, and since he was only the deputy county architect, without formal responsibilities for the expanding programme, he was reasonably free to move. In August 1948 he started work as joint head of the new Architects and Building (A & B) Branch at the Ministry of Education. With momentary diffidence Part had suggested that the new appointee head the team, but the bureaucracy demurred; Maud was even 'ticked off' by the head of the civil service for supporting such a deviant suggestion. So a rare compromise was reached, whereby Johnson-Marshall and Part ran the branch together.

In the first instance A & B Branch consisted only of a team of 'territorial' architects and administrators who vetted incoming plans; there was no broader role. At Johnson-Marshall's urging this soon changed. He had not become a civil servant without circumspection. He did so because he believed passionately that there was a proud and vital task to be carried through in building better schools for British children, and that if power was available it should be seized and exploited for good. But he always saw himself as an operator, as an intriguer within the establishment. Bill Allen recalls: 'I saw him in a black felt hat on almost his first day going to the Ministry. I said, "What the hell are you wearing that for?" He said, "Well, if you had the intentions upon the civil service that I have, you'd want a disguise too".' Johnson-Marshall therefore went to the Ministry on certain conditions. Above all, he must be allowed to build. A & B Branch could not instruct and advise on school-building, he reasoned, unless it could offer leadership by example. 'You must be able to show you've got the ability of your own convictions and you can design as well as the next man and indeed better': this was the attitude. Otherwise the Ministry's architects would become remote from practicalities, ossified and bureaucratic.

This proposal aroused widespread displeasure and opposition. The RIBA saw it as a further blow to the job prospects of the private architect and complained to the Ministry; the stronger county architects like Conolly of Essex and Stillman of Middlesex feared encroachment; and school-building authorities generally interpreted the suggestion as another symptom of centralization in the wake of the Butler Act. But the administrators stood by their new architect and tenaciously damped down opposition, dispatching Tomlinson to tell the RIBA to be less myopic. The Ministry would only build a tiny handful of experimental schools, they promised, and these would conform absolutely to all the conditions which local authorities had to observe. With the population rising so rapidly, any help in increasing the number of schools completed ought to be welcomed, they argued. In any case, the technical and educational knowledge which would accrue from committing part of the Ministry's team to responsible experimentation would, if properly promulgated, help both private and public architects enormously.

Thus, through Part's administration, Maud's suavity and Johnson-Marshall's vision, a way of working was created in A & B Branch which renewed and improved upon the model of Unwin's inter-war building partnership between central government and local authority. In this new version, the central team would act as enablers, advisers and investigators on behalf of the hard-pressed local authorities, like an industrial research outfit working ahead of but in concert with production. In Johnson-Marshall's mind it was a way of extending the cycle of design, use and development already established at Herts into an ambitious series of interlocking cycles, with the whole country's educational problems addressed and the issue of national resources confronted.


## THE DEVELOPMENT GROUP

The early hurdles once cleared, the way was free for recruitment to the 'Development Group' which was to shape the Ministry's technical philosophy on building and design its modicum of schools. Without such a team, dedicated to intervention and removed from the daily round of approving submitted plans, Johnson-Marshall's ambitions could have found no adequate outlet. Henceforward, A & B Branch was split into two: the Development Group, charged with research, building, theory, collaboration and experiment, and the territorials, who vetted the annual programmes and individual school plans submitted by authorities.

If the more glamorous role fell to the Development Group, the territorials were crucial in promoting and 'selling' the new ideas as they emerged. As their work put them in regular contact with the counties and boroughs, they were able to drop hints and pass on enthusiasms to the more receptive authorities and architects. 'The real interest was in persuading people to do better things,' says Pat Tindale, the first territorial architect appointed under the new régime. For the time being this was done light-handedly enough. Because school places were needed urgently, building was on no account to be delayed by the bureaucracy. At an early stage Johnson-Marshall and Part decreed that sketch-plans would no longer have to be submitted to the Ministry. From 1949 onwards, territorials scrutinized only final plans and dispensed with detailed lists of furniture and equipment. In future once an authority's annual programme had been settled, its schools went only once through the mill of ministerial approval. This simple change saved greatly in time and expense. It also convinced suspicious local authorities that A & B Branch's policies were going to be anti-red-tape and, essentially, liberal.

The idea of a development group, of a vanguard removed from everyday tasks to find some radical solution of general applicability to a pressing technical problem, had grown by degrees in British architecture. It can be traced back in part to the experiments in cottage-building sponsored by government after 1918 which led to the foundation of the Building Research Station. But it only became a conscious ideal as a result of pre-war and wartime enthusiasms for science, research and 'group-working'. The London, Midland and Scottish Railway's Development Group of 1939–48, led by Leslie Martin and Richard Llewelyn-Davies, was the first to use the term. Though its work was largely frustrated, the fashion spread to the Ministry of Education, the Scottish Special Housing Association, the London County Council, and then more broadly. The Ministry of Education's group was to be the most important, by virtue of its own work and influence on school-building and because it in due course supplied the model for later architectural teams within British government, in the Ministry of Health, the Ministry of Housing and Local Government and the War Department. At the time it was set up, nothing comparable existed. In other ministries, the parallel vertical hierarchies of administrators and professionals and the ancient curse of departmental jealousies prevented anything like A & B Branch flourishing until the structure of post-war building had become too rigid to change easily. Until 1957 only the Ministry of Education's Development Group could design, develop and deal with contractors and industrialists, and thus influence as much through example as through circular and regulation.

First, Johnson-Marshall had to pick people who could define this role in practical terms. Clannish by instinct, he turned to known colleagues or contacts who shared his philosophy of education and building. So into the budding Development Group in April 1949 came David and Mary Medd from Herts. Appointed with them to head the group's technical work was Anthony Pott, wooed away from BRS by persistent blandishment from Johnson-Marshall. An AA-trained architect, Pott (Fig. 6.8) had been a founder member of the Architects' Co-Operative Partnership in 1939. During the war he gravitated, like other technically orientated architects, to BRS, where he amassed an encyclopaedic knowledge. Pott was a perfect second fiddle to Johnson-Marshall, sceptical, deliberate, precise and organized where the latter was ebullient, strategic but vague. Maurice Lee remembers his 'totally incorruptible mind. He would never gloss over any technical problem.' Guy Oddie saw him as

nearer to being a first-division civil servant than he was to being an architect. He was the nicest chap I ever met in my life. He was a hopeless leader, but he made a very good sparring partner for Stirrat because he called a spade a spade, which Stirrat on no account would ever have done. He would puncture all Stirrat's bright ideas, and if they survived Anthony's onslaught then they would be all right and Anthony would back 'em.

If I had a problem, I'd go across the corridor to Anthony's room. Anthony would say: 'Well, have you read the code of practice on so-and-so? What about BRS Digest No. 24? And anyway what about this?'. By the time you'd finished, where you thought you had one problem you found in fact you had ninety-nine, ninety-eight of which you'd been too stupid to notice. So you came out of Anthony's room completely dejected and trooped along the corridor to Stirrat's. And Stirrat would say, 'Do come in and sit down'. He would waffle (he was a marvellous waffler), he would waffle away and flatter you (he was a tremendous flatterer), and you would think 'I didn't come here to be flattered, I'm really rather pressed for time. I wish to hell he'd help me with this problem—or rather these ninety-nine problems I've now got'. But as he flattered you, by the time he'd finished you'd hit your head on the door as you went out because you'd grown about three feet. That was Stirrat's great gift.

The combination of Pott and the Medds ensured that anything built by the Ministry would be thorough and practical. Other early Development Group architects were hired for similar qualities of commitment and care. There was a strong contingent of Herts or BRS people. Michael Smith was one ex-Herts man; Donald Barron another; Maurice Lee, a mature student from the Birmingham school who had fallen under the Johnson-Marshall spell and worked one brief summer at Herts was (in a manner) a third; James Nisbet, junior quantity surveyor at Herts for a couple of years, a fourth. Bruce Martin was enticed but declined to leave Herts. By 1952 the team included also John Price, Pat Tindale, Barbara Price (from the LMS Development Group), Guy Oddie (ex-BRS), John Kitchin, Dargan Bullivant and Peter Newnham. Most gifted of all was a young polymath from the AA, Michael Ventris. Well before this 'superior being' joined the Ministry in 1950, he had begun immersing himself in the logical mysteries of Linear B, the arcane Minoan language. Ventris brought his genius for organization and method to the tasks of the Development Group for a couple of years only. His progress in deciphering Linear B was by then so far possessing him that he left the Ministry to complete it. He had not long cracked its rudiments when his life was cut short by a road accident in 1956.

Others came in to A & B Branch along with these architects to realize Antony Part's vision of the inter-disciplinary team. Though education had only a middling status within the civil service, Maud managed to secure for the branch four successive chief administrators of flair and ability—Part himself, David Nenk, William Pile and Derek Morrell. Nenk in particular had a reputation for brilliance and all were tinged with greater idealism than is usually conceded to the civil servant. Then there were the schools inspectors (HMIs) who worked full-time with the Development Group in formulating briefs, expounding educational ideas and putting the architects in touch with exciting teachers and schools. The first of these, Leonard Gibbon, hid a rich knowledge of teaching practice and a loyalty to progressive ideals in education behind a discouragingly formal manner. His deputy and successor Eric Pearson shared his views but was more approachable. Over the activities of the HMIs hovered the influence of Christian Schiller, then housed on another floor in the Ministry as staff inspector for primary education and the most powerful advocate of a schooling which encouraged choice and activity.

## COST AND VALUE

How then to begin to bring the flexibility, the joint skills, the mixed talents of this commando-type team to bear upon the issue of getting universally better schools? So behindhand were most counties with their programmes, so sluggish their educational thinking and so dated their technical know-how, so desperate were many of them to be told what to do, that the branch could have started anywhere. A first task was to disseminate information on primary schools, trying to explain what Herts had done and how; the next was to start thinking about secondary schools. But the issue which immediately dominated the branch and threatened to smother its infant liberalism from the start was money. Cuts—drastic cuts—loomed on the horizon, as Britain's puny post-war economy writhed in the clutches of 'dollar convertibility'.

Local education authorities build Britain's schools, but central government decides how much they may spend upon the task in a given year. This division of responsibilities shaped the whole of the Ministry of Education's post-war building apparatus. Under Part's system of 1947, the authorities each year proposed a programme of so many schools. At the same time the Treasury fixed a limit to the money available on loan for school-building in that year. In reconciling these figures lay the Ministry's chief means of influencing the building of schools.

Directly after the war the situation had been abnormal. For a while, as has been said, the Attlee administration bothered less about the building costs of its programmes than about getting them going by securing the needed materials and labour. In 1946–8, with the construction industry creaking slowly back into action, the total value of the school-building programmes gave no cause for alarm. The great aim was to get 'roofs over heads'. Once huts had been abandoned, the new schools enjoyed a measure of spatial generosity. They had big halls, separate dining areas and ample corridors, since the Ministry encouraged plenty of circulation space.

Then the size of the post-war baby-boom became apparent and, with it, the scale of accommodation which would be needed. 200,000 new school places were required every year up to 1955 to cope with war damage, defective premises (some condemned as far back as 1925) and the leap in the birthrate. Confronted with a worsening economy and a hefty claim on capital to pay for the 1949 schools programme, the Treasury jibbed. Stafford Cripps inspected a wastefully planned school in a London suburb and came back with a curt threat. If the Ministry could not get the costs of school-building down, they would have to revert to huts, perhaps also to the 'double-banking' or 'warm-seat' traditions of schooling then common across Europe, whereby one set of children were taught in the morning and another in the afternoon. This was the threat hanging over the newly formed A & B Branch in 1949.

British architects had never been educated to think broadly or imaginatively about money, especially about controls upon costs. Johnson-Marshall and his team, it may be claimed, were the first to venture into this treacherous arena and take on the contradictions of social and financial accountability. They were able to do so only because of the branch's structure. Had the architects been separate from the administrators, the financial implications of building on so vast a scale would have been decided upon by the latter alone. Soon, schools would have been built to a lower standard; probably every feature would have become a little smaller, with services and finishes suffering most. Jumbled up together as they were in a mixed team, architect and administrator alike saw things differently. How could building costs be controlled in such a way as not to harm and perhaps even benefit the quality and number of new schools? Johnson-Marshall's attitude was unequivocal. If architects really wanted to influence school-building, they must put away their old-fashioned financial ama-teurism. 'Money is a factor in design,' he affirmed. 'It's not something you can ignore. You can only build within the funds available.'

Before the war, the Board of Education had struggled to contain school-building costs. But its methods had been empirical and haphazard. There were recommended minimum floor areas for classrooms and other parts of a school which, in the way of such things, tended to become maximum areas. In periods of stringency the Board's architects would ask, after plans had been submitted, for reductions in floor areas, finishes, wall-thicknesses or foundations. This process was tiresome and time-consuming. The method still theoretically obtained after 1945, when the new school-building regulations for the first time laid out statutory (and higher) minimum standards of accommodation and amenity for post-war schools. But it was lightly applied in view of the exigencies of the time.

The saner, clearer but more stringent system introduced by the Ministry in 1949 was that of 'cost per place'. Before each year, commencing with 1950, the Ministry would announce for both primary and secondary schools a figure of expenditure for each child accommodated, within which each school built in that year had to fall. This figure was arrived at in A & B Branch by combining a notional number of square feet per place and an estimated cost of building per square foot; but no separate figures were prescribed or published for these factors, beyond the minimum space standards ordained in the building regulations. Architects and authorities therefore had a degree of freedom, so long as the cost limit per place was not breached. They could build larger classrooms and a cheaper structure, if they chose, or they could have smaller classrooms and better structure and finishes or services. But the Ministry vowed never to honour those who built at a figure well below the cost limit by providing minimum classrooms with inadequate circulation, cheap structure, poor finishes and skimped services.

The first figures for cost per place had to be pitched at an attainable level. They were fixed at £195 for primary schools and £320 for secondary schools for the year 1950. But the Ministry warned that there would be quick successive reductions, to £170 and £290 respectively in 1951 (when the building regulations were revised and some minimum areas reduced) and then to £140 and £240 in 1952. This was a period of rising building costs, so that the real reduction was greater—perhaps as great as fifty per cent, according to Part. Despite a continued increase in prices, the cost limits did not rise above the 1951 level until 1961.

So described, this looks like the crushing of the school-building flower just as it came into bloom. The promissory notes of Butler, it seems, were being savagely discounted by a usurious Crippsian bureaucracy. Certainly many authorities had their tribulations in keeping within the plummeting cost limits of the early 1950s, especially when building secondary schools. But the story of school-building costs during this period is more instructive and encouraging than these cold figures suggest.

At the time of Cripps's warning, the Ministry had only hazy ideas about building costs. They employed no experts on the subject. The civil servants knew that the costs of completed post-war schools were wildly at variance and they suspected, like the Herts architects, that too much money was going on 'circulation'. Because of the shortages and the various experiments in 'alternative forms of construction', anomalies were natural. But A & B Branch could only devise a target cost per place if it knew accurately how much schools were costing. And it could only influence their design for good if it could say why they cost what they did—to put it more precisely, if it could break them down into 'elements' and see where the money was going.

To address these questions, Johnson-Marshall and David Medd brought in a young quantity surveyor, James Nisbet, to work in the branch. Nisbet had gained his professional grounding with a busy local authority in Scotland, where estimating and costing enjoyed a higher status than in England. In 1946–8 he had been at Herts as one of a small group of quantity surveyors working with the schools architects and sharing their aims. To get a better grasp of English building practice, Nisbet began while at Herts to collect detailed costs of all the jobs he could lay his hands on. He soon began to ask himself why, when the Herts schools were mainly built of standard components, they differed so much in cost. Thus far he had only an inkling of an idea: that if buildings were broken down into the generic parts or elements in terms of which they were designed or used, a comparison between the costs of these elements might be revealing. This was the experiment which Nisbet was hired by the Ministry to undertake.

They could establish that the same size of primary school cost, say, £100 in North Yorkshire and £300 in Middlesex—they had that range of costs. What they couldn't get was any rational explanation of why. The first thing I did was to develop the method. Stirrat got the various county architects to send in priced bills of quantities and the drawings for a number of schools. I had about six, I think. My first job was to see if what I was talking about would work. All I did was get down to it. When I'd got the analysis of the one in Yorkshire and the one in Middlesex, I said, 'Good God, *that's* where it is and *that's* where it is and *that's* where it is. Look at the floor finishes in Yorks, they must be damned cheap and awful,'—and so on. When I'd drawn these conclusions I needed moral support, and we said we'd better check it. So we paid visits to the schools, to see whether what we were concluding was right.

Which it was: thus was born 'elemental cost analysis'.

In principle it seems obvious that building costs should be broken down in terms of the different elements familiar to the designer, owner or user, and strange that this had not been tried before. Perhaps in a few instances it had. But there had been little previous call from architects for such a technique, since most of their buildings had been 'one-offs'. The crude old method of 'cubing', in other words calculating the cubic content and applying to it a rough, rule-of-thumb cost per cubic foot, gave a designer some notice of how much a building (or a hunk of it) might amount to, while later the bill of quantities broke down the price by materials and trades. These methods gave architects no serious pause for thought about cost, except perhaps to discourage them from using unduly costly materials. But analysis by elements was of limited use, if the next job was entirely different in kind. Only when a large quantity of similar, economical but non-identical buildings was in prospect, such as the schools programme, could such an innovation in thinking about costs take place. The previous such revolution in British attitudes to building costs had come during the Napoleonic wars, when the government was faced with the need to run up a large number of barracks quickly in case of invasion. From this crisis had emerged the 'contract in gross'. Now, in an equally urgent situation, new ideas about costing were again making themselves felt.

The simplest single merit of cost analysis was that it allowed architects and others to see where money had been spent. With cubing, says Nisbet, 'you were pricing this cubic bit of air which has got no relationship to anything which costs any money.' The first analyses by the new method, with their scrutiny of elements and of area rather than cubic content, were dramatic, remembers Part:

> We were surprised to find what many architects had done with their clients' money. Some hid it in the roof, a lot of them buried it in the ground, and not a few of them spent it on removing all the interesting features from the site. An analysis of cost per square foot is a very searching test. It demonstrates, sometimes with painful clarity, whether the amount of money spent on a particular part of the building reflects the importance of that part in the scheme of things.

In other words, cost analysis was more than a Scrooge-like device for sniffing out extravagances. It taught designers to reflect hard and deep before they chose their priorities.

Along with cost analysis went another simple tool, again inexplicably novel: area analysis, whereby Nisbet and his colleagues broke down the total floor area of each school into teaching space versus the rest. The early fruits of this technique were hardly less startling, especially when it was applied to the 'bay' style of school. In terms of savings, it was area analysis which chiefly justified the successive, harsh reductions in the cost limits between 1950 and 1952. These bit less deep than the figures suggest, because the Ministry was able to persuade authorities to cast out acres of space from their school designs. Doubtless the same reductions would have been urged without Nisbet's backing. The very implementation of cost limits forced architects, teachers and inspectors everywhere to re-examine their schools and decide which portions were underused or where two activities could take place in the same space. But Nisbet's work confirmed this by identifying areas of 'fat' in schools and setting figures of cost upon them. The key document in persuading authorities to replan their schools was *Cost Study*, the briefest of the Ministry's early Building Bulletins, written by Nisbet and Pile in 1951. It was to be the most widely used and quoted of A & B Branch's early publications.

Cripps's cuts, followed by the further savings insisted upon by the incoming Conservative government in 1951, put extra power into the hands of A & B Branch. Authorities were stopped in their tracks and forced to revise, if not entirely scrap, their building plans—especially for secondary schools. Middlesex, for instance, tried for a while to build schools with classrooms first and halls later, much to the Ministry's disapproval. Others found in the early 1950s, while Florence Horsbrugh was Minister of Education, that they were not able to build anything like the number of schools they needed. All this meant that they were obliged to listen to the branch's suggestions on cost and design.

Later, when economies had been pressed too far, many teachers came to deplore features of the reduced, jammed-up school plans of the 1950s and '60s: the elimination of corridors, the rampant spread of 'dual use', and the occasional naive innovation like the infant WC stuck behind a partition within the classroom space. Though these changes might be and were defended on educational grounds, they were without question first adopted for reasons of economy. Nevertheless before 1950 there was much unquestionable 'fat', much genuinely wasted space, in British schools. They do not seem to have suffered from this first economizing campaign of 1950–2. Some gained for being more tightly planned and became more coherent and communal. And at a time when numbers were critical, the savings allowed more schools to be squeezed out of the limited overall capital sums that the government would permit.

In 1952 an accolade to the success of A & B Branch's assault upon costs appeared in the form of the Pilkington Report. Potentially this was the earliest of many, wearying, distracting threats to the branch's existence. It was commissioned by Florence Horsbrugh, seemingly in the expectation that it might corroborate some charges about extravagance in educational building that had been flying around the Conservative Party since the days before cost limits were introduced. In the event, it resoundingly vindicated the Ministry and provided the first official encouragement for spreading A & B Branch's methods to other government departments and local authorities, 'with particular emphasis on those uses where some degree of repetition in the buildings provided or their components is practicable, such as Post Office buildings, Hospitals and Housing'. The Pilkington Report's conclusions were too embarrassing to the Minister for it to be published. But it further strengthened and consolidated Johnson-Marshall's hand.

## FROM COST ANALYSIS TO COST PLANNING

Cost analysis in its original form was only a passive process, a kind of 'consciousness-raising' for architects who were obliged by the cost limits to build to a strict budget. The next stage, developed by Nisbet together with Clive Wooster, hitherto one of A & B Branch's territorial architects, was 'cost planning'. This meant using analytic technique to design 'elementally', in other words, seizing the implications of choice and priority made manifest by cost analysis and taking them through into the design of new buildings. The attractions of so doing are put by David Medd:

Through cost planning you could decide at the start that you were going, say, to afford a certain lighting system, generous pin-up space, a pool or whatever, and build them into the cost plan at the start, instead of such things hanging precariously on the end of the cost sum and thus liable to being easily cut off. Thus such things as drains and foundations could be made to pay for what was going to give pleasure.

The cost-planning technique was used in all the buildings designed by the Ministry's Development Group. At the start of each job, cost targets would be placed upon every main element—walls, floors, foundations, heating and so on. The elements were then divided up among members of the team, who had to do their level best to stay within them by means of diligent research, development and design. This practice sprang directly from the Herts custom of giving each architect in a year's school-building programme an element to develop. But in the early Herts office money had not been a serious issue, whereas at the Ministry the cost targets were a discipline within which the whole Development Group was pledged to work. The group's schools had to be an advertisement proving that exemplary schools could be built within the limits imposed by the Ministry, and that the methods promoted there for monitoring and controlling costs would work. Inevitably, the conditions facing the local authorities could not be identical to those under which the Development Group designed. The group had the benefit of expertise in research, and was not tied to a rolling programme of production. On the other hand, each school project handled by the Development Group represented new departures in brief, technique and structural method, so that few lasting advantages accrued to the team from refinement and familiarity. All in all, the balance of difficulties in designing schools which gave 'value for money' was about even.

Wokingham, the Development Group's first school, was the guinea-pig for the cost-planning method. Designed in 1949–50, it was then delayed and built in 1951–3 and could have taken advantage of the 1951 cost limit of £290 per place. But such was the commitment to example that the group built the school within the forthcoming 1952 target of £240, to see if all the accommodation for this type of secondary modern school could be provided within the stiffer limit. The results vindicated the decision and the methods of cost planning. John Kay, an AA-trained architect who transferred from BRS to the Development Group in 1957 describes the process, by then well established, as it was applied to the Arnold Grammar School in Nottingham (1957–9):

> The cost plan for the Arnold project was established at the beginning, based on previous experience. This was broken down into elements, and if you were responsible for certain elements, say internal partitions, doors, ceilings, the whole of the internal lining of the building, you got awarded targets for your elements through discussion within the team. You would then develop an element choosing things that were off the shelf if there were any, or you would design new ones within these targets. If you found you weren't able to meet these targets by your design being quoted for on a provisional basis by some manufacturers, you then had to pinch and save within your own little group of components. If you weren't able to do that, you had to go back to the team and say, 'I'm very sorry, I can't make it. I need an extra shilling per square foot on such and such.' At the end of the day, to get a tender for a building that was almost entirely innovatory, often within five per cent of the target, gave you a feeling of confidence as a young designer.

The adjusting of the targets in cost planning from project to project constantly reflected educational and architectural choices, as well as mere economic adjustments. Guy Oddie:

> We'd look at earlier buildings and we'd say, 'What a lot of money we've spent on that steelwork'. We could be spending that on better finishes.' David Medd's phrase was 'You ought to be able to see your money'. When you'd spent it, you ought to be able to enjoy it, and you don't enjoy steelwork because it's all hidden, like foundations. In fact, the steel-frame developments which followed Wokingham were all directed to reducing the cost of that element.

As the word 'element' betrays, the techniques of cost analysis and cost planning grew out of the bias in favour of prefabrication which informed A & B Branch then and for years to come. Prefabrication prompted architects to think of building elements as fitted together from a kit of parts—separate, recognizable, neat components whose price was readily ascertainable. Prefabricated techniques of school-building were introduced in the first place and promoted by the Ministry on grounds of necessity, speed and diversification, not because they were cheaper than traditional construction. But they were held to offer the best value for money. In other words, the designer familiar with a given system of standard construction and with cost-planning technique could make better decisions about where the limited sums available to him could be spent. Hitherto, much of the cost in schools had been dissipated upon traditional walls and foundations, to the detriment of teaching spaces, finishes and services. The prefabricated schools of the 1950s and '60s usually offered more space and better facilities for the same sum. For the many teachers who were trying to expand classroom activity beyond traditional 'chalk and talk', often with classes of forty children, it was a boon to have more space than the minimum prescribed by regulation—which the politicians all through the 1950s set their face against raising. This must be remembered when critics carp about leaky roofs and shabby cladding on prefabricated schools.

Nisbet's costing methods, however, were entirely applicable to traditional building. In the long run, traditional construction gained more from them than did the systems from which they derived. Without the help which cost planning offered for working within the cost limits, traditional methods might have fallen behind as a means of building economical yet decent schools. In the event, so effective was the jolt that when A & B Branch finally overcame its structural prejudices and put its back into improving traditional construction, starting with the Woodside Junior School at Amersham (1956–7), schools which answered educationally just as well as their prefabricated rivals and looked more pleasing externally into the bargain began to appear. The 'rationalized traditional' or 'rat. trad.' approach to construction embodied in these schools stemmed directly from the pioneering work of

A & B Branch on costing and priorities in design, originally undertaken with prefabrication uppermost in mind. Later on, some upholders of 'rat. trad.' were to clash with the unregenerate prefabricators. But the more thoughtful antagonists of prefabricated schools acknowledged how much they owed to the study of 'elements' and to the questioning, analytic approach of Johnson-Marshall, Pott, Nisbet and the rest of the branch. Fred Pooley, long the county architect of Buckinghamshire and the staunchest of anti-prefabricators, concedes: 'Their great contribution was that they made everybody think. They pummelled us with new ideas, they kicked us in the pants.'

The issues of cost and value are fundamental to all programmes of building, and will recur. They were not unique to educational building. But the schools programmes of the 1950s did enjoy special advantages of bi-partisan political approval, continuity of development and experiment, and an unorthodox organizational structure. Despite the cutbacks of 1951–4 (modest by later standards), they were sheltered from the stop-go cycle of investment which made progress in public housing elusive. This allowed A & B Branch to pioneer a fair and imaginative way of sharing limited funds and making the best possible use of them. At the time, its authors hoped that cost analysis and planning could be applied to a whole range of building, private and public. Anticipating only greater prosperity and securer future funding, they did not foresee how a responsible, helping hand proffered to lead local authorities through a crisis could in less happy times become a fist pressing down public expenditure regardless of social consequence.

Here it remains to trace briefly the spread of the cost-planning gospel within the architectural profession in the 1950s. Building Bulletin No. 4 had in 1951 introduced cost analysis to those involved in school-building, and the Pilkington Report encouraged the Ministry to do more. Meanwhile the methods were becoming tried and tested. In 1955 Colin Boyne, John Carter and Lance Wright, aware that building costs had never been responsibly and regularly scrutinized by the British architectural press, took up the issue in the *Architects' Journal*. Relying upon the work of A & B Branch, they inaugurated a system of publishing buildings with a proper breakdown of costs, starting with a Herts school. They also brought in 'guest editors', including Nisbet, to contribute a long series of articles on costs and thus spread the word to the gentiles, beyond the world of school-building. These articles explained cost analysis and planning in fuller detail than hitherto. But their main burden was simple: if architects could not understand, anticipate and control costs, they would eventually lose more power and freedom than they would by submitting themselves to the necessary discipline. Reaction was unexpectedly strong. Architects, especially those in public offices, were mostly encouraging; but the quantity surveyors were hostile. John Carter:

> They wrote to the correspondence columns to say that (a) you couldn't split up a total cost into little bits and (b) if you could, you could make no use of the information and (c) it was really little different from what surveyors had been doing all along! This is a slight (but only a slight) burlesque. The quantity surveying profession was nettled that a technique that should have come from them had first hit the headlines in an architects' journal. Quantity surveyors had been little more than bill preparers for decades, and their awakening was bound to take time. Some of those letter writers later became convinced advocates of cost analysis and cost planning.

There was, however, a note of justifiable anxiety among the criticisms. Might not elemental costs come to be averaged as a 'yardstick', and the whole system used to screw down costs to a minimum, rather than to allow designers and clients room for manoeuvre and choice, as had been intended? This was exactly what was to happen when the age of rampant inflation arrived in the 1970s.

For the time being, however, the architect seemed to have taken the first steps towards resuming his ancient responsibility for costs, abrogated at the end of the eighteenth century. So influential were the *AJ* articles and building analyses that the RIBA was persuaded to hold its 1956 conference on the theme of 'Architectural Economics' and to set up a Cost Research Committee chaired by Anthony Pott. Other ministries were showing an interest in methods of cost planning, and the hope for the future was bright. This was the state of the subject at the end of the 1950s, where for the time being it may be left.

5.2. Bramcote Hills School, Nottingham, in course of erection, 1948: a typical scene from early post-war building. The structural frame is complete but awaits covering while the brickwork rises slowly, course by course. Delays due to shortages of bricks and labour can be confidently anticipated; and after the brickwork is finished, roofing and plastering have still to be done.

## THE BUILDING BULLETINS

It is hard now to grasp the plight of English school-building authorities in 1950. The Herts achievement, the aspirations of Middlesex, the LCC and a few other places, distort the picture. In other counties and cities, understaffed departments were mired down in a morass of plans and projects. Many contracted out as much as they could to private architects while concentrating themselves on what they knew how to do—designing traditional brick-built schools which carried over the educational styles and attitudes of the 1930s. Solid-looking enough now, they were often desperately slow to build; shortages of one kind or another could mean that one modest primary school might be two or three years on

5.3. Litherland Secondary Modern School for Girls, Lancashire, c. 1950. A proud pile of brickwork erected by Lancashire County Council's architects, characteristic of the old scale and solemnity which the Ministry of Education's architects shunned in the new secondary schools.

Assembly hall, Ormesby Primary School, Yorkshire (North Riding). Denis Clarke Hall, architect, 1949–50. Following pre-war success at Richmond, Clarke Hall designed several schools in the North Riding. The cheapness of the system he devised for Ormesby, combining load-bearing brick walls and welded steel portal frames, astonished the Ministry. James Nisbet investigated its costs and helped determine that its quality fell below an acceptable minimum.

the ground and prevent further schools from being built. Educationally, the grim old atmosphere and finishes of the board schools could still be sensed in some new schools of this period. Sometimes an enterprising private architect (Denis Clarke Hall was one, Ernö Goldfinger another) would devise a structural system to combat shortages or problems of cost (Figs. 5.4, 5). But the position of the private architect was such that the concerted development needful to turn his system into something coherent and worth further pursuit was never there. Most private architects wanted to take their written brief, design their school or schools to the best of their technical ability and have done with the process. With few exceptions, they had no desire to pose as educational reformers or experts. An occasional local authority (like Lancashire under G. Noel Hill) came up with a system of economical

Another private architect's structural system for schools: Brandlehow Road Primary School, Putney, London, 1950–1. One of two schools with an ingenious reinforced concrete frame designed by Ernö Goldfinger for the London County Council.

5.6. Covers of some of the Ministry of Education's early Building Bulletins.

school-building which was to be applied throughout its programmes, but lacked the drive and breadth of vision which made the Herts architects' approach unique.

In these circumstances, A & B Branch saw their foremost national task as that of instructing, informing and convincing both local authorities and private architects. How was this to be done? Over the years, Johnson-Marshall developed a many-sided armoury for winning the propaganda war and selling the kind of school-building approach he believed in. Tireless in the arts of persuasion, he himself cultivated county architects and others behind the scenes, while the branch's territorial architects made the best of their official status in the vetting and discussion of authorities' plans and programmes. But there had to be a formal side to the process as well, in which A & B Branch's attitudes and advice were set out clearly for all to see. This side was represented by the Building Bulletins.

Since the *Post-War Building Studies* got into their stride towards the end of the war, government and semi-official publications on building had showered down like confetti. Though they were much thumbed through and ransacked for information, few were attractive or readable. Likewise, Ministry of Education circulars were austere, unprepossessing documents; they might have to be obeyed, but they neither encouraged nor persuaded. With the Building Bulletins A & B Branch aimed to do better, reasoning that the flow of technical information had to be linked with authoritative educational advice if it were to be any use. At heart, the bulletins were a compromise between the directives dear to the official mind and the better type of technical literature which diligent architects sometimes take home and read. They were not 'official' statements of ministerial policy, but ways of conveying educational and technical experience together in a helpful form. They were published in a tidy, practical format, with illustrated covers, a spread of drawings and diagrams and, for the day, a tolerably relaxed style of text (Fig. 5.6). They were sold nationally and, to a degree, internationally. They were never bedtime reading, however. Technicalities could not be simplified out of existence, while the spirit of the age and the conventions of public service conspired to maintain anonymity. Individual architects were never named. Even the identity of builders and manufacturers was coyly suppressed lest they should appear to be favoured, as indeed was the case.

Starting up the bulletins was one of the branch's first tasks. Straight after joining the Ministry, David and Mary Medd sat down to write up in veiled form the lessons of the Herts experience for Building Bulletin No. 1, *New Primary Schools*. This appeared in October 1949. Better than the incomplete, spasmodic summaries in the architectural journals, it set out for local authorities the methodology built up at Herts. It probably had more influence than any other bulletin except No. 4, *Cost Study*, which appeared in 1951.

Most of the bulletins took on broad topics of direct and immediate value to local authorities. As repositories of lucid information and opinion, they became 'in a way a bible', and not just for those in the school-building business. The earliest ones confined themselves to outlining the Ministry's thoughts, in the light of the drastic changes implied by the cost limits, on the main building types which local authorities were asked to design—primary schools, secondary schools and colleges of further education. Next, technical studies predominated. No. 7, *Fire and the Design of Schools* (1952), composed by John Price, is a good example of how the bulletins could ease life for local authorities; by laying out uniform criteria for evaluating construction, it gave them an authoritative defence against having to adjust new methods of construction to the differing prejudices of each county fire officer. It was succeeded, for instance, by No. 9, *Colour in School Building* (1952), again largely drawn from the Herts experience, and by No. 11, *The Design of School Kitchens* (1955). For most of these early bulletins, one or two architects in the Development Group were seconded to do the research, come up with the principles and draw the diagrams, while William Pile shook their drafts into good order and 'official' English.

Given the heavy workloads of the time, these were the practical priorities. In retrospect it seems a pity that the branch did not better record the schools built by its own Development Group, let alone articulate the general slant of its activities and policies. St Crispin's School, Wokingham, the first development project, did earn itself a bulletin, No. 8 of 1952, compiled by the Medds and Michael Ventris; but this was not repeated until Woodside Junior School at Amersham was published in No. 16 of 1958, followed by Arnold Grammar School in No. 17 of 1960. In the press of work the group's educational and technical experiments in secondary school-building fell by the wayside unrecorded, so that those interested had to judge them from personal recommendation and cursory publication in the building magazines. In the case of the two comprehensive schools built at Coventry, the Conservative Government's suspicion of comprehensives seems to have inhibited their proper publication. The *Architects' Journal* and other magazines tried to fill the gap, the *AJ* in particular using every occasion to expound the branch's philosophy of public-sector building. But full adjudication of these experiments never appeared. Later, the Ministry tended to slip in accounts of its own building ventures in bulletins of a more general nature. When the Department of Education and Science superseded the old Ministry in 1964, the format of the bulletins altered and the tenor of their contents became less evangelical. But the basic purpose and philosophy of the series survived. To date, over sixty bulletins have appeared, together with a subsidiary series of nearly forty 'design notes'.

## LEADERSHIP BY EXAMPLE

In 1949 Johnson-Marshall, Pott and their early colleagues in A & B Branch began to ponder what sort of schools their newly approved Development Group might best build by way of experiment and example. At this date the constraints upon building were hardly less acute than they had been in the first aftermath of war. Labour was easier to procure and there had been some easing in the supply of materials, but shortages of timber and steel were still endemic and could last for as much as a year at a time. For this reason, building licences and the rationing of materials remained in force until 1953. Meanwhile the factors of number and cost were starting to dominate the equation.

If Pott's Development Group was to have value, it had to draw out the best technical and educational ideas which the harassed local authorities had no time to investigate, and to demonstrate them in buildings which could be seen, understood and emulated. As it could only build sporadically, it was obliged to begin with prototypes. But these prototypes had to be linked by a sense of purpose and development: in other words, they had also to be compendia of ideas carried forward and improved from one project to the next.

In addition the Development Group had to think ahead, to anticipate national needs, like a teacher keeping a few pages in front in a textbook before the pupils catch up. In 1949 this meant tackling secondary schools. Most of the schools completed in the 1940s had been primary schools, small in size, simple in facilities and quick to build. In Johnson-Marshall's view, Herts had essentially solved the building problems of the primary school; A & B Branch must help to spread the Herts message and promote improvement, but no fundamental work needed doing. Secondary schools would soon be needed in quantity, as the children born in and after the war grew up. They were much more of a headache. They were bigger, they cost more and they were subject to closer public and political awareness. But they lacked the clear sense of educational opportunity that enriched the post-war primary school. The Butler Act, in response to the 1926 Hadow Report, had seemed to tackle the reorganization of English secondary education. Of the four types of secondary school built after the war—the secondary modern school, the grammar school, the technical school and the comprehensive or 'multilateral' school—two were practically new inventions and offered fresh educational and architectural challenges. Yet it took years of fumbling for secondary moderns and comprehensives to cast off the burden of being regarded by many authorities, inspectors and teachers as second-rate copies of the academic grammar school, and to acquire authentic standing and expression of their own. Weighed down by a tyrannous, university-derived examination system, some would say that they never did so.

The post-war secondary school had scarcely come into being before it became an object of political contention. The one new model of school which commanded wide support and enthusiasm among teachers was the comprehensive. Despite the advocacy of the teaching unions, the Attlee government did little to encourage comprehensives of the kind planned by bolder authorities like Middlesex (Fig. 5.1), the London County Council and West Yorkshire. When administrations changed in 1951 the new Minister of Education, Florence Horsbrugh, did everything she could to make the creation of comprehensives difficult, especially in the urban areas where they were likely to work best. The Ministry's officials also gained a reputation for opposition to the comprehensive experiment. All this might have mattered less if a proper alternative had been to hand in the shape of the secondary modern school. But the secondary modern, despite some high talk, was bereft of much educational cogency; it was just the place to which children went if they failed to get into grammar schools.

Under these circumstances, the Development Group found it easier to make technical decisions than educational ones. They chose to pursue the logic and direction of the Herts initiative and make more prefabricated school-building systems available to meet the coming spate of secondary schools. The Ministry would undertake a selection of different types of secondary schools in different systems and different parts of the country. In this way educational theories could be tried out, techniques tested and relationships fostered with a variety of authorities, teachers and manufacturers. A whole set of 'languages' would then be available when the educationists got a clearer grasp of what they wanted to 'say'.

For Johnson-Marshall, tackling the principles of prefabrication anew at the Ministry, the key issues were choice and control. Choice meant that there ought to be several independent, reliable, structural systems available for schools. They had to improve upon traditional building, to do anything that an education authority might require in a secondary school, to compete with each other and to cover for each other's limitations. If steel were short, then an authority had to be able to turn to a system built out of timber or concrete. And if each system could be designed to the same module, the 3 feet 4 inches horizontal and ten-inch vertical dimension recommended in the recent Cleary Report of 1948, then in due course of development the components, cladding and so forth could become interchangeable, so leading to an infinite variety of choices and a proper 'open' method of industrialized building. That prospect did not seem unduly optimistic in 1949.

5.7. Hackenthorpe Primary School, Derbyshire. Prototype of Vic Hallam Limited's Derwent timber system, designed in the Herts tradition by Samuel Morrison and Partners, 1953, on a 6 foot 4 inch module, with a cladding of Lagos mahogany.

Control was thornier. Of the systems-built schools of the 1940s, a few were designed as 'one-offs' or perhaps 'two-offs' by private architects. Others, like those of Herts and Middlesex, were developed and built in systems for multiple use by a particular local authority. Others again were built in 'proprietary' systems, bought 'off the peg' from a few private firms who had worked up a kit to sell on the expanding school-building market. These proprietary systems were beginning to interest and concern the Ministry. Compared to the proprietary types of prefabricated house then on offer they were few in number, but they were starting to make some headway. They varied in range, ingenuity and responsiveness. If the Ministry was to get large numbers of schools built quickly, these particular gift-horses could not be looked in the mouth. It was part of the A & B philosophy to reconcile industrial production with building, not to keep them separate. But the makers had first to be persuaded to put their technical ingenuity to better educational ends, as the Herts architects had done with Hills of West Bromwich.

The biggest single proprietary manufacturer of schools at this time was the Bristol Aeroplane Company, a technically go-ahead firm whose ingenious aluminium school-building system served chiefly as an outlet for excess capacity following the post-war slump in aircraft orders. Hills, by contrast, marketed a proprietary 8 feet 3 inches system (Fig. 4.25) which, thanks to the work done at Herts, possessed many virtues of technical and educational flexibility. But in their case the purchaser had to buy cladding and other components along with the frame as part of the Hills 'package', though other firms made these items better. The best of the proprietary systems made its début a little later. This was the Derwent timber system, designed for the building firm of Vic Hallam by an ex-Herts architect, Samuel Morrison, with A & B Branch's encouragement. It came to prominence during the steel shortage of 1953. Morrison first tried the system out on schools built for old employers of his, Hackenthorpe Primary School near Sheffield for Derbyshire (Fig. 5.7), and Belswains Infants School at Hemel Hempstead for Herts. The Derwent system was quite flexible and its hardwood cladding gave it a warm, friendly appearance. Because A & B Branch approved of the Derwent schools, it made no attempt to revise or supplant them with a timber system of its own. But Derwent was devised for single-storey schools and never made much impact on the secondary scene, for which some multi-storey construction was usually needed.

There was another motive for intervening in the proprietary school-building market. Some

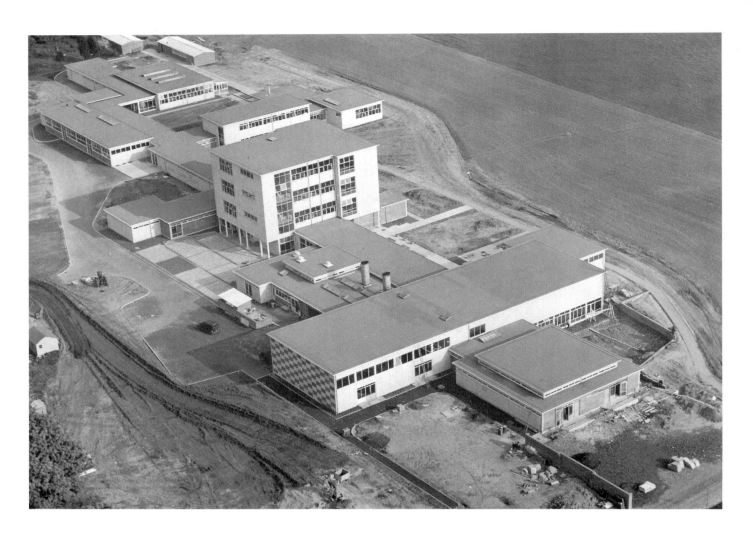

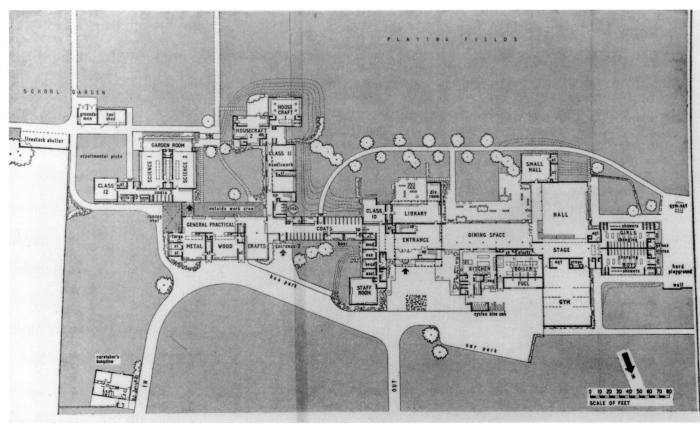

PLAYING FIELDS

SCHOOL GARDEN

grounds man

tool shed

livestock shelter

experimental plots

GARDEN ROOM

HOUSE CRAFT

HOUSECRAFT 2

CLASS II
needlework

SCIENCE 1

SCIENCE 2

CLASS 12

coats 3

SMALL HALL

CLASS 10

LIBRARY

HALL

gym. st.

outside work area

canopy shed

GENERAL PRACTICAL

forge
st.

METAL

WOOD

CRAFTS

COATS

boys

Entrance 2

ENTRANCE

DINING SPACE

STAGE

showers
GIRLS
changing

games
stores

STAFF ROOM

KITCHEN

BOILER

FUEL

BOYS
showers

changing

hard
playground

cycles bins oak

GYM

wall

caretaker's bungalow

IN

OUT

car park

bus park

0  10  20  30  40  50  60  70  80
SCALE OF FEET

manufacturers were being discouraged from staying in school-building or improving their product because every authority seemed to want something a little different, thus diminishing potential profit. 'There is a tendency at present,' wrote the Coventry schools architect William Glare in 1950, 'for fabricators to expend their energies in producing numerous slightly differing schemes to suit the varying requirements of individuals'. Unless the Ministry could help these firms, their aid in reducing the deficit of school places might be lost.

To surmount these problems, Johnson-Marshall and Pott decided to go further along the road which had been travelled with Hills at Herts. The Development Group would design a series of school-building systems, each in partnership with a single manufacturer or builder. The onus of inventing each system's kit of parts, finding suitable sub-contractors for supply and determining its educational range, would fall upon the Ministry. The nominated manufacturer would make, test and develop the system's structure and in the end would own it and market it, just like an ordinary proprietary system. No money changed hands: the arrangements grew out of an atmosphere of opportunity, challenge and fair collaboration. The manufacturers had the benefit of a Ministry-designed and approved system which could meet all foreseeable educational and structural tasks in secondary school-building. But they had to invest time, money and plant in making prototypes for the system without any guarantee of its success. The Ministry promised only one initial school, designed and to some degree publicized by the Development Group in partnership with a particular local authority. After that they were on their own. They could expect the Ministry's support when authorities were seeking advice about systems of building, but authorities could only be pressed so far. The Ministry-designed systems had to be marketed, just like Derwent or any other proprietary system.

Between 1949 and 1957 the Development Group's small staff of architects devised five separate and complete systems for building secondary schools. They had some basic technical features in common, with a view to the future interchangeability of components. All (including those built in pre-cast concrete) were in 'light construction' with cladding, all had to be able to rise to three or four storeys, and all tried to eliminate or economize upon brickwork and other wet trades; all except one were based on the module of 3 feet 4 inches accepted by the Ministry in 1948. The basic differences were structural, and other differences in components, fittings and services tended to follow from this. There was a system using hot-rolled steel, developed with Hills and first tested at St Crispin's Secondary Modern School, Wokingham (Figs. 5.8–13); another using cold-rolled steel, developed with John Brockhouse

5.11.  Rounders at Wokingham. Suburban secondary schools of the 1950s tended to appear marooned in an undifferentiated expanse of playing field.

5.12.  Looking into the dining area at Wokingham. The plants and the informal arrangement of tables help to create a civilized atmosphere. Mural by Oliver Cox to the right.

5.13.  Science laboratory, Wokingham. Good natural lighting is supplemented by the new Percon fitting. The wooden furniture is stout and practical.

and Company and tried out at The Parks Secondary Modern School, Belper (Figs. 5.35; 6.9, 10); the Intergrid pre-stressed concrete system, boldest of all in structural terms, represented by the Worthing Secondary Technical School and evolved in partnership with Gilbert-Ash Limited and the Pre-Stressed Concrete Company (Figs. 5.27–32); and a steel and aluminium system, produced with the Bristol Aeroplane Company and really a major revision of that firm's proprietary system for schools, first built at Lyng Hall Comprehensive School for Girls, Coventry (Figs. 5.22–25). As an afterthought a second concrete system, Laingspan, was developed for Laings the builders and tried out at the Arnold Grammar School, Nottingham (Figs. 5.33; 7.11, 12).

## WOKINGHAM

By a clear margin St Crispin's, Wokingham, designed in 1949–50 and built in 1951–3, was the first of these schools. Though it never led on directly to a commercial system of school-building, it has probably had more influence than any other British school built since the war. For the Ministry, it offered a first focus for the educational ideas which it wanted to try out in secondary schools, for the concept of collaborating with a manufacturer without the guarantee of future production, and for getting a school of high quality within fierce financial limits by using the methods of cost-planning. For architects and educators seeking guidance on the elusive subject of how to design a secondary modern school, Wokingham offered an approach, a model and an interpretation where none had existed before. It was possible to accept or reject it. But its distinctiveness and the clarity with which its creators explained the thinking behind it helped even those who were disposed towards rejection. It was more often visited than any other of the Ministry's schools, and the long Building Bulletin on the school was thumbed through in architects' offices for years.

Like so much that Johnson-Marshall promoted at the Ministry, Wokingham followed on without ambiguity or apology from the Herts schools. David Medd designed the system, working with Ernest Hinchliffe's familiar team of tracers and engineers at Hills, and the technical principles which underlay it were those worked out by the self-same individuals for the earlier Herts 8 feet 3 inches system. The chief difference was that the team was working now to the smaller grid of 3 feet 4 inches and had also to take into account a vertical module of ten inches. From the way the wind of modular theory was blowing, Hinchliffe knew that he would have to adopt this smaller dimension to supplement his 8 feet 3 inches package, so he was happy to go along with the Ministry. At the same time as Wokingham, Hinchliffe's tracers were sorting out the complexities of a proprietary 'tartan-grid' school-system in 3 feet 4 inches, designed for Hills by Richard Llewelyn-Davies and John Weeks and adapted by Bruce Martin for Herts (see p. 105). The Development Group looked askance at the modular ambitions of this system, preferring the kind of pragmatic approach which would be most serviceable for teachers and children. So Wokingham's structure was simpler than the rival tartan grid. Medd saw the school as a piece of scrupulously cautious development upon what had been started at Herts. When so much in the brief was new and there was such pressure to get the first example of the Ministry's work built, it had to be right. So it seemed only practical to go back to tried friends. Many Herts sub-contractors came back to help on this and the Ministry's subsequent schools: Weatherfoil supplied the heating, Adamsez the sanitary fittings, Econa the plumbing, ESA and Hammers the furniture, Gerald Holtom the curtains, and so on. So far did camaraderie go at Wokingham that Oliver Cox, previously at Herts with the Medds but by then a housing architect with the LCC, secured with his friend Fred Millett the contract to paint the murals, which they carried out over weekends (Plates IX, X). At this early stage there was little sense of 'jobbery' about the sustaining of such partnerships. Anyone willing to co-operate closely in the shared endeavours of design was welcome to A & B Branch, but few could be found.

There were some technical novelties at Wokingham. But the real departures lay in the educational thinking and its architectural expression. David and Mary Medd had spent their first months at the Ministry in 1949 compiling the account of the educational principles adopted in the Herts primary schools which appeared as the first Building Bulletin. This brought them together with Leonard Gibbon, the branch's first HMI. Gibbon had an abiding sympathy for the underdog, and longed to see secondary modern and comprehensive schools develop identities of their own. From pre-war days he recalled schools in Lancashire where girls had had to make shrouds for the local mortuary, and he resented the inspectorate's heavy bias towards grammar education. It was with Gibbon, after many visits to schools and talks with inspectors and teachers, that the brief for Wokingham and the text of the second Building Bulletin, *New Secondary Schools* (rushed out in 1950 to help architects struggling with the cost limits), were settled.

The outcome was a school which combined meticulous care and precision of function with an informality which was almost flaunted. The arrangement, says the bulletin on Wokingham with an air of defiance, 'is based on no preconceived plan pattern, but was allowed to grow out of the problem itself—the educational needs and activities of each of its parts'. In other words, the school's educational style was specific and strong but its architectural expression shrank into the background. Johnson-Marshall argued that it was too early in the development programme to produce anything like 'assertive architecture'. In the belief (mistaken, as it transpired) that most secondary modern pupils at Wokingham would end up in farming or horticulture, the plan (Fig. 5.9) was laid out with outside activities uppermost in mind. This, coupled with the generous suburban site and the architects' belief in good natural lighting, kept the buildings mostly down close to the ground (Fig. 5.10). Only towards the centre of the loosely linked plan, where a four-storey block housing classrooms tested the new system to its structural limits, was there the smallest hint of assertion. Yet inside, the Building Bulletin's diagrams show precise arrangements of furniture and equipment in each space and so give their blessing to a highly particular approach to teaching and use.

This type of accommodation between architecture and teaching—a relaxed treatment of plan and elevation playing second fiddle to a precise educational philosophy—drew deep upon the Herts primary schools. But there were salient differences and difficulties with secondary schools which Wokingham and its successors never entirely overcame. One was size. British secondary schools are far bigger than primary ones. Most of those built since 1945 occupy suburban sites surrounded by a flat, ample acreage of recreation space in districts lacking strong visible tokens of identity and community. Whether the architectural self-denial of Wokingham and the Ministry's later secondary schools is right for such contexts may be questioned.

This leads on to a deeper point. The new philosophy of the 1940s and '50s about primary schools evolved clearly, directly and without much controversy, however slow some may have been to embrace it. But secondary education was still a muddle in the early 1950s. Wokingham's flouting of grammar-school formality arose out of a desire to create a distinctive type for the secondary modern school. Floundering about without models, architects and educators had been turning out secondary moderns which were pale copies of the formally organized grammar school. By borrowing from the new primary approach to school-planning, Gibbon and the Medds hoped instead to create an atmosphere of positive informality for the secondary modern, to give some intelligible meaning to the vacuous phrase of the time that secondary moderns were 'places where you learn to live'. Only if an alternative to grammar-school arrangements could succeed would teachers, parents and pupils believe that those who failed the 'eleven-plus' examination had not been slung upon the educational scrapheap.

This dream never came true. Political and educational strife destroyed any chances of success that a separate secondary modern tradition might have enjoyed. When comprehensive secondary education grew in strength in the 1960s and '70s, the existing secondary moderns had to be restructured and often enlarged to fit the new styles of organization and teaching. In these circumstances, any precision in previous arrangements was lost. That is why the visitor to Wokingham today will see a school extended and changed in function out of recognition. Even the murals by Millett and Cox have gone. In a world of shifting social circumstance, such are the drawbacks of putting some particular social aim or brief, however convincing, before the issue of expression in building. Styles—or the lack of them—remain in the eye of incurious future generations. But the meticulously devised particularities of brief soon grow obsolete and forgotten.

In plan, the secondary schools which the Development Group built after Wokingham followed closely upon this first experiment. Leonard Gibbon, Mary Medd and the others had fashioned a basic approach which they felt to be right for planning the new, civilized type of secondary school whether 'modern', 'technical' or 'comprehensive', and they wished now to explore and develop it. By their nature, the Ministry's schools had to be 'one-offs'. But it would have run counter to A & B Branch's thinking to fritter away the opportunity in unco-ordinated experiments. So although for example's sake the Ministry undertook at least one of each of the new types of school—a technical school at Worthing, secondary moderns at Wokingham and Belper, two comprehensives of different types at Coventry—their layouts and educational philosophies were comparable. The Coventry comprehensives, for instance, Woodlands and Lyng Hall, were larger and more complex schools which developed the 'house' principle of social organization, a fashionable feature of comprehensives for a decade and more. But their dispersed, pavilion-like informality followed on from Wokingham and was quite unlike the comprehensives built by the LCC in the same years. Wokingham, Worthing and Belper, with their squarish, three or four-storey blocks in the centre, their low classrooms spreading all around and their dour concrete cladding, are superficially so alike that they can easily be confused at a quick glance (Figs. 5.8, 22, 27; 7.11).

Structurally, nothing could be further from the truth. Each of these schools represented a prodigious investment in time, energy and innovation. Since most of them involved starting from the beginning and inventing a new vocabulary of design which might be called upon to shoulder a complete building programme of schools, they could take up to four years to develop and build. To describe every system in detail would be a lengthy task. But two repay special attention: the most problematic one, the Bristol Aeroplane Company's Mark II system employed for Lyng Hall, and the most adventurous and commercially successful one, the Intergrid pre-stressed concrete system pioneered at Worthing. The next chapter will look in passing at a third experiment, in the end the most influential of them all, the Brockhouse cold-rolled steel system used at Belper.

## THE BAC DEVELOPMENT

The Ministry's collaboration with the Bristol Aeroplane Company started from a different footing than any other. In this case the Development Group approached the manufacturer as a suitor. When the advent of peace threatened their plane-making capacity, BAC had been quick to diversify. Like other engineering firms that shifted into building at this period, they first entered the housing market, producing large numbers of aluminium bungalows. BAC were the senior partners in the fabrication of the well-known 'AIROH house', of which some 70,000 examples, temporary and permanent, had been erected when production ceased in about 1949 (Fig. 2.10). The AIROH house was remarkable for the level of factory fabrication involved in its production, but notorious for its expense and, later, for its tendency to corrode (the partners having used the aluminium alloy from which their aeroplane bodies were made, taking scant account of dampness and condensation).

The BAC proprietary school first came forward in 1948, when it was clear on economic grounds that the AIROH house could not be sustained much longer. To develop and build it, the company brought in the architects Richard Sheppard and Geoffrey Robson and an enterprising middle-sized building firm, Gilbert-Ash Limited. Sheppard was a determined, up-and-coming architect, interested in schools and imbued with the spirit of reconstruction. Gilbert-Ash too, under the engineering guidance of Wilfred Ash, regarded schools as one of their specialities; they worked a little with Herts, were the contractors for Wokingham, and became the Ministry's chosen partners for the Intergrid concrete system. BAC's original school system, therefore, was ingenious. Everything possible, from the structure and the

5.14. Romney Avenue School, Lockleaze, Bristol, the prototype of the Bristol Aeroplane Company's Mark I school-building system. Richard Sheppard and Robson, architects, 1948–9. The design adopts the orthodox 'finger-plan' arrangement, with side corridors to a run of classrooms.

5.15. (*facing page, top*) Early interior of a BAC Mark I school, probably Romney Avenue School, Lockleaze, Bristol. Aluminium light-fittings, lockers, chairs and desks.

5.16. (*facing page, bottom*) Schools by air. Components of a BAC Mark I school being loaded on to a plane *en route* for France, 1949.

cladding down to the very doorknobs, was made of heavy-duty aluminium, and everything down to the fins for wind-bracing was conceived on aeronautical principles (Figs. 5.14, 15). The degree of prefabrication was again high. The walling panels arrived on site entirely made up, with insulation, window frames and even the glass pre-fixed; not even painting was needed. For this reason the BAC system, though never cheap, was competitive for primary schools and was widely employed by local authorities before the cost limits started to bite.

But it had disadvantages which could not be overcome without development. Because of their aluminium structure the schools, like the bungalows, were confined to a single storey and were therefore suitable only for primary education. The system was also inflexible. It had been geared to the plain, 'bay' method of classroom planning which dominated British school design for the first few years after the war. Every aluminium school offered the same weary combination of corridors and classrooms, outmoded educationally and impossible to plan economically in the reduced circumstances of the 1950s. For these reasons it suited BAC and the Ministry to come together. BAC hoped by developing further and getting a more economical and flexible system to break into the secondary-school market. Johnson-Marshall and Pott believed that for the mutual good of architecture and industry, the level of factory production already achieved in the aluminium schools ought to be put to wider and better educational ends. Above all, the BAC system had to be got off a 'bay' means of articulation and on to a 'grid'.

The setting for these developments was Coventry, then in the throes of the intensest rebuilding and expansion of any English city. Donald Gibson, Johnson-Marshall's pre-war chief at the Isle of Ely and his closest equivalent in temperament, ideals and manner of working, was still city architect of Coventry. In 1950 Gibson was up to his ears in plans for reconstructing the city centre and for a series of outlying districts to house Coventry's rising population. He was therefore delighted to act as 'Stirrat's tame client', if this would relieve pressure on his staff and get extra schools on the ground. William Glare, Gibson's deputy in charge of schools, enjoyed much freedom and initiative. Then chronically short on building labour, the city had already made a contribution to prefabricated school-building by getting John Brockhouse and Company to develop a system of cold-rolled steel construction for primary schools (see pp. 159–61). It had also used the BAC system, notably at Whitmore Park Primary School, opened by the Minister of Education, George Tomlinson, in January 1951. It was the biggest aluminium school to date, housing 880 children. Whitmore Park showed how quickly sharp architects like Sheppard and Robson had taken up the Herts innovations; the heating was by Weatherfoil, there were fabrics by Gerald Holtom and splashes of bright colour inside and out. Externally the pitched roofs, corrugated siding and fins were attractive enough, but the interior was like an endless series of half-humanized

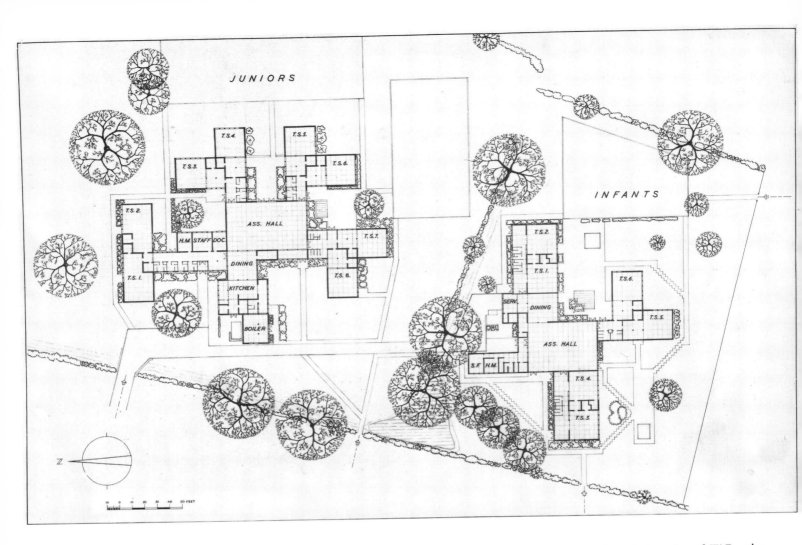

JUNIORS

T.S.4.

T.S.5.

T.S.3.

T.S.6.

T.S.2.

INFANTS

ASS. HALL

H.M. STAFF DOC.

T.S.7.

T.S.1.

DINING

T.S.2.

T.S.1.

T.S.8.

T.S.6.

KITCHEN

SER.

DINING

T.S.5.

BOILER

ASS. HALL

S.F. H.M.

T.S.4.

T.S.3.

N

10 0 10 20 30 40 50 FEET

5.17. Limbrick Wood Primary School, Tile Hill, Coventry, plan. Separate junior and infants schools, with the 'hen and chicks' arrangements of two-classroom groups off the hall: an example of the primary planning introduced in response to the coming of cost limits.

barrack blocks, with corridors stretching into the distance and serried ranks of WCs: the kind of plan which Johnson-Marshall always likened to a prison, with points at which warders or other enforcers of discipline could stand and look rakingly in two, three or even four directions. A proper, civilized, modern school must not be like this, he felt.

Gibson therefore agreed to lend a hand in developing a BAC Mark II version which would be first tried out in Coventry. His schools architects would have preferred to develop the Brockhouse system, but in Gibson and Johnson-Marshall they were up against a combination of irresistible persuasiveness. The collaboration was a tangled one, involving several partners. BAC contributed the engineering skills and manufacturing capacity, with Sheppard and Robson holding a watching brief on their behalf over the architecture; Gilbert-Ash continued to build the schools and advised on questions of site-assembly; Coventry supplied the educational and planning briefs and some architects' time. Michael Smith led the Development Group's architectural team, while at Coventry the architect most involved in the early stages was Edmund Tory, who had worked with Smith at Herts and so knew the required method of operation.

Limbrick Wood Primary School in the Coventry suburb of Tile Hill, built in 1951–2, was the first fruit of this endeavour (Figs. 5.17, 18). It is the least-known of the Development Group's early jobs and the only primary school which they undertook before Woodside at Amersham. It was designed to see if the single-storey BAC system could be adapted educationally and got within the cost limits. Since it was not an entirely new system it was known as BAC Mark IA. As at Cheshunt, the separate infants' department served as a kind of 'hand-made' prototype and the bigger junior school followed on. To avoid redesigning the aluminium cladding, the architects amended rather than abolished the bay

system and kept to BAC's four-foot planning module, though a vertical module was added. Limbrick Wood ended up like an early Herts school built in aluminium. Its closest companion was Greenfields School at Oxhey, designed at the same time to a similar plan by the Herts primary group. Their simultaneous, independent appearance did much to reinforce the tighter approach to planning primary schools.

Limbrick Wood had at least one successor at Coventry and there may have been others elsewhere. But it was only an intermediate step. For the Ministry, bent on establishing its range of systems for secondary schools, and for Coventry, eager to unleash its pioneering programme of large comprehensives, Mark II was the goal. Together they earmarked a comprehensive to be built at Tile Hill close to Limbrick Wood, eventually called Woodlands, as the prototype. Smith was to plan it and Peter Newnham, who joined A & B Branch in 1952, took charge of developing the system. This time there was to be a complete structural overhaul, to take the system up to four storeys and put it on a par with Intergrid and the other Ministry projects. Newnham went to the BAC factory at Weston-super-Mare to work on it. Then a hitch occurred.

I came up with a proposition for a double-beam system of extruded aluminium beams. We went a long way down the road of developing an aluminium frame and trying to hang on it the existing aluminium cladding units, which weren't generally being changed; and I developed a very elaborate aluminium flat roof designed to fall and drain itself and also be prefabricated, which was immensely complicated. Finally James Nisbet's quantity surveyors and/or BAC got round to costing these things and its cost was absurdly high. Meanwhile Michael Smith was well along with designing a school for Coventry, and Gibson's chief education officer needed the school. So in order to avoid loss of face, the Ministry of Education had to turn round very quickly and get this school built. Michael Smith had to go off and rapidly design it in 'Hills'.

So the Development Group, generally scrupulous about spreading its work around, built not one comprehensive school at Coventry but two. Woodlands is the only early school designed by the group to repeat a structural system that had already been tried. It is rather the better for this: Smith's meticulousness, combined with the chance of refining some features of the Hills system first tested at Wokingham, made the school perhaps the most satisfactory of the Ministry's early projects (Figs. 5.19–21; Plate XI). The effort needed to design a model comprehensive of untried size with the experimental 'house' arrangement was enough, especially since the Government as a means of discouraging Coventry's educational policies had stipulated that its new comprehensives should be divisible into separate parts, in case the day should dawn when this type of education could be scrapped. The added complication of a new structural system might have been too much. But it left the problem of finding a secondary school on which to try out the BAC Mark II system.

The crisis over the aluminium frame coincided with increasing friction between BAC and the Ministry. The directors had been drawn along a path in the hope of future orders, but they had no real feeling for what Johnson-Marshall and his colleagues were aiming at and little grasp of the impure complexities of building. This episode shook what confidence they had in the partnership. Moreover, the firm's outlook was changing. The Korean War had revived the demand for planes and precipitated a sharp rise in the price of aluminium. This, more than any failing on Newnham's part, had caused the fiasco over the aluminium frame. As costs rose, the firm retreated back into its shell, lost interest in schools and concentrated upon planes which—such being the priorities of governments—it knew it could sell, whatever the price. BAC saw the Mark II project through to the end of the development phase, submitting to an orthodox steel frame to support the aluminium cladding, and they used their marketing powers to secure just enough school contracts for Mark II to justify the 'tooling-up' process. But in 1955 they backed out of school-building completely and converted their Weston-super-Mare plant to aircraft production. A few employees branched out on their own to make aluminium components for schools, but for all important purposes the aluminium adventure was over.

So before Lyng Hall, the girls' comprehensive for the renewed attempt to build a Coventry school in BAC Mark II, had been finished, the Ministry knew it would have few successors. But it was never a 'one-off'. To keep it company, the Coventry schools architects (now under John Barker, Glare's successor) built two other aluminium secondary schools, Whitley Abbey and Green Farm (later Finmore Park). Whitley Abbey (Fig. 5.26), a mixed comprehensive, was consciously built for comparison with Lyng Hall; it housed the same number of children (1,650), it was erected in similar phases, and the schools were published together in the *Architects' Journal*. Despite a less fetching site, Lyng Hall (Figs 5.22–25) today looks in better shape. Whether that is due to vicissitudes of care and maintenance, to the less savage treatment meted out to buildings by girls, or to some extra skill exercised by Newnham, the architect chiefly responsible for its plan and design, is hard now to say. The system itself has given no appreciable trouble.

The BAC episode was neither a humiliation nor a disaster. But it did not in the end further the Ministry's aim of providing a means of secondary school-building which an authority could take up in the knowledge that the firms and the components would be ready and waiting. It also suggested some morals. Industrial collaboration in buildings of the kind which Johnson-Marshall was promoting could only work well when the partners could look beyond the motive of profit and show some imaginative sympathy for the programme's broader aims. Unless the sums added up, on the other hand, it was idle to expect a private manufacturer to enter into such a collaboration. The AIROH house programme had collapsed because it bore too hard upon the taxpayer; the BAC schools were curtailed because they did not recompense the fabricator. By 1955 it was becoming evident that the large economic inducements expected of prefabricated building production were as elusive as ever. As circumstances shifted, the architects and administrators of A & B Branch had

ate VII.    Stage curtain by Gerald Holtom for Whitley Abbey Comprehensive School Coventry, 1955.

ate VIII.    Stage curtain by Gerald Holtom for Looe School, Looe, Cornwall.

5.19. Three-storey block in course of erection, The Woodlands Comprehensive School, Coventry, May 1953. A modified version of the 3 foot 4 inch Hills frame used at Wokingham.

5.20. The Woodlands Comprehensive School, Tile Hill, Coventry. MoE development Group (Michael Smith, John Toomer and Guy Oddie, main job architects) with Coventry City Council, 1952–4. A corner in 1985, showing the cladding in good condition and the planting near maturity.

5.21. Metal-working shop at Woodlands. Heavy uses of this kind required modification and extension of the nascent industrialized schools-systems.

2. Lyng Hall Comprehensive School, Coventry, prototype of the BAC Mark II system. First phase as completed, 1953–5. DE Development Group (Peter Newnam, Dargan Bullivant and Michael Greenwood, main job architects) with Coventry City Council. The old farm buildings are in the centre, surrounded by BAC additions.

to start thinking hard about adapting the constructional and organizational methods which had worked so well in the first post-war years.

## INTERGRID

Intergrid, by contrast, looked by 1955 to have a promising future. When, five years earlier, Johnson-Marshall and Pott had pondered the diversification of secondary school-building systems, no avenue seemed more promising than that of developing a concrete system of construction. Hitherto all the structural innovation in school-building had been made in metals. Hills, BAC and Brockhouse, the firms best established in proprietary schools-systems, were experts in 'meccano'. Most British architects and engineers still preferred steel to concrete for structural work. Concrete as a cladding material and poured concrete for foundations and floors were well understood. But reinforced concrete, despite the leaps and bounds it had made during the war, was still widely regarded after fifty years of use as 'foreign' (specifically as French), right for heavy engineering structures but hardly applicable to much else. Yet in the post-war years concrete was reliably available whereas steel was not, and by most measures of cost tended to come out cheaper than structural steel, even for smaller buildings.

There were, however, obstacles to overcome. Reliable British engineering firms which could design, manufacture and fix prefabricated concrete frameworks within narrow tolerances did not seem to exist. To develop such a system, the Ministry resolved to take a

Plate IX.  Autumn and Winter. Two of the four murals of the seasons by Fred Millet at St Crispin's Secondary Modern School, Wokingham, Berkshire, 1952.

Plate X.  External mural in acrylic by Oliver Cox, St Crispin's Secondary Modern School, Wokingham, Berkshire.

## KEY

b p — biology pond
bh — boiler house
biol — biology
ch — changing room
chem — chemistry
cl — classroom
cts — caretakers
cw — craft & weaving
dep — deputy head
div — division room
drpa — drawing & painting
dypr — dyeing & printing
gds — gardeners
gr — garden room
hc — housecraft
hd — head
hr — houseroom
lcl — library classroom
lk — lockers
med — medical
mod — modelling
mu — music
p — preparation
pks — parks dept.
pm — pottery & modelling
qt — quiet room
ss — school societies
st — staff
t — tools

SECOND FLOOR

needlework
needlework
cl

science
p
science

FIRST FLOOR

pks
gds
ss
ss
ss
ss

0        100
FEET

BLACKBERRY LANE        MAIN GATE

sub station

cycle sheds

school garden

caretakers' houses

pks
gds
ss

chem   biol
p
biology

old farm yard

dypr   cw        cts
pm
mod
service yard

bh

kitchen

mu
mu
mu

gr  t    drpa

b p

FIRST FLOOR

pond

FIRST FLOOR

wc   hr

lk        qt
hc
hc        st
        st
lk        qt
wc   hr

cl
cl
cl
cl

to tennis courts →

staff
hd    med
dep
office

lcl   lcl
library
entrance hall

small
hall

wc
hc
hr
qt
st

lk

hr

middle
court

div   cl
cl
fountain
court
ch    stage
hall

hall

pond

wc
st

lk   hc   hc   wc   lk
herb
garden
hr   qt        qt   hr
st        st

play
court

gymnasium        ch

cl   cl   cl   cl

FIRST FLOOR        paddock

playing field

23.  Lyng Hall Comprehensive School, Coventry, plans. The arrangement shows the complex, informal nature of the MoE Development Group's approach to comprehensive-school planning. Buildings round three sides of the farmyard are old; all others are in the BAC Mark II system. The social organization of the school divided into five houses, numbered on the plan.

5.26. Whitley Abbey Comprehensive School, Coventry. BAC Mark II school designed by Coventry City Architects' Department (W. A. James, main job architect), 1953–5. In the foreground, a pedestrian bridge in pre-stressed concrete designed by Alan Harris.

24. (facing page, top) A corner of Lyng all in 1955. The pond and planting await aturity but a surviving oak gives pleasant mmer shade.

25. (facing page, bottom) A house room lunch time, Lyng Hall. Decentralized ning in separate houses was a feature of is and other Development-Group-fluenced designs of the 1950s as part of e thrust to impart a more 'civilized' tone the life of secondary schools. Because school reorganizations and economies school meals services, these arrange-ents rarely survive.

nominated contractor into partnership. If the shortcomings of the concrete houses of the 1920s and 1940s were to be overcome, the contractor had to be paired with an expert, independent engineer. And since concrete is heavy, that engineer would have to devise components of unusual ingenuity if the system was to be on all fours with its steel-framed competitors. Despite some improvements in labour supply and an increasing availability of small cranes on site, the Development Group's early schools were all subject to the rule of the 'two-man load'. Heavy, wet methods of concrete construction were out of the question. The group was looking for a concrete equivalent to steel and aluminium, something which would be 'dry and light'.

The engineer who supplied the answers was Alan Harris, an old crony of the Johnson-Marshall brothers. As a young engineer, largely self-taught, Harris had shared humble status and heated debate about the aims of architecture first with Stirrat and then with his brother Percy in the Willesden Borough Engineer's Office in 1936–8. He had then followed Percy Johnson-Marshall on to work for Coventry City Council briefly before the war, so he knew much about the brothers' aspirations and beliefs. During the war Harris found out a little about pre-stressed concrete, hitherto unknown to all but a handful of British engineers. He then went to learn the techniques with Freyssinet in France and worked there for three years before returning in 1949 as an employee of the Pre-Stressed Concrete Company, the only British firm to command the technology. It was a subsidiary of the respected firm of Mouchel; Mautner, a Jewish engineer whom Mouchels had prised out of Dachau just before the war to start up this operation, had died and Harris took his place. The company's only sizeable contract was the making of pre-stressed concrete sleepers for the railways—a wartime innovation. But with the spasmodic shortages of steel, Harris could now see openings.

Steel was very difficult to get. Pre-stressed concrete used the absolute minimum of steel, but almost a condition of using pre-stressed concrete was that there should be no consumption of reinforcement. As soon as you asked for some reinforcing steel to make a beam

5.27.   Beam components of the Intergrid system as designed for Worthing Secondary Technical High School.

5.28.   (*right*) Tensioning an assembled Intergrid beam on the ground. Worthing.

5.29.   A portion of the completed 'grillage', Worthing.

5.30.   (*right*) Raising one of the main beams into position, Worthing.

you had to get a licence, and this in many ways affected design because you designed the bloody thing to need no reinforcement. This was one of the characteristics of Intergrid.

Pre-stressed concrete joists were briefly contemplated in connection with the upgrading of the BAC system, to reduce the amount and cost of aluminium. It was thus that Harris re-encountered Stirrat Johnson-Marshall, on the introduction of BAC's contractor Gilbert-Ash Limited. Already A & B Branch was conferring with Wilfred Ash about a concrete system, though little progress had been made. So the Pre-Stressed Concrete Company teamed up with Gilbert-Ash to develop what became known as Intergrid. The name, redolent of the dour technical enthusiasms of those years, has a dull ring today. But the system broke more new ground than any other building technique of the period outside the sphere of tall buildings. Harris:

It was all new. Nobody had done a triangulated beam in pre-stressed concrete, nobody had done a grillage, nobody had done a pre-stressed column, and there were a hundred and one details which were quite novel. Coming back from France, where I was concerned with harbour works and big bridges, to building, the 'numbers-off' went up but the scale was tiny. It was a major effort to adjust the techniques of pre-stressing to a smaller scale. I regard it as my masterpiece. It is the most carefully integrated, carefully detailed thing I've ever done.

Michael Ventris was the Development Group architect first chosen to work with Harris and Gilbert-Ash on Intergrid, but he soon left and was replaced by Maurice Lee. Lee had come into the group to work on the later stages of Wokingham, doing his apprenticeship on the cladding and then on preparing material for the Building Bulletin,

which taught me an enormous lot about the intricacies and variations in the system and about rationalizing things like corners and changes of level. All of this prepared me, I think, for trying to translate this into pre-cast concrete. For each material, for each industrial technique, you have to solve the same problems in a different way, not only in design for the material but also for production methods.

Harris, Lee and Ash settled down late in 1951 to create a system in pre-cast, pre-stressed concrete which would do everything that Wokingham could do: go up to four storeys, change directions and levels in accordance with the established grid of 3 feet 4 inches and vertical module of ten inches, span up to thirty feet, support timber or concrete cladding without leakage at the joints, and so on. Particularly clever were the two-way beams, a series of interlocking, triangulated units with open interstices, like steel lattice work, so that services could pass through them. These were assembled on the ground like a jigsaw, post-tensioned by uncannily simple means and then hoisted into position by a light crane (Figs. 5.27–30).

By October 1952 the main development work was done. The biggest sub-contractor, Monoconcrete Limited, had agreed to make the pre-cast units, critical components had been tested to destruction in Gilbert-Ash's Cricklewood works, and the cladding (like Wokingham's) had been drenched with power hoses to test for water penetration. The West Sussex County Council now offered a technical school at Worthing as the guinea-pig for the system. Mary Medd and John Kitchin joined Lee in planning and designing the school (Figs. 5.31, 32), which was built in 1953–5. The Intergrid method was used for the whole school except the staircase wells, which were constructed from concrete cast *in situ* to provide the necessary wind-bracing. Later, Intergrid was adapted to accommodate the pre-casting of stair wells, but in general the prefabricated schools systems never discovered a complete answer to the problems of staircase design.

A & B Branch thought of Worthing and the Intergrid development as the outstanding success of their experimental secondary programme. Despite its harsh appearance and some typical later problems with cladding and flat roofs, it is easy to see why. Technically it made the other systems look tame. Yet it took no longer, cost no more and caused less aggravation than the cold-rolled frame used for Belper or the BAC Mark II system at Lyng Hall. Moreover it succeeded commercially where other systems did not. Before Worthing

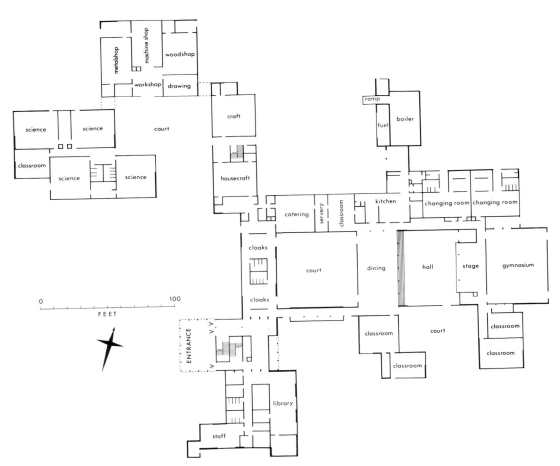

5.31. Worthing Secondary Technical
High School, ground plan. The sequence
of hall, stage and gymnasium is arranged
to allow 'dual use' for these spaces.

5.32. Worthing Secondary Technical
High School, Worthing, Sussex, prototype of the Intergrid system. MoE Development Group (Maurice Lee, Mary
Medd and John Kitchin, main job architects) with West Sussex County Council,
1953–5.

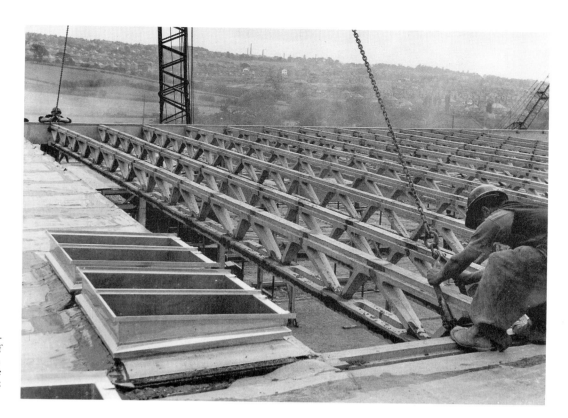

was complete, Gilbert-Ash were girding themselves to build a second school at Southam in Warwickshire, and nine education authorities were expressing interest in Intergrid. Soon afterwards Gilbert-Ash was taken over by Bovis, whose greater size and ability to sell brought in more schools, many of them in Scotland. Some few hundreds of schools were built in Intergrid, and the system was adapted on a modest scale to other types of building—notably a variety of commissions for British Railways' Eastern Region.

More schools would have followed, had not the era of the 'schools consortia' supervened and made the proprietary systems, even those designed under the Ministry's aegis, less and less marketable. This was why the second concrete system promoted by the Ministry, Laingspan, again evolved in collaboration with Harris (by then in partnership with James Sutherland) never made much of an impact. By the time its prototype, the Arnold Grammar School, Nottingham (Figs. 5.33; 7.11, 12), had been built in 1957-9, CLASP was under way and Laings, as a major contractor with many irons in the fire, preferred to abandon so uncompetitive an offspring rather than to promote it against the odds. Few Laingspan schools were built after Arnold.

The modest 'take-up' upon Worthing, Arnold and the Ministry's other secondary schools of the 1950s makes it hard to see them as they were conceived. They were intended not as isolated experiments in their own right but as vehicles for creating a set of proprietary systems which could help hard-pressed local authorities and eventually carry up to twenty per cent of school-building requirements. By taking the burden of technical development off the backs of local-authority architects, A & B Branch hoped to give them more time for the task of designing the actual schools. And by submitting the various systems to the latest and freshest ideas about planning, educational use and servicing, the branch tried to ensure that technical limitations would not hinder educational progress, as had previously been the case.

Part of the thrust in each of these projects was to build on the cumulative Herts approach and refine some aspect of the finishes and services so as to enrich the general 'language' of school design. So the fact that only one of the systems (the cold-rolled frame developed for Belper) was taken up in a big way did not condemn them to failure as a whole. Few

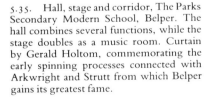

5.34. Rubber flooring and 'stack-back' chairs in the dining area of St Crispin's Secondary Modern School, Wokingham. This was the first use of studded rubber flooring in Britain.

of the technical and educational advances embodied in these schools were linked directly to the systems, and in due course a number were taken up by architects and the building industry at large. Studded rubber flooring is the most graphic example. It was introduced for the first time in English building by David Medd at Wokingham in an attempt to find a quiet, hard-wearing, non-slip surface for circulation areas (Fig. 5.34). The sheets were first manufactured by the Brimsdown Rubber Company of Lord Forrester (a firm friend of 'socialized' architecture) during the brief heyday of his spectacular Brynmawr Rubber Factory. Since rubber was costly, the studs had to be further apart and were less pronounced than they later became. Such adjustments were made in the light of experience and further development in the later schools, so that by the time the Development Group had finished with it, studded rubber flooring was a tried and tested finish ready to become a standard 'vernacular' feature of modern British design. Successes like this were the justification of Medd's claim that 'we were creating a vocabulary of school design for nothing'.

The effort devoted to creating an insulation barrier between the hall and the stage at Belper (Fig. 5.35) furnishes another example of how the development process could be put to wider ends. This was a case of the cost limits forcing hard thinking, through the imperative of 'dual use'. Patricia Tindale:

5.35. Hall, stage and corridor, The Parks Secondary Modern School, Belper. The hall combines several functions, while the stage doubles as a music room. Curtain by Gerald Holtom, commemorating the early spinning processes connected with Arkwright and Strutt from which Belper gains its greatest fame.

At Belper we wanted to use the stage of the hall as a separate music room. Local education authorities wanted great big stages so that they could have tremendous dramatic performances. But the feeling was that this was a poor educational use of space because they only occurred now and then, so it would be very good if the stage could be used for other purposes as well. In terms of the planning of the school as a whole, the most sensible thing was to use it as a music room. Therefore a very high level of sound reduction was required between the stage and the hall, whereas normally there was a great big opening. So we thumbed through some Post-War Building Studies and found a lightweight construction of timber-framing and asbestos—one of the few materials then available. This construction was to be made into a great panel which would move forward on the ceiling tracks and could be bolted through to the proscenium arch against a rubber seal. When it was at the back of the stage it would be the perfect backdrop. All this needed testing to see if it was really possible to get a worthwhile amount of decibel reduction. So we had prototypes made and put into the anechoic chamber at BRS and tested, and we got a fantastic reduction. When I came on to housing and the development of low-rise systems, we had to have a lightweight party wall and that's where we started from. We used plasterboard, not asbestos, because it was cheaper. I think it is fair to say that this was the key technical innovation which made lightweight terrace housing possible.

Formally, the Development Group was able to call on BRS's facilities and expertise because its investigations were the spearhead of a huge public building-programme. But this ease of access and warmth between architects and experts would have been impossible without the fostering of relationships which Johnson-Marshall had started at Herts. The 'development ideal' also justified, in his mind, the Ministry's continued recourse to the same set of sub-contractors and suppliers. Education and partnership, he averred, not competition, were the road to better building. The Herts manner of working continued on through these schools in other ways as well. There were specially commissioned murals in several of them and, to relieve the unredeemed vista of concrete cladding and playing field, planting and landscaping always received plenty of attention, Maurice Lee in particular taking such tasks under his wing.

## 'RAT. TRAD.'

From 1955 onwards the Development Group was obliged to look anew at its priorities. The experimental programme of secondary schools ushered in by Wokingham had nearly run its course with the exception of the Laingspan system, an afterthought of 1957–9. The huge, unfolding programme of local-authority school-building still needed support. But a divergence of opinion in A & B Branch gradually became manifest. Up to this point all the Ministry's experimental work had been with prefabricated systems. Circumstantial reasons apart, Johnson-Marshall believed in prefabrication and the Development Group had gained momentum from exploiting this belief imaginatively. But from about the time that building controls ended in 1954, the first niggling doubts began to surface.

Powell and Moya, architects much respected in the branch, had designed a handsome and effective traditionally built school for the LCC, Mayfield School, Putney, well within the cost limits, and came to talk about it at one of the informal lunchtime discussions which were a feature of the régime. Johnson-Marshall was sceptical of their claims, but Pott put Peter Newnham on to the task of scrutinizing its costs. 'I came up with some very uncomfortable facts about how cheap it was' recalls Newnham. 'They at first wouldn't believe the figures that derived from these very simple classrooms I was looking at.' Scepticism was natural. The branch was still basking in the glow of the 1952 Pilkington Report and in the knowledge that its approach to building, while not necessarily the cheapest, was the most productive—in other words, it offered the best value for money and the best means of monitoring and controlling costs. A few stretches of cut-price brick walling, built during a brief slackening in the demand for housing, were not going to divert the school-building

5.36. The beginnings of 'Rat. Trad.'. Garden court at Woodside Junior School, Amersham, Buckinghamshire. MoE Development Group (David and Mary Medd and Clive Wooster, main job architects) with Buckinghamshire County Council, 1956–7.

ship from the course which, given the bigger programmes which the authorities were having to take on, it was still believed would yet offer tremendous economies of scale.

Of prefabrication's acknowledged shortcomings at this stage, the chief was the cladding. After nearly a decade of experiment, the architects were still using concrete cladding but they had not yet managed to get it right—that is to say, technically satisfactory, delivered on time and tolerably attractive. It had been an issue in the Herts days and continued to be so at the Ministry. At Belper, for example, the team had striven to find something which looked good yet was light enough to be carried by the cold-rolled steel stanchions. Slabs, trays and panels of all kinds, foamed slag, shock concrete, Holoplast and so on: all were investigated. In due course a new kind of asbestos-cement cladding, used previously only on industrial buildings, was adopted for the upper storeys. Here and elsewhere the architects tried to cheer up the cladding by mixing in aggregates to give different colours, but after a few years of English weather the results rarely looked full-hearted. This was something about which the laymen in A & B Branch felt, if anything, more strongly than the architects. Part recalls:

> It became evident to me fairly soon that the claddings would not do as a long-term thing in the form in which they were using them, because they were very few of them really comparable in attractiveness of finish with brick, which is an extraordinarily difficult material to beat. I kept on saying to them, 'Do for God's sake do something about at least the concrete.' They spent a long time trying to improve the concrete finish and they did make some progress.

In addition, despite the Ministry's promotion of prefabricated school-building systems only a quarter of British schools were being built by these methods in the mid 1950s. If A & B Branch was to spread its favours fairly, it was high time it came to the aid of the other three-quarters and take cognizance of traditional construction. It needed in particular to show local authorities and private architects less sharp than Powell and Moya how traditional methods might be rationalized in the light of Nisbet's elemental cost revolution. This was the origin of 'rat. trad.' or rationalized traditional, a form of orthodox building adapted to the new and simpler approaches to foundations, roofing, partitions and internal finishes.

David and Mary Medd, working as ever together, started this line of investigation with their Woodside Junior School at Amersham, Buckinghamshire (1956–7) and followed it up with two small village schools at Finmere, Oxfordshire and Great Ponton, Lincolnshire (1958–9). All these were primary schools which, following the period of concentration upon secondary schools, the Ministry felt could benefit from fresh thinking. By this time the Medds had built up a unique body of knowledge and network of contacts in matters pertaining to primary-school building, educational as well as technical and architectural. So Amersham and the two village schools sprang from a minute examination of the needs of the new primary teaching, whether in allocation of space, design of furniture or quality of lighting. This campaign continued in later schools designed by the Medds like the Eveline Lowe Nursery and Primary School in Camberwell, South London (1965–6) and the Delf Hill Middle School, Bradford (1966–9). In these schools the construction became increasingly an elegant, simplified backdrop for a philosophy of teaching which the Medds and Eric Pearson, Leonard Gibbon's successor as chief HMI with the branch, wished to expound and develop.

The Woodside Junior School at Amersham (Figs. 5.36, 37) deserves a closer look. As it was the first 'rat. trad.' school, it in some measure united the experimental ardour of the Development Group's early years with the more settled atmosphere which gradually prevailed. Partly because it was built in brick, it has worn better than some of the Ministry's prefabricated schools. In addition its aims and organization were written up by the indefatigable Medds in one of the longest and most lucid of the early Building Bulletins.

5.37. Corner of a 'workroom', Woodside Junior School, Amersham. The furniture represents the culmination of ten years' development work by David Medd, resulting in the publication of a new British Standard for school furniture shortly after Amersham was built.

The school was commissioned by Buckinghamshire, where Fred Pooley, previously Donald Gibson's deputy at Coventry, had recently become county architect. At Coventry, Pooley had much to do with industrialized building and became increasingly wary of the claims made for it. Moving to Bucks, he found a county with a population growth second only to Herts, an ingrained conservative educational tradition, and thriving brick-making and furniture-making industries. He wanted to see if his school-building programme could reconcile these factors. If the Ministry's architects were to design a school, ideas might come up which could be taken up, refined or discarded by Pooley's own staff in the seemingly infinite run of primary schools which loomed before them. This was exactly how the relation between the Development Group and a local authority was supposed to work.

The task at Amersham was twofold. One was to rationalize customary load-bearing brick construction. This meant submitting it to a dimensional discipline based on brick sizes, employing a cross-wall structure with flat roofs, limiting and standardizing the other components, and contriving that brickwork's advantages in durability and appearance were not bought at the expense of poor or costly services. In the past, it had been the cost and time involved in installing services in brick and concrete structures which had given prefabricated school-building the edge in productivity. Since many of the innovations in services for schools had been geared to prefabricated structures, at Amersham it was often necessary to go back to first principles. There was renewed collaboration, for instance, with Ralph Hopkinson of BRS over lighting. The thicker reveals of the brick walls acquired splays, mullions were tapered to reduce their internal profile, and to improve the quality of light and colour a subtler approach to the use of reflected light was taken throughout the school.

The other brief which the Medds took up at Amersham was the further advancement of primary teaching opportunities. Few authorities were building junior schools of this type. But by concentrating for a time on the exact needs of children between seven and eleven, the architects hoped to consolidate upon changes which were now becoming accepted in infants' departments and see how far they could be extended up into junior teaching. Practical equipment in particular exercised them. How could the skills of children in this age-range be harnessed and developed without the full crafts and science resources which a secondary school could expect to have? The answer they came up with was the 'workroom', a space rather larger than the standard classroom equipped with wall benches along the perimeter and a variety of movable chairs and tables. Furnishing these rooms gave a new impetus to the aim, long in David Medd's mind, of evolving a complete range of school furniture at the Ministry which could be made economically available for schools throughout the country. It took many years before this range became a reality (see p. 192). But from Amersham onwards Medd was constantly extending the scope of his furniture designs and researches with this end in mind.

Woodside School at Amersham represented the first of the new rather than the last of the old. By the time that it was built, Johnson-Marshall had left the Ministry of Education; CLASP, the original school-building consortium of local authorities, had sprung up; and the tasks of A & B Branch had diversified beyond mere schools. Henceforward, the branch had to work its way towards a maturer role in which direct intervention was balanced with strategy and advice. Experimental schools continued to be built, but as at Amersham their technical content counted for somewhat less, their educational approach for somewhat more. To understand the dynamics of English educational building in the 1960s, it is time to turn away from the centre and trace the percolation of the Herts ideals elsewhere, in particular into the architectural offices of another county council—Nottinghamshire.

# CHAPTER 6

# THE STORY OF CLASP

CLASP was—and is—two things. It was a system of building based upon light-steel construction, adapted to combat the difficulties of sites liable to mining subsidence; and it was the earliest venture in bringing British local authorities together and pooling their resources to build more and better schools. Both these advances sprang from the post-war tradition of co-operative research, experiment and development in architecture, always strongest in the educational building world, where ideals were high, clients amenable and approachable, and the Gropian vision of long-term production could be turned from dream to reality.

## THE BROCKHOUSE FRAME

The history of the structural system which was at the heart of CLASP goes back, like many novelties of the period, to the necessities of war. In 1937, J. Brockhouse and Company, an established West Midlands engineering firm specializing in drop-forgings and castings, took over the Vulcan works at Southport, Lancashire. They did so in the expectation of arms contracts. 'The Vulcan' was a small motor manufacturer already engaged in armaments for the aircraft industry, and Brockhouse planned to expand the works and make artillery trailers and other military vehicles there, in whole or in part, under licence. They retained the services of the chief designer at the Vulcan, a thirty-six-year-old mechanical engineer, F. W. Lister Heathcote. Heathcote (Fig. 6.1) belonged to the pragmatic tradition of British engineering. A graduate of Owens College, Manchester, he was an insatiable, independent, empirical designer, adept at making tools and setting up production lines but ready to turn his hand to anything. He had been trained at Crossley Motors and then worked with 'The Overland', 'The Sunbeam' and 'The Ford', but as yet he had no experience of structural engineering.

1. F. W. Lister Heathcote in Home Guard uniform, c. 1942.

In 1939 Brockhouse moved Heathcote down to their headquarters at West Bromwich, to help set up a foundry for making track links for tanks. The task completed, he was at something of a loose end. Then in 1942 a member of the Brockhouse board, Group-Captain Baldwin, asked Heathcote to look into the prospects for cold-rolled steel in building. Already post-war reconstruction was in the air, and livelier industrialists were wondering what might be done in peacetime with all the extra capacity that they had amassed during the war. Through the Iron and Steel Board and the British Iron and Steel Federation, the Government was pressing for economies and experimentation with steel. Cold-rolled steel sections used less material than hot-rolled steel, but they were not so strong, nor were they competitive in price if the order was a short one, as they needed an elaborate set of rollers. Hitherto cold-rolled steel had been used for products like bicycle-wheel rims and drip moulds on cars. It had been little exploited for wartime work, and there was excess capacity. But several people thought it had a future in building. One was George Wright, engineer to the firm of Gyproc Plaster Partitions. Wright, who had previously worked on braced steel structures with a Canadian bridge company, had a vision of Gyproc's light partitions being

6.2. Gyproc houses in course of erection, Mitchell Avenue, Canley, Coventry, 10 November 1943. The first cold-rolled steel houses in Britain: structure by John Brockhouse and Company, F. W. L. Heathcote, engineer.

fixed on a light steel frame. Gyproc and Brockhouse therefore got together. Heathcote designed a machine to produce stronger cold-rolled sections than before, 'mugged up' on the necessary welding technology for joining them, and brought in a local welding firm on the project.

Housing was the first market in the minds of manufacturers equipping for post-war reconstruction, and the next step was to build a prototype house somewhere. The choice fell on Coventry. Here, because of a drastic housing shortage preceding but exacerbated by the blitz of November 1940, experimental wartime housing was being allowed to proceed in the suburb of Canley. So in Mitchell Avenue near a couple of other experiments was raised late in 1943 a bald, semi-detached pair, flat-roofed and asbestos–cement-clad (Figs. 6.2, 3). This was Britain's first essay in prefabricated building with cold-rolled steel.

Brockhouse, Gyproc and Sankey, a third firm involved, went on to build two further houses on an improved model at Edinburgh; and in 1944 the British Iron and Steel Federation promoted for the benefit of its member companies a set of experimental steel houses, one using hot-rolled sections, another cold-rolled, and a third sheet-steel. Each involved several manufacturers, of whom Brockhouse was just one. The cold-rolled model used only some sixty per cent of steel in weight compared to its hot-rolled rival, but it needed more welding and was altogether more costly. In the event, only the hot-rolled BISF house went into production. The hopes for cold-rolled housing receded, and the plant laid out by Heathcote for Brockhouse seemed to have lost the chance of mass production which it needed to prove itself:

> For cold-rolled, you've got to make it a factory-production frame. I don't think there's
> much outlet for individual members. The only hopes for factory-built frames is in big

6.3. The finished houses in Mitchell Avenue, April 1944.

production. You can't do a one-off. We thought that forty an hour was the minimum. I suppose perhaps you'd use double that number in a house. You could do the steelwork for a house in a couple of hours; you could do four houses in a day's shift.

But where housing failed, schools came to the rescue, just as had happened with Hills and Company, manufacturers of the steel frame for the Hertfordshire schools (and also based in West Bromwich). When the Coventry houses were building, Heathcote had been surprised to find Donald Gibson, son of his old engineering professor and mentor at Owens College, Manchester, A. H. ('Hydraulics') Gibson, at the reins as city architect. From his pre-war days at the Building Research Station and his first essay in prefabrication, the little nursery school on the Lache estate outside Chester (p. 50–1), Gibson had a taste for technical innovation, and he knew something of the revolution in attitudes which his friend Stirrat Johnson-Marshall was just beginning to get going at Herts. With a shattered city centre, a deficit of housing and precious little labour or materials to hand, Gibson had scant time to think about schools. But he had a technically competent and thorough deputy, William Glare. In 1947, therefore, he persuaded the Coventry education committee and treasurer to allot a proportion of the city's primary school-building programme to the development of a cold-rolled system and place a bulk order with Brockhouse, sufficient to make tooling-up worthwhile. Glare and his colleague Patrick Powell were then left to work with Heathcote and the education department, and evolve a satisfactory system based on the module of 8 feet 3 inches then recommended by the Ministry of Education.

Coventry was not Herts. Bereft of hindsight, the Brockhouse cold-rolled system used for the three Coventry primary schools built by this method, Henry Parkes School at Canley (1949–50) and its two successors, Parkgate Road and St Christopher's, looks like just another

6.4. Henry Parkes School, Canley, Coventry. Cold-rolled frame in course of erection by three men, 1949.

6.5. Henry Parkes School, Canley, Coventry. William Glare and Patrick Powell, job architects for Coventry City Council, 1949–50. A conventional Wood-Report arrangement, with entrance and administration buildings in brick, and 'bay' classrooms constructed from a light steel frame with uprights at 8 foot 3 inch centres.

6.6. Infant classroom at Henry Parkes School, c. 1950. An early instance of informal classroom arrangement, within a conventionally lit space.

of the sundry experimental methods of prefabricating schools tried out by bolder local authorities and architects during these makeshift, dearth-ridden years (Figs. 6.4–6). The technical problems were well solved, there was careful thought about light and colour, and the partnership between the Coventry architects and Heathcote, wearing a new hat as structural engineer, worked happily. But there was no strongly self-conscious spirit of enterprise. The schools were of the usual 'bay' type with 'finger' plans. Nor was Coventry of a mind to commit itself absolutely to Brockhouse. Schools were a side issue, and a choice of solutions commended itself. Glare:

> The City Architect having embarked upon the lightweight steel frame nevertheless was concerned not to place all the 'eggs in one basket'. This was wise and necessary because we were working out a prototype, and the design and fabrication problems could not be solved sufficiently quickly to involve several projects simultaneously . . . New primary schools had to be built quickly and development of a new system of building required time. We were open-minded, and it remained to be seen whether the system could usefully be extended to serve others.

Some early primary schools, therefore, were farmed out to private architects: Whitmore Park, built in the Bristol Aeroplane Company's aluminium system and mentioned earlier (p. 136) was one. Of those designed by Coventry's own architects, two used a conventional rolled-steel system devised in partnership with a local engineering firm, and another took up the Hills system. But the Brockhouse collaboration remained the favourite for future development. When Glare and his colleagues set about planning Caludon Castle, the first of Coventry's purpose-built comprehensive schools, it was the Brockhouse cold-rolled frame that they employed, duly developed and extended. This interesting school, plagued by delays, political opposition to comprehensives and the advent of the Ministry's cost limits, was built in phases in 1952–5 (Fig. 6.7). By then Gibson had entered into partnership with the Ministry's Development Group to make the BAC system educationally responsive using schools in Coventry as the guinea-pigs, as explained in the previous chapter. No further schools using the Brockhouse system were planned for the future. Glare left in 1955, and it seemed like the end of the cold-rolled experiment in Coventry.

Once the arrangement with Coventry was under way, Brockhouse meanwhile had started to market their system to other education authorities. Production was based at West

6.7. Caludon Castle Comprehensive School, Coventry, aerial view. Coventry City Council, architects, 1951–5, using the Brockhouse cold-rolled steel frame. Five separate 'houses' in the foreground, with the core of the school in an arc round a sloping court. This thoughtful contribution to comprehensive design had no successors.

6.8. Some of the architectural team involved in the Belper development, 1952. Left to right: Geoffrey Foxley of Derbyshire County Council; Hamer Crossley, county architect of Derbyshire; Barbara Price, MoE Development Group; and Anthony Pott, head of the MoE Development Group.

Bromwich and assembly at Southport. But they soon ran into snags. Every authority wanted something slightly different, especially after the increasing complexity of school plans undermined the 'bay' approach to construction. This took away all commercial incentive. 'The Southport people had a drawing office employing about thirty people,' recalls Heathcote. 'They got jobs overlapping and different specials involved. It was a very *ad hoc* process.' Unlike the Hills frame, Brockhouse had not yet got on to a grid, nor could the frame be bought along with its own cladding, roofing and the other accoutrements of a full 'proprietary' system. As Glare told the Ministry in December 1950, the system amounted to 'little more than a steel frame'. Unless it could be made more flexible, 'its use cannot be justified in these times'.

At this point, Johnson-Marshall and Anthony Pott stepped in and prevented Brockhouse from abandoning school-building by inviting the firm to become partners in one of the four systems for secondary schools which the Ministry of Education was planning to sponsor. John Brockhouse, the managing director, agreed, and Heathcote came down to London for a prolonged period of collaboration with the architects of A & B Branch's Development Group. Pott was in overall charge of the project; under him, Barbara Price, Donald Barron and Patricia Tindale were assigned to the 'Brockhouse Standard System', Tindale having special responsibility for the frame and cladding. Hamer Crossley, the county architect of Derbyshire and a student colleague of Johnson-Marshall's from Liverpool days, volunteered a secondary modern school at Belper as the prototype, and Geoffrey Foxley from the Derbyshire office joined the team (Fig. 6.8).

Belper (Figs. 5.35; 6.9, 10) witnessed a more radical overhaul of the cold-rolled frame than anything done at Coventry. It had to be put on a grid geared to the vertical module of ten inches and horizontal module of 3 feet 4 inches, and made to change level smoothly at re-entrant corners (the *pons asinorum* of prefabricated design, according to Heathcote). To be compatible with Wokingham and the Development Group's other experimental 'secondaries' of the early 1950s, the Ministry wanted it to go up to four storeys, a headache for cold-rolled technology. Two storeys had been encompassed without difficulty at Coventry, but four spelt complications and 'specials'. Heathcote therefore demurred, arguing that his firm could only provide what was consistent with economy and the normal needs of production, and a compromise of three storeys was agreed upon. Brockhouse also now became, with the Ministry's help, charged with finding satisfactory cladding and other components. All this was resolved, and the Parks Secondary Modern School at Belper built in 1953–5. Technically, the Ministry did not look back on Belper as a 'howling success'. On site, discrepancies arose between the frame and the new light-weight asbestos–cement cladding devised for the slight, cold-rolled sections. The builder got behind, and it was only through pressure applied by William Pile that a claim—rare indeed in those days—was avoided. Pott was never convinced by the Belper system, and expressed surprise when Nottinghamshire first proposed to adapt it. Nevertheless it did attract some adherents. Essex County Council, for instance, built several schools on the 'Brockhouse Standard System', and the Southport works had incentive enough to stay in the school-building business. But no one then could have dreamed that, with a subtle transformation, the Brockhouse frame was about to take off in a way that would dwarf all the existing schools systems—Hills, BAC, Intergrid, Derwent and the rest—and make them obsolete.

## 'THAT SINKING FEELING': NOTTS AND THE SUBSIDENCE ISSUE

Early in 1955 Donald Gibson (Fig. 6.11) resigned as Coventry's City Architect. His departure was abrupt, and regretted on both sides. After seventeen years of struggle, Gibson felt that he and his staff were being shabbily treated by some of the Coventry councillors. Emerging from a specially irksome meeting, he asked his secretary if there were any good jobs open. There was one: Nottinghamshire had been advertising for a county architect, but the shortlist was already made. Gibson immediately lodged an application. Notts, a less prestigious authority than Coventry, could hardly believe it. The clerk to the council, Alan Davies, promptly met Gibson on neutral ground to ask if he would take the job, should

6.9. The Parks Secondary Modern School, Belper, Derbyshire, in course of erection, November 1953, with Anthony Pott looking sceptically on. MoE Development Group (Barbara Price, Don Barron and Pat Tindale, main job architects) with Derbyshire County Council (Geoffrey Foxley, job architect). The new Brockhouse cold-rolled frame, designed to a 3 foot 4 inch module with pin joints and diagonal bracing, was to be the starting point for the structure of CLASP.

6.10. The Parks School, Belper, main entrance, 1955. Concrete cladding on the ground storey; light but troublesome asbestos-cement cladding on the upper storeys.

6.11. Donald Gibson at the time he left Coventry, 1955.

it be offered. He agreed, and stuck to his guns despite a procession of Coventry dignitaries to his door. Gibson arrived at the West Bridgford offices of the county council at the beginning of February 1955.

He found a troubling situation. Like most county authorities, Nottinghamshire's chief architectural responsibilities were for schools. But they were badly behind with their programmes. Schools were taking far too long to build, and in many places there had been a reversion to huts. In large measure the difficulties were administrative. The councillors, a blend of landowners, miners and others, were well disposed and reasonably harmonious, but the education department was at daggers drawn with the architects. They were hardly talking to one another; communication was mainly by way of written, formal briefs and memoranda, date-stamped on the education side in anticipation of any inquest.

Pressing down upon them all and threatening to reduce the county's building programme to chaos was the burden of mining subsidence. Notts and its neighbour Derbyshire were the two coal-mining counties where the industry had enjoyed most growth in the post-war decade. Miners had moved south with their families; new housing had been built in a score of Notts colliery communities, and with the new housing had to come schools. But the very source of this livelihood was proving a hazard to the new buildings. As the pitface advanced, the land above subsided with a wave-like movement, and the lengthier and heavier buildings on the surface fissured, sometimes becoming dangerous and requiring heavy repair. If you wished to build on a possible subsidence site and could afford it, you could pay compensation to the National Coal Board and it would leave the seam unexcavated, as it did around its own shafts to provide security for colliery buildings. Local authorities could not afford such sums. Yet they were obliged to build on subsidence sites, because miners' families needed homes and schools near the pit. Housing was manageable, so long as it was not built in terraces, since single or semi-detached houses with strong lintels could 'ride' the subsidence wave as little rigid boxes. But schools, being bigger, tended to fracture. Subsidence-area authorities had naturally taken advice on this. The conventional engineering consultants had told them to build 'egg-crate' foundations of reinforced concrete up to six feet deep. Even Arups, among the best engineers available, had counselled the Architects' Co-Partnership to do likewise when they were building schools in Derbyshire. These foundations (Fig. 6.12) sucked up the whole of the subsidence allowance offered by the Ministry of Education and were of no value to the teachers and children in whose name the schools were being built. In Notts many had proved a dismal failure, as Gibson found.

> I went to see a few of the new schools which had cracked. I didn't say it to anybody, but I knew that if they had cracked with all this expenditure, it was a waste of time doing that. You might just as well have built the things without any foundation, and they wouldn't have cracked any worse.

Gibson therefore had three tasks before him. He had to promote a 'crash' programme of school-building to make up the deficit. He had to reform affairs within his own bailiwick, mend—or remove—fences with the education department, and build up an integrated team. And he had to lick the subsidence problem.

Things moved fast. The first priority was to find breathing space for the needed reorganization. The senior officers at Notts knew they were in a fix, and therefore went along when Gibson put a radical proposition to them:

> I said, 'You've got a good answer here. You've been building individual huts. Why not build individual schools which won't be any trouble or need any foundation? Just build them in timber. You've got Vic Hallam [the proprietor of the Derwent timber system for schools] based on your doorstep in Derbyshire. We could do a deal with him to get fourteen new schools built this year. Let's commission private architects, one for each school, and give them the programme from the Director of Education. We'll get a quick start and all the schools built. In the meantime we have twelve months in which we can set up a development group to sort out a new system of building. Can I suggest we take the Black Horse pub; I'll choose the architects, we'll invite them all to come to lunch and tell them what we want and we'll see if they agree. I'll arrange

6.12. Foundations at Benjamin Outram School, Ripley, Derbyshire. Architects Co-Partnership, architects, 1957. A preposterously massive sub-structure by Arups carries a light, 'Medway' proprietary timber school in order to withstand subsidence.

also that we'll have one contractor to build the fourteen schools: I'll get a set of contract documents and the same bills of quantities and we'll obtain a tender from them to do all the schools. The rates for the gravel and the aggregate and everything else will be identical for every architect on every school.'

In this way, the Derwent system for timber schools became a stopgap solution for Notts, while the architects sorted out their problems. At the same time, before CLASP had been thought of, 'serial contracting' put in an appearance. The contractual arrangements for school-building were to be a very important part of the Notts story.

There followed a fast turnover of staff, allowing Gibson to set up his development group. With his friend Stirrat Johnson-Marshall at the Ministry to counsel and enthuse (he had suggested a slate of architects for the new Derwent schools), it was to the Herts manner of doing things that Gibson turned. In the summer of 1955 Dan Lacey and Henry Swain, among the leaders of the primary group and the keepers of the Johnson-Marshall conscience at Herts, arrived at West Bridgford, Lacey to be assistant county architect under Gibson and his deputy Ernest Frere, Swain to head the development group. They had hardly settled in when Alan Meikle joined, also from Herts. By the end of the year Alan Goodman, David Moizer, Derek Lakin, David Meylan, Bevis Fuller and Wally Wilson were also at work, with Bill Hill as quantity surveyor. The ethos was co-operative: Gibson provided the cover, courage and backing which in the murky matter of mining subsidence was vital, while demanding initiatives from others:

> He was a team man. He came here at 8.30 in the morning, took his coat off, and if you didn't give him bloody difficult problems to solve he'd go swanning off and find interesting things to do which were not so relevant. He expected to be made to work, he expected to contribute, he expected people to tell him what the problem was.

From the beginning, everyone agreed that they needed a light-weight, prefabricated and jointed system of construction that would 'ride' the subsidence wave. Gibson, a railway enthusiast, was struck quickly by the anomalies between the treatment of moving and static loads:

> I knew about railways and I used to go and watch when there were heavy goods trains. I found that our loads with a three-storey building would come to far less than goes per axle on a railway sleeper with a heavy load of waggons. I used to watch them shunting at Ruddington where we lived and see how much the rails sprang. If you can do that with a moving load, why can't you do it with a static load? It seemed much simpler. So the idea was that we ought to have an articulated frame so that nothing could ever fall down, and a very light building. You'd simply put sand on a level site with nothing sticking down at all and vibrate it with a roller, which imposes about three times the load any school will ever bear. Then you'd spread concrete over it and subdivide it, a bit like a chain of armour that will hold together and never tear apart, and put the frame together on these pads.

But simple analogies like this were not enough to work from. Before the architects could pick a method of construction, they had properly to understand what happened to ground and to buildings under subsidence conditions, in terms both of horizontal strain and of vertical movement. At first they were on their own. The existing literature on the subject was thin, none of the private consulting engineers had defined the problem correctly or studied it in depth, and the National Coal Board's own experts were deeply sceptical about Nottinghamshire's efforts except for one ally at headquarters in London, R. J. Orchard, who admitted that they 'were contending against a tremendous deadweight of reactionary prejudice about mining subsidence among Area Engineers, Architects and Mineral Valuers'. With the help of W. H. Ward of the Building Research Station's Soil Mechanics Division, the horizontal problem proved not too difficult to solve. Predicting the rate and degree of vertical subsidence was harder. But after Swain had stumbled across a paper by Kenneth Wardell on the relationship between time and subsidence and applied to it a certain amount

6.13.   The mature CLASP frame, seen at Bingham Comprehensive School, Notts, c. 1966. Pin-jointed steel frame on a thin concrete raft with spring-loaded bracing and a timber roof-deck. The staircase on the right is also shackled and braced.

of primitive geometry, the architects were able accurately to predict the degree of movement which would be needed in their hypothetical framed structure.

Armed with these calculations, Swain now made the rounds of the various existing systems to see which was the most suitable. Concrete structures were inadmissible on subsidence sites. Timber frames, like the Derwent system that Notts had adopted for the 'year of grace', were flexible enough and satisfied Gibson, but they ran into complexities over structure and fire regulations when they rose above two storeys. That left steel or aluminium, with some sort of new cladding. The choice fell on the Brockhouse cold-rolled frame at Belper, then in the latter stages of building. That frame was lighter than any of the hot-rolled frames then in common use and had the advantage of resisting wind pressure with diagonal bracing, not with rigid joints. And Gibson could bear witness from his Coventry days to Brockhouse's good record on school-building and in particular to Lister Heathcote's precious ingenuity, responsiveness and mechanical know-how. Heathcote was a 'spring chap', they figured. Before the war he had designed sprung frames for motor engines which had to withstand a perpetually bumpy road. If he had the know-how for designing moving structures on a still ground, surely he could cope with still structures on a moving ground? The principle was not dissimilar.

In this way Notts forewent a conventional structural engineer or consultant to help them with their daunting task, and put themselves instead at the mercy of a mechanical engineer. Collaboration with Heathcote began in the autumn of 1955, with a view to devising a school-building system which could be tested in the 1957–8 programme. Ninety per cent of the schools scheduled for building in this programme were on subsidence sites: eleven schools altogether, about the minimum number needed to make the venture viable for Brockhouse. Heathcote and Swain, with some help from Lacey and (for the floor slab) from Rex Coates of Nottingham University redesigned the Belper frame for subsidence sites in the winter of 1955–6. The crucial novelties were a pin-jointed frame with rocker bases for the uprights (hence the topical nickname, the 'rock and roll' system), and diagonal spring-loaded wall bracing at points between the columns, so as to allow for 'lozenging' under the strain of subsidence while withstanding wind loads. The site slab and the roof deck were divided into lengths of no more than 200 feet and a gap allowed for expansion. Only on subsidence sites were the braces equipped with pre-loaded coil springs and the stair flights shackled to cope with 'lozenging' (Fig. 6.13). Otherwise, practically the same frame

6.14. Brick and timber house of the 1930s at West Bridgford, showing 'lozenging' effect of mining subsidence.

without these special features was to serve for the rest of the schools, on the Herts principle that only a unity of development could raise technical and educational standards in the county. Light, cold-rolled steel dominated for the columns in the early stages of structural development, when single-storey primary schools were the main type of building in mind. But as secondary schools and multi-storey work entered into the programmes, the heavier hot-rolled sections came into play. They made no material difference to the system's capacity to deal with subsidence and eventually displaced the cold-rolled steelwork.

## A SYSTEM FROM SCRATCH

On this structural basis the architects of the Notts development group could proceed. The arrangements were the same as at Herts. Each architect took an element and prepared to design it to fit the technical requirements of the brief. They began, in other words, by creating a vocabulary of building rather than any kind of building in itself. For the participants, mostly keen young architects who jumped enthusiastically into the gaps created as the old guard took fright at Donald Gibson's innovations, it was a strange, exciting experience. At Herts there had been a Hills prototype, but Notts lacked even this. Alan Meikle:

> I can't recall having any real concept of what the buildings were going to look like. I remember asking Dan Lacey and Henry Swain about this because we were all designing the components, and Dan saying 'Never mind the *buildings*, get the *components* right'. I had a sort of dreamy idea of a kind of building that I'd never really ever seen before, like a pack of cards you could walk in and out of, which wasn't all walls, because we were talking about bringing the landscape inside the building. It was a strange sort of phenomenon because there was nothing you could relate this to. It wasn't going to look like Hertfordshire, and as there were gaps in our thinking because we hadn't designed something, then there was no *image* to put there. There was no image of a finished building.

In practice the tradition of Herts and of A & B Branch as interpreted and expounded by Lacey and Swain, plus the subsidence conditions, determined much of the vocabulary and appearance (Figs. 6.15–17,21). The module of 3 feet 4 inches with walls and partitions 'on the grid' drew upon the trials of 1951–5 at Herts, tempered by the lessons of the Ministry's best experimental schools of the period, Wokingham and Worthing. The planning of primary schools also carried forward from the two-classroom units with pockets of space between

167

6.15. Intake Farm (formerly Bancroft Lane) Primary School, Mansfield, Notts. The first CLASP school: Bevis Fuller and Henry Swain, job architects, 1956–7. The debt to Herts primary schools is plain.

which the Herts primary group had developed. The subsidence conditions and lightweight frame made timber the natural material for the roof deck and flooring (which were an integral part of the structural concept) as well as for the window frames. Meikle again:

> We were much influenced by a house not far from where we worked at West Bridgford [Fig. 6.14], where there'd been a very bad dose of mining subsidence. It was a Tudorbethan house complete with leaded lights and everything. It had lozenged and nothing had fractured. It had a most dramatic subsidence and was standing there, with the windows still opening. We used to look at this and say that lozenging was a very good principle. Clearly timber was a soft material, so that if the glass actually did hit the timber, it was less likely to fracture than if it was in a metal frame. There had been a lot of problems with glass exploding in metal windows in schools where there had been subsidence and we'd had to put sticky paper over them, like during the war, to stop the children being injured by flying glass.

Because of the light frame and the problems encountered with concrete and cement claddings at Belper, many of the external elements were first designed in timber too. There was little concrete cladding in the original 'mark' of the as yet unnamed system (Mark II as it was numbered in homage to Belper, which became Mark I). Instead the architects went for variety—the 'cocktail solution', they called it. Deliberately, the early Notts system was 'never a clear structural, one-material concept', says Syd Bell, one of Gibson's new recruits. Traditionalism found a firm place in this early vocabulary. Black weather-boarding, much admired on barns and early industrial buildings, made an appearance. So, more curiously and pervasively, did panels of tile-hanging, the theory being that the overlapping tiles would shift slightly on their battens, should movement take place. These seeming throw-backs to the age of handicraft made a strange costume upon the flat-roofed, assembly-line bones of the system. But designers and teachers appreciated their colour and unorthodox charm, and most early CLASP schools display them. They have suffered sorely from the neglectful maintenance of recent years. They were supposed never to be used in exposed places at ground level, a rule too quickly forgotten. Few are the schools now where energetic

Plate XI. The Woodlands Comprehensive School, Tile Hill, Coventry. A view in 1985, showing the Hills 3 feet 4 inches system in good condition and the planting approaching maturity. MoE Development Group (Michael Smith, John Toomer and Guy Oddie, main job architects), with Coventry City Council.

Plate XII. Corner of a CLASP school: James Peacock Infants School, Ruddington, Notts. Alan Willis and Gilbert Dabbous, job architects, 1966–7.

footballing or small prying hands have not dislodged their meed of tiles, leaving a patchy wall where the elements eat silently away at battens and brown paper.

The first school in the new Notts system, Bancroft Lane Primary School, Mansfield (now known as Intake Farm), began on site in January 1957 and was finished in September of the same year (Fig. 6.18). It caused a panic, not because of any defect in the system but because of its cost. As the Derwent schools seemed to be proving the benefits of serial contracting, the builder chosen for them, Simms Sons and Cooke, was asked also to erect the first bays of the new prototype in their works and was awarded the first few schools in the system after submitting a schedule of prices. Their preliminary quotations looked good, but at the last moment the final schedule turned out too high. In desperation to get the job done in time and at the right price, Swain ruthlessly cut out insulation and thinned down the foundation slab. No one seems to have noticed and the system received the go-ahead.

Decisive proof of the subsidence system took five more years to achieve. By 1962 hundreds of CLASP schools had been built in different parts of the country, many on known subsidence sites with the subterranean coalfaces edging ominously in their direction. These were far from relaxing years for the congenitally nervous Swain and his colleagues, for they had staked their reputation not once but hundreds of times on a solution whose validity had still to be tested. Then, by a freak of chance, in 1962 five CLASP buildings underwent the subsidence wave. Two suffered trivial damage; the rest were unscathed. Heathcote took the one case which could prove that the structure had met all the necessary conditions, a three-storey block at Heanor Gate School in Derbyshire (Fig. 6.16), as the basis for a definitive technical exposition of the CLASP structural system at a meeting of the Institution of Civil Engineers in March 1965. It showed, to universal relief, that the ideas arrived at by starting from first principles nearly ten years before and the risks taken to solve the subsidence problem had been vindicated. Millions of pounds of public money had been saved from being poured into useless, hidden foundations; and extra schools had been built with the money thus spared, for Notts had persuaded the Ministry to commute its subsidence allowance into extra cash for further schools.

Were the Brockhouse frame's special features, the spring-bracing and the rocker bases, really needed to combat subsidence, or were they unnecessary gimmicks, and might any pin-jointed frame of timber or light steel mounted on the same type of concrete pad have stood up to subsidence just as well? On the pure evidence of what did happen to the schools under subsidence, the spring-bracing may well have been redundant, as the Notts architects came to realize through gradual experience. Many of the Derwent schools built during Gibson's 'year of grace' were on subsidence sites and underwent little appreciable damage. But none of this was known at the time. That is why when, at an early stage of development, Lacey voiced a similar suspicion, Gibson would not go along with him. Without the confidence engendered by the 'special features', CLASP could never have been accepted by the Notts councillors, the Ministry of Education, the NCB, a visiting delegation of civil engineers, or the many other local authorities for whom subsidence was a headache. These are retrospective criticisms of a 'purist' kind, made at a time when the CLASP system had proved itself and commanded power and widespread acceptance. In 1957 it was a small, intrepid experiment which needed all the security it could get.

6.16. Heanor Gate Secondary Modern School, Heanor, Derbyshire, main classroom block in 1986. One of the first CLASP buildings to undergo subsidence, it was chosen by Lister Heathcote to study how well the system stood up.

## THE CLASP CONSORTIUM

By the time that Bancroft Lane was complete and years before the frame had passed the imponderable test of the subsidence wave, the new Notts system had outgrown its origins as a parochial, nameless method of school-building to combat mining subsidence. It had turned into CLASP—the Consortium of Local Authorities' Special Programme. How did this occur?

Successful innovations must enjoy luck and good timing, and so it was with CLASP. When technical development on the Notts system began in 1955, it seemed to the leaders

7. Barnby Road Infants School, Newark, Notts. Trevor Prosser, job architect, 1957–8. Mature use of the early CLASP vocabulary.

8. A corner in the Barnby Road Infants School, showing Nottinghamshire's homespun versions of the wooden furniture designed by David Medd for Herts
   the MoE.

Plate XIII.   Exterior of the CLASP Triennale School built at Milan, 1960.

Plate XIV.   Interior of the CLASP Triennale School at Milan, over-zealously cluttered up with objects to catch the visitors' attention and impress upon them the info
ality of English educational arrangements.

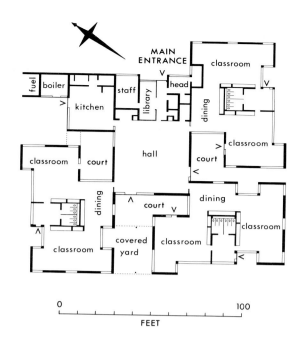

6.19. James Peacock Infants School, Ruddington. A small school of 1966–7 showing Nottinghamshire's mature approach to the planning of CLASP primary schools. Classrooms in clusters of two sharing a common dining space lead off from the hall, with open pockets in between.

of the school-building movement a throw-back, an anachronism. In the aftermath of war, Herts had spread its favours among a variety of manufacturers whom its architects had bullied into developing and supplying the components they wanted. Once the building industry had settled down, Stirrat Johnson-Marshall, Anthony Pott, and their administrative counterparts in A & B Branch changed tack and settled for a series of controlled partnerships with one or two industrial sponsors as the only means of building enough schools in the re-established capitalist Britain of the 1950s. Hence the Ministry's experimental schools of the early fifties. In 1955 the Ministry was in transition. Johnson-Marshall was growing restless, and Pott and he were vainly waiting to see the local authorities adopt the several systems which the Development Group had pioneered. They were sceptical that any local authority architects' department, beset by the burgeoning programmes of schools, could again find the time and expertise to do as Herts had done a decade before and alone command the interest and compliance of suppliers. Now Gibson and his architects were trying to do just that. The 'cocktail solution' of which they spoke was to be a system which Notts would originate, develop and control. Brockhouse, their chief commercial partners, were to play a smaller role than Hills had done at Herts; the firm was to supply the frame but not even to erect it, and it lacked the proprietary interest it enjoyed in the Belper system. In the Notts system as first devised, the only commercial incentive was the principle of serial contracting.

This may explain why at the outset the Ministry's attitude towards the enterprising Notts

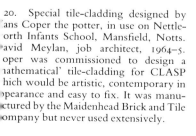

20. Special tile-cladding designed by [H]ans Coper the potter, in use on Nettle[w]orth Infants School, Mansfield, Notts. [D]avid Meylan, job architect, 1964–5. [C]oper was commissioned to design a ['m]athematical' tile-cladding for CLASP [w]hich would be artistic, contemporary in [a]ppearance and easy to fix. It was manu[fa]ctured by the Maidenhead Brick and Tile [C]ompany but never used extensively.

6.21. Early extension of the CLASP system. Fire and Ambulance Station, Sutton in Ashfield, Notts. Ralph Iredale, job architect, 1959–60.

architects seems to have been lukewarm. Gibson at an early stage invited Pott to help in beating the subsidence problem, but having satisfied himself that Notts was making good progress on its own, Pott declined to bring in the Ministry's Development Group. A little later, when Notts was starting to co-operate with other local authorities, Johnson-Marshall advised Swain and Lacey against a wider permanent arrangement, on the grounds that development would be difficult to control and the calibre of staff in other authorities could not be guaranteed.

The historic collaboration with other local authorities arose from a point which seemed to confirm the Ministry's view of things. Midway through the early development, Brock-house contacted Notts and told them that the schools programme which they had scheduled for 1957–8 was simply too small for them to proceed. Gibson's reaction was spontaneous. He picked up the phone and made calls to two allies: to Hamer Crossley, the county architect of Derbyshire, and to John Barker, the schools architect at Coventry. Both were authorities afflicted with subsidence problems and aware of what Notts was up to. Barker in particular was in close touch with Gibson, Swain and Lacey and had shown an informal interest already in somehow joining up with the Notts development, since Coventry was already familiar with Brockhouse schools and had been left in the lurch without an established system when the Bristol Aeroplane Company gave up school-building (p. 140). Gibson's question was this: could they chip in with a school or two from their 1957–8 programmes, and offer a little help in designing components in return? Quite quickly the answer came back: they could. In none of the three authorities did the architects encounter obstruction from officers or councillors over this unprecedented step. The hope of help on an experimental scale with the vexed problem of subsidence was enough to offset anxieties about loss of autonomy. Once again, opportunism in school-building had been rewarded.

These three partners therefore came together on the later stages of early development, under the command of Notts and without formal agreement. Neither the name of CLASP nor the term 'consortium' had yet been invented, but the prospect of spreading the work, saving on manpower and getting hitherto undreamt-of economies of scale had suddenly become thinkable. The Notts architects now set about finding collaborators in other coal-mining areas. The idea proved easy to sell. Most county and city architects tended to view such a school-building partnership between local authorities as a convenience, a mere help for them in building their programmes. But a few—Stephen George at Leicester was one—saw it unselfishly as an idea with great potential.

By now the Ministry had been drawn in again. The take-up of the Ministry-sponsored schools had been only one-fifth of what was anticipated; a fresh minister, Lord Hailsham, was at the helm from January 1957; and Pott and Pile had been promoted to head A & B Branch in succession to Johnson-Marshall and Nenk. The time had come for a new method of organizing school-building.

The age of the consortium dawned on 24 July 1957, when Hailsham presided over the inauguration of CLASP. Notts, Derbyshire, Coventry, Durham, Glamorgan, the West Rid-

ing of Yorkshire and Leicester City, all authorities with subsidence problems, pledged fealty at this meeting and swore to build schools to a collective value of 2.87 million pounds in the new CLASP system in 1958–9. Hailsham contributed the word 'consortium' (pronounced, to the architects' and mandarins' perplexity, in the judicial way, as 'consorshum'), plus the inducement of converting the old subsidence allowance into a bonus for authorities who used the system. The happiest feature to the arrangement was its informality. Lest local authorities should fear loss of power, CLASP began without legal standing, cumbrous bureaucratic rules, or permanent staff. Because the system was a vocabulary, the architects to the local authorities availed themselves of standard details and could, if they wished, contribute to the evolution of the 'language', but they continued to design their own schools. Tenders for supplying components were arranged across the whole consortium, but main contracts were always with individual members. An authority could entrust most of its building programme to CLASP, as Notts tended to do (Fig. 6.21), or merely a reasonable proportion. And until 1961, when a CLASP Development Group was set up, the lion's share of administrative work was done at Notts for a nominal fee.

CLASP was always a different animal from the later school-building consortia. It started earlier, it grew to be bigger, and it has lasted longer. Its originators saw it as a way of promoting a philosophy of building in quantity which could fulfil the old Herts ideals about production, collaboration, development and use. The later consortia were mostly contrived geographical groupings with little of this ideological baggage. Further, CLASP grew spontaneously out of a specific opportunity created by the subsidence crisis. So it suited other places where the same difficulties obtained. The Brockhouse spring-loaded frame not only solved a pressing problem and saved money; it also forged another bond between scattered regions of the country already linked (and scarred) by a common industrial history. Many of the elected councillors in the coalfield authorities which came together in the CLASP collaboration were miners. Some already knew each other through the National Union of Mineworkers, others had some practical experience of subsidence, and all could grasp the scale and implications of the problem. This shared background meant that CLASP enjoyed solid political backing from the member authorities in its crucial early years. Because of its special features, local authorities in mining areas had every incentive to extend CLASP to their other larger buildings: police stations, fire stations, ambulance stations, law courts and so on. If the system was confined at first mainly to schools, that was because the overwhelming building priorities up to the mid 1960s were for schools. Some authorities, too, felt that the schools must undergo trial by subsidence before they wantonly let CLASP loose on other more complicated structures, particularly inhabited buildings.

## GLIMPSES OF THE FUTURE

In the early 1960s it seemed for a moment as if CLASP might represent the breakthrough

6.23. CLASP in military mould. Army Pay Corps Building, Worthy Down, Hampshire (designed by Robert Matthew, Johnson-Marshall and Partners (Michael Keyte and Hugh Morris, job architects) for the War Office (chief architect, Sir Donald Gibson), 1959–60.

in a socially owned and controlled form of industrialized building long ago dreamt of by Wells and Bernal. The horizons of the system were expanding all the time. The consortium had grown to the limits of manageability and was starting to spawn others, with the Ministry of Education as the willing, admiring midwife. In 1961 the Ministry, *pour encourager les autres*, published a building bulletin called *The Story of CLASP* which explicitly traced its pedigree back to the early work at Herts and the policies of A & B Branch. That same year, CLASP set up its own independent development group under the architectural leadership of Sydney Bell of Notts—the upshot of difficulties experienced in carrying out the first major overhaul of the system, leading to Mark III, by the process of to-ing and fro-ing between several different local authorities. Meanwhile, a CLASP school built at Milan for the Triennale in 1960 (Fig. 6.22; Plates XIII,XIV) had won publicity, plaudits and awards and made even the educationally more rigid nations of Europe curious about British school-building; the prospect of export orders in Germany and Italy put CLASP even higher in government favour.

As always in the tightly knit world of public-sector building, old friends did much to help. Donald Gibson, promoted to the War Office in 1958 after only three years at Notts, brought his new department into the consortium and, with it, an entirely new set of needs (Fig. 6.23); while Stirrat Johnson-Marshall, converted by CLASP's success into its warmest admirer, badgered his colleagues in private practice into extending the system for building nothing less than a university, at York (see Chapter 8). With York under way, a complicated collaboration linking the private and public sectors and known as the CLASP Joint Development Programme was to follow. This would stretch the CLASP frame to its uttermost limits, putting heavy as well as light construction within its grasp. In less than a decade, CLASP had come further towards offering a real breadth of alternative vocabulary for architecture than any preceding system. Logic demanded that expansion must continue: a revolution in building technique seemed around the corner at last.

Hindsight can supply the glib reasons why this faith was mistaken. The peculiarities which made CLASP strong and successful obscured the fact that it was 'bucking a trend'. It came into being just at the time when the building industry was settling down after the long-drawn-out years of post-war shortages and controls. A movement away from systems was just beginning, and though it was stemmed for many years through the creation of the various consortia based upon CLASP's success, the arguments for prefabricating schools were never as clear-cut as they had been in the 1940s, except in special circumstances like those of mining subsidence. Labour and materials could still be hard to find in the 1960s, but the shortages in capacity were patchy and sporadic. Local-authority architects had a decade of varied building experience behind them, and though some departments were still weak and grateful for help, others were less easily persuaded to submit to the binding discipline of an industrialized vocabulary. Private architects had always been jealous of their individuality, and were now more powerful than they had been in the post-war decade.

Deeper lay the vexed issues of economy, productivity, efficiency and value for money. As the better school-building authorities learnt under the pressure of cost limits to apply elemental cost planning to all types of design, it became increasingly hard to ascribe successes in this field to prefabrication alone. Notts, for example, under the successive command of Gibson (1955–8), Lacey (1958–64) and Swain (1964 to date), grew from a sluggish authority into one of the most productive building outfits in the country. The invention of CLASP and the county's readiness to commit virtually the whole of its building programme to that system were tremendous spurs to concentration and efficiency. In the early years of CLASP, designing was a formidable discipline: 'it was a sin of the first order to design a "job-special"', remembers Meikle. But how far were these virtues due to the system or to the broader resolve to run the office with a clear-headed, consistent philosophy of building? *The Story of CLASP*, based on the consortium's first four years, claimed impressive economic advantages for the system, among them the annual competitive tenders for components, serial contracting, and elemental bills of quantities. Two of these techniques could apply outside the world of systems, while serial contracting was not even universal within the CLASP consortium. Though the 'club rules' obliged authorities to use CLASP for a proportion of their work, few members cared to go as far as Notts had done, and for them the benefits of serial contracting were less certain. Notts, the founder, has always been dominant ideologically in CLASP. Second in importance were Derbyshire and the West Riding of Yorkshire, counties adjacent to Notts and with large building programmes and strong educational traditions of their own. These three authorities constituted the 'inner circle' of CLASP, and stood to gain most from the economies of scale offered by its bulk-tendering and serial-contracting procedures. Such economies were certainly made all through the 1960s, when building programmes were full and prices had not risen beyond control. But in the event, the great victory over costs which was still anticipated in the early 1960s from the mass production of components never took place. CLASP and the other consortia were able to keep their heads above water because of their size, but by the end of the decade the tables had turned. Prefabrication had revealed its own inflexibilities and drawbacks, just as traditional building had done twenty years before.

## RESEARCH INTO SITE MANAGEMENT

By the mid 1960s, then, prefabrication was proving to be far from a panacea. But among architects, it remained true that only those who had been drawn to programmes and systems had the courage to confront some of the more fundamental issues of modern building. Cost planning had been a fruit of this in the 1950s. And in 1967, with CLASP at the peak of its repute, Notts took a further bold step with its experiment known as 'Research into Site Management' (RSM). It was to last seventeen years before it closed down in the face of the cold wind of reaction in 1983.

Co-operative endeavour had been the watchword of the movement started by Johnson-Marshall at Herts. In any large programme of building, its proponents held, lasting improvements could only occur if designers worked continuously alongside clients, users and makers. Encouraging progress had been made, at least in schools, with clients and users. But to come close to the makers seemed harder. Prefabrication had attracted because it took much of the making away from the site, where conditions were messy, confused and fragmented, and entrusted it to manufacturers with whom architects could deal more coherently. It seemed in the 1940s only a mark of progress and civilization to lure workers away from the mud and wet and install them in a warm, dry factory.

Two decades of experience had exposed the weaknesses of this faith. Despite their best efforts, the architects and their fellow-professionals had shifted much less work away from the site than they had hoped. Even in that amount, benefits only accrued when they could work directly and regularly with nominated sub-contractors. But many sub-contractors answered to the main contractor alone. The tangle of relationships between architect, builder and the sundry sub-contractors had delayed some of the early Herts schools. Meanwhile the great residue of site operations showed no signs of diminution, as the Ministry of Education's bulletin on the subject, *Site Labour Studies in School Building* (1955), had had ruefully to admit. It was hard enough to try and make work on site more efficient, competent, safe and humane, and well nigh impossible to improve standards from job to job, when the rules and vicissitudes of competitive tendering, insisted upon by local authorities as part of their fiscal duty to ratepayers, meant that the contractor for one school might not build another with the same architects for several years. In such circumstances there could be no prolonged exchange of information, no opportunity to store up experience. This predicament, the gap between hand and brain, was exacerbated by the bad old British class system, rampant as ever in the 1950s. The caricature of the architect in his suit and tie self-consciously donning shiny boots to tour the site with the builder, half-feigned authority on one side meeting half-guarded hostility on the other, still rang true.

From the start of CLASP, the Notts county architects did what they could to improve this. They soberly acknowledged that the root-and-branch reform of the building industry envisaged in the 1940s was too vast a task even to contemplate. For the time all that could be tried were some careful, local experiments. Donald Gibson, as has been said, instituted a policy of serial contracts for schools to clear a backlog of work. Serial contracting, whereby builders tendered for a string of jobs at one time on the basis of a schedule of prices, was

6.24.  Henry Hartland Grammar School, Worksop, Notts. Alan Goodman and J. C. Stone, job architects, 1962–3. CLASP Mark III in orthodox use on a secondary school.

not wholly new. But a local authority could not use it widely, because it aroused charges of favouritism among local builders. Continuity, feedback and the chance of cumulative improvement had also to be weighed against the danger that a builder would grow slack, secure in the promise of jobs to come.

CLASP, with its new structural system and promise of long production runs, allowed the architects to venture beyond the crude device of serial contracts. Going on their sense of the local situation and their experience of building the Hills system at Herts, Swain and Lacey began by returning as much responsibility as they could for assembling the CLASP system to the main contractor. They hoped if possible to establish the sense of partnership with the builder which had never been present at Herts. The frame and the partitioning, for instance, were designed for the contractor to assemble, and so with a few exceptions were the other elements. At first many of the timber components, including the whole of the roof deck, were made by the main contractor as well. Thus the architects hoped to avoid some of the muddles that had previously arisen and foster feelings of responsibility and inter-dependence. 'What we set out to achieve,' says Swain, 'was a gang of men committed to building a building with a variety of skills, but starting building it and seeing it through to the end'. Serial contracting continued, but on the basis of annual tendering for a whole programme of schools. Local builders thus had the chance of entering the lists once a year. Simms, Sons and Cooke was the firm first favoured, but in due course various Nottinghamshire builders became expert in the system. Searsons was the firm which probably built most Notts schools during the golden years of CLASP.

As the CLASP consortium blossomed into a big organization the relations between architects, manufacturers and builders shifted. A conflict arose between the ideals of partnership and continuity, and the search for lowest immediate cost. Very good prices could now be had for components by organizing tenders annually throughout the consortium. This made it sensible to take much of the manufacturing back again from builders, leaving them as specialist assemblers. During, for instance, CLASP's first major technical revision of

6.25. Chilwell Lower School, Chilwell Comprehensive, Notts. Roger Beardsmore, job architect, 1975–6. CLASP Mark V deployed on a comprehensive school.

1961 (Mark III), the window-frames were massively rationalized (with outside encouragement from Bruce Martin). Some fifteen hundred arbitrary types, previously made by the contractors, were reduced to about twenty frame-units, manufactured for the whole consortium and assembled into different patterns on site. This process proved too drastic, as the new window-range leaked and rotted and had rapidly to be redesigned. But the principle of reduction and centralization remained, and was applied less drastically to other components. At the same time Syd Bell and the new CLASP Development Group started (with help from BRS) to look at the sequence of site operations in order to get greater efficiency by reducing site labour—a process culminating in CLASP Mark IV of 1966. This made the CLASP builder yet less involved. He could expect a predictable but low profit, he employed few skilled men on site and he made few independent decisions. Even a clause in the CLASP contracts offering incentives for time-saving ideas on site brought no perceptible response. Swain describes the situation thus:

> My picture of the drawing office was of the job architect ringing up suppliers and contractors and telling small local firms how to build CLASP. The job architect was effectively running the site, because although the contractor had quite a lot of assembly work to do, it was very much in the hands of the architect to get component deliveries in advance, and so on. It was the nature of the CLASP system to change the role of the architect from letting the contractor do the building while he did the design, to having by the nature of prefabrication to set the scene for the contractor too. Although under the terms of the contract the contractor was really supposed to have the power, in equity, since there were nominated suppliers, we had the power. It seemed to me that half the architects in our office ought to be contributing to the smooth production of a major British industry, not ringing up and complaining.

And: 'What we were not getting was innovation from the production end.'

After years of circumspection, Swain decided in 1967 that the only recourse was to go directly into the building business. His caution was realistic. Since the infant days of 'municipal enterprise' in the 1890s, some urban local authorities had striven to bypass the contractor and set up a 'works department' or 'direct labour organization', often with a measure of success. But they had always faced formidable political opposition, and the relations between architects' departments and DLOs had been fraught with suspicion and managerial difficulty. Like most county authorities, Notts had never had a fully fledged DLO, and it was unlikely that a newly created one in the 1960s could have withstood the enmity of local private builders. Only something more modest in its aims and free from political pressures had any hope of success. Swain and Alan Meikle, who was to be in charge of the project, careered southwards one night to ask Johnson-Marshall if he had any thoughts on the matter. They came away, says Meikle, with one clear piece of advice:

> In all my conversations, Stirrat Johnson-Marshall has tended to simplify rather than complicate issues for me, and has always left me with the most important single thought that I needed. He said: 'If you're going to be involved in building, then you must do this directly yourselves. You must put nobody between the architect and the men. If that is what you want to do, to find out how the designer influences building, how brain and hand are inter-connected, then you must shorten that to the shortest possible point. Ideally you would build your own design, but if you can't do that then you must have this direct relationship. Do not have site agents or anybody like that.'

The RSM experiment started in a quiet way. The notion was to take a proportion of the annual Notts building programme (seven per cent at most, and therefore modest enough to contain the envy of the local building employers' federation) and build it directly. The staff for the project consisted of a small group of architects, surveyors, technicians, accountants and labourers, all employed by the county architect's department. The 'professionals' were among the best available in the Notts office; they included, under Meikle, Henry C. Morris, Roger Cheney, Alan Willis and John Bennett. This team was set up so that in any comparison of costs it should not be sheltered from competition; equipment, office time and other overheads, perceived or hidden, were included. Essentially the purpose was pedagogic: to dispense with the normal hierarchies of building, to provide architects with the practical experience of building in CLASP, and to wrench from the sites the secret lessons which they had held for so long. It was a tentative experiment, confined at first to a year, then another year, then (so long as politics allowed) prolonged but scarcely widened. The buildings chosen were mainly primary schools: simple, familiar architecture on which the team could cut its teeth. A few old people's homes followed, but never anything on a grand scale.

Mistakes were naturally made at the start, through ignorance of organization and technique. On the early jobs, the primary schools at Cotgrave (1967) and Bingham (1967–8), nobody really knew what happened on site, says Swain:

> We started off with no confidence. We ignored Stirrat's advice and tried to buy in foremen. But when we realized they weren't any good for our purpose, our own men were promoted to leading positions and from then on, with joiners and architects, we were all right, it was a success.

Working side by side with the men on site and arguing out details of the job proved a shocking and maturing experience for many of the participants. Alan Meikle kept a diary of the first three years of RSM which records some unpleasant necessities. Site discipline had to be imposed, and sluggards who thought that public-sector employment might be comfortable and undemanding had to go:

> Alan Willis dictated the dismissal notices to Barbara and then we decided that somebody

26. Hollywell Primary School, Kimberley, Notts. Alan Feakes, job architect, 1981–2. CLASP at length submits to the pitched roof. This school was one of the last built under the RSM (Research into Site Management) experiment.

6.27. Women students at work, Ernehale Infants School, Arnold, Notts, 1969, as part of Nottinghamshire's Research into Site Management (RSM) programme.

ought to break the news to the men first. Henry Morris said Alan ought to do it. I said, 'Which Alan?'. Henry nodded at Alan Willis who was looking rather glum. I reminded him of our agreement that the man took them on was also the man who sacked them. So that was that.

It was even more shaking to realize that much preparatory work done by architects in their warm offices was useless at best and often a great nuisance. 'The discipline of doing things manually is that you try and avoid things that are unnecessary': that, in the words of Meikle's diary, was the overwhelming lesson from the sites. Simplification and clarity were the qualities which the builder needed on site and which the architect very rarely supplied. Working drawings were the worst cause of offence:

> They are intended for use by the architect on site and by the work gangs. This really should not need saying but we suspect that drawings are often prepared for the next man in line. Architects draw for the benefit of the q.s. who prepares a bill for the estimator and in the end the man on the site works from the foreman's interpretation of the drawings on a cigarette packet. Quite soon in the project we found that our ordinary joinery details had to be redrawn by the architect on site to show his joiners what he really meant them to do.

Time after time, the men on site at RSM jobs were able to show a better or quicker way of performing an operation. Because of the rigid demarcation of tasks, it had never found its way back to the architects before; or perhaps the suggestion had been made, but until the architects had helped to lay a yard of concrete or clean up the site, it had never sunk home.

On the strength of these lessons, fed back as a matter of principle into the next job, RSM settled down at Notts into a regular pattern. The preparation of jobs—cost-planning, organizing the sequence of operations and size of workforce, and so on—absorbed more time than before. But by contrast there were no bills of quantities, no tenders, no schedule of components and less working drawings. The sites, to the architects' surprise, turned out to be civilized and amicable places, not the profane, threatening morasses of their imagination. Women students were employed to assemble the steel frame at one site (Arnold Ernehale Infants School) in 1969—a rarity at the time which 'made *The Sun* and Radio 4' (Fig. 6.27). Minor decisions were left, as far as possible, to the last minute before building. 'Success or failure', declared Swain, 'depends very much indeed on deciding what matters are strategic and settling them at the beginning, and what can, indeed should, be left to tactical decisions on site.' The RSM sites and office practices were open for builders and others to examine, since it was part of the experiment to amass information and make it as widely available as possible. Swain lectured on RSM and the *Architects' Journal* published articles on the subject, but the architectural profession seemed in no mood to take much notice. Despite some encouraging figures on cost, Swain and his colleagues were careful not to make undue claims for RSM. They never asserted that RSM as a building unit was more productive than the best Notts builders, nor that it was exceptionally quick; indeed, one lesson had been to confirm the adage often expressed in the building trade, that 'faster building using more men loses money'. But they did insist that for any organization like Notts concerned in the continuous development and production of buildings, the combination of design and management under one control, as in RSM, could lead to greater overall efficiency, better buildings and better architects and builders. Searsons, the builders who at this stage were winning the most serial contracts from Notts for CLASP, were delighted to find that the experiment had taught architects how to run all their jobs more intelligently.

Officially, the RSM experiment was another phase in the refinement of CLASP. Its results were absorbed into the design and organization of CLASP Mark V, introduced in 1972, for which Henry C. Morris, the chief surveyor on RSM, in due course became the technical director. But ideologically RSM amounted to rather more. It marked the first attempt in Britain to integrate architects responsibly and systematically into the practical building process and to tackle certain persistent faults in the construction industry since Lethaby, Ashbee, Gimson, Blow and some other leaders of the Arts and Crafts Movement, had tried to do the same, more sporadically, around the turn of the century. The comparison is not fortuitous. Swain had been a Lethaby fan since his days under Furneaux Jordan at the AA. His RSM team were spiritual heirs to these pioneers in the sense that they were grappling, as Lethaby and the more radical Arts and Crafts architects had done, with the difficult and elusive issue of rational building. Lethaby and his contemporaries faced huge problems: the opposition of established builders, the demarcation between the professions, and the lack of continuity from one job to the next. Under the patronage of an enlightened county council, RSM had advantages over these, but it could not survive the apathy of the architectural profession in the 1970s towards ventures of this kind, or the re-emergent dogma of competition in its narrowest, most blinkered form towards the end of that decade. Faced with the prospect, under new legislation, of submitting all RSM jobs to the orthodox tendering process and making the unit conform to conventional rules of accounting, Swain let it die at Christmas 1983. The challenge of organizing an integrated 'design and build' team under proper social control remains.

Meikle's RSM diary concludes with a summary written in 1971, when he left Notts to become county architect of Worcestershire. It remains relevant today:

> What RSM has shown is that if the relationships between the people concerned with the building process are right then communications are no more or less of a problem than they are between any other people who are in the habit of talking to one another . . . To be a master builder should be the ambition of many of us, not in the eighteenth-century way, but working towards the twenty-first century in which problems of building both rapidly and economically must be solved if the increasingly large population of the world is to be housed in anything like a civilised way.
>
> If our profession fails to get this point we shall be pushed aside by the politicians.

# CHAPTER 7

# AFTER JOHNSON-MARSHALL

In 1956 Stirrat Johnson-Marshall announced abruptly that he was leaving the Ministry of Education. Robert Matthew, previously chief architect at the London County Council, was by now Professor of Architecture at Edinburgh University. On the strength of his reputation at the LCC, more and more private architectural work had come his way and he wanted a partner of equal weight to set up a London office. Basil Spence is said to have declined the offer; Johnson-Marshall accepted. Thus was born Robert Matthew, Johnson-Marshall and Partners, private architects and planners.

The decision shook his colleagues, some of whom openly thought of themselves as his disciples. No architect had shown more clearly than Johnson-Marshall that working in the public sector need not be a second best, but required special qualities of commitment, idealism and breadth of thought. Now he was going over to the vagaries of private practice, with its discontinuities, its hand-to-mouth approach, its preoccupation with image-making and, above all, its powerlessness. In short, the captain of the school-building ship seemed to be leaving in midstream. He even took with him two of the Architects and Building Branch crew, Peter Newnham and Maurice Lee. 'I felt the bottom had dropped out of my world,' remembers one architect. 'This was the key office and one felt it was kept going by his personality.'

Johnson-Marshall well knew that all this would be cast in his teeth. But he felt that he had done as much as he could at the Ministry, that circumstances were growing less favourable to the kind of working upon which he throve. At Herts, having changed the face of school-building in under three years, he had moved on; at the Ministry, having shifted attitudes to the subject throughout the country in less than eight more years, he must move on again before he became bogged down. His stated intention in joining up with Robert Matthew was to create a model of private architectural practice which would serve as a kind of 'third arm' for the public sector, taking up the new ways of working, experimenting with them and developing them in directions which local-authority offices were too preoccupied and cumbersome to consider. Higher education in particular seemed a promising field. 'Academic independence' being what it was, private architects were going to shoulder most of the coming load of universities, polytechnics and colleges of further education which would soon have to be built, as those with educational prescience could see in the mid 1950s. In the event these hopes were only in small part fulfilled; Johnson-Marshall never again found continuously worthwhile outlets for his energizing and organizing talents. This tends to make his departure from the Ministry look less logical than it seemed to him at the time.

## A CHANGE OF CLIMATE

The timing of the move was shrewd. From about 1954 the climate in which A & B Branch operated had begun imperceptibly to alter. In retrospect the watershed was the lifting of

1. Mies takes a trip to Norfolk. Hunstanton Secondary Modern School, Norfolk. Alison and Peter Smithson, architects, 1952–4.

2. Industrial finishes at Hunstanton: technology triumphant and celebrated, but subordinated to the priorities of teaching and learning.

building controls. From this point private commissions, private clients and private architects (Robert Matthew's growing firm was an example) clawed their way back to their traditional pre-eminence in British architecture. For the time being the public sector's workload was swelling. In terms of output, local-authority architects' offices had years to go before they reached the crest of their wave. But as they grew in size and experience, this presaged a shift in relationship between the wings and the centre. Gone were the early post-war years when bewildered school-building authorities begged what crumbs they could in the way of materials and skills from the table of central government. Henceforward the main route to further technical progress would come not from direct building initiatives by the Ministry, but from the pooling of new ideas emanating from the better authorities. Hence the rise from 1957 onwards of CLASP and the later school-building consortia.

The celebrated Hunstanton Secondary Modern School, opened in 1954, was a symbol that from now on the Ministry's architects were not going to have things all their own way. This school's origins went back to a competition of 1950, for which Denis Clarke Hall had been the assessor. At this time Clarke Hall was engaged on Woodfield Secondary Modern School at Cranford for the Middlesex County Council. Because cost controls had arrived and the county lacked spare acreage, Stillman, the county architect, had opted for larger, more compressed and formally arranged secondary schools than the Ministry cared for. Woodfield followed this pattern with some refinements of its own and the winning entry for Hunstanton, by chance or design, took the same approach to layout. Its authors were Alison and Peter Smithson, two young architects of aesthetic persuasion temporarily working in the Schools Division at the LCC.

When the Hunstanton school came to be built, the Ministry's architects were troubled by the formality and tightness (qualities less logical in Norfolk than in the cramped spaces of Middlesex) and unapologetic image-mongering of the Smithsons' design. It appeared (Figs. 7.1, 2) an arbitrary, individualistic essay in the Miesian aesthetic, in stark contrast to so delicately tuned an educational instrument as Wokingham. Its architects claimed that it not only fulfilled its educational brief but was also a handsomer, cooler, stronger design than any other secondary school built since the war. This the Ministry's partisans disputed. Etiquette required that the argument should be carried on obliquely in the pages of the *Architects' Journal*, which appraised the Hunstanton school before and after its completion. A leader of September 1954 by Colin Boyne began flatteringly on the planning and detailing. But then it lashed out:

Architects should walk into the assembly hall and the classrooms and see for themselves the gault brick walls, the exposed RSJs, the exposed rough pre-cast concrete floor units painted white, the troughed asbestos ceiling in the assembly hall, everywhere the exposed pipes and conduits, the black and dark brown thermoplastic floors, the unpainted, galvanised steel door frames, the unpainted, galvanised pressed steel switchgear, the calorifier pushed under the stairs, and the industrial, steel, light-shades. There is not one single piece of soft material anywhere in the building. It will be interesting to know the noise level when it is full of children ... Indeed, in that this building seems often to ignore the children for which it was built, it is hard to define it as *architecture* at all. It is a formalist structure which will please only the architects, and a small coterie concerned more with satisfying their personal design sense than with achieving a humanist, functional architecture. It is likely to prove an expensive venture into a blind alley.

'Architecture': here the hoary issue of meaning and intention, dormant since the war, raised its head anew. Did building only become architecture and take on meaning, as the Smithsons and their formalist friends believed, when it asserted something about itself? Or rather, as those in the Ministry felt, was modern architecture devoid of significance unless it enriched and extended opportunities for the citizens of a democracy?

It seemed sad that the two aims could not come together. A later and gentler article in *The Times Educational Supplement* made this point in comparing Wokingham with Hunstanton. It conceded deficiencies of coherence in the former but deplored far more the barrenness, noisiness and want of collaboration between architects and educators over the latter. Hunstanton, the author claimed, had also suffered delays because the Smithsons for reasons of fashion chose to use a special steel at a time of prolonged steel shortages. Charges—hotly contested by the Smithsons—were also levelled about the frustrations experienced by teachers in the school.

For A & B Branch, immersed in the raising of technical and educational standards, Hunstanton was no more than a passing irritation. It had no serious influence on school-building and the Smithsons never designed another English state school. But it showed the potency of style, so long suppressed in school-building. The cool, empty publicity photographs of Hunstanton made it a rapid *succès d'estime* and shot the Smithsons into the smart flight of British architects. Hitchcock, Richards and the rest of the critical establishment in architecture could warm to these kinds of image but not to the thorny, intractable issues of cost and building. Even the discerning Reyner Banham used the excuse of Hunstanton to pour scorn on 'educational sentimentalists'—a veiled reference to A & B Branch. Such was the allure of novelty.

For similar reasons there was a certain estrangement between A & B Branch and the biggest single school-building team of the time, the London County Council's schools architects. By the mid 1950s the LCC was in the throes of a hefty school-building programme. Many London primary schools of this period were built in an adapted version of the Hills 8 feet 3 inches system, which the hard-pressed LCC architects had been glad to take over for their own ends. But on their more prestigious programme of comprehensive schools, there was scant exchange of information and ideas. Johnson-Marshall had been instrumental in persuading Robert Matthew to scrap the old, pyramidal structure of responsibilities in the LCC Architect's Department and allow younger architects more leeway, but he had no influence on what was produced in the Schools Division. When Leslie Martin succeeded Matthew in 1952 he ran the vast department by giving individual groups of architects their heads, both in housing and in schools. Some, like the Smithsons, were budding *prima donna* architects of the re-emergent type, wedded to style and fashion rather than social objectives. In addition, Leonard Gibbon and the other educationists in A & B Branch found the LCC Education Department rigid, proud and unwilling to seek advice. The result was a series of one-off comprehensives, varying in style, quality and plan and having little in common besides the 'house system'.

To the branch, this incoherence in school-building by the country's leading local authority represented a sad shortcoming, summed up by the perverse but handsome Strand (later Tulse Hill) Comprehensive School (1953–6), a nine-storey slab block in curtain walling (Fig. 7.3). Like Hunstanton, Tulse Hill seemed to be the opposite of what a modern, humane

7.3. Tulse Hill Comprehensive School, Tulse Hill, London. LCC Architect's Department, Schools Division (J. M. Kidall, main job architect), 1953–6. Nine storeys of Hills patent glazing on the approved 3 feet 4 inches steel frame in order to cater for 2,210 boys on a restricted site. In the eyes of the MoE's architects, another aberration in school-building.

school should look like. To the LCC architects on the other hand, the Ministry for all its lucid bulletins and circulars seemed to stand aloof from their inner-city problems. In part because of political decisions by the Conservative Government, all the Ministry's early development projects were for suburban, green-field sites. The A & B Branch philosophy had been nurtured in the county of the garden city and it appeared as yet to have few messages for the urban school. It was a pity that this relationship failed to prosper, for in range of talent and commitment to a municipal architecture, no other authority could compare with the LCC. In the absence of such a close understanding, the Ministry's cost controls, always harsher on the inner city, seemed to bear down heavily on the LCC architects. Kenneth Campbell, then deputy schools architect at the LCC, remembers his division's view of A & B Branch thus:

> It's unfortunate because it wasn't fair, but we always felt that their major task was to try and cut us down on cost, that to some extent they were prostituting themselves to give the skinflints the ammunition with which to shoot us down, for them to cut down and to make schools tighter and smaller and tighter and smaller. There was a certain resentment among us. We knew it was for the best of motives, but we thought they were stupid to go on doing it beyond a certain point. There was a tendency therefore to scoff as each refinement became more refined, as space became double-used and treble-used and quadruple-used. There came the feeling that these chaps don't have to sweep the floor before the next class can use the room. So it was a very ambivalent relationship. But at the same time there's no doubt the lines on which we were working, particularly on primary schools, came from them, and we saw the advantage of the reduction in corridor space and the clustering of classrooms.

## ADJUSTMENT

The task confronting A & B Branch after Johnson-Marshall's departure was delicate. Given the growing strength and independence of local authorities, it had to shift the balance of its attention to educational problems without jeopardizing its leadership. Educational dialogue and experiment had always been integral to the branch's work. But as the post-Butler schools system came to something like maturity, as the children of the baby boom grew up and new fields of building endeavour like higher education hove into view, it became vital to anticipate demand; to select, interpret and test the proliferating body of educational theory on behalf of local authorities and thus guide them to wise choices. Technical issues of basic construction now began somewhat to recede in importance. But the branch had to keep on asserting its strategic role if it was to avoid falling back into a mere regulatory agency, as other government departments concerned with programmes of building still were in the 1950s.

All this took time to become clear. It fell to Anthony Pott, joint head of the branch from 1956 until his sudden death in 1963, to preside over the architectural side of the transition. The excitement of the early years, when an entire philosophy of school-building was being created, could not be sustained for ever. With the Development Group's crop of prefabricated secondary schools practically complete, some momentum had disappeared even before Johnson-Marshall moved on. Superficially, things ran on well. On schools, local authorities went on being advised, informed, encouraged and monitored; and the Development Group continued to build demonstration projects. But, for a time, there was also some uncertainty of direction.

Harris College of Further Education at Preston was a case in point. The Development Group's first venture into higher education, it took the best part of a decade, on and off, to build. Universities never fell within the remit of A & B Branch, much to their regret, but colleges of further education did. A building bulletin on the subject had been rushed out as early as 1951 and its revision was put in hand to accompany the job. The brief asked for a series of large extensions to an existing college. It was a hard job, therefore, in which to express a clear philosophy. Nor were the clients attuned to the intense, collaborative way of working which the branch embraced. To everyone's embarrassment the job got behindhand and the Architects Co-Partnership had to be brought in to help out. Guy Oddie analyses the mistakes thus:

> What went fundamentally wrong was that we tried to apply the techniques of observation that David and Mary Medd had applied in primary and secondary. We tended to assume that the architecture could play a role in technical education that was as important as in primary and secondary, whereas in point of fact its role is limited. In short we fastened on the wrong aspect of architecture for design. We were looking at things in minute detail instead of taking the broad view, instead of working out what kind of building form *en gros* is most likely to lead itself to the enormous flexibility that a technical college needs.

This self-criticism raises issues basic to the whole practice of interdisciplinary group-working as exemplified at Herts and the Ministry. If a good client could be coaxed to articulate his views, if enthusiastic colleagues in other disciplines and trades were willing to share in the vision of development, if a philosophy of teaching could be brought to life in a building, then worthwhile architecture might result. But if the project were too unwieldy, if no reliable and knowledgeable client could be identified or reached, if there was no body of ideas to interpret or develop into built form, what then? In traditional architecture, the architect imposed his personality, skills and design philosophy to fill the void. But for the A & B architects, to put personality so brazenly forward ran counter to all their beliefs.

In schools, the solution since the days with Newsom at Herts had been to identify the leaders in educational thought, translate their ideas into architecture and then convince clients to try them out. This essentially was how A & B Branch worked in the early days. It was often hard to find these 'leaders'. They were few in number, and the institutions which might have balanced this approach—the teaching unions, for example, or university departments of education—showed little interest in school-building. Probably the branch could have done more to promote such links. But before educational information ran riot in the 1960s, the branch garnered its expertise and enriched its ideas mostly through individual contacts: HMIs in the Ministry, enlightened county education officers, talented teachers whose names were communicated on one grapevine or another, and so forth. The process was laborious and often painful, as Pat Tindale remembers:

> The biggest conflict was between the people who were 'up front leading' and your actual client in the local education authority. You'd make tours round the country, you'd see all the leaders, you'd develop ideas about arts-crafts areas or what the future of science was going to be. You'd be enthused and uplifted by all that and produce some ideas. Simultaneously you would be talking to the client or the specialist in the county education office, and they of course would be seeing it in much more practical terms. There was then the hard graft, the bits of compromise between what they felt to be practical, and oneself not wanting to close off options about how the school might be operated in ten or twenty years.

The Ministry's work, in other words, both through its bulletins and in the schools it built, aimed for a high standard of imaginative teaching which might or might not materialize. In Oddie's words: 'Their determination to go for what they saw as the best teaching was questionable, because the best teachers were so different from the average teacher. So a lot of the influence of the schools has been much less and nothing like as good as one might have hoped.'

An example of this dilemma arose over the two village schools designed simultaneously by David and Mary Medd for Finmere and Great Ponton (1958–9). In 1955 the Ministry promoted an initiative on village schools, many of which had been sorely neglected for fifty years. After so many suburban schools, the change of scale stimulated the architects to produce a pair of sympathetic, simple buildings of somewhat Scandinavian feeling, with pitched roofs and intimate plans. Finmere (Fig. 7.4) in particular became famous as the first English primary school to carry through the logic of informal classroom planning

Finmere Village School, Oxfordshire. MoE Development Group (David and Mary Medd and Pat Tindale, job architects) with Oxfordshire County Council, 1958–9. The first English primary school with a semi-open plan, well and poorly imitated over the next two decades. The classes have their own 'bases' but share a common area in the centre.

Great Ponton Church of England School, Lincolnshire, shortly after completion. MoE Development Group (David and Mary Medd and Pat Tindale, job architects) with Lincolnshire County Council, 1958–9. A two-class rural primary school: infants to the left with a covered verandah, juniors to the right with a smaller verandah in front of a library corner. The space to the left of the lobby is shared.

started in the nursery schools of the 1930s and remove the barriers between the teaching space and the areas for other activities. Instead, it had an arrangement of interconnected spaces varied to suit groups of different sizes and purposes. Great Ponton (Fig. 7.5) followed similar lines, though its classrooms were not so closely linked. But the two schools had very different histories. At Finmere the Medds worked with Oxfordshire County Council, among the most enterprising authorities in the country. Together with the deputy education officer, Edith Moorhouse, an ex-village teacher with a rich, practical imagination, they 'observed' children in existing village schools (now a standard preliminary procedure), formed the brief and discussed every detail of equipment and placing. Finmere became Edith Moorhouse's special care. By appointing hand-picked staff, she was able to see that

it functioned in the way that she and the architects had envisaged; and by encouraging architects, teachers and education staff in the county to go and see it, she ensured that its philosophy contributed to the design and the teaching in later Oxfordshire schools. Finmere, after Wokingham, became the Ministry's most visited school. Great Ponton, by contrast, though designed on the same principles, was never a showpiece. It was a Church of England school, the education authority was more traditional in sentiment, and the headteacher first appointed used the building unadventurously. Though a serviceable school, it never became the outpost of fresh ideas of the kind which A & B Branch liked to feel it was scattering strategically around the country.

Another limitation to the exercises in participation and research undertaken by A & B Branch in the 1950s was that they rarely looked back. The few building bulletins devoted to individual schools came out soon after their completion and said little about how they were being used in practice. Such was the urgency of work, the need to get on to the next burning topic before the local authorities were inundated with programmes, that the branch had not yet found time to appraise in detail any of their own schools in use. The ethos of the Development Group was one of continuity and progress, and an architect assigned to build a secondary school would certainly go back to Wokingham or Worthing and try to fathom what had or had not worked. But the branch remained closed to anything more widely based. Preferring informal contacts with the 'best' teachers and inspectors rather than the nebulous conclusions of social surveys, they never had a picture of what the mass of teachers, let alone children, thought about the post-war schools, or what effect if any they were having on the ideas and psychology of children. In 1962 the *Architects' Journal* tried to remedy this last omission by asking a sociologist to talk to a selection of teenagers, half of whom had been to a pre-war and half to a post-war secondary school. The results pointed only to the familiar adage, that a good teacher in an old school was worth more to a pupil than a poor teacher in a new school. If architects were to design imaginatively and responsibly, they had to believe in the liberating, enabling and encouraging effect that good schools could have on pupils and teachers alike. Perhaps this was why no further surveys of the kind were carried out for the time being. Later, some 'user-based appraisals' of a few development projects were conducted and published.

## THE DEPARTMENT OF EDUCATION AND SCIENCE

Two developments of the early 1960s helped to dispel the doubts and to complete the transformation of A & B Branch from commander, vanguard and standard-bearer all in one, to the role of enabler, providing the cues and backing for others to be educationally imaginative and productive. One was the 'consortia' movement, the spread of technical partnerships between groupings of school-building authorities. The other was a renewed burst of educational experiment and activity which coincided with the return of Labour to power in 1964. From that point the previous pattern of energy and innovation went on unfolding for another ten years, reaching a peak in 1972–3; broader became the range of activities served and facilities provided by local-authority architects' departments; and richer became the skills which these departments could call upon from A & B Branch. For veterans in the school-building process, the integrity and intensity of their early post-war struggles remained a point of reference. They did not doubt that the schools built in those days were naive and simple vehicles, long surpassed in sophistication. But the same framework of operation, comprising development, research, user-requirement and building to cost, endured.

The origins of the school-building consortium have been examined in the previous chapter (p. 170–3). Here it is enough to say that CLASP, the earliest and longest-lasting consortium, was the only one to encompass broad social aims in the Herts tradition. Though its establishment in 1957 was formally due to the Ministry of Education, in most important particulars CLASP stemmed from the initiative of a single authority, Nottinghamshire County Council. But its successors, from SCOLA (1962) onwards, were more or less instigated by central government after CLASP had proved itself. They were intended to save time and money by spreading the expertise in prefabricated school-building garnered by the stronger authorities, and thus to give local-authority architects everywhere the chance of building more and better schools. The technical level of competence assured by the consortia also released A & B Branch's architects from the obligation to devise systems of building and allowed them to pursue more fruitful and strictly educational lines of research.

A flurry of coincident changes gave A & B Branch the sense of a fresh start in 1964. In that year the Ministry of Education became the Department of Education and Science, Labour replaced the Conservatives, and John Hudson took over as chief administrator to the branch. Also, following an interregnum after Anthony Pott's death, Dan Lacey (one of the two ex-Herts architects most responsible for promoting CLASP) left Notts to become chief architect to A & B Branch. Lacey came from a modest background and had started in architecture as an articled pupil. He lacked the charisma of Stirrat Johnson-Marshall or the flair of Henry Swain, his bosom companion at Herts and Notts. But he understood and could wield power, he was firm, energetic and thorough, and he had the gift of getting others to work together. He felt deeply that the principles inculcated by Johnson-Marshall were the only right ones for public-sector architecture. At all costs, he believed, the branch must press on with the task of making educational opportunities available.

Of these changes, the most invigorating for educational building was the political one. Under the ministerial hand first of the taciturn Michael Stewart, then of the debonair Anthony Crosland, Labour at last took the plunge and 'went comprehensive', a decision enshrined in the celebrated circular 10/65. The government also announced the raising of the school-leaving age to sixteen; this, like previous commitments of the kind, was deferred, but only by a year, until 1967. These two promises put fresh urgency into the search for a better model of secondary school, and in particular for means of dealing with the growing size of sixth forms. At this age, architectural and educational problems became similar to those faced in colleges of further education. The branch was also grappling now for the first time with polytechnics, into which some of these colleges were being transformed. With universities, the senior partner in higher education, A & B Branch's relationship was of a different order. University-building was in full spate all through the 1960s. But the prior existence of the University Grants Committee, a body with its own ways of doing things, and the jealousy with which academics defended their privileges and independence, made it hard to get them to spend their sudden shower of gold with the consistency and humility shown in school-building. Nevertheless the branch's influence was felt in university-building in several ways: through the recruitment of ex-A & B staff (Guy Oddie, Robert Castle Cleary and Clive Wooster) to the small architectural team that advised the UGC; through the consequent adoption of certain A & B criteria on cost there; and through the choice for a few universities, notably York, of architects who believed in the approach to building pioneered in the branch. The nearest that the branch got to working directly on the new universities was through its membership, in a team led by John Kay, of the CLASP Joint Development Programme of 1966–8, whose purpose was to upgrade the CLASP system for use in heavily serviced or loaded university and college buildings like laboratories and libraries.

Under Lacey and Hudson, with John Kitchin and John Kay as assistant chief architects, the branch did its best to apply the old philosophy of development and partnership to this diffuse pattern of activity. It was by now an accepted constituent of the DES and suffered no longer from the entrenched suspicion which Johnson-Marshall had met fifteen years previously; its methods were valued, and until 1970 it rode the tide of renewed educational initiative. After the lull of the early sixties the Development Group started building more projects again, but on a footing of greater equality with local authorities. Previously the Ministry's hand had been dominant in design, once a brief had been hammered out. With the structural technicalities of schools in the hands of the consortia, the group was mostly content to use whichever mode of construction the authority in question subscribed to. In its interventions in orthodox school-building, technical needs now came second to educational development. Much technical work still went on, but it was more specialized and supportive and impinged most on the extra building types with which the branch was also now involved. One team investigated laboratories (in ostensible independence from the DES, to placate the jealous universities), another took on sports buildings, while a third looked at the problems of polytechnics. Often these enquiries bore fruit in some building venture, like the Science Department at Bristol Polytechnic or the Student Union at Leicester Polytechnic. But the advisory and information-gathering side to this work was almost more important. By now the relationship between A & B Branch and the local authorities was firm enough for the latter to call confidently upon the branch for data or research, if they cared to. The building bulletins went on mounting up quietly, but there was less missionary zeal about their language and production.

In terms of building philosophy, the most important technical work of these years concerned 'performance specifications'. Like cost analysis and cost planning, this innovation sprang from the techniques of systems-building but had repercussions far beyond the world of systems. A performance specification defines a portion of a building or a component not in precise terms of design—what it looks like—but in terms of performance—what it can do. Most architects were (and are) attuned to the belief that the designer can and should control every basic product or unit in a building above a certain size. Thus when the Herts architects invented their own 'language' of school-building, they translated their understanding of their clients' and users' needs into specifically designed components, each made exclusively for their system by a single manufacturer. This relationship between designer and maker encouraged monopoly and led to a 'closed' system of building. Broadly speaking, CLASP and the other early consortia perpetuated these arrangements. But in the mid 1960s, with the consortia in full swing and the building programmes riding higher than ever, mutterings about favouritism and inflexibility made themselves heard. The performance specification was a response to this. For certain items which were similar everywhere, like internal partitions, it now became possible to lure manufacturers with the size of the programmes and specify standards of performance on the basis of which they could tender varying solutions and offer local authorities a real choice of appearances, materials and even structure. To write these specifications well required minute co-ordination of educational and technical knowledge on a national scale. This task fell naturally to A & B Branch. But it was the Consortium for Method Building, the west-country grouping, which took this approach furthest off the ground and made most progress in Britain towards an open system of building, in which the designer could take advantage of a choice of guaranteed products and solutions.

## FURNITURE

The development of British school furniture through the DES in the 1960s and '70s shows how the principle of the performance specification could work in tandem with the design of a specific 'product range'. No clearer example could be given of the science of development central to all A & B Branch's work: the laying-down of general principles, guidance and advice combined with empirical investigation and experiment. It seems self-evident that the two should go together, yet in post-war architectural practice they have been more commonly divided.

We have seen how David Medd, Oliver Cox and others embarked upon the basis of a range of primary-school furniture at Herts (pp. 91–2). Piece by piece, Medd added to the range all through the early schools of the Development Group. It drew upon the Birmingham Anthropometric Survey of Zuckerman and Clements, which amassed data previously guessed at, assumed or unknown about the size, shape, reach and movement of schoolchildren, and upon dialogue with the British Standards Institution's committee on school furniture and the Furniture Industry Research Association. By the time of the Woodside Junior School at Amersham (1956–7) the range comprised several types of table (the locker-desk, common habitat of the inter-war schoolchild, having been roundly condemned because it confined movement and led to poor posture), chairs, benching, locker and storage units and various moveable trolleys and bins on castors (Fig. 5.37). At Eveline Lowe Primary School, Camberwell (1965–6), Medd took development on to the point where a virtually complete 'language'

7.6. Civilized mealtime in groups at Eveline Lowe Nursery and Primary School, Southwark, London. DES Development Group (David and Mary Medd, John Kay and Norman Reuter, main job architects) with GLC architects for the Inner London Education Authority, 1965–6.

of primary-school furniture existed. It was designed (Fig. 7.7) to encourage the modern teaching methods of group-work, activity and movement rather than inhibit them, as much school furniture tended to do. Some secondary-school furniture had also been designed, and the principles enshrined in these efforts were making their way slowly into British Standards—the equivalent of performance specifications.

Because the Development Group designed schools only sporadically and local authorities had their own traditions of school equipment, the furniture-makers had been reluctant to market the range. But the coming of the consortia, which enjoyed bigger markets and had provisions for bulk-purchasing, allowed manufacturers to take up innovations like this. In 1962 the Counties Furniture Group was set up in order to develop and buy its own joint range of furniture, chiefly for use in schools built by the new SCOLA consortium. This provided the germ of an idea which A & B Branch took up. The CLASP organization had found school furniture slow and costly to install, as well as uneven in quality. So it undertook to buy the Development Group's range if the DES would complete it and arrange for its manufacture and marketing. There followed a four-sided collaboration which took up much of Medd's time from 1966 onwards. It comprised the Development Group as the designers of the furniture; Pel, the firm appointed to make it; the Ministry of Public Buildings and Works (later the PSA Supplies Division) in whom ownership of the range was vested; and CLASP, which offered the original market. Most of the FORME range, as it was called, had been first conceived in wood and one of the reasons for the appointment of Pel, a firm best known for pioneering tubular steel furniture, was to adapt parts of it for manufacture in steel and plastic. Once Pel had taken over the marketing of the range in 1969 it spread far and wide, internationally as well as within Britain. At a time when British furniture was often dismissed for stodginess, this publicly owned, 'official' range (Figs. 7.8,9) made good headway on the European schools market. It did so not because it was smart, but because it helped teachers to use classrooms freshly and imaginatively. At the same time the example of FORME, together with the fruits of the branch's broader work on furniture, led to widespread imitation and thus to changes in the whole style of British school furniture. Had such a range been privately promoted, its secrets might have

7.7. Corner with a view, Ysgol Glant-wymyn (Cemmaes Road Primary School), Powys, Wales. One of a set of small community schools built to help revitalize depopulating areas of rural Wales, with advice from the DES Development Group. Montgomeryshire County Council (J. Richard Evans, main job architect), 1970–1.

been guarded; but because it was in public ownership the promulgation of its principles was earnestly encouraged. With the dwindling of school-building in the late 1970s the FORME range naturally dwindled too, but it had completed its work of influence. In this respect British school furniture remains an international leader. It represents another vindication of the Herts ideal, of the results that can be reached when policy, design, manufacture and development are consistently linked to worthwhile ends over long periods.

## COMMUNITY SCHOOLS

What was involved in the development of educational initiatives by A & B Branch in the 1960s? Many examples could be chosen, such as the growth of middle schools, nursery schools or special schools. But the one which most merits comment was the architectural response to 'community education', the movement for breaking down the barriers between the life of schools and the adult world.

During the early years of compulsory education in England, urban schools were deliberately distinguished and walled off from their surroundings; they were thought of as havens

7.8 and 9.   The FORME range of school furniture, developed by the DES Development Group in the 1960s and made by Pel. Above, fixed and heavier movable items; below, chairs, tables, etc. The transition from wood to plastics in this period of school furniture development reflected the economics of production.

of higher values and refuges from infection, physical or moral, all around. Slowly the British urban condition improved, and the better education authorities fostered evening classes in their schools. Yet this notion of shelter and separation proved recalcitrant to change. Though Henry Morris did his best to integrate the rural schools and communities of Cambridgeshire in his village colleges of the inter-war years (pp. 41–4), his arguments seemed for a time to have fallen on deaf ears. In the press of post-war school-building, Morris appeared almost forgotten. He still urged his case, especially in the New Towns, but he met with little success. Bristol, one of the first authorities to adopt a comprehensive policy, put the occasional library on a site together with a comprehensive school, and Oxfordshire experimented with the odd 'wing' for adult education. But most new schools still stood aloof on suburban sites, surrounded by a sward of playing fields, occupied for some forty hours a week during the term-time, then locked and barred all through the long holidays.

By the 1960s secondary schooling for all had been thoroughly enough established in England for the old anxieties of policy-makers to ease, and for them to see the folly of this enforced separation of childhood and adulthood. Morris died in 1961 but his ideas were kept alive by a handful of enthusiasts and disciples. Community education was a movement fathered by liberal county education officers like Stuart Mason of Leicestershire and Gordon

7.10. Chaucer Nursery and Infants School, Ilkeston, Derbyshire. DES Development Group (Dick Thompson, Graham Parker and Liz Berkson, main job architects) with Derbyshire County Council, 1973–4. A development project built in CLASP. Nursery and family centre to left, infants school to right.

Bessey of Cumberland who, in succession to Morris, were well placed to observe the wasteful compartmentalization of educational, social and leisure services. Leicestershire, for instance, began building on Morris's foundations from as early as 1954 onwards.

The example of Henry Morris was familiar in A & B Branch from the first. All its architects admired Morris's Impington Village College (Figs. 3.5–7), more perhaps for the novelty of Gropius and Fry's design than for its educational arrangements. Stirrat Johnson-Marshall knew Morris personally and at an early stage of the branch's history, while Morris was still working in Cambridgeshire, the Development Group nearly designed a college of further education for him. The experimental secondary schools built by the group in the 1950s from Wokingham onwards were all imbued with the idea, basic to Morris's philosophy, that older schoolchildren could be best taught if they were treated as responsible citizens with legitimate wants and habits, and housed in enabling rather than repressive environments. Beyond that, for the moment, they could not go; the schools remained schools only, distinct from the traffic of the world all around.

It was in the remoter, poorer districts where facilities were few and far between that the idea of community schooling first resurfaced. Cambridgeshire belatedly tended the flame by adding Melbourn Village College to Morris's pre-war four in 1959. But it was the Wyndham School at Egremont, designed for joint school and community use by the Cumberland county architects and opened in 1964, which most alerted educators, architects and administrators to the opportunities of the 'community school' and revitalized secondary-school planning. To the educators it offered a way to lessen the stultifying segregation of older children from the pursuits of adulthood; to the architects, the challenge of combining facilities for children and adults; and for administrators, the chance of making better use of the large and costly complexes, 'beached and stranded' on the edges of towns, which post-war school-building had spawned. In the words of Michael Hacker of A & B Branch:

> Society is no longer prepared to make available a set of valuable buildings and resources for the exclusive use of a small, arbitrarily defined sector of the community, to be used seven hours a day for two-thirds of the year. School buildings therefore have to be regarded as a resource for the total community available to many different groups, used for many different purposes and open if necessary twenty four hours a day.

For school-building authorities, the chance to put these high sentiments into practice came when the DES in conjunction with other ministries issued circulars encouraging them to join hands with district or borough councils, pool money and build community facilities within their schools. In this way, schools were able to get extra space and equipment without

196

transgressing the cost limits. The process began in 1964 with a circular on sports facilities; in 1970 the principle was extended to broader types of community use. These inducements set the bolder counties off in several directions: Leicestershire, for instance, into a range of 'community colleges' upon the lines mapped out by Henry Morris, Nottinghamshire into grand sports complexes within their CLASP-built comprehensives. Full-heartedly or half-heartedly, many other authorities toyed with community schools of one type or another.

For A & B Branch, integrating schools with other facilities was inseparable from the issue of building fitly for older children. In 1963 the Development Group had collaborated with Surrey County Council on a Sixth Form Centre for Epsom. But the Labour Government's decision in 1965 to endorse comprehensives and to raise the school-leaving age lent urgency to the problem. Henceforward there would be bigger secondary schools with more technical demands, and a larger proportion of older pupils who had to be reconciled to staying on at school. Only if adults used these costly facilities could they be justified.

It became the branch's task to plan a strategy for the physical changes in schools entailed by these policies. Converting schools into comprehensives was not easy, because no new money was reserved for the changeover. Many secondary modern and grammar schools were therefore thrown together and added to piecemeal over the years. This was frustrating. The school-leaving-age problem, on the other hand, attracted new money and could be tackled more robustly. The Development Group designed a series of units which offered joint facilities for sixth forms and adult education and could be tacked on to existing schools. In the event, most of the needed accommodation was built into new schools or special colleges instead. But the effort was the prelude to a range of pioneering projects with community use which the group designed. Additions to Maiden Erlegh Comprehensive School, Berkshire (1972–4) showed how to adapt a secondary modern to the new principles of organization while adding some facilities for adults; the Chaucer Infant and Nursery School at Ilkeston, Derbyshire (1973–4) embedded a family centre at its heart (Fig. 7.9); while the Abraham Moss Centre in a blighted inner suburb of Manchester (1971–4), amalgamated a secondary school, further education college, library, sports facilities and an old people's day centre in one enormous CLASP-built complex. Abraham Moss represents the furthest point in the physical amalgamation of different uses. In the next big project designed by the branch, a community comprehensive school for the Central Lancashire New Town, the various services and uses were scattered around in a kind of 'village' arrangement, as the architects stood back from the ambitious scale of the 1960s. The Central Lancashire project was never built, but its relaxed layout bore fruit in the planning of the social and

1. Victoria Centre, Crewe, map showing the relation between the centre itself, to the south of the Ludford Street school, and the town's educational and community facilities as a whole.

2. Victoria Centre, Crewe, isonometric drawing. The new buildings are introduced in the midst of the town between the shopping centre and the Ludford Street School, with pedestrianized circulation linking them.

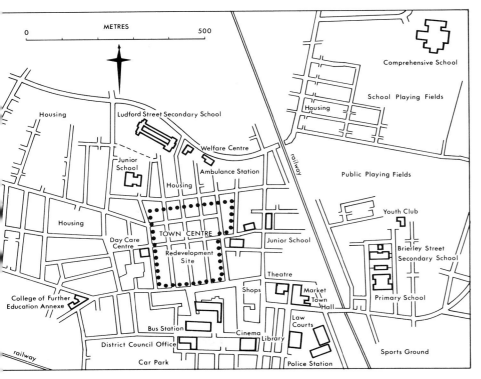

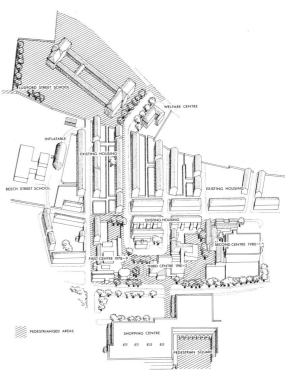

7.13. Tuxford Secondary Modern School, Nottinghamshire. Alan Goodman, main job architect for Nottinghamshire County Council, 1957–8. One of the first CLASP buildings to go multi-storey, in a school strongly influenced by Wokingham in plan and educational principle.

educational buildings at the Victoria Centre, Crewe, which are spread in modest clusters across a segment of the town centre (Figs. 7.11,12).

Most of the 'community schools' that mushroomed all over Britain after 1970 drew in one way or another upon these examples. 'Architecture' in any exalted sense was rarely the result, though the buildings looked for the most part smoother and pleasanter than hitherto. As in all its work of these years, the branch's influence was subtler than it had been. But it exerted influence still because of its strong, inter-disciplinary tradition of working and its habit of eliciting and expounding for others the pattern of activity that had to be accommodated in such complex projects. The principles remained the same: to promote educational choice and imagination, to show how if opportunities were seized, if the occasional puff in the political wind could be caught, the average standard of provision could be lifted.

The diversification implied by community schooling had hardly commenced when the slump in public-building programmes set in—the consequence of inflation, a static population and the cumulative collapse of political commitment to the British welfare state. This makes the movement hard to assess. 'Community education' is an open-ended term. Defined as the appreciation that to isolate schools makes scant educational, social or financial sense, it has an obvious future. But its hopes cannot be realized unless and until the winter of parsimony lifts and the British education service is again treated by central government with courage, respect and imagination.

7.14. Ordsall Secondary Modern School, Retford, Nottinghamshire. J. Griffin, main job architect for Nottinghamshire County Council, 1957–8. Another early CLASP secondary modern.

## NOTTS AND EDUCATION

In most places the movement of the 1960s and '70s towards integrating and civilizing the English secondary school was 'education-led', and so owed only modest debts to A & B Branch's pastoral hand. But one authority, Nottinghamshire, already the leader in developing CLASP, enjoyed peculiarly close ties with the branch and a continuing belief among its architects that conscious, consistent building methods could be used to open up educational opportunity—the old Herts ideal. At Notts therefore, the search for a better model of secondary school was largely 'building-led'. It is worth looking away once more from the centre to see how this process unfolded.

When technical work on what became CLASP began in 1955, relations at Notts between the architects and the education staff, it has been said (p. 164), were at low ebb. One symptom was the briefs for new schools, peremptory, standardized documents without latitude for imagination or discussion. A first goal was to alter this. Fresh as they were from Herts, Dan Lacey and Henry Swain knew it was crucial not to impose their beliefs upon mistrustful education officers. So they asked to be taken out by the education staff to spend time looking round and observing in what were considered the best and worst of the Notts schools, so as to fill out the briefs and get a grasp of local traditions of teaching. This brought the architects into easier, extra-mural contact with their educational counterparts and allowed them to get to know some of the county's best teachers. It required only that underrated quality in a good architect, to listen and watch, before teachers and education staff alike started to articulate ideas which had hitherto been dormant within them.

By degrees, allies began to emerge and strengths to be discerned. Notts had no leading

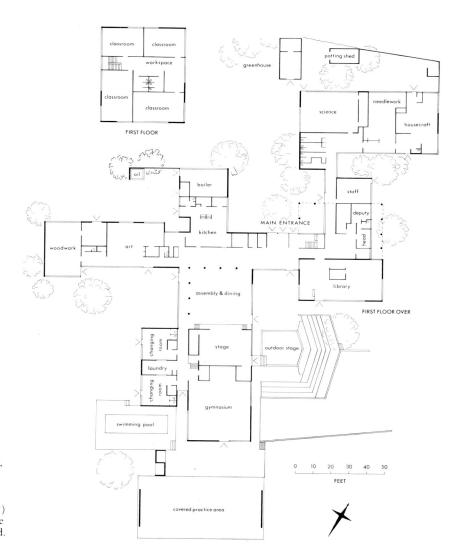

7.15. Ordsall Secondary Modern School, Retford. A Nottinghamshire secondary modern of 1957–8 on the Wokingham model, with sequence of hall, stage and gymnasium as at Worthing (Fig. 5.31) and covered practice area at the south end.

7.16. Arnold Grammar School, Nottingham. MoE Development Group (John Kitchin, John Kay and David Parkes, main job architects) with Nottinghamshire County Council, 1958–9. Prototype of 'Laingspan', the last of the experimental secondary-school systems sponsored by the Ministry in the 1950s. The 'barn' used as a sports hall is seen to the right.

educational figure ruling its counsels like Newsom at Herts or, for that matter, the powerful education officers in the three neighbouring counties, Mason of Leicestershire, Longland of Derbyshire and Clegg of Yorkshire's West Riding. Perhaps for that reason the officers and members seemed refreshingly open-minded. A particular ally turned out to be the physical education adviser, David Barnes.

It was in secondary school-building that Notts tried especially to make progress. The muddle of ideas surrounding this subject had by no means dissipated at the time that Notts began to build in CLASP. Notts was an authority which changed political control now and again, and neither the members nor the officers felt inclined to rush into comprehensive education. So the architects sharpened their teeth on a medley of small grammar schools and secondary moderns, influenced educationally by Wokingham but often arranged on a courtyard plan and rising to three storeys at most. Tuxford and Retford Ordsall (Figs. 7.13–15) were the earliest secondary schools of this group. They were meant to be unintimidating, civilized places where children could be coaxed into behaving like adults. The same principles applied when in the early 1960s comprehensives started to be built. Notts began by imitating Coventry and the LCC and broke down its comprehensives into units of tolerable size by means of a 'house system' of organization, but soon discarded this in favour of a sequence of specialized departments, distinct and apparent but linked by little social spaces.

So far the county's schools were respectable and alert to A & B Branch's experiments, but hardly exceptional. It was physical education which most stimulated the architects to be bolder. Early in the talks between architects and educators, David Barnes had remarked on the absurdity that the schools produced physically fit children, but that nothing was done to keep them fit as adults, while school games were often unpopular because they were regimented and over-disciplined, unlike the games for which adults showed an increasing preference. On the one hand, there was in schools the standard-sized obligatory gym for 'exercises' only; on the other, 'the tyranny of the national games', cricket and football, which were played outside. Barnes urged that the tendency in modern sports was a social one, towards tennis, skating, swimming, climbing, sailing and games with small teams. A decent secondary school ought to foster socialized sports of this type, not perpetuate the old class-linked barbarities.

Like physical education teachers everywhere, Barnes hankered for proper sports facilities and particularly for swimming baths in all state secondary schools. For the time the iron

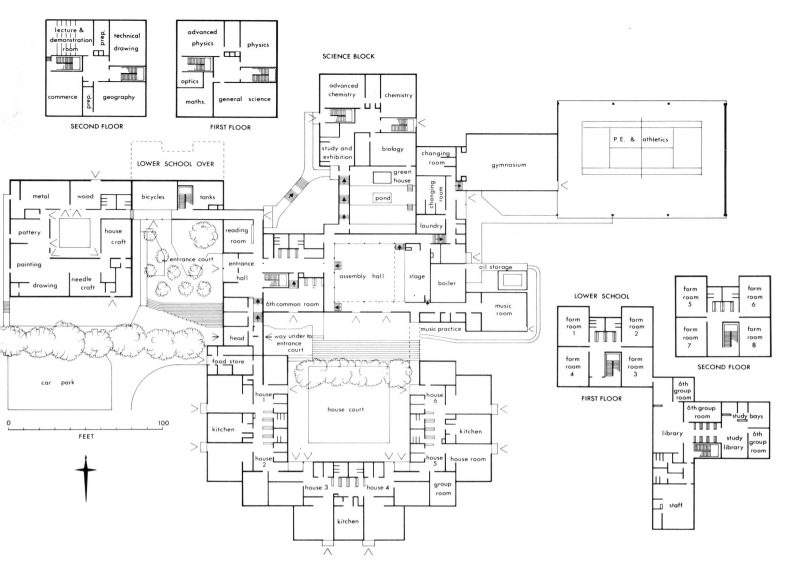

17. Arnold Grammar School, plan. A ew form of arrangement for 'maintained' rammar schools, with a 'house court' for rdinary classes and social organization, nd distinct spheres for separate special- ms. In the north-east corner, the covered ractice area for indoor games and exer- se.

hand of cost limits ruled this out, so the first reaction of the Notts architects had to be makeshift. At Tuxford and Retford Ordsall a pair of agricultural Dutch barns appeared, bought 'off the peg' and with the ends enclosed—an idea dreamt up between John Kitchin of A & B Branch and Alan Meikle at Notts. These were crude and cheap tools compared with what came later. But they permitted a wider range of games and the protection from the elements which most of these games needed. The same idea was used at Arnold Grammar School (1958–60), the last of the Ministry's experimental secondary schools of the 1950s where, as part of the campaign to win over the county's education staff, Notts and the Development Group joined forces in a concerted attempt to 'match social accommodation to the maturing needs of the boys and the girls' (Figs. 7.16,17).

When Dan Lacey ceded his place as Notts county architect in 1964 to take over at A & B Branch, the relationship between the two teams was further strengthened. In the same year authorities, urged on by an enthusiastic Minister for Sport, Denis Howell, acquired their first chance to pool education and 'district' money in order to build recreational facilities within their schools. Notts, now under Henry Swain, rapidly shot off along the path of 'joint use' towards the community school. The Dukeries Comprehensive School at Ollerton, where a theatre was grafted on to an expanded secondary modern, came first. Then in the late 1960s the austere 'athletics sheds' of Tuxford, Retford Ordsall and Arnold matured into the sports halls of Bingham Toothill, Worksop Valley, Carlton Cavendish (Fig. 7.18) and Balderton Grove comprehensive schools, replete with swimming baths and equipment for tennis and other games hardly acknowledged before in English state schools. Out went

7.18. The community school in action. Women's 'rhythm and movement group' in full swing at Carlton Forum, the CLASP sports centre attached to Cavendish Comprehensive School, Carlton, Nottinghamshire. Gilbert Mellers, main job architect for Nottinghamshire County Council, 1968–9.

the children late in the afternoon, at least those that did not stay on to play; in came their parents after work to supersede them, sometimes even to join them and compete with them. When that happened, the word 'community' ceased to be a piece of welfare-state jargon and took on meaning. The CLASP system had to be stretched to cope with the scale of these grand sports halls, which represented a first coincidence of practicality and monumentality in post-war school-building. Typically, Notts resolved to build all these halls in CLASP and design most of them 'in-house', so that the lessons of one should benefit the next and there could be a gradual gain and enrichment of architectural and educational experience.

The revitalized movement for community education reached a climax in Notts with the Sutton Centre, Sutton-in-Ashfield, begun in 1972 and built in stages up to 1976. Just as Nottinghamshire's secondary schools of the early CLASP era looked for educational example to Wokingham, so the germ of Sutton depended upon A & B Branch's preparatory work for the Abraham Moss Centre, Manchester. Over and above this, it required the support of a convinced educationist at Notts, Joe Stone, newly arrived from Stuart Mason's department in Leicestershire, to translate the limited concept of 'joint use' exemplified by the sports halls into a proper, integrated community school. But the architects were the unquestioned initiators of the project.

Sutton Centre brings together under one roof and in the very centre, not the outskirts, of a small mining town a comprehensive school, a crèche, a theatre, a recreation centre with sports hall and ice rink, a community centre and a scatter of bars and cafeterias. There were plans too for a civic centre and a clinic, but the health and district authorities stood aloof to the disappointment of the county council. Of the many schools and colleges planned in the burst of activity after 1970 which aspired to the 'community' tag, few ventured even half as far as Sutton Centre. Scale in itself is no virtue, and there are powerful arguments for the dispersal of services, especially in big cities. The strength of Sutton was that it argued the case for integration with a boldness and conviction which obliged others to take note.

Like many buildings in the Herts tradition, Sutton Centre (Figs. 7.19–21) is deceptive architecturally. It is built in the tight, mute, flat-roofed idiom of CLASP Mark V, with chip-faced concrete cladding and the odd peaked roof-lights developed for the system at

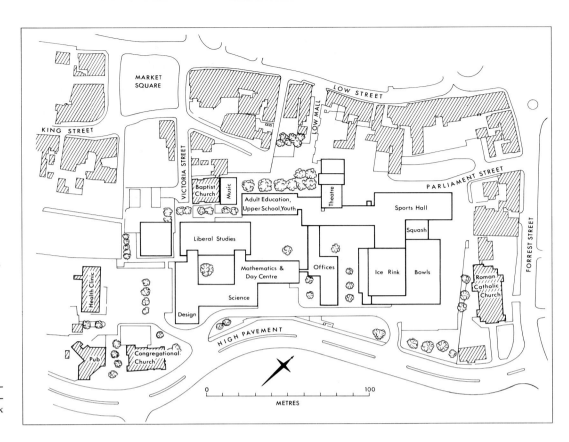

the time of the University of York. From the outside it could be taken for a shopping
centre. Inside, one encounters a warren of stairs, wells, corridors and meeting areas leading
from one seemingly undifferentiated sphere of activity to another. The critic bred to the
familiar architectural values of elevational expression and clarity of plan may conclude that
here was a job which did not exercise its designers greatly. Nothing could be further from
the truth. Nine architects wore themselves out over Sutton Centre. But drawing-board
drudgery was only a fraction of their labour. One motive in Nottinghamshire's long loyalty
to CLASP had been to free its architects from such self-absorbing tyrannies by offering
them a ready-made range of details, so that they could concentrate their efforts on the clients'

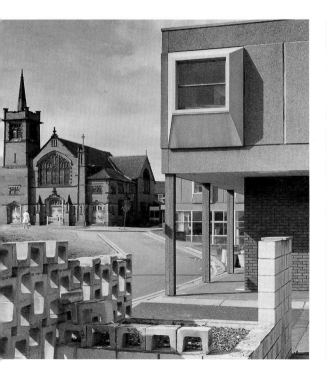

needs, opportunities and constraints. At Sutton the needs were more exacting, the opportunities more enticing and the constraints more contradictory than ever before. It was in exploring and reconciling these that the designers exhausted themselves.

In the process some startling novelties arose. Many were not in the province which people commonly call architectural, but it needed the architects either to suggest them or to translate them into something practicable. The most fundamental one concerned the siting of the building. Up until 1970 the intention had been to build at the edge of the town on a conventional, green-field plot. It was Alan Meikle who, following the trend set at the Wyndham School, Egremont, put the provoking question: 'Why not build the school on the vacant plot in the middle of the town?'. The facilities for welfare, recreation and entertainment followed on from this single, heretical proposition. For a centre which was within walking distance and of genuine use for most inhabitants of the town, local people were willing to sacrifice the time-honoured relationship between school and playing field. Once this had been negotiated, it became the architects' burden to break down the compartments of social, educational and recreational convention, so that different parts of the building could be accessible to other constituents yet could also function efficiently and quietly on their own. The children had to be able to share the sports hall with the adults in a reasonably co-ordinated way, and the untoward interest of a pensioner in one of the school workshops was not to be rebuffed merely because he or she wanted to visit it in school hours.

These were the tasks which taxed the architects of Sutton Centre. In the 'higher' architectural criticism they had little interest. If the plan confused the first-time visitor, they argued, that was because it was not geared to visitors but to the people of Sutton who would use it regularly and familiarly. Where mistakes were made, they could be remedied on the next occasion by building on the same basis. That had been the Herts philosophy in the 1940s, and it remained the philosophy of Sutton Centre and the A & B Branch community projects thirty years later. The difference is that so far there have been few 'next occasions'.

## RISE AND DECLINE OF THE CONSORTIA

In retrospect, the spread of the schools consortia during the 1960s looks like a mixed blessing. At the time there were few doubters. When SCOLA, the second consortium, was established in 1962, CLASP was already acclaimed; it had realized major savings and seemed by the scale and precision of its operations to presage a breakthrough in building costs, once production had grown a little bigger. Local authority chief architects welcomed the consortium idea because it seemed to guarantee a degree of freedom. Previously the Ministry of Education had pressed them to take on trust one of the proprietary systems originated by A & B Branch in the 1950s; now they were invited to participate with fellow authorities in designing and developing systems themselves. It hardly needs underlining which they preferred. Under the consortium arrangements smaller and weaker architects' departments, of whom on their own admission there continued to be many, could opt to pay a development levy and leave the actual design of the system to the stronger members. At the least, work was shared out and the load of development work correspondingly lightened; and once the system was established, the 'bank' of working drawings and details allowed the hard-pressed architects more time to reflect upon the planning and general design of their buldings. As long as the cost limits remained tolerable, as they did until 1970, there were distinct advantages to designing with the schools systems. And on the whole they delivered larger classroom areas, which educators and teachers liked.

In the conventional understanding of architecture, any system would always constrain 'freedom of expression', and it needed a certain temperament to accept this and seize the compensating advantages. Complete systems of prefabrication could be elegant enough on a small scale, when joints and components had to be devised to fit neatly together, but they never seemed so alluring or satisfactory when it came to composing the whole building. The close focus of systems-work suited the technically minded, but for those many architects who thought in terms of the single building and its appearance rather than the good of

7.22 and 23. Schools designed by the Consortium for Method Building, showing the choice of vocabulary at last beginning to emerge in school-building systems from the late 1960s. Above: Worle Lower School, Worle Comprehensive, Somerset, with ample use of brickwork, 1971–2. Below: Exeter Central Middle School, Exeter, Devon, in the more conventional language of the schools systems, 1975–6. The dimensional discipline, fenestration and roof zones are the same in the two schools.

the whole programme, its limitations were irksome. Some of the consortia tried to overcome these difficulties by building in a large number of options within their particular system. CLASP, at one end of the scale, was a tightly closed system with a clear function and philosophy and a limited vocabulary. 'Method', at the other, the consortium formed by Somerset and a number of neighbouring authorities in 1963, chose the small, internationally approved module of four inches (or ten centimetres), a variety of structural solutions and facing materials, and an open attitude about where the system should be employed, in whole or in part. A system like Method was not far removed from many rationalized versions of traditional building, in which the designer merely takes account of the materials and goods which are available on the market. With the plethora of components and materials and the growth of the performance specification and dimensional co-ordination, hybrids like Method were possible by the 1960s in a way they had not been earlier. Technically, the future lay with them rather than with the enclosed philosophy of CLASP, which adhered to the tradition of the self-contained system for most coherent development. In due course even CLASP was to succumb to the pitched roof and brick wall (Fig. 6.26) and become, somewhat sheepishly, more 'open'.

One further reason for the rounding-up of the counties into school-building consortia was that demographers were constantly (and wrongly) warning government in the early 1960s that a new explosion in population was about to happen. The local authorities were

already fully stretched in school-building, so it seemed only sensible to plan for production. With virtually every English county rounded up into consortia by 1970, it would be possible if the crisis came to step up production fast and thus avoid any recurrence of the old Crippsian threat of huts. For the moment, many consortium members put only a share of their school-building programme into their system. Only sixteen per cent of schools in value terms were built by consortia in 1964–5, and the highest figure ever reached was 52 per cent in 1970–1. But the option to build more schools quickly was there, should it be needed.

After 1970 support for the consortia dwindled, as the mighty public-building programmes fell away. While authorities committed more of their schools to the consortia, younger architects, unconvinced by the arguments about production, numbers and costs, grew frustrated by the fetters with which the systems bound them, especially in regard to the appearance of buildings. Periodical revisions of the systems were no substitutes for starting from scratch and designing something better, as many architects who had had no hand in the first development work itched to do. Some stronger authorities like Herts and the Greater London Council felt that they had done better when hunting singly than when they were dragooned into packs. Much depended on the strength and sensitivity of managements in the individual consortia. In the better ones like CLASP, SCOLA and 'Method' (Fig. 7.22–3) there was give and take, but in others gulfs of opinion appeared between one authority and another.

All this was reflected in a graver trend, the beginnings of a profound public suspicion and resentment about the whole concept of systems-building. Some of this was, and remains, rational; some of it was not. The differences between the heavy, prefabricated, contractor-owned 'panel systems' which caused such havoc in public housing, and the light-weight systems developed and controlled by local authorities through the consortia and used mainly for schools, are significant, but they have proved hard to explain and convey. Prefabricated schools have certainly suffered, though never to the same extent, from most of the faults experienced in housing: failing roofs, leaky cladding, inadequate insulation and high maintenance costs. All these drawbacks were coming to public attention. It was fruitless to show, as an independent report on CLASP did in 1976, that its buildings were 'no better or no worse than other forms of construction with regard to maintenance', or that traditionally built schools suffered too from leaky roofs, rotting windows and the new sports of vandalism and fire-raising. The upshot of a general policy of parsimony, of building too cheaply and for too short a timespan, of having shifted resources from the building 'envelope' to what went on inside the school—all this was suddenly cast in the teeth of the systems. The wrath of righteous reaction was heaped upon a symptom, not a cause.

Individual building systems devised for schools certainly turned out to have their Achilles' heels. The reputation of CLASP was deeply dented by a pair of fires which caused loss of life: the first at the Edouard Pailleron School at Ballancourt sur Essonne outside Paris in 1973, the other in 1974 at the Fairfield Old People's Home, Edwalton, Nottinghamshire, one of the earliest residential buildings constructed in the system. There were special circumstances in both cases; in the French fire, for instance, fateful modifications had been made to the system by the Brockhouse subsidiary which marketed CLASP buildings abroad—a process in which the consortium itself had no direct responsibility. But there had been other fires as well, less appalling in their consequences. The shaken architects had to go away and overhaul the system radically.

Inflation dealt a further savage blow to the consortia. As costs leapt upwards between 1970 and 1975 the whole building industry in Britain was cast into disarray. So cost-conscious already was the designing of school systems that a bare minimum was being spent on structure in order to get liberal floor space, decent finishes and good servicing. When inflation supervened, it was not easy to economize on structure by omitting a coat of plaster or thinning down the roof, as could be done in conventional building; spaces, finishes or services had to be cut instead. While cost limits kept pace with prices the situation could be contained, but in order to rein in expenditure the Government was reluctant to allow this. In these years the cost limits rose sluggishly, in line with the national rate of inflation rather than of building costs; they increased by 175 per cent between 1966 and 1973, while building costs rose by 257 per cent. Design teams using systems at least had the advantage of knowing

7.24. MACE and its causes. A jet flies over Poyle County First School, prototype for the MACE system, and adjacent to the west end of Heathrow Airport. The system was designed to reduce external noise. Surrey County Council, architects, 1972–3.

the price of their standard components a year or so in advance. But this still left them with stark and disillusioning cuts to make.

Thus the rational tool of cost planning and cost limits, forged by architects, quantity surveyors and administrators in local and central government in order to build schools responsibly, became a blunt instrument in the hands of the Treasury for slamming down the lid of the Pandora's box opened by a property boom. The quality of new schools was forced down. The average area per place in primary school-building, constant since the mid 1950s, fell to unworkable levels and took some years to recover. Again the systems were blamed. 'The use of building systems in a régime of rigorous cost control is rather like the introduction of the potato as a stable diet in a peasant economy', wrote the usually sympathetic Colin Ward in 1976. 'It reduces the peasantry . . . to a potato level of subsistence.'

In the midst of this crisis there took place a massive reorganization of British local government. This gave some authorities the excuse they wanted to withdraw from the consortia. The reorganization 'hurt CLASP most severely,' says Henry C. Morris, the quantity surveyor who took over its development group in 1974:

> It took away the powerfully run counties of West Riding and Glamorgan, and the resulting fragmented authorities seized an opportunity to 'do their own thing'. (It was an almost childish reaction; if one Metropolitan District adopted CLASP then its neighbour would do the reverse.) Two other authorities were overwhelmingly enlarged: Staffordshire, who seized the opportunity to withdraw from CLASP on the basis that newly absorbed Stoke didn't wish to be associated with it; and Lanarkshire, suddenly absorbed into the monster region of Strathclyde. All this led to a very unseemly scramble of professional people to get even more highly paid top jobs and the welfare of the community . . . assumed a lesser priority.

One casualty of this period is worth brief mention, to show what could happen to a system which grew in the wrong way at the wrong time. That is the *débâcle* of the MACE consortium. MACE, the Metropolitan Architectural Consortium for Education, was established in 1966. As its name implies, the bent of the MACE system was urban. Its technical brief was probably the most ambitious and self-conscious in British school-building since the days of Bruce Martin's experiments at Herts. There was the same search for elegance, flexibility and a 'universal junction', and the same urge for exactness, coupled with provision for easy maintenance and insulation against noise in cities (Fig. 7.24). The Development Group of the member authorities which designed the system in 1968–9 came up with some plausible technical ideas about jointing and components, but it was already plain that the system would not come cheap. Then came the test of production. At this juncture (1970) six of the member authorities pulled out, finding MACE too elaborate and technocratic for their needs. This left the Greater London Council, the Surrey and East Sussex county councils and a handful of urban boroughs. The Surrey architects were the main enthusiasts, but the consortium relied for its future upon the numerical strength and reputation of the GLC's architects (working on behalf of the Inner London Education Authority). By 1973 the GLC junior architects were in outspoken rebellion against the system. The effects of inflation had forced them to opt for the cheapest possible components, with harsh striated concrete cladding and a second-rate heating system. The vaunted flexibility had turned for the job-architects into a nightmare of rigidity. When the Edith Neville Primary School near Kings Cross in London was opened by Margaret Thatcher in 1973, the new headmistress inveighed publicly against the meanness of the space standards, to the ill-concealed delight of authority and architects alike. Shortly afterwards the GLC and ILEA resigned their membership and the consortium swiftly collapsed, having built just over a hundred schools. It was regretted by few. Yet there was not much technically faulty in the idea of MACE. It was merely a reminder that only the most thoroughgoing empiricism in matters of technique can make headway in times of economic pressure. Inflation and idealism make sorry bedfellows.

At the time of writing, the organization of school-building in Britain is still the same as has been described in these chapters. A & B Branch advises local authorities and takes practical initiatives, though it has endured intermittent threats to its methods, its ideals and very existence. After the trauma of the mid 1970s, it used its unique position in British government to campaign successfully for a restoration of the area per pupil to workable levels; and it can claim leadership and international respect in its approach to the new educational issues of the era of 'falling school rolls'.

CLASP and some other of the consortia survive, weakened yet wiser and broader in technical outlook: ready, too, should the birthrate rise or state education acquire a happier share of funding, to build schools in quantity again. Only the occasional school is being built just now, in districts of rising population. Architects have more time to lavish on these few schools, and they are anxious above all to make them more handsome and individual than the products of the post-war decades. With this estimable trend, for which Hampshire County Council is best known (Fig. 7.25), the remainder of the chapter need not concern itself. When the great programmes of building collapsed in the mid 1970s, English schoolbuilding ceased, after thirty years, to be at the forefront of the issues which are at the heart of this book—how to develop fair, imaginative and responsive means and institutions for building on behalf of populations as a whole; how, in a phrase, to create a genuine social architecture.

## THE IMPACT ABROAD

All through the 1950s a trickle of visiting architects, educators and others found their way to Hertfordshire, as to the LCC's Alton Estate at Roehampton and to the British New Towns. Some were lured by the ethos of what promised then to be in the making: a western version of social democracy, broader than anything that even Scandinavia could show. Others went to see the Herts schools for specific reasons. They represented the first peacetime programme of industrialized building of any scale outside the field of housing, and the first of all with a real claim to social or architectural merit. For many Europeans seeking redirection, the little Herts primary schools pointed promptly and convincingly forward. So small and primitive do they seem now that it is hard to recapture that significance.

Visitors studied the Herts achievement for many reasons, educational, technical, sociological and organizational. Among some architects there was even mathematical and theoretical curiosity. The grid-planned schools of the early Hills system afforded a first chance to see modular co-ordination in practice, bay-planned systems and standardized housing having done without it. Modular co-ordination could be easily linked to ideal proportion in architecture, a recurrently fashionable topic to which the advantages of dimensional planning, the theorizing of Le Corbusier and the historical researches of Rudolf Wittkower lent renewed respectability in the 1950s. Few of the education architects at Herts or the Ministry of Educa-

7.25. *(facing page)* Well-groomed children of the 1980s at Yateley Newlands School, one of Hampshire County Council's recent schools. Assured, relaxed, even stylish school architecture, yet strongly indebted still to the post-war pioneers.

208

tion had the time or the patience to ride this hobby horse far. But among the visitors was Ezra Ehrenkrantz, a young Californian architect with a strong mathematical bent. Ehrenkrantz spent some time at the Building Research Station around 1954 trying to develop a theory of number patterns as the basis of a universally applicable system of modular coordination, or 'preferred dimensions', as he called it.

The attempt fizzled out. But Ehrenkrantz, a persistent and persuasive advocate of his ideas, kept in touch with English school-building when he returned to the United States. In 1961 he fathered School Construction Systems Development (SCSD), a Californian response to the schools consortia movement just then gaining momentum in Britain. SCSD was a brilliant but limited technical experiment, geared closely to the American school-building market and to the urgent needs of California, where immigration was putting heavy pressure on the state's schools. In the United States, school boards covering limited districts controlled the building process, private architects designed all schools and had little continuous contact with clients and users, while anti-trust legislation made it unlawful for any one supplier to monopolise the production of components. On the other hand manufacturing was more diversified, advanced and flexible, affording a wider choice of components. At the same time Ehrenkrantz believed that English schools were too precisely designed. So he sought to relieve some of the pressure on Californian schools by means of a contained version of the English school-building programmes. Instead of a complete, 'closed' approach to design, SCSD adopted the 'performance specification' approach: in other words, it defined functional requirements precisely enough for suppliers to devise and make their own competitive alternatives for certain 'elements' or groups of components within the schools, notably the structure, the lighting and ceiling, the air-conditioning, and the partitions.

In the writing of these specifications, SCSD achieved a technical elegance far beyond the English schools consortia; in due course its example influenced the design of the ill-fated MACE system and the infancy of the 'high-tech' movement in British architecture. Every school had its 'custom-designed' envelope in recognition of the wish for individuality, and other elements like ground floors and foundations were left out of the development. This allowed architects and builders to take up some pieces of the 'system' but not others. But the products of the SCSD experiment (Fig. 7.26) were limited. The building programme in which all its elements were deployed came to only thirteen schools altogether. Ehrenkrantz tried to expand the initiative elsewhere. But the main successor-programme to SCSD, Educational Facilities Systems Development of Toronto, quickly foundered (like MACE) on grounds of cost, ugliness and a damaging exaggeration of the need for future adaptability. Though Ehrenkrantz was alive and sympathetic to the educational thrust of English school-building, the lessons of SCSD were in the main technical and procedural.

SCSD represents the most tangible fruits of a long interchange of ideas on school-building between Britain and North America. The 'progressive' teaching philosophy which lay behind the planning of the Herts primary schools had made as much (if not more) headway in pockets of the United States by the 1940s. A few British architects and educators knew something about the efforts of liberal school boards in the suburbs of Chicago and San Franscisco which had produced some cheerful, informal schools, memorably those designed by Richard Neutra. These were 'classroom statements' springing from Neutra's delight in simple timber craftsmanship rather than from a specific educational approach. And the mild California climate meant that their planning and details could hardly be translated to Britain.

Many Americans perhaps first heard about English post-war school-building through Antony Part, who seized the opportunity of a visiting fellowship to the United States in 1954 to speak and then to write on behalf of the Ministry of Education's methods; Gropius, originator of so much of the movement's technical ideology, attended one of Part's talks and growled his whole-hearted approval. There ensued a period of quite intensive to-ing and fro-ing. One or two architectural firms like Caudill Rowlett Scott of Houston and Perkins and Will of Chicago shared the basic English philosophy of school design. Lawrence Perkins, for instance, an educational 'progressive' by background who had worked with the elder Saarinen, studied English schools in the mid 1950s and applied some of their ideas in a set of commissions for the liberal and wealthy Scarsdale community outside New York

26. Test-assembly of School Construction Systems Development (SCSD), California, *c.* 1963. The helicopter is dropping an air-conditioning unit. The roof beam has a seventy-foot span and a five-foot cantilever.

City. The Medds in their turn visited the United States in 1959 and published a full building bulletin about what they had learnt there.

These and later exchanges had some impact on the planning of a few individual schools. But the basic features of the English experience, the regular cycle of inter-action between designers and clients and its outcome in complete programmes of building, could not be transferred to North America because different administrative arrangements obtained there. Because of the variation in space-standards, even the exchange of planning ideas was fraught with danger. In the 1960s, many American schools took to the fad of the 'open' or 'loft' plan—undifferentiated big boxes, flexible and fully serviced in theory, often very constraining in practice. But the generous space-standards which prevailed in the richer American school-board districts gave the concept some plausibility and success. Britain succumbed to a short-lived clamour for the open plan, an easily grasped idea which excited the shallow-minded, less among teachers than in the architectural profession. It was opposed by A & B Branch on the grounds that with the lower English space-standards the results would be claustrophobic and rigid, not flexible at all. Only a few English 'open-plan' schools were built, though many primary schools have taken up the semi-open approach started at Amersham and Finmere. It was always the view of the English school-builders that space in schools, however desirable in itself, should be linked to a clear educational philosophy of its use. In England there was constant conflict between the cost limits and the universal desire for more elbow-room. Elsewhere, in Sweden, Denmark, West Germany and some parts of the United States, they lamented to see more generous space-standards simply going to waste.

In Western Europe, industrialized building raced ahead of Britain in the 1950s and '60s. But the systems which it spawned were geared chiefly to housing, were developed for profit and lacked regular architectural involvement or control. When these systems were

7.27. CLASP abroad. Amended CLASP frame for single-storey housing at the University of the Ruhr, Bochum, West Germany, *c.* 1962. The system marketed by Brockhouse at this date differed from the version used at home by the CLASP consortium, but the steel stanchions and timber roof deck were the same.

imported to Britain, they were to damage the reputation of the architectural profession more than that of the commercial interests behind them. A few systems bore some slight resemblance to the light-and-dry example of English school-building, but these were devised (again by private entrepreneurs) for factories or low-rise office accommodation. The consequences for post-war school-building in Europe varied from country to country. In France, targets of cost, time, and quantity were met as successfully as in Britain, but only at heavy sacrifice of quality. Other countries fell behind with their programmes and were obliged for years to teach their children in two intakes per day or otherwise, as in the case of some German Länder, their costs rose to levels which roused political criticism. Most were rescued from their predicament only by the eventual fall in birthrates.

The prize-winning CLASP school erected for the Milan Triennale in 1960 (Fig. 6.22) concentrated European attention upon English school-building anew. In comparison with the ponderous, rigid teaching-boxes then still being built all over the continent, it appeared a triumph of simplicity, enlightenment and modernity. Milan set Brockhouse, as makers of the CLASP frame, on a long saga of export-chasing—with mixed success. The promise of really large export orders never materialized. Hungary was the country where most CLASP schools were eventually built, but other buildings were constructed under licence of one kind or another in France, Germany (Fig. 7.27) and Portugal. The dangers of a loose licensing arrangement were brought home by the fire at the Edouard Pailleron School, mentioned above. Here Brockhouse had had to modify the system almost out of recognition to comply with local regulations and the CLASP organization had no control over the result, but the fire naturally damaged its reputation. Later, when the English school-building programmes collapsed and Brockhouse withdrew from the fray, the CLASP Development Group owed its survival to a willingness, at the instigation of Henry C. Morris, to get more seriously and responsibly involved in exporting. First came an experimental school-building project in Venezuela (1981–2), intended as a prototype geared to local conditions and for a programme which, as so often, has failed to materialize. More recently CLASP International secured the contracts for two large hospitals in Algeria designed by the Percy Thomas Partnership. For these (in contrast to earlier arrangements) the components were overwhelmingly shipped out from Britain.

Since the 1970s there have been other examples of the trade in technical know-how based on the educational development approach of A & B Branch. But exporting for exports' sake never interested the better schools architects; they cared more about the free promulgation of ideas and methods. A means for doing so occurred when the Information Centre for School-Building, founded as an offshoot of the Bouwcentrum at Rotterdam, made English experience the first focus of its attention. Then in 1962, following an international conference on school-building in London, the Organization for Economic Co-operation and Development (OECD) mounted a programme to help member countries in the Mediterranean region to overcome their school-building bottle-necks. Guy Oddie, an ex A & B Branch architect, was hired to run the programme and set up small development groups in each of the countries concerned. This led on in 1966 to the still-operational Programme on Educational Building, to which a wider range of countries subscribes. Ever since the 1962 conference, it is no exaggeration to claim that countries in the OECD region have looked to England for leadership in tackling the changing problems of school-building. In some countries the English influence has gone further. In Portugal, the outstanding case, the whole development of planning, construction and furnishing in primary and middle schools has taken English models as its point of departure and reference, starting from the example of the Woodside School at Amersham.

It would be pleasing to record equally happy results flowing from English school-building methods in Third World countries, always short on money and in need of educational help. Apart from a few schools built in special places under special conditions, anything tangible is hard to discern. But a kind of negative influence has sometimes been helpful. In several countries, Nigeria for one, English architects trained in value-conscious attitudes to building have been able to persuade their impoverished clients not to build vast monuments to ambition and technology but to make the best use of skills and resources to hand. More such guidance could have been given, had the British Government and its agencies been alert to the expertise developed by architects in public service and aware of their potential value for technical assistance in the Third World.

Despite these successes, one may look in vain anywhere in the world for any considerable group of schools to reveal a direct trace of English ancestry. This is not because other countries employed no comparable system of industrialized building. It is because the child-centred, activity-oriented approach to primary education which inspired the school-building movement started at Herts never found such firm support in national policy elsewhere; and because the architectural and administrative arrangements which bore such fruit in England had no parallel. Even in those European countries with centralized traditions of government and education, those who decided educational policy normally belonged to a different ministry from those who built schools. Since the 1970s the selective and exclusive *lycées* and *gymnasia* of Napoleonic and Prussian origin have in some measure yielded to more democratic and 'comprehensive' forms of secondary education. Yet the new types are still essentially formal in their approach, while the educational significance of scale and social organization often goes unrecognised. Frequently the only imperatives have been those of numbers and cost.

The English achievement in school-building is respected elsewhere not because of any special brilliance among its proponents, as they would be the first to admit, but because of its context. The system created after 1945 for building schools nurtured a productive tension between educational demand and constraints upon cost, between creative direction from central government and imaginative response from local authorities. Above all, it allowed architects to work side by side with educationists, both employed together in the same public service and sharing their accumulating experience. This context was, and is, unique to England; it has been the upshot of history, geography and national assumptions. Because it is unique, the English approach to school-building has proved in the main to be unexportable.

# CHAPTER 8

# YORK

As a coda to these chapters on the post-war schools, it is fitting to add the story of the one British university in which the methods and ideals of Hertfordshire and A & B Branch were carried over into higher education with any show of success. This was the University of York, commenced in 1961 to the design of Robert Matthew, Johnson-Marshall and Partners. Among the products of the academic boom of the 1960s, York has proved one of the happiest. To claim it as the best new British university would beg questions and set up unanswerable comparisons. But nowhere else did concentrated thought about what a university ought to be like in a modern democracy come so close to finding integrated physical expression. And its early growth escaped the acrimony between architects, administrators and academics which attended the infancy of other of these raw foundations.

York (Figs. 8.1–4) was the high point of Stirrat Johnson-Marshall's twenty-five years in private practice. It preoccupied him for a decade, and its continuity sustained him through a professional vale where despite his own firm's prestige and success he was something of an outsider, self-condemned to wander in an alien world where jobs did not follow on logically from one to the next, where development, growth and collaboration had to be fostered artificially rather than coaxed and allowed to evolve.

Like the spread of community schools, York also represented a kind of posthumous vindication for the shade of Henry Morris, an example of how that difficult and elusive man's inspiration jumped a generation and filtered back into education in the 1960s. The link began with John West-Taylor, one of many younger disciples whom Morris gathered about him at Cambridge. In 1951 West-Taylor, inspired by Morris to do something for educational development and hearing of an idea to set up a university at York, forsook Cambridge and took the post of secretary to a committee answerable to the York Civic Trust. At that point the university was little more than a dream, an ancient dream of an ancient city with aspirations to renewed medieval glories. In 1947 two respectable luminaries of the York Civic Trust, Dean Milner White and a local businessman, J. B. Morrell, had revived the dream. The University Grants Committee, the national body responsible for government finance for the universities, could promise nothing, certainly not money; but it encouraged the trust to set up a pair of small institutes in further education to deal with subjects for which the city of York seemed suitable, archives and architecture, with emphasis in either field upon preservation and restoration. All through the 1950s West-Taylor administered both, taking special interest in the York Institute of Architectural Studies (later the Institute of Advanced Architectural Studies). As this organization grew in scope, West-Taylor got to know many architects. Through Henry Morris, by now in retirement near Welwyn, he became friends with the Johnson-Marshalls, then living nearby.

As the post-war birth bulge moved steadily through the secondary schools, higher education began to stir. In 1958 Sussex got permission from the UGC for the first of the new British universities, to be designed by Basil Spence. York and the University of East Anglia were the next to be approved, in 1960. This allowed West-Taylor's Academic Trust to spawn

8.1. University of York, aerial view in *c.* 1969. Robert Matthew, Johnson-Marshall and Partners, architects. Bottom left: Heslington Hall, with formal garden above. To its right, the CLASP-built Derwent College; above it, Langwith College (centre), linked by walkway to Vanbrugh College (top centre); opposite (jutting into lake), Goodricke College. Other CLASP buildings include the Chemistry Laboratories (right foreground) and Alcuin College (centre right). The Central Hall overlooks the bottom of the lake.

a Promotion Committee, chaired by Archbishop Ramsay and with local-authority representation; its primary duty was fund-raising. At the same time the UGC set up an Academic Planning Board for York under Lord Robbins. The board appointed Eric James, High Master of Manchester Grammar School, as Vice-Chancellor in February 1961. Architects were then to be chosen, to take the final report of the Academic Planning Board and translate this into a 'development plan' for the 'idea of a university'. West-Taylor escorted a succession of them around the unprepossessingly marshy site (which the Academic Trust had acquired) and dilapidated Heslington Hall, the future administration building. Some touted, others behaved well. But Johnson-Marshall, known to West-Taylor personally and to James by reputation for his work at the Ministry of Education, must already have been the favourite. According to West-Taylor, it was a rare aesthetic remark that clinched the matter:

> I had great fun bringing the architects out here and showing them this great bog and just seeing what their reaction was. When I showed it to Stirrat he took one look at the site and said, 'What this needs is a lake to unify it'. No one else said that at all; he was the only man to make that remark. Most of the others looked a bit daunted.

Matters were formalized late in 1961. When at the end of the year Patrick Nuttgens arrived to take over the Institute of Advanced Architectural Studies from West-Taylor, he heard that York was in the hands of RMJM. So he rang up his old mentor in Edinburgh, Robert Matthew, to ask if there was any chance of his being project architect, only to be told that the job belonged to the firm's London office, over which Matthew had declining influence.

The architect chosen by Johnson-Marshall to work with him on York was Andrew Derbyshire, hitherto in the Sheffield City Architect's Department. The two already knew each other through a small group of 'activists' (the 'Chain Gang'), who had been organizing to get public-sector architects better representation in the RIBA. Derbyshire was immersed at the time in the first big survey of British architectural practice, published in 1962 as *The Architect and his Office*. He had a background in Cambridge science, the Building Research Station, the AA, and local-authority housing and schools, so he possessed the perfect pedigree for Johnson-Marshall's methods of working. Derbyshire was becoming disillusioned by

8.2. Langwith College, University of York, from the garden of Heslington Hall.

public practice 'because of the political penchant for quantity rather than quality', and was eager to move. He had even been approached by West-Taylor to take the job at the IAAS, with the prospect of becoming the first professor of architecture at York. But like Nuttgens he had cast covetous eyes upon the site and thought better of becoming an academic. Hearing of this, Johnson-Marshall asked him to join RMJM in order to write the development plan for York. Such had been the impression made by Derbyshire upon West-Taylor, that the university stipulated that Johnson-Marshall and he should lead the team.

Their original brief was not to design buildings at all, but to develop a plan for the university's first ten years. The Academic Planning Board had assumed that this would be done in a matter of weeks; then would follow the business of appointing architects for the buildings. But Johnson-Marshall and Derbyshire insisted on six months to do a proper job, even at the cost of deferring the date for completion of the first permanent buildings to 1965. They were being asked, they argued, to produce a plan for a micro-city or small new town with a crucial time-factor involved. No such thing had been done before for a British university. Spence had produced some sketch-plans for the University of Sussex but no real logistics. The University of Leeds had the nearest equivalent, a plan written by Dargan Bullivant, an ex-A & B Branch architect. Since a university existed already at Leeds its philosophy had been taken for granted, whereas at York the philosophy was still in the throes of evolution. 'Nobody had talked about the architectural implications of academic and social ideas,' says Derbyshire, 'and nobody had produced theoretical relationships and developed them into a plan with a time-dimension in it.' The university needed something that it could use as a reliable, specific framework for development, as a document for raising money, as a statement of aims for potential academics applying for jobs, and as a 'design guide' in case RMJM were not retained as architects. Nothing less than a full Geddesian survey of all the factors would answer, they decided. In the end, the time lost in producing the development plan would seem well spent.

While the plan was in preparation and in the period that ensued, Johnson-Marshall and Derbyshire were indefatigable in their collaborative zeal. They conferred with the Estates and Buildings Committee (successor to the Academic Planning Board), they listened to newly appointed professors, and they fought with each other. Most of all they badgered James and West-Taylor. Nowhere was Johnson-Marshall's oligarchic instinct of working so patent as at York. No committee, he believed, had the stamina for the exhaustive discus-

sions, dialectic and investigations which alone could lead to good building. At University College, Oxford, RMJM had lately put up a small building. The dons, indulging in their petty, common-room variant of Athenian democracy, had bickered and offered late, conflicting and intransigent opinions. At York, Johnson-Marshall was going to have none of that. With the connivance of the committees, the idea, shape and future of the university were largely planned by four individuals, James, West-Taylor, Johnson-Marshall and Derbyshire. But the debates between them were of a breadth, intensity and continuity which it would be hard to match in other discussions between architect and client in modern British architecture. James took time at the outset to get into his stride. Until the end of 1961 he was still trying to run a major school and could hardly fulfil his formal duties towards the university, let alone contend twice a week with the architects. But they bullied him and made him think; and at heart there was nothing James liked better than a good argument. He soon became an equally zestful debater and eventually the architects' most fervent admirer, as the account of their collaboration which is appended testifies.

The outcome of these sessions was a university more deeply pondered and clearly conceived than any of its potential rivals. It was to be a monument neither to any abstract aesthetic, nor to the glory of individual departments; in fact, it was not to be a monument at all. The nearest that Johnson-Marshall would allow at this early stage to a visual image was the vague proposition that it should be 'in the style of the Cambridge backs—grass, trees, water, buildings'. James was intent upon a collegiate structure and had long preached the integration of living and learning, as at the ancient universities. To this vision the others added, consciously or half-consciously, dashes of the idealistic spirit of Patrick Geddes and of Henry Morris, parallel thinkers who in their different spheres each saw educational, civic and architectural reform as one. Not for any of them the dull banality of halls of residence; social space, teaching space, residential space and eating space, for both students and staff were to be mingled together and the patterns of circulation were to run right through the middle of the colleges. All this was new, complicated and (for some) uncomfortable. It threatened existing hierarchies, administrative and academic alike. Because the university paid for student accommodation and the UGC for teaching space, it meant mixing budgets—a source of irritation to UGC officials, who liked their universities in tidy chunks of building devoted to one use each and now had to do some work to come up with fair formulae for the combining of learning and living. It also entailed dividing the academics of the non-scientific departments between the various colleges. The braver ones went along with this, but others objected. Eventually a compromise had to be reached and the economists secured their ivory tower in the shape of Alcuin College, the third in the series of colleges. Unquestionably the original idea was too extreme; but without teaching space, the colleges would never have worked as they have done.

The University of York Development Plan was presented in May 1962. Despite inflation, recession and the consequent easing of growth in student numbers, its decisions and projections have been quite closely confirmed. But at the time it aroused some disquiet, because it failed to tell the expectant academics and donors what the university was going to look like. Only through the support of James and West-Taylor were RMJM retained and able to proceed to the physical design of the campus. The first job was to restore the university's two existing buildings, Heslington Hall and The King's Manor, which could proceed while the first new buildings were on the drawing board. Bernard Feilden was appointed architect for these jobs, so that RMJM could mature the new work without distraction.

It was at this stage, in 1962–3, well after the development plan had been issued, that the university agreed to use CLASP for the colleges and many of the smaller buildings. As so often, the question of whether it was rational to use prefabrication at York permits of claim and counter-claim. The historian can render best service by setting out the story.

Johnson-Marshall was undoubtedly intent that York should continue into higher education the work he had done at Herts and the Ministry. He had always been a 'systems man' and kept in his repertoire an assorted medley of arguments to refute the doughtiest opponent. At York he overcame a full ration of adversaries. James was willing to trust the experts, so long as they delivered on time and at cost. However, some of the fund-raisers on the Promotion Committee found it hard to part with the long-cherished prospect of ivy-covered stonework in favour of thin concrete cladding on a flimsy steel frame. Nuttgens, who sat on the Estates and Buildings Committee, was also wary at first, in part because Johnson-Marshall had tried to 'nobble' him and get him to go along with his plans. And his own colleague Andrew Derbyshire had to be convinced. Before agreeing to the novel step of prefabricating a university, Derbyshire insisted on testing every argument in turn, during and after the development plan. Johnson-Marshall, trusting to instinct, simply waited. In due course Derbyshire conceded and agreed they must build in CLASP, as his partner had no doubt wanted to do from the start.

Three main reasons were advanced for prefabrication at York. Firstly, said the architects, there was a long-standing shortage of building labour in and around York. Stone was out of the question on grounds of expense, and even brick buildings on the scale contemplated were bound to be delayed. The methodical Derbyshire went deep into this matter to test its truth:

> We talked to the building employers' federation, both centrally and locally, we talked also to the various government departments about their future building plans. There were two things on the horizon which were very major construction projects, a new hospital

8.4. A courtyard, Derwent College. The peaked rooflights invented for York's CLASP buildings stick up behind.

and new barracks in York, due to begin at the same time as our construction period. There was also a projected growth of private house-building, as the market was picking up at the time. The general conclusion of all these things was that if we wanted to attract a labour force of 600 with an existing labour force of 3,800 and the other competing demands, then we would get very high tenders, tenders which would bust the UGC cost limits. The contractors would be fighting for labour. They would have to assume that they would import from either the West Riding or Tyneside or Humberside, or they'd have to build a labour camp, also very expensive. There'd be a concentration of local demand for aggregate, bricks and timber, which were all in short supply.

Here was an issue which only those architects trained to see beyond the buildings at the end of their pencils were likely to see. Next, in order to get the university going as a proper community from 1965, as many buildings as possible had to be brought into operation as quickly as possible. This was James's special shibboleth. He was not going to preside over a new university which opened with students arriving at York Station without anywhere to lay their heads for the first night. The architects had already borrowed time with the development plan: now they had to pay it back, and get a mass of buildings up fast—and to cost. Lastly, the ground on which it was proposed to build was poor and waterlogged. Even after drainage, costly piling would be needed unless the university adopted a light mode of construction.

All these arguments pointed towards prefabrication, which was economical on site labour and fast to construct. They centred upon cost, but other issues were also bound up with them. As in the school-building programmes, prefabrication was never claimed to be cheaper at York *per se*. Instead, the architects asserted that it supplied better value for money because it offered greater predictability, speed and better and more flexible accommodation and services for a given sum of money. On the former counts the architects were vindicated. No building in the first ten years suffered a major cost overrun, and none was finished behind schedule. These virtues were at least as important as low first cost. Here the contract with the building experiences of other British universities was dramatic. At Sussex, the first of the batch, Basil Spence had gone way over the estimates expected and the UGC in reaction imposed sharp cost limits, in Ministry-of-Education fashion. Many architects hired for the new universities were soon in deep trouble with these and badly behind with their programmes, while York sailed serenely on. This was because Johnson-Marshall and Derbyshire knew and approved of cost limits and cost planning, and were determined to make the best of them. Johnson-Marshall and one of his lieutenants, David Parkes, even published a paper to rebut the argument, popular among free-booting academics, that 'university standards of architecture are damaged by the application of financial discipline'. In their view, the attitudes of those who pushed for as much as they could get away with were tantamount to sabotage, imperilling the whole future of university-building. Derbyshire:

> Stirrat insisted that we should be absolutely open with the UGC. Nothing should be hidden, because he'd been used at the Ministry to architects trying to cut corners, conceal things, put things under carpets and so on. Trying to control a building programme with a tight budget is difficult enough. But if you have people who aren't telling you the truth it's hell. He wasn't going to play that game with the UGC. Equally Eric James supported that entirely. He wasn't going to have any jiggery-pokery. He was a man with a great respect for the civil service, for budgetary control, the right kind of creative administration, and a good honest relationship between the consumer and the producer. So we entered naturally into a continuous dialogue with UGC. We told them everything.

'Everything' included, for instance, the extra price of the lake, York's glory, as opposed to a concrete tank. The consulting engineers had said they must have one or the other as a 'balancing reservoir'. The UGC pressed them hard and for a moment it looked as though the lake would have to go. Then Johnson-Marshall dug in his heels, and the equivalent sum had to be taken out of the buildings. It might have been possible to disguise the figure somewhere, but this the architects declined to do. The lake had become a priority in the cost-planning process.

On the issue of costs and the standard of accommodation, the arguments for prefabrication

8.5. Wing of Derwent College under construction. With the roof deck on at an early stage, the contractors can proceed with cladding and other tasks unimpeded by the worst of the weather.

8.6. Cladding for the CLASP buildings at York on trial at Evans Brothers' yard. This picture shows the 'Siena Cathedral' finishes which proved too costly to manufacture.

8.7. Another attempt to cheer up the cladding. Concrete panels designed by Fred Millett at the end of a walkway, Langwith College.

turned out in the long run to be less convincing. It provided a flexibility in the colleges which was often turned to advantage later on, and made it easier to link up the larger teaching and social spaces with the little study-bedrooms. But as the building programme went on and inflation started to bite, the difficulties which all systems had in coping with cuts became increasingly manifest. The buildings became simpler, more repetitive, less imaginative. Eventually the residential blocks got detached from the teaching and social nucleus and at Wentworth, the final college, the Brockhouse steel frame became so costly that it was abandoned altogether for load-bearing blockwork in the study-bedrooms. Systems, as the school-building programmes also proved, were less easy than traditional methods to reduce and skimp upon in cost when penny-pinching began—not such an ignoble failing.

The choice of CLASP as opposed to any other prefabricated system for York was in Johnson-Marshall's mind from an early stage. RMJM had already designed a few CLASP jobs before York. But Derbyshire refused to be rushed into using the system, insisting on a full appraisal of what was available. That sense of choice seems to have communicated itself to the clients. 'We were by no means stampeded into having CLASP,' insists West-Taylor. 'We really made that decision ourselves.' But its selection was nearly inevitable, once it had been agreed to use a system. Most of the builders' proprietary systems were for larger things, used a coarse module and did not enjoy the architects' trust. Intergrid and the other schools systems of the 1950s were entertained but all rejected for one reason or another. CLASP was still novel, exciting, 'client-sponsored' and expanding all the time. The boundless capabilities of the system as they appeared in the early 1960s, the opportunities it offered for development of the long-sought universal language of architecture, appealed strongly to the architects. It needed some technical development before it could be used in university-building, but for Johnson-Marshall that was more of a lure than a drawback. It was no financial disincentive, for though the university paid a fee on joining the CLASP consortium, it did not have to bear the burden of development costs. The RMJM office did most of the work in collaboration with the CLASP Development Group, and when they were ready the drawings were available for use throughout the consortium. Later CLASP buildings drew heavily on the development work done for York.

The tasks involved in adapting CLASP for use at York included revisions to the steel frame (in which Lister Heathcote continued to play a major role) with long girders for the wider spans, new roof-lights, new partitioning to meet fire regulations for multi-storey buildings, and sound insulation between the bedrooms. Above all, there was to be handsome new storey-height concrete cladding to impart scale and dignity to the buildings. Here the architects met with disappointment, all too common in the saga of claddings. There had been high hopes of a splendid set of panels, some white and some green. Derbyshire and James had 'discovered a common love of Siena Cathedral' and set to work, rather to Johnson-Marshall's suspicion, playing with aggregates of green-granite chippings and fluorspar (Fig. 8.6) Then came the moment of costing and of truth; it was out of the question, and so were several cheaper alternatives. 'We went gradually down the scale until we finished up with river gravel dredged out of the Trent down the road from the factory,' recalls Derbyshire ruefully. So the colleges and other CLASP buildings at York, though cleverly planned and splendidly sited and landscaped round the lake, are let down like so many others of their type by the drabness of their cladding.

Even after these developments, CLASP could not be used for the biggest buildings on the site, the library, the physics teaching block, and the central hall, which were designed by RMJM architects in varying styles and techniques. The contrast was deliberate, but it brought into question the system's applicability as a unifying feature of the university. Had CLASP's technical development allowed, Johnson-Marshall would certainly have used it more at York. The CLASP Joint Development Programme which followed on in the RMJM office in 1966–8 was intended to overcome this deficiency and make the system available for heavy university buildings. In due course this research found its way into the mainstream of CLASP development, but its applications in British universities were few. RMJM used it at Bath University, under the architectural direction of Hugh Morris. But at Bath the architects never found a James or a West-Taylor; there was development but no discussion, and the spirit of co-operative innovation invoked at York could not be recreated. This was the real achievement at York and the underlying reason for its success. The last paragraphs therefore are left to Lord James, who has written that rarest of documents—a client's testament to continued, cordial relations with his architects.

Of the relationship between architect and client I could write a small book . . .

Almost immediately a relationship developed between us that is, as I now realise, very rare indeed between architect and client. From the time they were appointed in 1961 until I left York no month ever passed without at least one whole day of intense discussion between us. They were uncompromising in their demands on the client, and as regards the overall plan they insisted I was the client. As specialised buildings were built then the academics were brought in, together with the Bursar and Roger McMeeking, the buildings officer. But from the start they regarded me as their legitimate prey who must be catechised relentlessly about his ideas and ideals. I remember well being asked at a very early stage how the students' time should be divided between lectures, seminars and tutorials, and replying that it had not been decided. I was told that it had better be decided fast, because the decision had very important planning implications. Those prolonged and exhausting dialogues were for me a profound educational experience. A session which began with the most mundane questions about accommodation ('How often will the students bath?') would quite often end with the question 'But Eric what do you think a university is really *for*?' . . .

Behind the visions and discussions there was a very down-to-earth attitude. Not for Stirrat and Andrew was the prima donna approach which outlines plans and then vanishes until the royal opening, leaving the actual work to junior assistants. Their visits, as I have said, were very frequent and intensely active. I remember them clambering about among the maze of struts which support the roof of the central hall without columns, and asking questions about the X-raying of the welds. The prima donna role was abjured in nothing more clearly than in the choice of techniques and materials. They were prepared to give up a cladding that we should all have preferred because it would take us outside the cost-limits. I remember sympathising with them because we couldn't afford the architectural luxuries of an Oxbridge college costing four or five times more per place than ours, and I was told that if they couldn't produce a good building within the cost-limits they must be bad architects.

Since the creation of a new university would have social repercussions they were concerned to explain what they were up to to the local community, whether by illustrated lectures in York or in the village which was to be transformed by our advent. No trouble was too great for them. I remember a meeting for the village on a night of driving snow, when the chairman explained very reasonably, that 'you couldn't expect people to turn out on a night like this.' Stirrat and Andrew had driven 200 miles to be there. But if they were prepared to work, the client was expected to work too. Before the start of any of the first building or landscaping operations I was instructed, not asked, to give a short address to the workers of every kind on the site, to explain how vital it was that we should finish on time, as students would actually arrive. This I did with considerable embarrassment and, I suspect, complete ineffectiveness. Above all they expected the client to be decisive. Up to a certain date nothing could be modified without imperilling the completion date, and it was my job to make this clear to my academic colleagues. The result was that no building was ever late and none cost a penny over the cost limits. This was due not only to the architects, of course, but to the Bursar and his colleagues, and to the contractors, the main one being Shepherds. I often wished then, and often since, that Shepherds' attitude not only to technical efficiency but to labour relations was more widespread . . .

And so the university was built. A main road was driven, and bridges built to avoid a division of the site. A fourteen acre hole was dug and lined with plastic, the spoil being used to create undulation, afterwards to be most splendidly planted by Maurice Lee. And as it filled with water the lake came into being, afterwards to be stocked with trout and inhabited with birds, and to provide a splendid background for the annual fireworks parties which my wife gave for children of the staff. It is the lake that now impresses visitors to say how fortunate we were to possess such a site, and it is a remark that causes me to remember the flat, largely treeless swamp that was, in fact, the site that some of us knew. Of course mistakes were made. Not all the buildings are of equal merit. If we had unlimited money no doubt some things could be more elegant. But the verdict of Pevsner in his volume on the East Riding is worth recalling. He begins his account of the university with the blunt statement 'As for the new buildings and their siting, they have resulted in the best of the new universities visually and structurally, thanks to one stroke of genius and one highly sensible decision. The stroke of genius is the large lake. It provides all the undulation and some of the variety that one wants to see, and it allows the buildings to be entirely reasonable and to keep away from all gimmicks. The decision referred to was to use the CLASP system.' His favourable verdict was echoed in a different way by *The Observer*'s architectural correspondent, who wrote: 'The client likes the architects, the architects like the builder. The builder likes the architects, and this architectural correspondent likes the buildings. This is obviously a success story all round.'

I have dealt at length with the physical planning of the university, not only because it bulked so large in my own life for some years, but also because I think there are lessons to be learned. First, if we are to expect good university buildings, or, indeed, good buildings of any kind, we must expect to take trouble. The involvement of the client at every stage must be a reality, and that client must in the last resort be a senior person, even if he is inexpert, who, together with a quite small group of colleagues can take firm decisions. Design by committee can lead not only to delays but disasters. Secondly, the people who are going to use a particular building, whether it be a kitchen or a laboratory, must be closely involved, providing, as I say, that there is someone senior enough to put a stop to further discussion. I have heard far too often architects blamed for faults which could have been avoided if the client had been prepared to clear his own mind as to the exact purpose of the building and discuss it in detail with the architect. From an experience of looking at plans, rather uncomprehendingly, I admit, much wider than when I was at York, through serving on the Royal Fine Arts Commission, and listening for many hours to architects' talk, I am sure that there are more bad clients than bad architects, and perhaps more bad junior planning officers, than either. I can only conclude . . . by saying in all sincerity that of all the experiences of my life none has been more stimulating than that of playing some small part in the translating of educational ideas into physical form.

# PART III

# ACHIEVEMENTS AND CONCLUSIONS

# CHAPTER 9

# CLAIMS, CRITICISMS AND COMPARISONS

A bold claim may be made for the English post-war school-building movement started at Herts. Alone in Britain, without exact parallel in other countries, its proponents grasped the chances for social development implicit in modern architecture since the 1930s and succeeded in applying its principles in such a way as to benefit a whole nation. This is the contention, and this the reason why the movement is still worth attending to.

Upon what principles of architecture did those who were central to English school-building in the post-war period fix their faith? In these days of architectural disillusionment, precision is necessary. The commandments of modern architecture which, consciously or unconsciously, they took as canonical amount to three. All relate to the process and aims of building, not to its appearances. Firstly, they held that everything about architecture and building ought to be submitted to the test of the most searching, rational scrutiny. Secondly, the benefits of a better architecture had to be conferred evenly upon the whole population, not reserved for one small segment. Thirdly, the methods of architecture had to be intensely co-operative and collaborative. From a combination of these tenets sprang a fourth. Buildings were to be the embodiment of a continuous, developing process between architect, client, user and maker, whereby the architect would regularly scrutinize every detail of the others' means, habits, hopes and requirements, set them in the broadest possible context, and strive to endow them with every advantage of modern technique and organization.

Even today, few people would be brazen enough to dismiss these familiar ideas altogether. As a complete philosophy of architecture this austere code may be incomplete, but it gets to the heart of the movement. Further thoughts, about expression, about technology, were tacked on to these basic ones by architects of varying temperament and differing cultural persuasion. Leslie Martin, to take one instance, attached as much weight to reconciling art and science in building as to any of the principles set out above. But most of these further ideas were in one sense or another introverted ones, addressed only to architects and a few others and therefore, from the social point of view, secondary. The more obsessive these lesser aims became, the greater was the distortion of the fundamental code and the less clear-sighted the architectural policies and decisions which ensued. The pioneering school-builders after 1945 were unique in keeping their sense of priorities and balance, amidst all the pressure of work and practical difficulties. Were production methods necessary for the sake of building schools urgently and in great numbers? Yes: but the lure of industrial methodology was never to obstruct teachers from pursuing their everyday aims and their higher ideals; therefore prefabrication had to be by components, not by units. Should architects design the best and most beautiful buildings possible? Certainly: but the opportunities had to be studied and exploited within the limits of available resources; otherwise there would be inequities, and in due course the authorities would cut funding and curtail everyone's freedom of manoeuvre, to the impoverishment of all. Such are two examples of how adherence to a basic creed led to decisions of moment in the school-building movement.

What, in material terms, were the achievements of the school-builders? Against a shifting backdrop of urgency, opportunity, shortage and stringency, they helped to develop policies and means of construction which housed a whole generation of children in state schools to a far higher standard of accommodation and services than anything thought imaginable before the war. There was no 'double-banking' of the kind common·elsewhere, no child turned away for want of a school place. The schools built were neither temporary nor identical. They could expect a medium- or long-term life-span, and they were tailored to the different local wants and aspirations of teachers and education authorities. Some were original and handsome, others were not special to look at, but most were practical. Imaginative practicality, in so far as such generalizations can be made, was the distinguishing mark of the post-war British school.

But what of the wider influence of these ideas and methods? The school-building movement in post-war Britain was no isolated phenomenon. It sprang, earlier chapters showed, from a broad urge among young architects before, during and after the Second World War to build upon the planning example of Unwin, the programmatic philosophy of Gropius, and the scientific spirit of Bernal. The methods of science, research, development and collaboration were to bear fruit in a complete national policy of building. If this movement still has claims upon our attention, we must first understand why the successes it attained in school-building were not repeated elsewhere, save perhaps in the New Towns programme.

Fortune, it must be stressed, smiled upon those who built on behalf of education in the post-war years. The separate heads of steam which issued respectively in the Butler Education Act of 1944 and in post-war reconstruction lent tremendous joint force to the school-building movement. There were remarkable teachers and thinkers, eager to put long-repressed ideas into educational practice; high-minded administrators, undaunted by Treasury caution; and confident politicians who believed that the nation's collective tribute should be spent upon the nation's collective future. While this alliance held, great things were feasible for those charged with the school-building programmes. When it so much as wavered, as it did over the structure of secondary schools, the quality of the building programme wavered too. Such is the delicacy and difficulty of building well for the state.

## SCHOOLS AND HOUSING

Public housing is the crucial area of comparison which must be weighed before it can be claimed that the school-building methods of Stirrat Johnson-Marshall and his disciples had broad or general validity. All the while that the post-war schools programmes were swelling and maturing, they were like the favoured little sister to the big brother of public housing; popular, demure, content, well-adjusted, patted regularly on the back by government and press alike. On every occasion for congratulation, there in the background skulked housing: the child of the same parents (government and local authority), larger, greedier, and all the more problematic for the chops and changes that mother and father kept making in its regimen.

It is vital not to fall for the easy heresy of the moment and assume that the history of British post-war public housing has been a disaster. Much of it was created by the same kinds of architect as the schools, working in the same offices. If it had been the *débâcle* it is now simplistically assumed to be in some quarters, the verdict on the schools too ought to be a savage one. When the statistics are examined, the amount of post-war housing built by local authorities to have had severe building failures is small, if significant and agonizing. Even of tall blocks, the gravest mistake of building policy, the proportion actually to have caused real concern is not usually put at over a quarter. But certainly the building of decent housing on any scale has long proved tough and dispiriting. When a group of architects moved from Herts to the LCC in 1950, they found matters far more intractable. Others promoted or encouraged by successes with schools to make similar moves into housing, later discovered the same. Why was this?

The crux of the matter was failure of political will. What housing lacked and schools enjoyed was a straightforward commitment from successive British governments dating back through numerous education acts to 1870 and strengthened by the historic compact of 1944, to the effect that where there were children, there too would be state schools for them all, or for as many as presented themselves to be taught, conforming always to standards laid down by law. This is a contract which still runs unquestioned. Were Britain not now in a period of static population and 'falling school rolls', the questioning might well have begun. But for the moment, despite the collapse of social consensus and the merciless squeeze on public expenditure, wherever in Britain the population is growing, in Hampshire, Essex, Kent and other parts of the economically sunnier south-east, there new schools are still built by local education authorities. They have only to put projections to their ministry and have them validated, and in due course the relevant permissions will be forthcoming.

Housing never enjoyed these privileges. From the time of its Victorian birth, public housing was tolerated by governments on sufferance, to avert strife, to prevent the spread of disease, to placate reformers and war-weary servicemen. After 1919 it became a limited obligation rather than a voluntary commitment. But the whole structure of housing provision by the state retained a deeply passive and negative tinge. Some cities built handsomely and generously, others with a bad grace. Endless reversals of government policy made continuity, hard enough to achieve in education, a nightmare in housing. So heavy did housing weigh upon the economy that at the earliest whisper of instability it was always the culprit singled out for correction. In reality, the state's undertaking to house has been a pious political fiction in comparison to its pledge to provide school places, which it has always met.

So much can be gathered from an elementary study of housing. But the comparison must be further pursued if a fair judgement is to be arrived at on the wider relevance of the methods of architectual working used in the schools programme.

Take first the organization of local authorities. Before 1974, public housing in Britain was built by city, borough and district councils, but not by the county councils which were building most of the new suburban schools. The number of these authorities was large, some twelve hundred in all, and they differed hugely in size and experience. The LCC (London being an exception to the usual structure for housing provision) enjoyed a budget and resources greater than some smaller European countries. Other housing programmes were trivial, rural, hole-in-the-corner operations, run quietly by the chairman of the housing committee (perhaps a local squire), the council's treasurer, and a builder or two. Discrepancies of size and staffing made policies for such authorities difficult to agree; when their representatives met or were consulted, they often clashed.

The Butler Act, by contrast, reduced the number of local education authorities in England and Wales from 315 to 146. These authorities were sizeable but not gargantuan. They all employed permanent professional staff, educational and architectural, and their relationships to their ministry were similar enough to prevent great conflicts of interest. Until about 1970, the post-war schools represented for most of them the biggest and most absorbing portion of their building programmes. Their architectural staff were able to concentrate upon them almost to the exclusion of other building-types and became experts in the field. The peculiarity is often remarked that the 'progressive' advances in post-war school-building should have stemmed so much from Herts and other 'shire' authorities rather than from more radical urban ones. There are two reasons for this. Firstly it was in the 'shires' (or more accurately on the outskirts of cities which remained in the areas of county authorities) that most of the new schools were built, especially in the Conservative years of 1951–64. Secondly, the urban authorities were so taken up with the burdens of city-planning and public housing that schools tended to take second place there for both politicians and architects. The LCC, for instance, was willing for all its pride and independence to borrow the Hills system from Herts in 1950 and adopt it without much new thought to their primary schools, because they were concentrating so much upon housing. To some extent the call of school-building upon professional time could be construed as another impediment to solving the urgent urban housing problem.

Next in importance was the marked difference in attitudes towards the organization of schools and of housing. Housing has never been permitted to become a professional matter.

We all live in dwellings, we all have opinions about them, and therefore we are all housing experts. Council committees wish to scrutinize housing plans in detail, and tenants too must have their say. We also went to school, many of us have children, yet few of us feel that we authoritatively understand a teacher's or a child's educational needs. Because of this difference, local authorities were able to take professional educationists on and trust them. This was vital for the school-building programmes. Here were people in the same organization with whom the architects could regularly talk, work and think; they had similar status, comparable aims and the same 'enabling' role. Anything upon which the architect and the educationist could agree was likely to be acceptable to the education committee, especially in the county authorities where, for the first two post-war decades, local politics was still a very part-time pursuit and the 'expert' was viewed as someone to trust, not to challenge. In housing, by contrast, there was no proper equivalent of the educationist or the schools inspector. Nearly a hundred years after the work of Octavia Hill and after all the inter-war lip-service paid to the ideal of research in housing, Britain lacked a working tradition of enlightened housing management. Well after 1945 the housing departments of many local authorities continued to be staffed by accountants, estate agents, maintenance engineers and rent collectors. There was rarely any 'feedback', any regular mechanism for dialogue between local-authority management and tenants, or any provision for architects to discover who would inhabit the dwellings to be built and in what way. Efforts in due course were made to overcome these obstacles, initially and notably within the LCC. Sociologists were hired, housing welfare roles expanded, tenants' and housewives' groups formed, and a new national institute of housing management was set up. But none of these could find the political clout to organize the 'upper client body' which housing so direly needed. These groups never achieved the consistent access to policy-making which the architects and educationists achieved within the Ministry of Education.

Further complications arose in housing over the role of the builder. Private housing is not an unduly specialized business. Historically, the part played in its design and construction by architects and other professionals has been small; it is the province of the independent, risk-taking builder. Private and public housing have always been in indirect competition, and builders' interests have been well represented on the housing committees of local authorities and on the many government bodies appointed to resolve the inexorable 'housing problem'. Therefore the design and construction methods of all housing, public as well as private, have been attuned to the most urgent of the independent builder's concerns—profit and loss. The evil reputation under which systems-building labours today has many roots, but the most devastating was the employment in the 1960s of heavy-panel European systems of reinforced concrete for tall flats devised and tested commercially and sold to local authorities as complete packages. They were geared to the convenience of the crane and the accountant, not of the tenant or housing committee. Government pressure for speed and numbers caused their adoption, later so bitterly regretted. Similar pressures existed in the schools programme. They were never so intense, but the crucial difference was that of control. The systems most successfully used for schools were devised by architects and educators within the public domain, and owned and controlled by local authorities. Economy and speed contributed to their creation, but the spectre of profit and loss had never to be appeased in the same implacable, impoverishing way. In school-building, the architects, educators and administrators were in command; where there was a difficulty they could put their case to the Minister and win. In housing, the architects had no rapport with the managers, no one represented the users, and a succession of ministers crumbled under the combined pressure of the fight for numbers and of the building industry.

Material differences about the nature of design also distinguished schools from housing. One concerns the size of the schemes built. A primary school is a project readily encompassed. It can be conceived, designed, approved, built and occupied under the direction of a small team within two or, at the most, three years. There is time for ideas to be tried and lessons digested before altered conditions have made them irrelevant. Secondary schools take longer and, as a matter of record, did often suffer delays, but to a degree the same was true of them. The larger and more contentious the project, the harder it proved to derive helpful lessons from it even in education, as the experience of colleges of further education and universities demonstrated. Not all housing schemes were vast, but many of the grander experimental projects were undertaken on a big scale, because of the pressure on time and numbers. And in housing the complicated mechanism for approvals, which obliged an authority to set out a scheme before even a site could be authorized for purchase, meant that the gap between conception and completion was far too long, from five to ten years. The ideas and conditions which had informed the original design were almost bound to be obsolete by the time that a mature judgement could be made on the outcome.

Another point follows from this. A school is a self-contained project, often in essence a single building with an 'inside' and an 'outside'. But housing schemes consist of many buildings, and also of their relationship to each other and to what is around them. How the semi-public spaces in which the buildings stand are used and maintained, where cars are parked, how rubbish is disposed of, are ingredients which make the difference between success and failure. Yet the control of these spaces and uses is nowhere near so simple a matter as it is for a school.

Finally, it is worth adding a subtler point about the difference between a school and a dwelling. One of the achievements of the schools architects of the 1950s and '60s was that they acquiesced in major cuts in the cost of school-building without serious attendant loss of quality or space. Arguably there was 'fat' to cut out of schools only because schools had always been in the public domain, shielded from the constraints of the market. Despite the Board of Education's pre-war attempts to economize on construction, the 'fat' had lain there, undiagnosed for want of a technique like cost analysis. But in housing the iron hand of speculative discipline had over the centuries pared down the small dwelling to minimum standards of construction and servicing. Consequently there was no excess 'fat' in housing. Space standards were about all there was to reduce, and the temporary reduction of these in the early 1950s caused great anger. The crying need was for higher standards, such as were adopted following the Parker Morris Report of 1961. Although the cost-planning revolution devised for schools was applicable to public housing and was so applied in modified form in the shape of the 'cost yardstick', there was just not the same room for manoeuvre or for dramatic successes. By contrast the effects of economies were more immediate than in schools, quickly impoverishing the quality of tenants' lives.

This litany of comparative advantage and disadvantage could be repeated, less starkly, for all the major types of building demanded by welfare state and government since the war. In every case, the balance of circumstance and privilege favoured the schools programmes. Hospital-building, for instance, started later, involved equipment of greater complexity, longer delays and endless tussles with the medical profession—a breed noted for its introversion, authoritarianism, quarrelsomeness, obsession with technology and intractability. Service-buildings for the armed forces, post-office buildings and some of the tasks entrusted to the old Ministry of Works enjoyed something of the continuity possible in schools and housing. But they lacked the appeal to draw in young architects of ability or the independence from central government which the peculiar British arrangement of architects employed by local authorities allowed.

## DEVELOPMENT GROUPS

If schools were so fortunate, how then can it be said that the way of building which scored such successes in this field has a general claim to validity?

For any great national improvement to succeed, the conditions must be right. For public administrators the school-building saga repays study because of these favoured conditions: the number, size, organization and strength of authorities responsible for schools, their relation to central government, the political continuity which permitted them to develop without major hindrance and their ability to cross professional and departmental boundaries. So many of these pieces were missing from the jigsaw of post-war public housing that it might have been better to reshape the puzzle altogether.

But governments rarely have the chance to behave like that with matters of such electoral moment. The shrewd public servant can only turn their conditions, enactments and opportunities to the people's advantage by getting access to policy and shaping it to beneficial ends. Such was the feat of Stirrat Johnson-Marshall and his colleagues—one exceptionally rare among architects. Their record offers a corrective to too cold and administrative a verdict on the causes of success in post-war school-building. If the situation they inherited had unique potential, it was also fraught with dangers and obstacles. Standardized classrooms, the sacrifice of numbers to quality or of quality to numbers, too much reliance upon technology, too absolute or remote an attitude from central government—any one of these could have wrecked the school-building ship. The material and economic hardships of the post-war decade, the indifference or hostility of many architects in private practice, the antiquated structure of the building industry were all powerful obstructions. To travel along the road embarked upon at Herts needed far-sightedness, balance of judgement, courage and conviction, coupled with a willingness to spurn the conventional prizes of architectural fame.

Above all it was because Johnson-Marshall and his team conceived their plans for school-building early, while the mould for Britain's post-war reconstruction was not yet fixed, that their manner of building could do so much for education. The same chances, it may be conceded, did not exist in other fields. Yet in other parts of the British public sector their manner of building was never applied, or applied only in a small way, late, half-heartedly or uncomprehendingly. In the rare instances where these principles were brought into clear-sighted operation, they proved their value.

The history of development groups affords the most tangible evidence of this. The concept of the 'development group' in architecture, of a small team of specialists withdrawn a little from the regular production of buildings to concentrate upon a technical task of wide applicability, had its origins in the pre-war and wartime enthusiasm for science, research and 'group-working' discussed in the opening chapters. In itself it had nothing to do with educational building, and was first tried out in a backwater, the wartime offices of the London Midland and Scottish Railway. It was broadly discussed as a way of organizing and controlling the evolution and quality of any big programme of building, but Johnson-Marshall was the first to give the idea practical substance and power. The Ministry of Education's Development Group, set up in 1949, anticipated by some years the initiative of any other ministry. Lively local authorities tried, within the bounds of their resources and responsibilities for regular production, to follow suit. Herts deployed Bruce Martin and a few colleagues as a small group to investigate new ways of building, while the LCC with its grander scale of operations set up its own group to look into methods and details of housing construction in 1950.

Between 1957 and 1964 most of the British building ministries and departments were persuaded to imitate education's success and set up their own development groups, in whose ranks a handful of ex-'schools' architects featured prominently. When Elizabeth Layton made a study of local-authority building in 1961, the Ministry of Works, the Ministry of Health, the War Office, and the University Grants Committee all had teams of this kind, and a further one was in process of formation at the Ministry of Housing and Local Government. At this date the reputation of the school-builders was at its height; and on the issues of organization, cost-control, research and development, her conclusions amount to a panegyric upon the Ministry of Education and an endorsement of the development group as the way forward in all public building. The joint group set up in 1957 by the Ministry of Works and the Post Office to scrutinize the design of telephone exchanges had, for instance, vindicated the philosophy of cost planning outside education and achieved some 'quite spectacular financial economies'. CLASP at this time was the only consortium in operation and had just set up its development group. Its imitators, both in school-building and in other forms of construction, tended to start with a development group and to work out from there. Between 1961 and the retreat from public building after 1974, the organizing principle of the development group went virtually unchallenged.

The achievement of these teams was, as a whole, disappointing. To emulate A & B Branch's method, they had to have a say in policy-making, see beyond matters of mere technique,

230

learn continuously from the process of building without being overwhelmed by production, and teach and influence by example. First in the field was the LCC's Housing Development Group, ideologically led by ex-Herts architects. This team had access to political decision-making and got off to a strong start, producing in its first scheme (the Portsmouth Road section of the Alton Estate at Roehampton) new types of layout, internal plan and standard details which were taken up throughout the country. But the loose structure of the LCC's ever-expanding Architect's Department under Leslie Martin undermined the group's authority. In time it became distracted by issues of technology, management and productivity—symptoms of the 'push for numbers' which bedevilled housing.

In due course the attempt to apply the Herts ideal in housing was renewed in the Ministry of Housing and Local Government, which set up a multi-disciplinary development group in 1960 under Cleeve Barr, abetted by Oliver Cox and a staff among whom ex-A & B architects were prominent. By then it was too late, as Elizabeth Layton already saw. Lines had long been drawn in the battle for housing production, the contractors were in command, and the outfit simply lacked 'clout'. Some promising development projects on the social 'A & B' model were built in the first five years—among them the adaptation of CLASP for residential use in some old people's flats at Stevenage (Fig. 9.1). But the administrators, under the eye of Dame Evelyn Sharp, frowned upon the development group's unorthodoxies and the projects were soon discontinued. The group survives to this day within the Department of the Environment and has had its minor successes. But the influence and sanity it tried to dispense were never strong enough, especially in the dire days of heavy-panel housing construction.

The same story could be repeated elsewhere. When development groups had the authority to build but no real contact with users, they tended to become preoccupied with technology. Such was the case of the unhappy Yorkshire Development Group in the housing field and, to an extent, of MACE, the schools consortium. When they had little or no power to build, like the University Grants Committee's modest development team, they could offer advice but did not stand much chance of being heeded. Once the structure of any great building-programme had been laid down, it was not to be expected that the institutional relationships could be renegotiated afterwards.

Timing, then, was all important. The development group was a powerful weapon in the armoury of social architecture. If the successes it won in school-building were not repeated, that was because it was used too late and too feebly. Even with schools, much less would have been possible had the fundamental technical and social thinking been deferred. By getting in 'at the ground floor' before the Attlee Government had started to wane, Stirrat Johnson-Marshall's development group was able to give a decisive lead. Even then and in a liberal ministry, its establishment encountered obstacles which would have thwarted architects less clear-headed and confident in their aims. Circumstances and luck undoubtedly attended Johnson-Marshall and his allies. But the instinct of knowing how and when to strike in such a vast and formidable field, and of doing so with force and will and vision, was no small virtue. It is a commonplace of history that opportunities must be seized; they do not recur.

## TECHNICS AND AESTHETICS

Much has been said about the special successes and opportunities of post-war school-building. But what of its alleged mistakes, and what do they have to teach? The failures most commonly diagnosed and the hopes least fulfilled lie in the realms of technical development and of aesthetics.

Many architects involved in the great post-war building programmes would dispute that their technical efforts had in any way ended in failure. On the contrary, they would argue, the relationship between British architects and technical innovation in building was revolutionized by the model of research, development and collaboration carried on in public-sector offices like Herts, A & B Branch and the LCC, and gradually imitated elsewhere. In school-building alone, the list of technical successes which sprang from this approach and which were refined in the process of continuous production is a long one: better washbasins and WCs, better school furniture, warm-air heating, good lighting (natural and artificial), rubberized studded flooring and, most spectacularly, a solution to the grave problem of building on mining-subsidence sites. Some inventions were tried and found wanting; others served for a time but became outmoded or were discarded because of their cost. But the wealth of innovation, of old ideas improved or new ones introduced, the care lavished upon component design in the search for a new industrialized 'vernacular' vocabulary of architecture, paid off. Because these techniques and concepts were arrived at with the taxpayer's money, it became part of the architects' duty to publish them and get them known about, not to hedge them about with secrecy and patents. In this way many products, duly developed, found their way into British Standard ranges and were put to the service of the nation.

At the same time the ideology of the 'meccano' set pioneered at Herts inspired architects and designers of many persuasions for many years. As late as the 1970s such architects as Norman Foster, Richard Rogers and Cedric Price variously attributed something of their approach to structure to the light-and-dry, steel-framed methods of the school-builders.

Overshadowing all this is the current hatred of prefabrication, a topic so emotional that reason on the subject is hard to attain.

In one sense, prefabrication undoubtedly failed. Although it was first taken up by government and local authorities out of need, not choice, to reconcile the shortages of the post-war years with the social ambitions and demands of the period, some saw in prefabrication a means for reshaping industry and society. They hoped that it might change the nature of construction from a messy and savage process to a clean, civilized one, and encourage people to live and work differently in structures with a limited span of life. Precious little of this took place. Building technique, we now know, cannot proceed forward by wholesale leaps and bounds, but only by meticulous development, adjustment and refinement. The building industry remains obdurately unreformed, for all its current panoply of technology. No vision of architecture which ignores ingrained habit can expect to succeed, especially when it encroaches upon so fundamental and instinctual a territory as the people's dwellings. Nor, we have learnt to our cost, can one generation presume upon a more prosperous successor to redeem architectural priorities, rectify mistakes and build better. The decision, born out of war and impoverishment, not to dictate to the future by raising solid buildings which would become impediments to progress, seemed like humility at the time but now appears an act of unwisdom.

The record of the school-builders on prefabrication has been mixed, but includes some profound successes. They saw from the outset that good prefabricated design must be based on a language of refined interchangeable components, not on the complete unit or classroom. They refused for the most part to be sidetracked by the allurements of modular purity and approached prefabricated building pragmatically, borrowing from traditional building technique to solve problems of joints, seals and profiles. They made sure that the systems which they devised should be properly controlled or supervised, by being developed for a commercial client by an accountable agency like A & B Branch. Most of all, they saw prefabrication as a means to an end, as a way of building more schools with more space and a better standard of services and opportunities. All this the systems delivered for a decade and more after the war. When they showed signs of falling short, the wiser schools architects adapted prefabricated techniques to refertilize traditional building. Others, loyal to the deeper ideology of prefabrication, carried it forward into the 1960s, then gradually, sometimes grudgingly, admitted the improved methods of traditional building back into their own fold. By 1974, when the programmes of building declined, the sharp old separations between 'closed' and 'open' systems of construction had become blurred. All this was a mighty achievement.

Against this must be set some failures and rigidities. Some oft-mentioned inadequacies of the prefabricated schools are hard to judge without statistics comparing them with traditionally built ones over the same period. Many objections to the systems apply in equal measure to other, *in situ* methods of light-weight construction, and are therefore by implication criticisms of the amount of money allotted to schools, not of the manner in which they were built. Prefabricated schools have burnt down; so have traditional ones. Their roofs have leaked; so have all types of flat roofs over the post-war period. They have grown shabby and costly to maintain; but no figures exist to confirm the conventional wisdom that they have been more onerous than brick-built schools. In all spheres of public building, present high maintenance-costs must be laid at the door of past cost limits, not of any one building technique. Two indictments seem to stick. The prefabricated schools are generally hotter in summer, cooler in winter, and lose more heat than their traditional equivalents. And their sound insulation has never been good enough.

Some of the schools architects (Stirrat Johnson-Marshall was one) were slow to concede the limitations of the systems, and thus contributed to the odium which currently attaches to this way of building. To labour the point would be to reinforce an irrational ideology which seems intent today upon attacking prefabrication itself rather than analysing the practical reasons for its shortcomings. Absolute opposition to prefabrication is absolute opposition to industrialized society. As is often pointed out, the brick and the nail are specialized, prefabricated 'components'. Unless we sanction the de-industrialization of our economy, we have to live with, understand, control, influence and extend the vast range of standard elements made available to us by modern industry. In building, as in other industries, the trend is still towards greater pre-production of components and will continue to be so. Sane men and women cannot turn their backs on this process. Better buildings can only come out of a partnership with industry, not from a crude and nostalgic idealization of the traditional crafts.

In pinning their faith in systems for so long, the public architects were contravening one of their own rules and attending too little to user-requirements and reactions, especially the latter. This is a failing which stems from the structure of the architectural profession. It is one thing to spend time and effort on exactly what a client wants when a building is in the making, another to analyse the drawbacks of the finished product with equal thoroughness, when the architect's time is distracted by new tasks, and clients and users cannot see the practical end of such an exercise. Some efforts were made in the school-building programme to institutionalize 'feedback' as a formal part of the architectural process; it was done, for instance, at Herts in the early 1950s. Under the shock of building failures and popular dissatisfaction, it has come into vogue again today. But there is still no mechanism for ensuring that it occurs regularly. This is something badly needed in all fields of building.

In the same way, professional priorities and values distracted the school-builders from heeding what clients and users had to say about the appearance of their buildings as carefully as they should have done. Whatever triumphs the school-building movement may claim, in the matter of external aesthetics they cannot be said to have succeeded.

From the outset, the 'architecture' of the post-war schools elicited conflicting attitudes. Their authors saw their highest task as a social one, that of delivering better, happier, more serviceable places in which children could learn. Aesthetics or, more exactly, the quality of the environment was a powerful constituent of this ideal. Care was lavished upon lighting and colour in the early Herts primary schools, works of art were encouraged on their walls and in their playgrounds, and sensitive landscaping was undertaken. At the same time, the designers rebelled against traditional attitudes to architecture in which the 'look' of the building had dominated the architect's contribution. Above all they shunned the formalism and symmetry which, they argued, had forced previous school-planning into brutal contortions and imposed a severity at odds with the modern psychology of education. Schools should not impose at all, they said, echoing Lethaby: 'a building which poses as imposing is an imposition'. Instead, they ought to be an assortment of modest, quiet, low, broken-up elements. If architects and critics took one look at them and turned away, so much the worse for them; they were meant for children and teachers, not for the paltry world of architectural fashion.

The outcome of these values was that the external architecture of the post-war schools lagged behind their interiors in looks and charm. The same may be said about architecture as a whole over the past fifty years; the insides of our buildings have improved in comfort and practicality out of recognition, but we are no nearer than ever we were to settling their outsides any better. In schools the contrast was especially strong, because the social ideals of the school-builders reinforced the stringencies of the cost limits. Again and again, when priorities had to be chosen, they took money out of the appearance of buildings and diverted it to maintaining or improving standards and services within. Who shall say that this was wrong? It often caused great pain to the architects. But it also pauperized the appearance of many schools.

It would be crass to imply that these architects did not bother themselves with the looks of schools. Endless thought went into the problems of siting, contour and grouping which followed from the determination to build broken-up, informal schools and the need to escape the dangers of monotony inherent in using a limited vocabulary of building. The Herts schools, so simple-seeming now, had a profound architectural impact when they first appeared; and the initial CLASP vocabulary was lovingly devised to give it a softer, more 'vernacular' appearance. Constantly also the architects endeavoured to upgrade the systems' external components, deliberating over eaves, refining re-entrants, searching for sightlier aggregates for the concrete cladding, redesigning window frames, and so forth. But the nature of systems, which force the designer to think the whole time in terms of small, determined components, seems to have inhibited many architects from designing as fluently or coherently as they might. In the long run it discouraged those with the strongest aesthetic sensibilities from staying within school-building.

Finally there was the issue of scale. Having cut their teeth on primary schools, the school-builders never sufficiently rethought their attitudes when confronted by secondary schools and higher education. They preferred to enlarge on what they had learnt, not to start from scratch. Educationally this was wise. But buildings of this bigger size could not be broken up in the same happy way as could primary schools. Often the result was a set of modest, muddly, semi-separate blocks, tentatively inter-related and swamped by the expanse of space all round them. In the suburbs, where the school was usually set in a large acreage of low-rise housing, some stronger landmark was often needful to enliven the locality and offer symbolism and leadership to a community which, in due course, the better educators were striving to lure inside its walls.

Some would counter these criticisms by reaffirming that the schools were designed for their occupants, and that to give much weight to appearances lends comfort to traditional architectural values and reinforces the bad old separation of makers from users. But for many people aesthetics, however confusing and disputed, constitute an absolute value. No burnt offering to social commitment or technical proficiency will convince them that architects ought not always as a first priority to offer the maximum pleasure, stimulation and subtlety to the beholder of their buildings, casual or customary. It is possible to disagree, but foolish to fly in the face of so influential and persuasive view.

In this context it is worth praying in aid of the pioneer social scientist Charles Booth's defence of the London School Board against the charge of extravagance in its East End schools:

> It was necessary to strike the eye and hold the imagination, it was worth much to carry high the flag of education, and this is what has been done. Each school stands up from its playground like a church in God's acre ringing its bell. It may be that another policy should now be followed, that the turn of economy has come; but I am glad that no niggard spirit interfered at the outset. We have full value for all that has been spent.

Aesthetics, therefore, must be appreciated as a crucial tool of propaganda or rhetoric even by those who cannot accept its absolute value. The A & B Branch architects could point till they were blue in the face at what they saw as the deficiencies of the Smithsons' Hunstanton school and of other egregious offenders against sobriety and practicality. Yet it was slick, smart Hunstanton rather than her country cousin, practical, ungainly Wokingham, which caught the fancy of the next generation of designers. Wokingham had a more instructive progeny; but it is Hunstanton that the architectural texts now remember. Somehow the two should have come together.

The public sector in British architecture won many battles for its recognition, status and methods in the 1940s and '50s, but one battle it failed to win was the battle for better appearances. Private architects, the continuity of whose work often relied upon appearances, were generally more sympathetic to the artistic aspect of architecture and more conscious of the publicity value of a handsome exterior. The result is familiar. Today British public architecture is ignorantly vilified as dreary stuff, the work of hacks and non-entities. To the amateur eye, one post-war school looks much like another. From the train or car can be seen in any suburb the schools erected indiscriminately by the consortia of the 1960s: low, flat-roofed, undistinctive, with thick, bland, white-painted fascia-strips disguising the service zone above the ceiling and emphasizing the monotonous horizontality of the whole. 'How can there be anything to learn from this?', people ask. There is a vast amount to learn: but the questioner will not stay for the answer. It is not enough to build more carefully and responsibly than others. The good social architect has also to alert people to that fact, to draw them in, convince them, take them by the scruff of the neck. He or she, in other words, must be superficial and pleasure-loving as well as earnest and puritan. There is no getting away from appearances and aesthetics.

## PRINCIPLES, APPLICATIONS AND OPPORTUNITIES

Opportunities, it has been said, do not recur. So cannot the school-building saga be left as a remarkable episode in post-war British history? Or does it have lessons to impart?

If the school-builders represent the best in that social strand of British architecture which grew out of the dissatisfactions of the 1930s and took hold after the Second World War, so in turn that movement as a whole was rooted in a philosophy of building which descends from Ruskin, Morris, Lethaby, Geddes and Unwin. The Herts tradition, in other words, applied a set of established historical principles in a new way. The austerity and anonymity of the school-builders, the value they set upon process, collaboration and community, their eagerness to transcend the superficiality of appearances and get to grips with social objectives and social justice, are legacies of the radical wing of the Arts and Crafts Movement. A few of these architects, particularly those who were at the AA just after the war, subscribed explicitly to these old values; others imbibed them indirectly.

It has been the fashion of late to propose that the continuity between the English Arts and Crafts Movement and architectural modernism has been overplayed. Certainly architects like Voysey were more than mere precursors, certainly also the impact of industrial production upon building confused and divided the disciples of Morris. Yet in Britain the basic social philosophy of the Arts and Crafts Movement remained strong after the war, stronger indeed and more unified than before, since the long-desired reconciliation of craft and technology, art for the few and service for the many, seemed at last to have been accomplished thanks to the work of the Dessau Bauhaus. The very rewriting of history by Pevsner, Furneaux Jordan and others was a conscious testament of debt and continuity. In English school-building, as in the New Towns, these old principles at last found broad social and architectural realization.

Any application of a principle is bound to wither, but the principle itself is harder to extinguish. In Britain, the public-sector model of architectural teamwork through which the school-builders made their mark may have had its day. The curbs in social spending over the past decade, the cuts in programmes, resources and maintenance, have shattered the standing and morale of many public architectural offices. Others have adapted well, and as long as the framework for their operation remains in place they will be able to respond in the former way to any sudden call upon their services, any boost to local-authority building programmes. But the call may not take this form again.

Principles, therefore, and the way in which they may be applied in future, are what matter. Here it may be helpful to distinguish between two currents in post-war school-building: the social and technical ideals on the one hand, and on the other the organizational means through which they were transformed into effective policy and action.

There is not, and never has been, any want of social idealism among architects. Equally, the openings for disinterested service in building may have shifted, but they have not disappeared. The urge for co-operation, in particular the movement among architects to bring responsibility, humility and patience to their dealings with those who live and work in buildings, has never been stronger. That is what the current passion for 'community architecture' is all about. It reiterates anew that old, plain truth with which the school-builders strove to come to terms: building is not really worth having unless it is rooted in people's needs, and those needs have constantly, painstakingly, precisely to be elicited and re-examined. Because of the divisions in our society, buildings and wants are for ever coming apart and having to be put back together.

The deeper difficulty is to find the means, as the school-builders did, through which such ideals may be translated on a scale sufficient to affect more than a few lives and to make permanent changes in building. Here the building team cannot stand on its own; it has to be helped by enlightened public policy. With the dissipation of the organizational momentum started by the Second World War, we are in danger of being thrown back to an earlier era. Pioneers of social building operating in the private sector, like Walter Segal, are relegated now by the structure of architectural practice to the sidelines. It is a matter of chance, whim and publicity whether their ideas and innovations are taken up or sink without trace. The community architects meet together, try to learn from each other and to lobby, but they are far from the centre of policy-making. Their status and their intermittent funding inhibit them from developing the consistency and continuity which they need to balance their admirably co-operative ways of working.

To an extent, the predicament in modern Britain stems from the illusion of affluence and peace. The post-war building programmes were the outcome of a national emergency, and their organization and techniques of construction reflected this. Once the crisis had passed, it was tempting to fall back on the hand-to-mouth habits and discontinuities of *laissez faire*. How feckless this may prove the British people have yet, in a declining economy, to discover. But there is another side to this particular coin. Impoverished economies and scant resources are not the exception in today's world but the norm. Many countries in sundry stages of development undertake crash programmes of social building, well or badly organized. Third-World housing, for instance, is the subject of animated arguments about methods, resources and organization. Underlying these disputes are the issues which actuated the English school-builders. How are people's needs to be met with a kind of building which is fair, cheap, responsive and quick, one which does not constrain by too much uniformity or technology, and one to which improvements can be made from project to project, so that the wheel does not have constantly to be reinvented? It would be unwise in the extreme to apply anything like the organization of English school-building elsewhere. But as the most sophisticated application yet seen anywhere in the world of the concept of the national building programme, the principles which underlay its achievement reward thought and study. To apply them, policy-makers and architects alike have to find and seize opportunities with the courage of Johnson-Marshall and his colleagues.

## AIMS, COSTS AND RESOURCES

'Can we build more simply?' was the title of a rare public utterance by Stirrat Johnson-Marshall—a brief talk broadcast on the BBC Third Programme in June 1950. The plain and challenging question addresses dilemmas of today as well as those of the post-war generation.

The text of this talk is reprinted as an appendix. It offers the clearest expression of the hopes of Johnson-Marshall's generation of British architects and of the faith which they invested in prefabrication, properly controlled and developed, as a means to solving certain great social and architectural problems of the time. The detailed history of this faith, these hopes, provides the subject-matter of earlier chapters. In conclusion it may be salutary to revert to the issues of resources and their distribution posed in the talk.

The post-war architects were confronted with a crisis. They were asked to build large numbers of buildings in a hurry. Johnson-Marshall put the position thus:

> We are forced to choose between three courses of action. The first is to build only the small amount we're likely to be able to afford. This is to acknowledge defeat. The second is to accept a drastic reduction in space and quality whilst maintaining the same total. This again is defeat, and why should we accept defeat in this, when we have accomplished so much in other fields—radar for instance, nuclear fission, or jet propulsion?
>
> The third course is to approach the whole problem of building afresh, with the object of devising a fundamentally simpler technique; a technique which will give us greater beauty, comfort and value at lower cost.

In the event, the state made an unwritten compact which encouraged the public sector in architecture to pursue the third of Johnson-Marshall's courses. While the Butskellite consensus ran, British schools in particular and other types of public building to a lesser extent were enriched by the energy and care expended upon them in order to stave off the 'defeats' which architects, educationists, politicians and administrators alike refused to contemplate. Through resourcefulness, it proved possible in education to prolong the chosen course successfully into the 1960s and in some measure beyond; in housing, the state was already falling back upon Johnson-Marshall's second course, his 'drastic reduction in space and quality', as early as the mid-1950s, during Macmillan's years as housing minister.

But with an economy in continuous trouble and governments of varying persuasion, the pact was never likely to be kept indefinitely. One day, the weapons of cost control were destined to be trained upon their inventors. Once the political will necessary to counter the restrictions imposed by insolvency disappeared, once the pressure on numbers let up and public programmes began to drop, the hopes for a radical reform of the building process were gone. The end of the public building programmes should be neither underestimated nor exaggerated. Any great social programme depends upon the will of governments. In economic retrospect it may be surprising that the building programmes were sustained for so long. Yet the scope and ambition of the programmes and the sophistication and success of the schools programme in particular will make them points of reference for centuries to come.

Can we build more simply? To this question, posterity seems to have answered 'no'.

The rigidities of the construction industry, the plethora of checks and regulations, the vagaries of climate, the unforeseen drawbacks of prefabrication, the fragmentation of the professions, the demands for higher standards of services: all these have conspired to obstruct the radical simplification of either the design process or the nature of site operations in the way that Johnson-Marshall hoped. The question which he was perhaps too circumspect to ask on the air was: 'Can we build more *justly?*' To this, the post-war programmes of public building, especially the schools programme, suggested a positive answer. They showed how public money for building could be apportioned evenly across the economy without drastic uniformity or loss of local autonomy. They indicated how technical improvements in building, small and large, could be made available without charge for anyone who cared to take them up.

Above all, they opened eyes in a way that had never been done before to the vision of a just relationship between architecture and resources. This point must be stressed, because the extravagances of architects are more quickly forgiven than their inelegancies. The critic who judges the post-war social movement in architecture by its physical manifestations alone will miss this piece of the picture. To take an example: the handsome brickwork of the University of Sussex, where the cost overruns were heavy, looks pristine today, while portions of the University of York, clad in concrete with a cheap facing of river gravel, begin already to look tatty. Yet the enrichment of Sussex contributed to the impoverishment of York. Anyone lax or cynical enough to build, as many consciously do, beyond the reach of known resources, must abrogate any claim to be building justly. If, as commonly occurs, he or she is asked to build for an unrealistic sum, the hard and bitter struggle for more money becomes an integral part of the job. It will not always be won. But its waging is part of the building team's duties, whereas the deliberate over-running of cost limits can do no good to the prospects of future buildings.

At the time of writing, no more critical task confronts all the skills involved in the construction industry than the struggle to win back resources in order to build justly. Derision and ignominy have been lately heaped upon post-war architecture, and particularly the architecture of the public sector. Some of this is fair judgement upon avoidable shortcomings; but in far greater measure it stems from the irresolution, cowardice and, now, cynicism of recent British governments. As in all the spheres of economic life today where public investment is grudged, hampered or maimed, the excuse of no resources or shrinking resources is no sort of excuse at all. Nothing in history suggests that technical, industrial or cultural progress follows when this withholding of social investment becomes the systematic and conscious aim of public policy.

The example of construction presents only one aspect of this overwhelming issue of our times. The case for construction's peculiar importance has often been made, but it would be wrong to indulge in special pleading on its behalf. This would be to perpetuate the crude idea of public expenditure as a cake of simply ascertainable size which governments make from the modicum of available ingredients and then cut into neatly defined portions. The reality is more complex and dynamic. Every sane and selfless group must acknowledge limitations to resources. All clients in building, and governments most of all as the most powerful of clients, are obliged to apportion, manage and control expenditure. If the story of the post-war schools proves anything, it is that with trust and encouragement those involved in building can understand and respond to shortages, overcome barriers and come up with remarkable answers to many of the technical and managerial obstacles to building justly. But if they are discouraged, abused, saddled with discontinuities and treated as means to macro-economic ends, if first cost is perpetually rated higher than value for money, the same story suggests that they will fail. If we wish to build justly, if we seek a more accountable and intelligible architecture and a saner, less savage construction industry, we have, as the Herts architects did after the war, to take up Stirrat Johnson-Marshall's challenge and 'approach the whole problem of building afresh'.

# APPENDIX I

## STIRRAT JOHNSON-MARSHALL: A BIOGRAPHICAL SKETCH

'The most influential architect in the United Kingdom died last Wednesday,' claimed the *Architects' Journal* in December 1981, breaking the tidings of Stirrat Johnson-Marshall's death. To most people that verdict is bound to be a puzzling one. Very few men and women under fifty could say with accuracy what his legacy to post-war British architecture has been; even fewer would claim to have been inspired by his example. Among older architects there are and long have been disciples, but most probably never knew who he was, how he operated, and what he achieved.

Stirrat Johnson-Marshall was an architect who did little of the three things upon which conventional architectural reputations are founded. During his prime he rarely designed, wrote or taught in the straightforward sense in which these words are usually understood. The little house which he and his wife built for their growing family baffled and tickled his colleagues, and its one-off designing caused him pain and exasperation. Seven years in local government, eight in the civil service and twenty-one in private practice produced no weighty report or technical study directly attributable to him. On paper, he preferred to express himself by means of marginal notes on the memoranda of others. When forced to write formally he tended, as in everything, to work with others, so that the final wording is rarely his own. This is a pity, since his own very occasional prose spoke with a directness and lucidity exceptional among architects. As for teaching, in the genuine sense of the term he never did anything else. His life's work was consecrated to spreading and inspiring in others a certain broad view about architecture, building and society. But, for self-chosen reasons, that talent never graced the platform of the lecture-hall. Sparing, shy and hesitant in public speech to the point where strangers could think him inarticulate, Socratic in manner of discussion and intolerant of formality in any guise, he declined to be drawn into academic circles. Getting things rightly built or, better still, enabling things to be rightly built, was his mission. For that, he believed, he must always be in practice.

Some have said that Stirrat Johnson-Marshall was hardly an architect at all; others believed that he was a genuinely great architect, the nearest equivalent that Britain ever had to Walter Gropius and, for reasons of circumstance, a more productive influence upon building than Gropius was ever able to be. That is the paradox of his career.

★ ★ ★ ★ ★

Stirrat Johnson-Marshall was born in India in 1912, the son of a civil servant of Scottish descent responsible for regulating and taxing the salt trade. There were two Johnson-Marshall boys: Stirrat, and Percy (born in 1915), who became his older brother's first, most loyal and most enduring admirer, following him dependently and then independently in his career (Figs. 10.1, 2). After Stirrat's death Percy Johnson-Marshall, the fluent writer and speaker which his brother never was, set down a vivid sketch of their early companionship. It evokes the privileges, rootlessness and isolation of Anglo-Indian boyhood, the shifts from

10.1. Stirrat Johnson-Marshall when chief architect to the Ministry of Education, 1955.

10.2. Percy Johnson-Marshall in the East End of London, *c.* 1955. While his brother presided over the nation's school-building, Percy Johnson-Marshall was grappling with the intractable problems of reconstructing Stepney and Poplar as an architect–planner with the London County Council.

pillar to post around the sub-continent and the occasional 'furlough'. For three years the brothers were left with austere grandparents at Ooticamund, where they went to a local 'prep' school. Already Stirrat was starting to show what in those days used to be called 'qualities of leadership':

I have memories of our father coming on leave, and taking us down to the lower Nilgiri jungles, hunting butterflies. He had a large and valuable butterfly collection which was all destroyed later. I remember falling into a river and being rescued by Stirrat—always there when needed, always reliable . . .

Sometime in 1922, we went down by ourselves from Ooticamund to Karwar on the Malabar coast, a considerable journey for boys of ten and seven. I had been dangerously ill (gastroenteritis?) and my grandmother decided that I should eat nothing but only drink milk. In an extraordinary gesture of self-denial, Stirrat also refused to eat anything. In those days one changed from the mountain railway at Metapallium at the foot of the hills to the main line, and changed again at Bangalore for Mangalore. Occasional Europeans kindly showed us from train to train, until at Mangalore we boarded a country boat. Half way to Karwar one of our father's staff came aboard with a large branch of bananas. We ate the lot, causing severe stomach aches . . .

Our father was transferred to Nasik in 1924, and we then spent a year there, away from any school, going with our parents on distant tours in one of the first T-model Ford cars; getting stuck in the middle of river crossings; seeing animals of various kinds, and having one long adventure. One incident comes clearly to me when Stirrat decided to strip the car engine, which he did with his usual efficiency. It was only after he had put it together that there was a new rattle which proved to be from a spanner left in the works. But he had done the job at twelve years of age, and had already demonstrated his competence and pleasure with machinery.

This routine of dislocations, excursions and excitements came to a climax in 1925–7 with two years in Baghdad, then an exotic, unruly city for two impressionable boys, with corpses dangling at the gates, bazaars and booths with other ogrish sights, and an apocalyptic flood when the Tigris burst its banks and threatened to engulf the entire town.

Then followed the sobriety, dampening for children rich in experience beyond their years, of a small English boarding school, the Queen Elizabeth School at Kirkby Lonsdale, which Stirrat attended until 1930, Percy until 1931. Holidays they spent at the school or with friends, as their parents were still in Baghdad. For Percy Johnson-Marshall this was a lonely time, atoned for by his brother's loyalty.

> It was during this period that I was most dependent on him in many ways, and, I suppose, I hero-worshipped him. But I was not alone, as in his last year he was Head Boy of the school and Captain of both cricket and rugby. In addition, he passed out with eight credits in the 'matric' exam. He was always preventing bullying wherever he saw it, and was almost an archetype of the public schoolboy ideal.

Out of this itinerant, Kiplingesque, old-fashioned start in life a whole batch of qualities developed in Stirrat Marshall: courage, stubbornness and patience; a deep-seated, chivalric idealism, focussed at first in a hazy, adolescent way on the British imperial destiny; a confidence to command, coupled with the obligation to serve; a certain propriety of manner, dress and address; a preference for male companionship and oligarchic organization; and a mild personal snobbishness ('he was always interested in the colour of your socks', remembers a more class-conscious architect). These almost hackneyed attributes of the high-minded Victorian gentleman remained with him for life. Some special characteristics asserted themselves too: a lack of sentiment for the conventional physical baggage of secure civilizations, a calculating strain which could be taken for coldness and, rarest of all, ambition combined with real, self-effacing modesty.

★   ★   ★   ★   ★

Stirrat was the kind of youth who was expected to shine at anything he undertook. Had he been bookish he might have been an intellectual, but reading for some reason never touched him deeply (though his culture was wider than he would readily admit). Practical with his hands, energetic and resourceful in emergencies, he wanted to do something useful. In the autumn of 1930 he set out by train for an interview to study civil engineering at Manchester. On the journey, in Percy Johnson-Marshall's words,

> a plump gentleman got into the compartment wearing a black cloak and a broad-brimmed hat. This gentleman engaged him in discussion and persuaded him that architecture was his real mission, and that he should accompany him to Liverpool for an interview with the Professor, who was none other than the plump gentlemen, Sir Charles Reilly.

Stirrat, no fantasist, insisted in later years on the truth of this story.

The Liverpool University School of Architecture stood then upon the threshold of a transition, described earlier (p. 5–7), from a training ground for mere designers of buildings to something offering its pupils wider scope and sense of purpose. While Reilly remained principal (till 1933) it remained a Beaux-Arts school, though one influenced more by American example and exchange than by anything going on in Paris. Students learnt still to draw the orders and submit highly finished drawings for highly theoretical projects. Stirrat had to do this, and he did it well (Figs. 1.5, 10.3). Later the canard got about that he could not 'design' in the conventional sense. But on the evidence of his student drawings, a thesis on the design and planning of a department store, and first-class honours at the end of the course, he was very capable of this at Liverpool. In time he grew dissatisfied with the limitations of conventional design, got out of the habit and found he did not miss it much.

During the 1930s the Liverpool school quietly shifted the balance of its teaching from classicism to modernism, from the aesthetic to the 'functional' conception of architecture, and from the idea of the independent gentleman-architect serving a select clientele to that

10.3. (*left*) Liverpool student project for a lakeside ferry station by Stirrat Johnson-Marshall, 1933. For the elevation, see Fig. 1.5.

10.4. (*right*) Granville Road Baths, Willesden, London. Borough of Willesden Engineer's Department, architect, *c.* 1936. Despite a resemblance to the ferry station, this building is not credited to either of the Johnson-Marshalls. Both are fashionably indebted to Easton and Robertson's Royal Horticultural Hall.

10.5. Electric House, Willesden Lane, Willesden, London. Stirrat Johnson-Marshall, job architect, for the Borough of Willesden Engineer's Department, 1936–7. Extant but in forlorn condition at the time of writing.

of a profession answerable to the whole community. In particular it was the course on civic design taught by Patrick Abercrombie in the neighbouring town-planning school which broadened Stirrat's and many other young architects' social horizons.

Since the shift in philosophy at the Liverpool school was accomplished without rancour, its implications took time to sink in. In Stirrat Johnson-Marshall's mind there was no sudden conversion or dedication to causes. Later in the decade some young architects became politicized in their efforts to make changes in their chosen profession. Percy Johnson-Marshall, who had followed his brother on to Liverpool a year later, was one such, but Stirrat stood aloof. He was always too circumspect and 'Fabian' to follow that path, believing that the best way towards reformation was for men of purpose to take hold of existing institutions and bend them to better ends. Some inkling at least of such a future had occurred to him by the time he graduated. A turning point, says his brother, was a talk given by Gropius at the Liverpool school in May 1934. Gropius's compelling description of the work of the Dessau Bauhaus and his gospel that the scope of architecture was total, for everyone, emboldened Johnson-Marshall to begin thinking deeply about how new techniques in architecture and engineering might come to the aid of social reform.

The first necessity in 1935, however, was employment. In that year he married Joan Brighouse, a fellow student whose father was an architect in Ormskirk nearby and had given him some part-time office experience. For the aspiring architect with a social conscience, local-authority work was the coming thing. Buttressed by a handsome reference from Reilly, who relished looking after and forwarding his own, he landed a job as an architectural planning assistant in the unromantic borough of Willesden, upon London's north-western fringes. No apter or busier employment could have been found. These were boom years for the outer London suburbs, and those like Willesden which had achieved municipal status but were beyond the London County Council boundaries abounded in responsibilities, for planning, housing, schools, and the fuller measure of social services which the better councils were beginning to develop. For nineteen months Stirrat Johnson-Marshall was immersed in this work, participating in a planning scheme for the borough, a school, a couple of housing estates, extensions to a hospital, and showrooms and offices for the municipal electricity supply in Willesden Lane. 'Electric House' was the building most completely designed by him, a neat clean block in the modern Dutch or Scandinavian manner then approved at Liverpool (Fig. 10.5). Percy Johnson-Marshall, who took his brother's place at Willesden when Stirrat left in 1937, helped to finish off the job and build it. It was published as the work of 'J. H. Parker and S. J. Marshall, A.A.R.I.B.A., supervisor F. Wayman Brown,

A.M.Inst.C.E.' At Willesden, as in most small local authorities then, architecture came under the borough engineer, and the Johnson-Marshalls were officially his employees. But Parker, an architect of talent and generosity held cruelly back by physical disabilities, was their real superior and teacher. The Willesden office around Parker was no stagnant backwater but the setting for continuous debate, even more so after Percy Johnson-Marshall replaced Stirrat and started to argue politics with Alan Harris, a sharp and witty young engineer of a heterodox turn of mind. 'We argued our way through the Spanish Civil War instead of fighting it,' recalls Percy. 'At Willesden,' Harris attests of the brothers, 'they were really starting to ask, "What exactly are we trying to do?"' Harris made fast friends with them; later, his inventiveness was to be helpful to Stirrat in his school-building ventures (pp. 147–9).

Willesden gave Stirrat Johnson-Marshall experience and allowed him a taste of the wider architectural groupings and discussions in and around London. But the prospects and pay were poor. February 1937 therefore saw him promoted to chief architectural assistant for a yet obscurer local authority, the Isle of Ely County Council, centred at March in remote fenland country. Here again a non-architect, this time a jealous and timid county surveyor, presided over the building programmes. But by good luck Johnson-Marshall was quickly joined by someone he already knew who came in above him as deputy county architect. This was Donald Gibson, who had taught briefly at Liverpool in 1934–6. Gibson's interest in building more simply, his curiosity about prefabrication and his readiness to try technical experiment and research (which he reinforced with a year at the Building Research Station after Liverpool) were in some degree legacies from his father, a distinguished hydraulics engineer. At Liverpool he had a nodding acquaintance with Johnson-Marshall, to whom he taught advanced construction; at the Isle of Ely, they and their wives soon became intimate friends. Henceforward they were to be close allies, their careers and purposes constantly interweaving. Gibson became 'almost a third brother, so close were our ideals', claims Percy Johnson-Marshall. Gibson was the senior by four years and the more knowledgeable on matters technical, but much of the vision and drive came from the younger man. At tactics, both were pastmasters.

Gibson and Johnson-Marshall had been brought in at the Isle of Ely to work on the 'mini-boom' in school-building of the immediate pre-war years. They designed a few brick elementary schools for the county, trying but generally failing to outflank the surveyor on issues of style and technique. This led them to give some initial serious thought to schools. Gibson started a night-school class as a pretext for some amateurish research on daylighting, while Johnson-Marshall joined up with his brother for an unsuccessful entry in the *News Chronicle* schools competition of 1937. Apart from this, there was not much to do at the Isle of Ely except fish. Gibson soon got restless. In 1938 he boldly applied to be city architect at Coventry, where a new Labour council was laying plans for revitalizing Britain's fastest growing city; Johnson-Marshall helped him prepare for the interviews. Aged only twenty-nine, Gibson won the post, moved to Coventry and began gathering allies round him, including Percy Johnson-Marshall. For the time being Stirrat stayed on at March, promoted to deputy county architect.

War came and Johnson-Marshall, already a territorial and still something of an imperialist, was glad to be called up along with several of his colleagues (Fig. 10.6). His company of Royal Engineers remained in England till 1941, when they joined 18 Division and were dispatched to Singapore. They were there, unscathed and disengaged, when the Japanese raced down the Malay peninsula, forcing the British into abject surrender in February 1942. Before the Japanese troops arrived, Captain Johnson-Marshall had made his decision. Among the demoralized men, heads hung low, he sought out companions with whom to make the near-hopeless dash for India and freedom. With two others he set out under the cover of dark, rowed out in a small boat, found a drifting launch and got it started. By dint of skulking and hopping from island to island they reached the Sumatra Coast after various adventures and privations. Thence they proceeded in a Dutch coasting vessel to Java, from where they were conveyed in due course with other escapees to Colombo.

Singapore was the dramatic moment in Stirrat Johnson-Marshall's life. As an episode in wartime valour, it conferred on him a stature which, many years on, can be too easily

10.6. Captain S. J. Marshall, Royal Engineers, c. 1940.

disregarded. But it had a deeper meaning too which contributed to his disinclination to talk later about these events. At Singapore he saw the British empire discredited, the world of his parents and grandparents crumble, the white man pathetic, jeered at and discomfited. It confirmed his personal belief in austerity and discipline, and made him more resolute to help build a firm and just society at home. Many went through similar feelings at this time, but for Johnson-Marshall the shock was acutely emotional. After 1945 he would rarely travel abroad, and never did so again in Africa and Asia, despite the architectural opportunities which opened to his firm there. In part perhaps he was haunted by the spectre of Singapore.

From Colombo, the survivors and stragglers from the *débâcle* were distributed all over India. Johnson-Marshall elected to learn camouflage (a skill in which the British were glaringly deficient compared to the Japanese) at a training school near Poona, and was then transferred to the camouflage directorate at Delhi. His brother crossed paths with him again at this time, on his way out to a whirlwind wartime career of his own in India and Burma. This was not a happy time for Stirrat. Then late in 1942 another blow struck. He heard the news that his younger son Michael, aged two, had accidentally drowned in a horse pond close to their home at March. He was sent back to England immediately on compassionate leave.

In 1943 Johnson-Marshall returned to camouflage work in England. This, as the allies grew stronger and cleverer, was developing from the passivity of concealment to the active and 'creative' process known as deception. At Farnham Castle, where the Camouflage Development and Training Centre was located, he was under the command of Major James Gardner, exhibition-designer extraordinary in civilian life, and he rubbed up against a bevy of architects, artists, engineers and assorted oddballs who had found a niche in this unorthodox arm of warfare. David Medd, not long out of the AA and for the next twelve years his closest collaborator, he first met in the vaulted mess at Farnham towards the end of the year. In the quest for devices that could be quickly mass-produced in anticipation of D-Day, the team was trying out every idea and technique conceivable, with plentiful resources and backing but precious little time and few formal arrangements. A flavour of these experiments is given on pp. 23–6. They helped to catalyse Johnson-Marshall's thoughts about the possibilities in construction for a continuous cycle of relations between designers, manufacturers, users and policy-makers, as well as about the type of buildings Britain might have after the war: light-weight, informal, flexible, prefabricated, produced in numbers by a co-operative team working intimately with makers and users. Here it needs only to be added that Johnson-Marshall played a key role in several of these experiments. Others were now turning to him for decision, leadership, discipline and philosophy.

★　★　★　★　★

Knowing that the architectural future lay with them, Johnson-Marshall was looking round before the war ended for fresh jobs in local authorities. He applied, or thought of applying, to be borough architect of Huddersfield. He was also offered a job at the Building Research Station, where preparations for reconstruction were in full spate. But by then he had accepted the position as C. H. Aslin's deputy at Hertfordshire County Council. He arrived at Hertford late in 1945. Immediately he started planning and organizing, surrounding himself with young architects of commitment and idealism and setting on foot the Hertfordshire schools programme.

The saga of the next eleven years, of Johnson-Marshall's brief but decisive sojourn at Herts (1945–8) followed by his move, with genuine misgivings, to become chief architect to the Ministry of Education (1948–56) forms the centrepiece of this book. They are the justification for any claim he may have to be ranked as a great architect, in some sense of those easily distorted words. They were a time of purpose, application, fertility, power and achievement; in retrospect they offer a model of public, co-operative architecture unmatched in range and depth of enquiry, however simple, amateurish and unpretending some of its products may look today. Here it is merely necessary to stress Johnson-Marshall's role as catalyst and central figure in the process, since he himself declined taking credit or drawing attention to himself. No one close to the decisions which shaped British school-building in these years doubted that he was the key figure, the 'umbrella-man', enabler, facilitator, and, on occasions, conspirer. Design, research and technical decisions he knew how to delegate to others. But it was Johnson-Marshall who spent evening after evening toping with Aslin, urging the need for a programmatic approach to building schools and badgering him for the kind of staff he wanted for Herts; Johnson-Marshall who persuaded Antony Part, the powerful civil servant in charge of school-building at the Ministry, to take on board the Hertfordshire approach nationally and set up a development group which would build; and Johnson-Marshall who cajoled and argued most to get a better attitude in the technical press and the RIBA towards the use of public money in building and towards the duties and dignity of the public architect. It was he who supplied the psychological confidence, inspiration and backing crucial to the success of any great collaborative conception. All through this period he was fertile in ideas, intuitions and stratagems, not all of equal merit. His colleagues had to learn to suppress the bad ones, pick the good ones and carry them through.

The least-known side of Johnson-Marshall's endeavours in these years was his struggle to get recognition for architects in public service, or 'official architects', as they were then known—a phrase he hated and helped expunge from the architectural vocabulary. In common with others he believed that if first-class architects were to be recruited into local government and devote their careers to 'social architecture' they must have better pay and conditions of service. This had been an issue before the war at Willesden and the Isle of Ely, it was still a stumbling block at Herts, and it contributed to Johnson-Marshall's own desertion of the public sector in 1956. The Association of Building Technicians (ABT) and its predecessor the Association of Architects, Surveyors and Technical Assistants (AASTA) had already organized and campaigned on this topic with some success, despite the hostility of private architects in the RIBA. But the ABT was identified with its communist leadership, and rapidly lost ground after the political reaction of 1949–51.

It fell therefore to those less identified with political ends, and especially to a small clique of senior architects among whom Johnson-Marshall was the most active, to fight for the public-sector architect and a socially responsible architecture in a different way. One token of this was the initiative launched by Johnson-Marshall through Colin Boyne of the *Architects' Journal* to end the bad old bureaucratic custom of crediting the top architect alone in public offices for every building. The anonymity, the hierarchy, and the concealment or real responsibility must, he believed, be abolished; job architects and others, competent or incompetent, should be credited or discredited. Over the years this little change was widely taken up by the journals and did much to improve the morale of junior architects working for local authorities.

More important was the task of winning over the RIBA, still then the stronghold of private practice, to a fairer representation of public-sector architecture and thus to a more responsible attitude towards building altogether. This meant getting candidates on to the RIBA Council and other key posts there, elective and non-elective. The campaign originated with an ABT group largely made up of LCC architects, among them Percy Johnson-Marshall (who by then was working with the team for reconstructing Stepney and Poplar). Realizing they needed allies, they approached Robert Matthew, the LCC's chief architect, and Stirrat Johnson-Marshall. Together with Donald Gibson and Robert Gardner-Medwin of the Scottish Department of Health, Stirrat Johnson-Marshall and Matthew briefly constituted an informal 'upper house' (Fig. 10.7). In 1952–3 they contributed to the *Architects' Journal* a series of articles (drafted by Percy Johnson-Marshall) on the role of the public architect which became a kind of manifesto for this little pressure-group. In due course the 'lower house' evolved into a more organized cabal known as the Chain Gang (later as QAG). Its members were mostly architects from the Herts, Coventry, Notts, LCC and Ministry of Education offices and they met regularly—sometimes in the Architectural Press's basement at Queen Anne's Gate, sometimes in the RMJM offices, to exchange ideas and arrange campaigning and voting for RIBA elections. Stirrat Johnson-Marshall was the only senior

10.7. Caucus-meeting on behalf of public-sector architects at the Bride of Denmark, Architectural Press, Queen Anne's Gate, London, c. 1952. Left to right: Robert Matthew, Donald Gibson, Stirrat Johnson-Marshall and Robert Gardner-Medwith.

member to attend these gatherings regularly: they were 'almost rudderless without him', recollects Colin Boyne.

These groupings achieved an extraordinary about-face in the RIBA from the late 1950s onwards. They helped to win a better status for salaried architects in public service and railroaded the RIBA into carrying out its first serious research into the state of the architectural profession and its problems, culminating in 1962 with the publication of *The Architect and his Office*. In these years hardly a candidate promoted by the 'Chain Gang' and its allies failed to win election. Both Johnson-Marshalls sat on the RIBA Council, but Stirrat spoke there in monosyllables, if at all. Often he had already sorted things out and arranged who would talk, perhaps on the phone, over a late-night drink or in a pre-council meeting. Though many failed to notice, he was commonly at the centre of things.

★　★　★　★　★

In 1956 Johnson-Marshall abandoned the Ministry of Education to set up a London office for Robert Matthew. By then Matthew was professor at Edinburgh University in his native Scotland and wanted to stay there, but he also enjoyed being in practice and had just landed the commission for New Zealand House at the bottom of the Haymarket in London. He needed a colleague of equal weight and authority in the south. Thus began the firm of Robert Matthew, Johnson-Marshall and Partners. It is impossible not to conclude that this was an error of judgement for Johnson-Marshall professionally. Personal reasons played their part in this unlooked-for change of direction. He had never saved, the Ministry at that time paid poorly, and he had considerable financial commitments, having growing children and a new house he and his wife had just built for their family at Digswell outside Welwyn Garden City. He was beginning to be bored at the Ministry, and though he could have had almost any job in the public sector for the asking (he nearly went to the LCC at about this time), could discern that the pendulum was swinging slowly back towards private practice. He believed (or so he argued) that with Matthew's powerful help he might by example be able to shift private practice in architecture towards standards of greater responsibility and continuity. He admired Matthew at first and had given him counsel when the latter was taking the gargantuan LCC Architect's Department to pieces and putting it back together again a few years earlier. They, if no one else, could surely bring the methods of the public sector to bear effectively upon private commissions.

The firm succeeded from the first. With his talent for picking men, Johnson-Marshall soon brought together at Park Square East (the handsome house which Matthew retained in London) a group of like-minded architects and old cronies. Many, like himself, were tiring of the frustrations attendant upon working in public offices and of the way in which politicians were already mistaking quantity for quality. There was little need to chase work. Matthew's and Johnson-Marshall's contacts in government, local and central, eased the way, and overloaded authorities were only too happy to 'farm out' schools and other buildings to architects who understood the objectives and constraints. These were the cake, on top of which was a layer of icing: New Zealand House and the Commonwealth Institute in the early years, followed by new universities at York, Bath and Stirling, growing numbers of foreign assignments and local-authority headquarters at Worcester and Hillingdon.

Much of this held scant appeal for Johnson-Marshall. He was indifferent to the adventure of securing, designing, building and publishing any single commission, however prestigious, though he knew it had to be done for his colleagues' sake. A monument like New Zealand House, really Robert Matthew's job, was to him something of an embarrassment, stimulating merely for the opportunities it offered for understanding another kind of user and for getting a tall building efficiently built. In such instances he might make a few small suggestions, and leave his partners to get on with most of the work. Some types of job he would if possible refuse, not on the grounds that they were socially distasteful but because he could not see a chance of entering into genuine dialogue with the client. Army barracks, for instance, the firm would undertake, but hospitals he would try to avoid, as he found the attitudes of doctors inconsistent, uncomprehending and intransigent.

The buildings which sustained him during his years with RMJM were those which promised some degree of dialogue and continuity. The new Cavendish Laboratory at Cambridge was one, built after animated debates with the Professor of Physics, Brian Pippard (1970–4). Then there were the new universities, which seemed for a time likely to allow him to open up to rational scrutiny the piecemeal methods by which they were being built and thus fulfil his claim of bringing the continuity of public practice into private work. Above all there was York, the one university where, with the help of exemplary clients, he was able to manifest his ideas on a large scale. York preoccupied him for a decade from 1961, a period during which the movement in public building which he had done so much to pioneer reached and passed its peak. After it he was struggling against the tide, with less and less effectiveness. His contribution had been made.

As RMJM took root and flourished, spawning subsidiary offices (one at Welwyn Garden City for the ease of Johnson-Marshall and other partners who lived in the area), he became somewhat remote from the routine of the practice—a pattern not unusual for senior partners in large firms. He insisted on equality among the partners and would efface himself to the point of concealment in meetings, but was always recognized as the senior figure in London and Welwyn Garden City and could get his way as of old, when he wanted, by way of obstinacy or prior negotiation. With Matthew remote in Edinburgh or circling the globe as salesman and architectural diplomat, relations became strained and the offices became virtually separate practices. It was a case of the Scottish cavalier and the English roundhead, the increasingly pleasure-loving monarch versus the stubbornly puritan co-operator. Johnson-Marshall found his partner's domineering hard to bear, while Matthew thought the southern offices too expensive, too democratic, too independent, and disinclined to be grateful for the foreign work which he brought in. He was right about the expense. Despite his preoccupation with issues of cost in building, Johnson-Marshall would spare neither time nor money nor staff in his own office to get a job right or a general principle elucidated. Much energy was lavished on committee work, reports and studies which were to the benefit of the client or the construction industry but could never bear fruit in the firm's finances. So the southern offices did not make the profits they might have done in the fat years, and never lined the pockets of the partners. The strain of social idealism and the disinterested traditions of the public sector continued to run strong in RMJM—at any rate in London and Welwyn Garden City.

Buildings themselves were only part of Johnson-Marshall's efforts in this period. He was still active in architectural politics, exerting his potent influence in appointments to key posts in the public domain or offering advice to the University Grants Committee, the Department of Education and Science, the National Buildings Agency and other bodies. But having relinquished the power he had once exercised, he more frequently went unheeded, He could only suggest, or show by example and urge that the example be taken up. His remaining dream was that the type of industrialized architecture started at Herts, socially controlled and managed, might be broadened to encompass as wide a range of building as possible. The CLASP system and organization in particular, earliest of the schools consortia, he believed could provide the key to this revolution. Most of the RMJM jobs which involved his personal commitment, therefore, he sought to build in CLASP, and many were so built; the Cavendish Laboratories, most of York, a little of Bath University, several schools and old people's homes. Even a set of flour mills were designed in the system. The CLASP Joint Development Programme, a costly collaboration to make the system suitable for heavy buildings, was housed in the RMJM offices and would never have taken place without his personal urging. But the 'take-up' that could have justified these endeavours was never forthcoming. They remained interesting, isolated, dead-end experiments.

The last years were not happy ones. Johnson-Marshall was out of sympathy with the style-conscious architecture like the Hillingdon Civic Centre which his partners were beginning to turn out, and felt keenly the waning of breadth of purpose and social concentration among younger architects. He had lived for his work and had no real wish or instinct for withdrawing from the fray. But, hard on himself as ever, he insisted against his own inclination on retiring when he reached sixty-five in 1977. He would have liked to stay on, but did not know how to ask. Joan Johnson-Marshall, a woman with a great breadth of talents and resources, a maker of things and a keeper of ducks, bees, and sundry other creatures, had long wished to live in the countryside. They moved from Digswell, therefore, to a small, dilapidated mill some miles from Stroud which Hugh Morris, one of the RMJM partners closest to Stirrat, had stumbled across while visiting 'Bobby' Carter and his wife nearby. This they thoroughly repaired. But Stirrat was at a loss. He did not read much, he had few hobbies except for sailing, without the constant ringing of the telephone he felt purposeless, and he drank too much—a habit first contracted, he claimed, in persuading Aslin to try out his ideas at Herts, and prolonged since in numberless late-night sessions of persuasion and debate. A tiny RMJM office was opened in Bristol, always something of a contrivance, but it had little or no work. Here, quite suddenly, he died of a heart attack on 16 December 1981.

★　★　★　★　★

For all who knew him well, Stirrat Johnson-Marshall was an enigma, a perennial source of fascination. Despite his neat turn of dress, he had no great physical presence in comparison with his imposing partner Robert Matthew. He was shortish, walked quickly and lightly, and had a habitual pipe perched at an angle from his mouth. He spoke in a hesitant, clipped manner, never blustered, and never ordered. He never lost his temper, and possessed an implacable, dogged patience. His manners were impeccable, his demeanour was modest, and his habits and relaxations were spartan. Money and possessions bored him, and he could never understand the eagerness of others to amass them. He was never seen in a shop, and relied wholly and traditionally on the good will and forbearance of his wife and family to sustain his austere pattern of life.

Among his wide circle of acquaintance, many may have thought there was nothing special about him. A small number knew that his influence, however mysteriously expressed, was profound and pervasive, while a few came close to worshipping him. Occasionally an outsider came close to penetrating his qualities; Gio Ponti, the Italian architect, for instance, had a deep admiration for Stirrat Johnson-Marshall. Some found him peculiarly indecisive for a man of such strong will and purposes; others thought him a master strategist, others again a tremendous opportunist. He had deep personal loyalties but could flatter or obfuscate or obstruct. He thought intuitively, not analytically. Yet the rarest of his talents was for making others think clearly and deeply, and for unravelling complicated problems into simpler ones which others could then address. 'He made me *think*,' say his devotees, as if in unison. James Nisbet, the quantity surveyor and originator of cost planning, is an example. Nisbet was sceptical of Johnson-Marshall when he first knew him because he was 'always praising'. At the same time he would come in and say,

> 'Why do you have slates on the roofs? Why do you have all these little bits of things? Surely that's nonsense. Why are you measuring all these things, all these bits of cutting and the rest? Wouldn't it be better to have something nice that just went over the roof like a tent?' He asked questions which made me think. Here was a chap who seemed to be undermining my future. It disturbed me and appealed to me at the same time.

Johnson-Marshall liked to operate within an oligarchy of architects, experts, clients and decision-makers. Nobody was ever so tireless in seeking out like-minded young architects, probing them, exhorting them, bringing them in, trusting them and backing them up if they passed the test, but rejecting them and opposing them with every adversarial skill if they did not. These colleagues were never expected to be yes-men; he was too modest a man and too good a listener for that. But they frequently found his arguments and manner hard to resist. The intimate sessions of debate which he loved, lasting into the early hours, belied his public reputation for inarticulacy. He would act in them as a kind of architectural psychiatrist. Others would do most of the talking and stagger away worn and drained, but often with a single phrase or idea which seemed to offer the key to a problem. Sometimes, especially in the early years, he simply inspired. 'He had the ability to fire you,' recalled

Dan Lacey. 'To talk to him I found a most wonderfully stimulating and motivating experience, because I found I shared his values and he was able to depict the opportunities and the sense of direction much more clearly than I could see.'

Johnson-Marshall was ambitious not for any self-recognition, but out of a deep-seated belief in the necessity for moral and social change. At Herts and the Ministry of Education, he saw it as his duty to ensure by whatever means that there should be enough good school-places for children, of the highest possible standard for the money available. Broad ambitions like this were shared by so few architects that he felt justified in seizing and wielding power, lest it be used against the public good rather than for it. His preference for working anonymously, his aversion to politics and his conventional habits seemed to make him the perfect civil servant. Yet he hated the blinkered, administrative orthodoxies of government departments and was always endeavouring to circumvent them and rebel against them.

When knighted in 1971 (an honour he grudgingly agreed to take for the good of his practice), he consented also to an interview. It stumbled forward with difficulty. What buildings or architects did he specially admire (he was asked)? He couldn't think of any. Did he have any remaining ambitions? After much hesitation: yes, to be architectural adviser on building to the Treasury, an answer that must have surely stumped his questioner. This was the summit of his later visions, not to raise great monumental buildings, but to change the short-sighted rules which govern capital expenditure for public construction and which, by economizing on first costs, heap up maintenance problems for the future. Only a change of this kind, he perceived, could secure better buildings for all.

On another, private occasion, Hugh Morris again asked him the former question. Were there really no buildings he loved? 'I suppose,' conceded Stirrat, 'a Cotswold village is *all right*'. Years earlier he had shown a modest interest in some Scandinavian and Dutch architecture, the more 'social' work of Aalto and of Van der Vlugt and Van Tijen, Dutchmen who were as much engineers as architects at heart. But as a physical object in itself, no individual building stirred his puritan soul. On a rare visit abroad, to Switzerland in the early 1950s with colleagues, others warmed to the social architecture of Moser and Roth, but Johnson-Marshall came back enthusing about the Volkswagen Beetle. He was just not greatly interested in what others called 'architecture', and anything which for a moment suggested monumentality repelled him. It was the idea of building rationally in the fullest sense, not for a few but for many, which excited him. He was by no means visually indiscriminating. He had an acute sense of how buildings felt to their users in such terms as scale, space, light, colour and order; and his hatred of the monumental was conditioned by years of trying to imagine how a child reacts within and relates to spaces. But he loathed the way in which architectural reputations are made and perpetuated on the strength of 'looks' alone—and usually external 'looks' at that. 'The right design in the right place in the right time at the right price', was one of his catchphrases, meaning that the emphasis on pure design without the broadest context poisoned the current of responsible endeavour in building and narrowed architects' horizons to an almost childish set of preoccupations. He despaired of styles, and regularly inveighed against what he saw as the hijacking of the possibilities of modern architecture by the stylists—'Renaissance in modern dress' as he called it, echoing Lethaby.

His attitudes to architecture were, in sum, peculiarly British. They came, consciously or unconsciously, from the rich Victorian vein of thinking about architecture as something more passionate, pressing and all-embracing than a pastime for the diversion of the eyes alone, something needing co-operation and moral commitment in the search for a just and deep way of building. They came from authors he would claim never to have read, from Ruskin and from Morris, from Lethaby, from Geddes and from Unwin, all quickened by the example and opportunities to which Walter Gropius opened his eyes at Liverpool in 1934. It is as an English, a very English, Gropius that Stirrat Johnson-Marshall deserves to be remembered. 'We could all chip splinters off this man.' says Colin Boyne, 'and some can write, speak, design, or organize better. But who inspired so much?'

# APPENDIX II

## 'CAN WE BUILD MORE SIMPLY?'

*A talk broadcast on the BBC Third Programme by Stirrat Johnson-Marshall, 11 June 1950*

Can we build more simply? The short answer is that we certainly can. But why have we got to try? Why does it seem so complicated to build simply, and easier to build in a more complicated way?

Well we all know that during the next fifteen years we have to fulfil the enormous building needs caused by wear and tear, the destruction of war, the fact that there was no normal building during the war, and that there has been a great increase in population. Of course even so, we shouldn't have to worry about simpler building methods if cost were not a vitally important consideration. But the provision of large numbers of buildings at present-day prices creates a huge financial problem, and I am certain that half-measures will get us nowhere.

We are forced to choose between three courses of action. The first is to build only the small amount we're likely to be able to afford. This is to acknowledge defeat. The second is to accept a drastic reduction in space and quality whilst maintaining the same total. This again is defeat, and why should we accept defeat in this, when we have accomplished so much in other fields—radar for intance, nuclear fission, or jet propulsion?

The third course is to approach the whole problem of building afresh, with the object of devising a fundamentally simpler technique; a technique which will give us greater beauty, comfort and value at lower cost. Now, considerable work has been done in the development of new techniques. I shall try to avoid generalisations by speaking from my own post-war experience in an approach to the simpler building of schools by methods which I think will prove equally appropriate for other types of large building. I shall not deal with housing.

You may well ask at this stage 'If this were possible, why was it not done long ago?' Well, let's look at the past. Before the Industrial Revolution the building industry was a simple organisation comprising only the architect, the builder and the craftsman. Buildings were relatively few in type—cottages, farms, country houses, churches. In addition they were comparatively small in number and were produced over a long period of time. They were constructed of simple materials such as stone, brick and timber which the architect, the builder and the craftsman understood well, as in fact did the client.

With the coming of the Industrial Revolution the structure of the building industry and its techniques remained much the same even though the process of building became more and more complicated. It increased greatly in volume and included a far wider range of building types. Added to our old list we find industrial buildings, hospitals, shops, flats, cinemas and airports, each of which has brought with it new planning and structural problems. Add to this the complications caused by the introduction of sanitation, plumbing, electricity and gas, of ventilation plants and of lifts. Each of these was added so gradually that the suitability of the industry to take it was never fundamentally questioned.

Apart from the reason that it is always difficult to bring an old industry up-to-date there are social causes for the resistance to change.

Old methods of building were admirably suited to the social conditions that prevailed in the past because they grew naturally out of those conditions. They relied first and foremost on an abundant supply of cheap skilled labour which moved from site to site fashioning buildings by hand out of small parts. As we became industrialised numerous fittings such as wash basins, balustrades and windows tended to be factory made, but site labour remained plentiful so the main elements of the structure continued to be hand-made on the spot. Our most common techniques of building today rely on much the same use of manpower. But in the meantime our social pattern has completely altered. Skilled site labour is no longer cheap and what is more, it is extremely scarce and is likely to remain so unless we abandon full employment.

On the other hand while our building methods have not changed fundamentally during the past hundred years, our industrial skill and capacity have increased enormously. Doesn't this indicate the type of new technique we need? We must make the best possible use of what labour is available on the site, and to do so our components should be erected with a minimum of effort. They must be larger for instance than bricks and tiles—large enough perhaps to cover 2,400 square inches in one operation instead of the 27 square inches covered by a brick, and they must be light enough for two men to carry. And if we are to take full advantage of a large industrial capacity, they must also be designed for factory production.

To get a better picture of these new techniques let us compare a room which has been built in one of them with a similar room constructed traditionally. The traditionally built room has smooth walls, a smooth floor and a smooth ceiling. They look deceptively simple but what lies behind them? A vast number of small components, many of which have had to be cut and all of them carefully fitted by hand to meet the dimensions of various parts of the room—round the fireplace for instance, and round the windows and doors. This cutting and fitting not only takes time but it wastes material. But in the other room behind the surface of the walls one might find no more than a dozen simple uprights to which the wall units are screwed. These wall units are slabs of about two feet by six feet. They fit snugly round windows and doors without having to be carved or chipped on the site. Whilst the ceiling, again in large sheets, needs no site plastering to cover the neat machine-finished joints.

These two rooms may not be very different to look at and their wearing qualities will be much the same but whereas the first was built with about 5,200 bits and pieces, the second needs only 200 today and soon may well need only 55; and I should like to promise you that neither the internal nor the external appearance of the second room will bear any resemblance to the emergency hutting of the war years; hutting which is sometimes referred to as 'prefabricated', which has done the whole idea of prefabrication a great deal of harm.

It is not easy to shift skill and knowledge, developed on the building site over many generations, to factories where an intuitive understanding of building does not exist. This is one of the main tasks of the architect. Cheap factory production makes certain other demands of course. For instance to make it economic large numbers of similar components must be made; this, incidentally, does not imply that all our buildings will look exactly alike. The components, when compared with the size of a building, are still relatively small and with skilful design they can be made for assembling in many different ways. If they are widely used, there will be many types, dimensionally related to one another but of different sizes, colours and textures. If we are skilful enough at design I think we can gain considerable advantages from this move to the factory. Furthermore the controlled conditions in a factory should offer exciting opportunities for a higher degree of precision, strength and refinement than we are able to attain in the relatively crude surroundings of the actual building site.

But we have to face the fact that if we are to solve new problems and take full advantage of new opportunities we must combine the skills of the architect, the Building Research Station, the builder and the manufacturer, in a team in which each member can make his contribution at the inception of a project and not at different stages in the process of building. The architect should design with a clear idea of what the factory is best able to make even if this entails spending half his designing time there. But the builder is the person who has to assemble the components on the site—perhaps 60 feet off the ground—so surely he must have a say in their design too.

Well, I return to my question of why these methods haven't been adopted before. The second part of the answer is that the present processes through which a project has to pass before it is completed make team work of this kind almost impossible.

To start with, the client or his representatives state the conditions to their architect. They say when they want the building, how it is going to be used, by how many people and for how long, and roughly the amount of money they can spend on it. They usually draw up a list of rooms based on some existing building, and too frequently they make no further contribution.

The architect in this set-up functions not only as the designer but as the main link between the client and the people who make or sell components and the builder who assembles them. By adopting a simple and effective procedure which has been devised to ensure that he meets his clients' needs at a reasonable price, the architect designs the building, produces drawings and specifications, and these he hands to the quantity surveyor who measures the amount of material or number of components and sets them down in a 'bill of quantities'. The main purpose of the bill is to enable suppliers of parts and builders to quote prices competitively and on a common basis.

This is a perfectly happy arrangement if the technique of building is unquestioned and is understood by all, and it may be appropriate in the future when our new techniques have become normal practice, but what effect has it on new techniques now?

It places a most effective barrier between the 'purchaser', who is represented by the archi-tect, and the 'seller', represented by the manufacturer and the builder, until the goods have been completely designed down to the smallest detail. They cannot pool their common experience until it is too late to affect the design. By adhering to this old system we force them to make their main contributions individually and separately.

One of the points made by Bertrand Russell in his Reith Lectures of 1948 is very relevant to this problem. He said something to the effect that in almost all the fields of human endeavour, significant advances could no longer be made by the individual because the field of contemporary knowledge was too extensive to be mastered and applied by a single mind. He said that the arts of painting and writing were exceptions, but I am sure that the art of building is not.

How are we going to bring our team together at the embryonic stage of development and keep them together to repeat the process; for this is the method that has produced our best aircraft, ships and motor cars? Who is going to take the initiative? The builder? He is not a designer and in any case he cannot be sure of a customer. The building scientist? He seldom builds. The manufacturer? Like the builder he cannot afford the capital outlay unless he is sure of a market. The architect? He is the most likely figure so far but the architect can't move unless his client is prepared to adopt a more dynamic role.

The trouble from our point of view is that most customers usually want only one or two buildings at a time: and small numbers of buildings can't pay for the initial cost of our work. But within the programmes of big concerns (and Local Authorities are good examples of what I mean) our prospects improve; especially when the need is for large numbers of buildings of similar type such as schools or health centres or hospitals. Where these needs are known in advance and can be planned ahead, conditions are almost ideal.

Given these conditions and continuing with the example of the large Local Authority, one then has to face the problem of how to achieve the administrative pattern we need, because these new requirements cut right across the long established practice of competitive tendering. It is clear that our new techniques will not thrive until this problem is solved. The Council, with the help of the Clerk, the Accountant and the Quantity Surveyor are between them well qualified to devise new but equally effective rules for protecting the public purse, which can be written into Standing Orders. If we can get the active collaboration of these several people our team is complete, and our difficulties begin to disappear when we can create a climate in which the team is encouraged to remain together long enough to repeat the process of design and building several times.

Well, perhaps you see some of the difficulties in the way of new building techniques. Remember too that the task is too complex to hope for absolute success in terms of quality and price at the first shot. Earlier on I mentioned our best aircraft. These nearly all represent the sixth or seventh shots by teams who have worked together for ten years or longer.

As you see I am not suggesting a panacea for all our building troubles, nor a technique which will replace traditional building overnight; but rather the immediate acceptance of a new approach which, if adopted now by enough large organisations, will take us forward towards higher standards at lower cost at a time when conditions might otherwise dictate the opposite. But I do want to stress that it is not sufficient for a team to develop new techniques unless they are prepared to expend equal thought and ingenuity on the development of the administrative organisations on which they rely.

Perhaps it wouldn't be fair to end my talk without mentioning a few of the organisations where work of this kind has been or is being attempted. There's the Architects' Department of the old LMS railway and the Hertfordshire County Council, both of which have put up buildings by the new methods I've been describing. And numerous bodies such as the London County Council, the Department of Health for Scotland, the Nuffield Trust for Hospitals and the Middlesex County Council are experimenting in new techniques. They are still in the early stages and the results are by no means perfect but good luck to them. I am sure that an enormous amount depends on their success.

# NOTES

The references below are organized as a concise guide to sources of information; they are not intended as verification for every statement in the book. The appearance of individual names without elaboration refers to taped interviews, discussions or correspondence with the author. The following abbreviations have been employed for periodicals and series of publications:

ABN         *The Architect and Building News*
AD          *Architectural Design*
AJ          *The Architects' Journal*
AR          *The Architectural Review*
BB          Building Bulletins of the Ministry of Education and Department of Education and Science
RIBAJ       *Journal of the Royal Institute of British Architects*

## CHAPTER 1

1. 'We were born in the war . . .': *Focus*, vol. 1, 1938, p. 1. On *Focus* generally: Sir Anthony Cox, Oliver Cox. There were four issues; a fifth failed to appear because of the war.
1. 'To determine . . .': Henry Swain.
1. 'One felt one was joining the profession . . .': David and Mary Medd.
2. An Admiral's House. Anthony Cox in reminiscences of the pre-war AA, *AA Journal*, vol. 67, 1952, p. 208.
2. 'Much experiment . . .': John Summerson, *The Architectural Association 1847–1947*, 1947, p. 43.
2. Rowse: Elizabeth Chesterton, Sir Anthony Cox, Percy Johnson-Marshall, Sir Denys Lasdun, Max Lock, Bruce Martin, David Medd, Sir John Summerson. He had taught and influenced Robert Matthew at Edinburgh: unpublished lecture on 'Sir Robert Matthew and His Work' by John Richards of Robert Matthew, Johnson-Marshall and Partners (Edinburgh), 1984.
2. 'The thing he used to talk about . . .': Sir Anthony Cox.
3. 'Besides being . . .': article by Architects' Co-Partnership on its origins and work in *RIBAJ*, vol. 84, 1967, pp. 230–1.
3. 'He argued . . .': Bruce Martin.
3. 'He was too clever . . .': John Brandon-Jones, quoted in *Architectural Design*, vol. 49, 1979, 'Britain in the Thirties' supplement, p. 101.
3. The AA units, 1938–9: Elizabeth Chesterton, Sir Anthony Cox, Oliver Cox, Max Lock, David Medd. *Focus*, vol. 1, 1938, publishes 'Tomorrow Town' thinly; it was to have appeared in vol. 5, which was cancelled because of the war. 'Rather to the group's disgust': Sir Anthony Cox.
4. 'We got to know . . .': David Medd.
4. 'Sketching in their urns and axes . . .': *AA Journal*, vol. 67, 1952, p. 207.
4. 'We didn't much like . . .': Sir Anthony Cox.
5. 'To stamp out . . . the political and sociological tendencies . . .': quoted by Alan Powers in *Architectural Design*, vol. 49, 1979, 'Britain in the Thirties' supplement, p. 50. Powers documents the AA confrontation of 1938 with some partiality for Goodhart-Rendel; contrast the account in *Focus*, vol. 3, 1939, pp. 79ff.
5. Liverpool. *The Book of the Liverpool School of Architecture*, ed. Lionel B. Budden, 1932; C. H. Reilly, *Scaffolding in the Sky*, 1938; Myles Wright, *Lord Leverhulme's Unknown Venture: The Lever Chair and the Beginnings of Town and Regional Planning*, 1982. On Liverpool before Reilly: Quentin Hughes in *Architectural His-*

*tory*, vol. 25, 1982, pp. 102–113 (with large claims). On Liverpool in the 1930s Cleeve Barr, Sir Donald Gibson, Percy Johnson-Marshall, Lady Johnson-Marshall.
7. 'Gropius's lectures . . .': Percy Johnson-Marshall, 'Emerging Architectural Ideas of the 1930s', unpublished manuscript, 1983.
7. On the Cambridge scientists of the 1930s see especially Gary Werskey, *The Visible College*, 1978.
8. Bernal and the history of science conference of 1931: Werskey, *op. cit.*, pp. 139–49; Maurice Goldsmith, *Sage: A Life of J. D. Bernal*, 1980, pp. 54ff. On Bernal see also Dorothy Hodgkin in *Biographical Memoirs of Fellows of the Royal Society*, vol. 26, 1980, pp. 17–84.
8. 'A sweeping revolution in the methods of building . . .': H. G. Wells, *Anticipations*, 1902, pp. 89–90; the passage was known to Lewis Mumford and others.
8–9. 'The main principles of architecture . . .': J. D. Bernal, *The Social Function of Science*, 1939, pp. 350–3. Some of this passage derives from a paper given to the RIBA in 1937, published in *RIBAJ*, vol. 44, June 1937, pp. 805–12. For the modification of Bernal's architectural views in the light of his wartime experiences, see *RIBAJ*, vol. 53, March 1946, pp. 155–8.
10. 'The distribution of purchasing power . . .': Lancelot Hogben, *Dangerous Thoughts*, 1939, p. 134, in his essay 'Planning for Human Survival'.
10. 'It is not far from the truth . . .': Hogben, *op. cit.*, p. 135.
10. 'I was doing the kind of architecture . . .': David Medd.
11. E. J. ('Bobby') Carter: Sir Anthony Cox, Colin Penn. Carter's papers at the RIBA Library reveal much about British architectural ideals before, during and after the Second World War.
11. Architectural research and the Tecton practice: Peter Coe and Malcolm Reading, *Lubetkin and Tecton*, 1981, pp. 69ff.
11. 'Bombarded with endless questions . . .': Solly Zuckerman, *From Apes to Warlords*, 1978, pp. 56–7.
11. 'A valuable habit of exhaustive research . . .': G. Nelson in *Pencil Points*, October 1936, quoted in Coe and Reading, *op. cit.*, pp. 86–7.
11. 'I didn't know anything about school-building . . .': Denis Clarke Hall.
12. On ARP, the ATO, the AASTA (later ABT) and the AScW: Cleeve Barr, Sir Anthony Cox, Stephen Parsons, Colin Penn, R. W. Toms. See also Werskey, *op. cit.*, pp. 223–37; Coe and Reading, *op. cit.*, pp. 44–6, 162–8; *Keystone* (Journal of the AASTA), 1937–40, *passim*. Coe and Reading however make too much of the ATO's importance and confuse its connection with the more significant

254

AASTA/ABT, whose papers are now at the Modern Records Centre, University
of Warwick Library.
2. Building Research Station. The standard history, F. M. Lea, *Science and Building: A History of the Building Research Station*, 1971, is inadequate. See also
H. W. Melville, *The Department of Scientific and Industrial Research*, 1962, and
R. B. White, *Prefabrication, A History of its Development in Great Britain*, 1965,
pp. 67–8.
3. BRS in the 1930s: William Allen, Sir Donald Gibson.
4. 'It was a sort of bible . . .': William Allen.
4. On the mutilation of the 1909 Planning Act: Kenneth D. Brown, *John Burns*,
1973, pp. 139–41, 149–51. On British town-planning history, the most illuminating accounts are in *British Town Planning: The Formative Years*, ed. Anthony
Sutcliffe, 1981.
5. Municipal architects. No proper study of the growth of public-sector architecture exists. Susan Beattie, *A Revolution in London Housing*, 1980, pp. 9–13,
70, gives a brief account of the development of the LCC Architect's Department.
On the Addison Act and local-authority staffing: Mark Swenarton, *Homes Fit
for Heroes*, 1981, pp. 139–41.
6. Quarry Hill flats: Alison Ravetz, *Model Estate*, 1974.
6. Coventry: Sir Donald Gibson, Percy Johnson-Marshall; also Percy Johnson-
Marshall, *Rebuilding Cities*, 1966, pp. 292ff.
6. Finsbury: Coe and Reading, *op. cit.*, pp. 140–4, 162–76, 178.
6. 'Stale chocolate'. This is how Goodhart-Rendel's phrase was remembered;
the actual words, at least as printed, were 'repetitive and slightly stale': Alan
Powers, *Architectural Design*, vol. 49, 1979, 'Britain in the Thirties' supplement,
p. 51.
6. 'One does not have to be particularly "left" . . .': John Summerson in *Horizon*,
vol. 6, October 1942, pp. 234, 242–3.

## CHAPTER 2

7. The hundred contractors, ordnance factories and hostels: Sir Anthony Cox,
Birkin Haward, Colin Penn; *Science in War*, 1940, pp. 107–13; *AR*, vol. 92, Dec.
1942, pp. 131–46; C. M. Kohan, *Works and Buildings*, 1952, p. 331; Myles Wright,
*Lord Leverhulme's Unknown Venture: The Lever Chair and the Beginnings of Town
and Regional Planning*, 1982, pp. 173–6.
9. 'I was given the drawings . . .': Bruce Martin.
9. 'We are always in these days . . .': John Ruskin, *The Stones of Venice*, 2.6.21.
9. 'The Germans never got their scientists . . .': Sir Andrew Derbyshire. On
operational research generally, P. M. S. Blackett, *Studies of War*, 1962, Part II.
10. Bernal, Zuckerman, BRS and Princes Risborough: Maurice Goldsmith, *Sage,
A Life of J. D. Bernal*, 1980, p. 83; Dorothy Hodgkin in *Biographical Memoirs
of Fellows of the Royal Society*, vol. 26, 1980, p. 53; Solly Zuckerman, *From Apes
to Warlords*, 1978, pp. 109–13.
10. *Science in War* and the Tots and Quots: William Allen; Gary Werskey, *The
Visible College*, 1978, pp. 262–4; Zuckerman, *op. cit.*, pp. 60, 109–11, 393–404;
Angus Calder, *The People's War*, 1971 edn., pp. 532–6. E. J. ('Bobby') Carter,
Allen and Holford were all peripherally involved with the Tots and Quots, and
Allen attended the dinner at which *Science in War* was planned.
10. 'A fundamental scientific discovery . . .': *Science in War*, 1940, pp. 7–8. 'As
executives to apply in their own special field . . .': *ibid.*, p. 111.
10. The scientists under Mountbatten. See particularly the memoir of Bernal
by Dorothy Hodgkin cited above, pp. 55–8.
11. 'In the early days of the war . . .': J. D. Bernal, 'Science in Architecture',
*RIBAJ*, vol. 53, March 1946, p. 155.
11. Camouflage and deception: see especially Guy Hartcup, *Camouflage: A History of Concealment and Deception in War*, 1979.
11. 'Deception was our business . . .': David Medd, 'Stirrat Johnson-Marshall,
Personal Tribute', *Performance*, April/May 1982, pp. 67–70.
11. 'A designer's dream . . .': James Gardner, *Elephants in the Attic*, 1983, p. 41.
13. 'These dummies . . .': James Gardner, recollections of Stirrat Johnson-Marshall at CDTC, communicated to Colin Boyne, 1983.
14. Reith and reconstruction: J. C. W. Reith, *Into the Wind*, 1949, pp. 403–45,
473; C. M. Kohan, *Works and Buildings*, 1952, pp. 69–81, 119, 427–33; *The Reith
Diaries*, ed. Charles Stuart, 1975, pp. 266–89.
14. 'I wished there might be an inspiration . . .': Reith, *op. cit.*, p. 429.
15. 'At the present time . . .': from 'Answering You: No. 19', transcript of North
American wireless transmission, 23/24 Nov. 1941, among papers of E. J. Carter
in RIBA Library.
15. The RIBA and the Architectural Science Group: William Allen; RIBA
archives; *Towards A New Britain* (RIBA publication), 1943.
15. Plethora of government plans. For this reason the ABT produced a *Guide
to Official Publications on Building*, 1946–7, with a foreword by Bernal.
25. BRS from 1943: William Allen, Sir Andrew Derbyshire, John Kay, Guy
Oddie.
25. 'The most impressive learning experience . . .': Guy Oddie.
25. Architectural Physics Division: William Allen, Ralph Hopkinson.
26. Early prefabrication: Gilbert Herbert, *Pioneers of Prefabrication*, 1978, is the
best but by no means an exhaustive text on Victorian prefabrication.
26. 'Modern civilization rests on machinery . . .': C. R. Ashbee, *Where the Great
City Stands*, 1917, pp. 3–4. The first two axioms had already appeared in Ashbee's
*Should We Stop Teaching Art?*; see Alan Crawford, *C. R. Ashbee*, 1985, pp. 160,
167.
26. Prefabrication of public housing in the 1920s: R. B. White, *Prefabrication:
A History of its Development in Great Britain*, pp. 44–84. The building industry's
lack of adaptability: Marion Bowley, *The British Building Industry: Four Studies
in Response and Resistance to Change*, 1966, Ch. 2.
27. Gropius and prefabrication: Gilbert Herbert, *The Dream of the Factory-Made
House*, 1984. Another wise early view on prefabricating houses was Lewis Mumford's, expressed in essays of 1929–30 reprinted in *City Development*, 1945,
pp. 61–83.
27. Cyril Sjöstrom, Scandinavian housing and Quary Hill: Cyril Mardall; White,
*op. cit.*, pp. 71–2, 93, 97–103; *Focus*, vol. 3, 1939, pp. 41–7; Alison Ravetz, *Model
Estate*, 1974, pp. 52, 67.
28. The Crystal Palace and architectural modernism: Robert Thorne in *AR*, vol.
176, July 1984, pp. 49–53.
28. 'Light, loosely grouped and "flexible"': Anthony Cox, review of H. Myles
Wright and R. Gardner-Medwin, *The Design of Nursery and Elementary Schools*,
in *Focus*, vol. 2, 1938, p. 94.
28. Committee for the Scientific and Industrial Provision of Housing: Denis
Clarke Hall (interview); Denis Clarke Hall, *Building Pre-Fabrication*, 1940 (typescript in RIBA Library); *Housing Production, or the Application of Quantity Production Technique to Building*, First Report of the Committee for the Scientific and
Industrial Provision of Housing, Jan. 1943.
28. Coventry prototypes: Sir Donald Gibson, F. W. L. Heathcote; *AJ* 18 July
1940, p. 41; 25 July 1940, p. 63; 24 Apr. 1941, pp. 273–81; 8 Jan. 1942, pp. 21–2,
25–9; 7 Oct. 1943, pp. 255–8; *ABN* 16 Nov. 1945, pp. 111–14.
29. Prefabricated prototypes during and after the war: White, *op. cit.*, pp. 139–65;
Bowley, *op. cit.*, pp. 83–103. Bernal's work on prefabricated house-types: Goldsmith, *op. cit.*, pp. 139–40; *The Builder*, 16 Nov. 1945, p. 502. On the AIROH
house: Brian Finnimore in *Construction History*, vol. 1, 1985, pp. 60–72.
31. The post-war AA: Colin Boyne, Oliver Cox, Andrew Derbyshire, John
Kay, Hugh Morris, Joseph Rykwert, Pat Tindale.
31. 'Familiar buildings took on a new life . . .': Oliver Cox (notes).
31. *Plan*. Started in 1942, this was technically the journal of the Architectural
Students Association and was first associated with the Manchester School of
Architecture. It began to be dominated by AA students from 1946. Vol. 2 of
1948, pp. 6–22, reports the symposium on group-working, addressed by Stirrat
Johnson-Marshall, Howard Robertson, Oliver Cox and others and edited by
Michael Ventris.

## CHAPTER 3

36. 'The dearth of secondary schools . . .': throughout this chapter I have relied
much upon G. A. N. Lowndes, *The Silent Social Revolution*, 1969 edn., and
Malcolm Seaborne and Roy Lowe, *The English School, Its Architecture and Organization, Vol. II, 1870–1970*, 1977.
36. *AJ* articles on schools. The series began in *AJ* 4 Nov. 1937, proceeded inter-
mittently to 7 Apr. 1938 and was republished as H. Myles Wright and R. Gardner-
Medwin, *The Design of Nursery and Elementary Schools*, 1938. A previous long
article on school-building appeared in *AJ* 28 May 1936, pp. 797–858. These articles
had much influence on school-building in the late 1930s.
36. Enthusiasm of the Spens report: *Focus*, vol. 4, 1939, pp. 53–7.
37. Stirrings of medical and architectural research. The Spens Report (Board
of Education, *Report of the Consultative Committee on Secondary Education*, 1938)
contains a brief section (pp. 301–4) with a footnote on research done to that
date on heating, ventilation and lighting of schools. The Board's *Suggestions for
the Planning of Buildings for Public Elementary Schools*, 1936, touches on similar
points.
38. Joint work of Medical Research Council and BRS: Ralph Hopkinson, David
Medd.
38. Denis Clarke Hall's *News Chronicle* competition entry: *AJ* 25 March 1937,
pp. 517–20.
38. Evening classes at the Isle of Ely: Sir Donald Gibson.

40. 'Monumentality should have no place . . .': *AJ* 7 Apr. 1938, p. 594.

40. Dartington: David Medd, Colin Penn; Lawrence Wodehouse in *AA Quarterly*, vol. 8, no. 2, 1976, pp. 3–14; Michael Young, *The Elmhirsts of Dartington*, 1982.

40. 'Your gangster age . . .': quoted in Jonathan Croal, *Neill of Summerhill, The Permanent Rebel*, 1983, p. 164.

41. 'At my prep school . . .': Anthony Cox in *Focus*, vol. 2, 1938, pp. 93–4.

41. 'It was an adventure . . .': Henry Swain.

41. Henry Morris and the village colleges: Harry Rée, *Educator Extraordinary, The Life and Achievements of Henry Morris*, 1973. For his writings, *The Henry Morris Collection*, ed. Harry Rée, 1984.

42. Morris as 'classical humanist': Harry Rée, *Educator Extraordinary*, 1973, p. 98. 'Let us say to the architect . . .': *ibid.*, pp. 30–1, 153–4.

44. Learning from the nursery. I have relied much here on Nanette Whitbread, *The Evolution of the Nursery-Infant School*, 1972; see also Phoebe E. Cusden, *The English Nursery School*, 1938, and *Friedrich Froebel and English Education*, ed. Evelyn Lawrence, 1952, Chs. 2 and 3. For an account of some early nursery building-projects: Henrietta Startup, 'Architecture and Nurture: Building for the Small Child and for Motherhood 1890–1939', Bartlett School of Architecture, University of London, M.Sc., 1985. For the earlier background to building for children: Deborah Weiner, 'The Institution of Popular Education: Architectural Form and Social Policy in the London Board Schools, 1870–1904', Ph.D., Princeton University, 1984.

45. Nurseries under the Butler Act: see, e.g., *Planning the New Nursery Schools*, Report of the Buildings Advisory Committee of the Nursery Association of Great Britain, 1945.

46. 'String of classrooms . . .': *Christian Schiller In His Own Words*, ed. Christopher Griffin-Beale, 1979, p. 66.

46–8. 'The form of the open-air nursery . . .': G. A. N. Lowndes, *Margaret McMillan*, 1960, p. 76. 'The old style of buildings . . .': Albert Mansbridge, *Margaret McMillan*, 1932, p. 105. 'On entering . . .': *ibid.*, p. 101.

49. Swiss Écoles Maternelles, Vienna kindergartens and Paris crèches are well illustrated in H. Myles Wright and R. Gardner-Medwin, *The Design of Nursery and Elementary Schools*, 1938.

49. 'Modern Movement' British nurseries: for Dulwich, *AJ* 11 Nov. 1937, p. 755, 9 Dec. 1937, p. 962. The Kensal House school was widely illustrated, e.g. by Wright and Gardner-Medwin, *op. cit.*

49. Timber-framed schools. Louis De Soissons' early example at Welwyn Garden City: *The Builder*, 20 Apr. 1923, pp. 652, 657. For a later and larger example by Hubert Bennett at Swinton and Pendlebury: *RIBAJ*, vol. 45, June 1938, pp. 744–50. Seaborne and Lowe, *op. cit.*, Plate 29, show a characteristic municipal example. Hartford Nursery School: Sir Leslie Martin; *AR*, vol. 86, 1939, pp. 127–8.

50. Nursery School Association, timber classroom: Ernö Goldfinger, Mary Medd; James Dunnett and Gavin Stamp, *Ernö Goldfinger, Works I*, exhibition catalogue, 1983, pp. 59, 60.

50. Hilary Haworth Nursery School, Chester: Sir Donald Gibson; *RIBAJ*, vol. 43, Dec. 1935, pp. 134–7; *AJ* 19 Dec. 1935, pp. 921–4. For the main Lache Elementary School: *The Builder*, 6 Sep. 1935.

52. Prefabricating British schools before the 1930s. Gilbert Herbert, *The Dream of the Factory-Made House*, 1984, p. 86, refers to an Edwardian school-building exported from Silesia to Leith, Scotland.

52. 'Alternative methods of construction' and the Board of Education: Seaborne and Lowe, *op. cit.*, pp. 73, 109, 117–20; *AJ* 26 Nov. 1942, pp. 342–9.

52. *News Chronicle* competition and Richmond High School for Girls: Denis Clarke Hall, Colin Penn; *AJ* 25 Nov. 1937, pp. 517–20.

53. 'I tried to use light quick building . . .': Denis Clarke Hall.

53. Stillman's schools in West Sussex: *AJ* 8 Sep. 1938, pp. 396–7 and 26 Nov. 1942, pp. 338–49; R. B. White, *Prefabrication: A History of its Development in Great Britain*, 1965, pp. 103–7; Barry Russell, *Building Systems, Industrialization and Architecture*, 1981, pp. 216–21.

53. 'Faded panache': Russell, *op. cit.*, p. 218.

54. 'The architecture was novel . . .': Seaborne and Lowe, *op. cit.*, p. 132.

55. Evacuation and building: Richard M. Titmuss, *Problems of Social Policy*, 1950, esp. pp. 209–12. The AASTA campaign: *Evacuation: The Under Fives*, Report of Evacuation Committee of AASTA, Aug. 1940; *Keystone*, March 1940; *ABN* 22 March 1940, pp. 259, 288–9.

55. Stillman's wartime plans for schools: *AJ* 26 Nov. 1942, pp. 342, 350–1.

55. Wartime huts and canteens for schools: C. M. Kohan, *Works and Buildings*, 1952, pp. 379–82.

55. The HORSA programme: Stuart Maclure, *Educational Development and School Building*, 1984, pp. 26–8.

56. The Wood Committees and *Post-War Building Studies No. 2*: see the discussion in Maclure, *op. cit.*, pp. 11–15; and the report itself, *Post-War Building Studies No. 2, Standard Construction for Schools*, 1944.

57. 'Unprecedentedly great', 'realities of the situation': *Post-War Building Studies No. 2, Standard Construction for Schools*, 1944, paras. 6, 8.

## CHAPTER 4

This chapter depends chiefly upon interviews and discussions, but I have also leant much on Stuart Maclure, *Educational Development and School Building*, 1984, Ch. 3, and M. P. K. Keath, 'The Development of School Construction Systems in Hertfordshire, 1946–64', Ph.D., Thames Polytechnic, 1983. I am specially grateful to Michael Keath, whose generosity in allowing me to draw upon his work has saved me from many mistakes.

58. New Towns and overspill estates: H. Orlans, *Stevenage: A Sociological Study*, 1952; Bob Mullan, *Stevenage Ltd*, 1980, Ch. 3; Jack Balchin, *First New Town: An Autobiography of the Stevenage Development Corporation*, 1980. For early social conditions on an overspill estate (South Oxhey), Margot Jeffreys in *London: Aspects of Change*, ed. Ruth Glass, 1964.

59. 'They were in the main ordinary people . . .': C. B. Purdom, *The Building of Satellite Towns*, 1949 edn., p. 59.

59. 'We have much to learn . . .': Stirrat Johnson-Marshall, 'The Construction of Primary and Secondary Schools', talk delivered to Building Research Congress, 1951, p. 7 (copy in RIBA Library). Pilgrimage to De Havillands: Colin Boyne.

60. Newsom at Herts: Maclure, *op. cit.*, pp. 38ff.

60. 'The chief officers were all . . .': Geoffrey Fardell.

60. 'No architect should design a school . . .': *AA Journal*, Feb. 1946, p. 46.

61. Mary Crowley. I am grateful to Mary Medd for information on her family background and career. Houses designed by her at Tewin near Welwyn before the war had received some notice: *ABN* 26 June 1936, pp. 388–91. For her father's views, see Ralph H. Crowley, *The Hygiene of School Life*, 1910.

62. Pre-war organization of Herts architects' office: Geoffrey Fardell.

62. C. H. Aslin: varieties of view expressed by Cleeve Barr, Oliver Cox, Geoffrey Fardell, Bruce Martin, David Medd, Jack Platt, Dan Lacey and Henry Swain.

63. Johnson-Marshall, Gibson and the Coventry houses. Among the few surviving architectural papers of Stirrat Johnson-Marshall were printed particulars of the 'Radiation House' built at Coventry in 1945.

63. Johnson-Marshall declines a job at BRS: William Allen, David Medd.

63. Stillman's West Sussex prototype, designed with Uni-Seco Limited: see R. B. White, *Prefabrication, A History of its Development in Great Britain*, 1965, pp. 226–8.

64. Memories of 1946–7: Sir Anthony Cox, Dan Lacey, Bruce Martin, David Medd. 'Herts were the happiest days . . .': Cleeve Barr.

64. 'Cheshunt was not a prototype . . .': Pat Tindale.

65. Hinchliffe: Oliver Cox, Geoffrey Fardell, Dan Lacey, David Medd; Keath, *op. cit.*, pp. 55–6; White, *op. cit.*, pp. 229–30.

65. 'The design of the components . . .': Keath, *op. cit.*, p. 77.

66. Hills schools for the LCC: Kenneth Campbell, John Weeks.

66. Experiments with six-foot grid: early plans for Croxley Green and Cheshunt among papers of Stirrat Johnson-Marshall.

66. 'The supply of steel . . .': Stirrat Johnson-Marshall, 'The Construction of Primary and Secondary Schools', talk delivered to Building Research Congress, 1951, p. 2.

67. 'The so-called building materials . . .': Bruce Martin in *Plan*, no. 8, 1951, p. 2.

70. 'With a grid you could build . . .': David Medd. For 'grid v. bay' generally Sir Anthony Cox, Dan Lacey, David Medd, Henry Swain.

70. Prefabricated schools 'more than a *pis aller*': Marian Bowley, *The British Building Industry: Four Studies in Response and Resistance to Change*, 1966, p. 263.

71. Cheshunt and Essendon. The fullest of many accounts is given by Keath, *op. cit.*, Ch. 9. See also particularly Michael Ventris in *AA Journal*, March 1948, pp. 172–5.

72. 'Do these scattered sheds . . .?': A. Trystan Edwards in *Financial Times*, 23 May 1950.

72. Distortion of the system at Essendon: Oliver Cox.

73. 'Forceful and also genial': *Financial Times*, 23 May 1950.

75. 'One had modelled oneself . . .': Henry Swain. 'Things I now take for granted . . .': Swain in *Stirrat Johnson-Marshall*, text of commemorative speeches given at Royal Society of Arts, 24 March 1982, p. 10.

75. 'The educationists became . . .': Dan Lacey.

75. Publicity lectures at the AA and Birmingham: Maurice Lee, Guy Oddie,

The Herts philosophy on school-building was set out for students in *Plan*, no. 6, 1949, pp. 22–9, and on group-working in no. 2, 1948, pp. 15–16.
75. Publicity for Herts. The first important article was in *AR*, vol. 101, Feb. 1947, pp. 63–6. Other significant articles appeared in *ABN* 16 Jan. 1948, pp. 47–53 and 30 Sep. 1949, pp. 319–265; *AR*, vol. 106, Sep. 1949, pp. 161–76; *AJ* 20 Oct. 1949, pp. 431–40; and *AR*, vol. 111, June 1952, pp. 367–87. Herts was well represented but not dominant at an RIBA conference of October 1947 on school-building: *RIBAJ*, vol. 55, Nov. 1947, pp. 7–28 and Dec. 1947, pp. 62–9.
76. Problems with Hills and the spreading of responsibilities: Geoffrey Fardell, Dan Lacey, David Medd; Keath, *op. cit.*, Chs. 10 and 11.
76. Schools farmed out to private architects. Oxhey Wood School, Oxhey (Gollins and Melvin) and South Hill School, Hemel Hempstead (Harrison and Seel), built in 1949–50, were the first primary schools farmed out. For South Hill: *ABN* 13 Sep. 1951, pp. 281–4. Scots Hill Grammar School, Rickmansworth (1952–4), by Robert Hening and the red-baiter Anthony Chitty, was sometimes cited as an example of the mess that could be made of the 8 feet 3 inches system.
77. Architects, educationists and 'user requirements': *ABN* 30 Sep. 1949, pp. 319–26. 'Fairly objective set of requirements': *ibid.*, p. 322.
81. 'I remember one component . . .': Cleeve Barr.
81. 'When I got to the Herts office . . .': Henry Swain.
82. Adamsez and Herts: Alan and Bryan Adams; Oliver Cox; David Medd. 'I have been thinking . . .': Alan Adams, typescript history of Adamsez Ltd., p. 37 (talk to staff in 1943). 'Imagine us, therefore, . . .': from 'Design in Sanitary Fireclay' by 'The Sanitary Fireclay Man' [Alan Adams], cutting of *c.* 1950 lent by the author.
85. Herts and BRS: William Allen, Sir Andrew Derbyshire, Ralph Hopkinson, David Medd. 'We sat down for about three days . . .': William Allen.
85. Forced warm air, John Fowler and Weatherfoil: William Allen, Dan Lacey, David Medd and Henry Swain; letter from Cecil Handisyde to Colin Boyne, March 1984; *AJ* 11 Aug. 1955, pp. 197–201. On temperatures: *Education*, 27 Apr. 1951. For the general post-war position on school-heating see the disappointing *Post-War Building Studies No. 27, Heating and Ventilation in Schools*, 1947, supplemented by the discussion in *RIBAJ*, vol. 55, Nov. 1947, pp. 20–4. Abbots Langley heating trials: BB No. 13, *Fuel Consumption in Schools*, 1955; *Journal of Institute of Heating and Ventilation Engineers*, 20, 1953, pp. 459–65; 23, 1955, pp. 88–123.
86. Lighting: William Allen, Ralph Hopkinson, John Kay, David Medd. For the position in 1947, see *RIBAJ* vols. 54, Jan. 1947, pp. 1–7 and 55, Nov. 1947, pp. 20–4. For a later view, R. G. Hopkinson and J. D. Kay, *The Lighting of Buildings*, 1969, Ch. 7.
88. 'Work that I had done . . .': Ralph Hopkinson.
90. Colour: William Allen, Oliver Cox, David Medd; contribution by Medd in *AR*, vol. 106, Sep. 1949, pp. 166–8. Articles by Ozenfant appeared in *AR*, vols. 81, 1937, pp. 41–4, 89–92, 195–8, 243–6; and 82, 1937, pp. 41–4, 77–80.
91. 'It enabled one to define . . .': William Allen.
91. 'The impact of these schemes': Oliver Cox.
91. Furniture: Oliver Cox, David Medd. Hertfordshire's own dimensional survey: *ABN* 30 Sep. 1949, p. 325.
92. Art in the schools: Oliver Cox, Rosemary Ellis, Dan Lacey, David Medd; Maclure, *op. cit.*, pp. 45–7, 58, with a list of 'original works of art' in Herts schools. One-third of one per cent: *AJ* 17 March 1949, pp. 248–9.
92. Landscaping arrangements: Cleeve Barr, Dan Lacey, Henry Swain.
93. 'The idea was to get the art students . . .': Oliver Cox.
93. 'It was an inspiration . . .': Gerald Holtom.
93. Econa plumbing wastes: Keath, *op. cit.*, p. 147. Switchboxes (by Hartley Electromotives Ltd): Sir Anthony Cox, David Medd.
93. The spark for cost analysis: James Nisbet; Keath, *op. cit.*, Ch. 23. Nisbet has emphasized that little concerted work on costs was started at Herts in the early years.
94. Site and sub-contracting problems: Cleeve Barr, Colin Boyne, Sir Anthony Cox, Oliver Cox, Alan Meikle, David Medd, Henry Swain. 'You've got a frame . . .': Cleeve Barr.
94. 'Out of a total . . .': Keath, *op. cit.*, p. 81.
95. Cladding: Sir Anthony Cox, Dan Lacey, David Medd; Keath, *op. cit.*, pp. 96, 110, 122.
95. 'C'est très jolie': Cleeve Barr, David Medd.
95. 'He lived in Berkhamsted . . .': Cleeve Barr.
96. Row with Aslin: Cleeve Barr, Oliver Cox, Geoffrey Fardell, Dan Lacey, Henry Swain.
96. Rivalry between primary and secondary groups: Alan Meikle.
96. Primary group: Dan Lacey, Alan Meikle, Henry Swain; Keath, *op. cit.*, Chs. 12 and 13; *AJ* 26 June 1952, pp. 785–8. 'Gave us a justification . . .': Dan Lacey. 'We used questionnaires . . .': Henry Swain. 'As we went on . . .': Dan Lacey.
102. Secondary group: Geoffrey Fardell, Dan Lacey, Alan Meikle, Jack Platt; Keath, *op. cit.*, Chs. 18 and 19; *AJ* 19 April 1956, pp. 379–84 and 2 Aug. 1956,

pp. 156–62.
103. Barclay School, Stevenage: David Medd; *ABN* 17 June 1949, pp. 526–7 and 16 Sep. 1949, pp. 265–72; *AA Journal*, March 1949, pp. 172–5.
103. Cleary Working Party, LMS Development Group, Architectural Science Board and beginnings of 3 feet 4 inches: William Allen, Bruce Martin, John Weeks; Keath, *op. cit.*, Ch. 17; *AJ* 23 Nov. 1950, pp. 420–30; *AR*, vol. 111, June 1952, pp. 371, 385–7. See also paper by Mark Hartland Thomas and discussion in *Journal of the Royal Society of Arts*, vol. 51, 1953, pp. 98–120, epitomized in *AJ* 18 Dec. 1952, pp. 741–7.
103. General Panel system and its fate: Gilbert Herbert, *The Dream of the Factory-Made House*, 1984, Part III.
105. First 3 feet 4 inches schools: Geoffrey Fardell, Bruce Martin, David Medd, Alan Meikle, Jack Platt; Keath, *op. cit.*, Ch. 17. Clarendon: *AJ* 23 Nov. 1950, pp. 420–30. Summerswood: *AD*, vol. 22, Aug. 1952, pp. 224–33. Beechwood Day Nursery: *ibid.*, March 1952, pp. 64–74.
106. 'I found the Holoplast buildings . . .': Alan Meikle.
107. 'There were lots of things . . .': Geoffrey Fardell.
107. Later experiments with 3 feet 4 inches: Geoffrey Fardell, Dan Lacey, Alan Meikle, Jack Platt; Keath, *op. cit.*, Ch. 20. Burleigh School, Hatfield: *AJ* 8 Sep. 1955, pp. 319–34. Simon Balle School: *AJ* 24 April 1958, pp. 615–26.
109. Ravenscroft School, Barnet: *AJ* 24 Feb, 1955, pp. 365–78. Dennis White and secondary-school furniture: Alan Meikle; *Municipal Journal* 10 Sep. 1954, pp. 2117–24.
109. Herts and modular co-ordination: John Kay, Jack Platt; *AJ* 8 Dec. 1955, pp. 783–9.
109. Herts from 1956 to SEAC: Geoffrey Fardell, Jack Platt; Keath, *op. cit.*, Chs. 21, 22, 24. For a critical view of Hertfordshire's later development: *Official Architecture and Planning*, vol. 29, Sep. 1966, pp. 1286–9.

# CHAPTER 5

112. British architecture and central government. For early nineteenth-century developments: *The History of the King's Works*, ed. H. M. Colvin, vol. 6 (1782–1851), 1973. Developments since 1851 are as yet uncharted.
112. Unwin in the Ministry of Health: Frank Jackson, *Sir Raymond Unwin, Architect, Planner and Visionary*, 1985, Chs. 5 and 6; Mark Swenarton, *Homes Fit for Heroes*, 1981, pp. 141–4. Thomas Adams and George Pepler were also important early 'officials' in government planning.
113. The MoE in the 1940s and the formation of A & B Branch: Stuart Maclure, *Educational Development and School Building*, 1984, Ch. 4; John Redcliffe-Maud, *Experiences of an Optimist*, 1981, pp. 52–4. Ellen Wilkinson at the MoE: *History Workshop Journal*, 7, 1979, pp. 157–69. Tomlinson: Fred Blackburn, *George Tomlinson*, 1954.
113–14. 'A very sparky, energetic . . .'; 'each quarter a central government committee . . .'; 'we thought it so important . . .': Sir Antony Part.
115. Maud 'ticked off': Colin Boyne.
115. 'I first saw him in a black felt hat . . .': William Allen.
115. 'You must be able to show . . .': Stirrat Johnson-Marshall's attitude as expressed by Pat Tindale.
115. RIBA opposition to A & B Branch: Colin Boyne, David Medd.
116. 'The real interest was . . .': Pat Tindale.
116. Scrutiny of final plans only: MoE Circular 191/1948.
116. Development Groups. For a summary of the LMS work, R. B. White, *Prefabrication, A History of its Development in Great Britain*, 1965, pp. 258–68. For fuller accounts: *AR*, vol. 94, Nov. 1943, pp. 135–6 (design of 'railbars'); *RIBAJ*, vol. 51, Sep. 1944, pp. 275–82 (canteen programme); and for the experimental stations *AR*, vol. 99, March 1946, pp. 79–83; *RIBAJ*, vol. 55, Feb. 1948, pp. 164–9; *AJ* 8 April 1948, pp. 325–31. Queens Park (1945) was the LMS prototype 'unit station'; few others were built. Development Groups in other ministries: Elizabeth Layton, *Building by Local Authorities*, 1961, pp. 317–33.
116. Pott's 'totally incorruptible technical mind': Maurice Lee.
116. 'Nearer to being . . .': Guy Oddie.
117. Ventris as 'superior being': Maurice Lee. At the time of his death, Ventris was working part-time for the *Architects' Journal* on presenting and organizing information for architects.
117. Part, Pile, Nenk, Morrell, and the civil servants' and inspectors' contribution: Maclure, *op. cit.*, pp. 63–5, 79–81.
117. Organization and finance of school-building programmes: J. A. G. Griffith, *Central Departments and Local Authorities*, 1966, pp. 97–166; Sir William Pile, *The Department of Education and Science*, 1979, pp. 43–8, 78–80.
118. Cripps and the threat of huts: David Medd; Maclure, *op. cit.*, pp. 67–70.

118. 'Money is a factor ...': Stirrat Johnson-Marshall's views as expressed by Pat Tindale.

118. Cost per place: John Kay, James Nisbet, David Medd; BB No. 4, *Cost Study*, 1951. Cost figures from 1949 onwards are set out in Maclure, *op. cit.*, p. 140.

119. 'They could establish ...': James Nisbet. See also the profile of Nisbet in *Building*, 10 Feb. 1978, pp. 68–72.

120. Origins of cost analysis: James Nisbet. The Napoleonic barracks: *Economic History Review*, vol. 8, 1955–6, pp. 167–76; vol. 20, 1964, pp. 94–110.

120. 'You were pricing ...': James Nisbet.

120. 'We were surprised to find ...': Sir Antony Part.

120. Area analysis: Guy Oddie.

120. Early Middlesex schools: *AJ* 1 Sep. 1949, pp. 223–5; *AD*, vol. 21, April 1951, pp. 92–108; *AA Journal*, vol. 69, Dec. 1953, pp. 129–32. MoE's opposition to partial building of schools: BB No. 2, *New Secondary Schools*, 1950.

120. Political restraints on school-building in the early 1950s: Brian Simon, *The Common Secondary School*, 1955, pp. 21–2.

121. Pilkington Report: Maclure, *op. cit.*, pp. 77–9. 'With particular emphasis ...': 'The Educational Building Practice of the Ministry of Education, Report by Mr. W. H. Pilkington', para. 51.

122. Cost planning: John Kay, David Medd, Peter Newnham, James Nisbet, Guy Oddie. 'The cost planning for the Arnold Project ...': John Kay. 'We'd look at earlier buildings ...': Guy Oddie. 'Their great contribution ...': Fred Pooley.

122. Spread of cost planning. Articles in the *AJ* continued from 27 Jan. 1955 to 30 June 1955; a lucid exposition of cost analysis occurs on 24 Feb. 1955, pp. 261–4, and objections are voiced on 14 April 1955, pp. 496–500. See also Andrew Derbyshire in *RIBAJ*, vol. 61, Sep. 1954, pp. 431–46.

123. 'They wrote to the ...': John Carter, paper written for Colin Boyne, 1984.

125. Alternative school-building systems. Denis Clarke Hall's: *AJ* 6 July 1950, pp. 13–18. Ernö Goldfinger's: *AD*, vol. 22, Oct. 1952, pp. 184–93. Lancashire system: *RIBAJ*, vol. 62, May 1955, pp. 286–90. Another short-lived method was the adaptation of the Orlit concrete housing system for schools. Carden School, Brighton (1947–8), was the prototype: *Concrete Quarterly*, 5, Jan. 1949, pp. 4–7.

126. Building Bulletins. To assess technical progress and sophistication, BB No. 7, *Fire and the Design of Schools*, 1952, is worth comparing with its predecessor, *Fire Precautions in Schools*, 1945, which is simplistic and unrelated to construction.

128. Problems of the first comprehensives: Simon, *op. cit.*, pp. 35–45, 75–7, 160–6. For early ideas on designing comprehensives: *AD*, vol. 26, April 1956, pp. 108–21.

129. Derwent timber system: *AJ* 18 June 1953, pp. 768–73 and 18 Oct. 1956, pp. 552–3.

131. 'There is a tendency ...': William Glare, report to MoE on schools systems, Dec. 1950.

133. Wokingham: Maurice Lee, David Medd. Maclure, *op. cit.*, p. 200, gives a bibliography. 'Based on no preconceived plan pattern ...': BB No. 8, *Development Projects: Wokingham School*, 1952, p. 11.

135. BAC: William Glare, Sir Alan Harris, Maurice Lee, Peter Newnham. On the AIROH house: Brian Finnimore in *Construction History*, 1, 1985, pp. 60–71. The original schools system was published in *ABN* 30 Jan. 1948, pp. 91–5. For the first school (Romney Avenue, Locklaze, Bristol): *AJ* 17 March 1949, p. 246 and 13 Oct. 1949, pp. 405–10. See also Barry Russell, *Building Systems, Industrialization and Architecture*, 1981, pp. 226–8.

136. Whitmore Park: *ABN* 23 Dec. 1949, pp. 654–60; *AJ* 19 July 1951, pp. 78–81; *Official Architecture*, March 1951, pp. 132–4.

138. Limbrick Wood: *RIBAJ*, vol. 59, Oct. 1952, pp. 446–9; *Official Architecture*, Nov. 1952, pp. 524–5. Its successor was called Aldermoor Farm.

139. 'I came up with ...': Peter Newnham.

140. Lyng Hall, Whitley Abbey and Woodlands: Peter Newnham, Guy Oddie. For the upgrading of the BAC system: *Prefabrication*, June 1955, pp. 359–64. Woodlands was published in detail in *AJ* 13 Oct. 1955, pp. 487–502, Lyng Hall and Whitley Abbey in *AJ* 28 Feb. 1957, pp. 321–39. For Coventry's early comprehensives, Bob Burgess in *Life and Labour in a 20th Century City: The Experience of Coventry*, ed. Bill Lancaster and Tony Mason, 1986.

143. Intergrid: Sir Alan Harris, Maurice Lee. Worthing: *AJ* 4 Aug. 1955, pp. 145–64; *Prefabrication*, Aug. 1955, pp. 449–54; *Architecture and Building*, Sep. 1955, pp. 332–8.

147–9. 'Steel was very difficult ...'; 'it was all new ...': Sir Alan Harris.

149. 'Which taught me ...': Maurice Lee.

152. Rubber flooring: Colin Boyne, David Medd; *RIBAJ*, vol. 61, June 1954, pp. 307–8. For the strange story of Lord Forrester and the Brynmawr Rubber Factory: *AA Files*, vol. 10, 1985, pp. 3–12.

153. 'At Belper we wanted ...': Pat Tindale.

153. Rat. Trad.: David Medd, Peter Newnham.

153. 'I came up with some ...': Peter Newnham.

154. 'It became evident to me ...': Sir Antony Part.

155. Amersham, Finmere and Great Ponton: Len Marsh, David Medd, Edith Moorhouse, Sir William Pile, Fred Pooley. Woodside School, Amersham: Maclure, *op. cit.*, pp. 160–3; *AJ* 1 Aug. 1957, pp. 516–19; BB No. 16, *Development Projects: Junior School, Amersham*, 1958. Finmere: Maclure, *op. cit.*, pp. 164–5; *AJ* 30 June 1960, pp. 1005–16. Finmere and Great Ponton: BB No. 3, *Village Schools*, 1961.

## CHAPTER 6

157. The Brockhouse frame: F. W. L. Heathcote.

158. Mitchell Avenue houses, Coventry: Sir Donald Gibson, F. W. L. Heathcote. The Brockhouse-Gyproc houses are briefly mentioned in *AJ* 7 Oct. 1943, pp. 245–8, but should not be confused with Edric Neel's 'Radiation House' and other experimental types built at Canley in 1940–5. See *AJ* 18 July 1940, p. 61; 25 July 1940, p. 63; 24 April 1941, pp. 273–81; 8 Jan, 1942, pp. 25–9; and *ABN* 16 Nov. 1945, pp. 111–14.

158. BISF houses: F. W. L. Heathcote; R. B. White, *Prefabrication, A History of its Development in Great Britain*, 1965, pp. 178–9.

158. 'For cold-rolled ...': F. W. L. Heathcote.

159. Brockhouse schools at Coventry: Sir Donald Gibson, William Glare, F. W. L. Heathcote; detailed notes kindly provided by William Glare. Henry Parkes School, Canley: *AD*, vol. 20, Oct. 1950, pp. 266–71.

161. 'The City Architect having embarked ...': William Glare. Caludon Castle: William Glare; *AJ* 2 Aug. 1951, p. 131; *Coventry Evening Telegraph*, 28 June 1952.

162. 'The Southport people ...': F. W. L. Heathcote.

162. 'Little more than a steel frame ... its use cannot be justified ...': William Glare, report to MoE on schools systems, Dec. 1950.

162. Belper development: F. W. L. Heathcote, Sir William Pile, Pat Tindale, plus Heathcote's file on 'Early Meetings, 1950–5'; *AJ* 15 Dec. 1955, pp. 797–814, 823–4. Belper not a 'howling success': Pat Tindale.

163. Gibson's move to Notts: Sir Donald Gibson, Dan Lacey. For a profile of Gibson on the eve of his move: *AJ* 20 Jan. 1955, p. 77. For his later views on education: *AJ* 26 June 1968, pp. 1492–5.

164. Notts under Gibson. Full accounts by Lacey, Swain and others appeared in *AJ* 26 Sep. 1957, pp. 465–8 (organization of the architects); 3 Oct. 1957, pp. 514–21 (client-architect relations); 10 Oct. 1957, pp. 557–70 (designing for mining subsidence); and 24 Oct. 1957, pp. 631–6 (development of the 'Notts' system'). For Gibson's own account of technical developments: *RIBAJ*, vol. 65, Dec. 1957, pp. 47–59. For an outsider's view: Stuart Maclure, *Educational Development and School Building*, 1984, pp. 100–4.

164. Notts and the subsidence problem: Sir Donald Gibson, F. W. L. Heathcote, Dan Lacey, Henry Swain. Arups and ACP: Sir Anthony Cox.

164. 'I went to see ...': 'I said, "You've got ..."': Sir Donald Gibson. For one of the Derwent schools, Bingham Secondary Modern by ACP: *ABN* 27 Aug. 1958, pp. 289–92.

165. 'He was a team man ...': Henry Swain.

165. 'I knew about railways ...': Sir Donald Gibson.

165. Technical investigations of subsidence: Henry Swain; *AJ* 10 Oct. 1957, pp. 557–70; *RIBAJ*, vol. 65, Dec. 1957, pp. 47–59. Notts 'contending against a tremendous deadweight ...': R. J. Orchard, memo of June 1956 in F. W. L. Heathcote's file on early Notts development. Wardell's paper: *Transactions of the Institution of Mining Engineers*, vol. 113, 1953–4, pp. 471–82.

166. Details and designing of early CLASP system: Syd Bell, F. W. L. Heathcote, Dan Lacey, Alan Meikle, Henry Swain; BB No. 19, *The Story of CLASP*, 1961, pp. 10–14.

167–8. 'I can't recall ...'; 'we were much influenced ...': Alan Meikle.

168. The system 'never a clear, structural, one-material concept': Syd Bell.

170. Bancroft Lane: Henry Swain; *AJ* 24 Oct. 1957, pp. 637–42.

170. Proof of the subsidence system: Sir Donald Gibson, F. W. L. Heathcote, Henry Swain. Heathcote's paper: *Proceedings of the Institution of Civil Engineers*, vol. 30, Feb. 1965, pp. 347–68, with discussion in vol. 33, March 1966, pp. 492–517. For a later report of the record of CLASP buildings and subsidence: Swain in *AJ* 8 May 1974, pp. 1047–54.

174. The CLASP consortium: Sir Donald Gibson, Dan Lacey, Sir William Pile, Henry Swain; BB No. 19, *The Story of CLASP*, 1961, pp. 14–19; Maclure, *op. cit.*, pp. 104–5. Maclure seems to put too much weight on the role of Lord Hailsham and the MoE in the founding of CLASP. A letter in *AJ* 30 May 1984 refers to the collaboration between Notts, Derbyshire and Coventry which preceded the formal consortium.

175. CLASP in the 1960s: Sir Andrew Derbyshire, F. W. L. Heathcote, John Kay, Hugh Morris, Henry Swain; BB No. 19, *The Story of CLASP*, 1961. The Triennale School at Milan: *AJ* 25 Aug. 1960, pp. 284–9. For CLASP applied (inadequately) to a British 'public school' (St Paul's, Barnes): *AJ* 13 Nov. 1968, pp. 1114–15.

177. 'It was a sin of the first order . . .': Alan Meikle.

177. Research into Site Management: Syd Bell, Alan Meikle, Henry C. Morris, Henry Swain; *AJ* 11 Dec. 1968, pp. 1389–96 and 12 Jan. 1972, pp. 75–96; *Architecture East Midlands*, Jan./Feb. 1977, pp. 17–29.

178. Production aspects of school-building: BB No. 12, *Site Labour Studies in School Building*, 1955; Marian Bowley, *The British Building Industry: Four Studies in Response and Resistance to Change*, 1966, pp. 276–83; University College Environmental Research Group, Building Economics Research Unit, 'Pilot Study on Schools Consortia', 1971.

179–80. 'What we set out to achieve . . .'; 'my picture of the drawing office . . .'; 'what we were not getting . . .': Henry Swain.

180. 'In all my conversations . . .': Alan Meikle.

181. 'We started with no confidence . . .': Henry Swain.

182. 'Alan Willis dictated . . .': Alan Meikle, RSM diary (quoted in *AJ* 12 Jan. 1972, p. 86).

182. 'They are intended for use . . .': Henry Swain in *AJ* 12 Jan. 1972, p. 85.

183. '. . . made *The Sun* and Radio 4': Alan Meikle, RSM diary.

183. 'Success or failure . . .': Swain in *AJ* 12 Jan. 1972, p. 80.

183. 'What RSM has shown . . .': Alan Meikle, RSM diary, concluding comments.

# CHAPTER 7

184. Stirrat Johnson-Marshall's move into private practice: Percy Johnson-Marshall, Maurice Lee, David Medd, Peter Newnham. 'I felt the bottom had dropped out . . .': Pat Tindale.

185. Hunstanton. Denis Clarke Hall's Woodfield Secondary Modern School, the precursor of Hunstanton, is criticized by Peter Newnham in *AA Journal*, vol. 69, Dec. 1953, pp. 129–32. For arguments on Hunstanton: *AJ* 10 Sep. 1953, pp. 323–8, 16 Sep. 1954, pp. 335, 341–52; *Education* 29 Oct. 1954, pp. 89–90; *Times Educational Supplement*, 11 March 1960. For a recent assessment of Hunstanton (now Smithdon High School): *AJ* 23 May 1984, pp. 39–42.

185. 'Architects should walk into . . .': *AJ* 16 Sep. 1954, p. 335.

186. Banham on the 'educational sentimentalists': Reyner Banham, *The New Brutalism*, 1966, pp. 19–20.

186–7. A & B Branch and the LCC: Colin Boyne, Kenneth Campbell, David Medd, Guy Oddie, Henry Swain. 'It's unfortunate because . . .': Kenneth Campbell.

188. Harris College, Preston: Cleeve Barr, Guy Oddie, Pat Tindale. The early BB No. 5, *New Colleges of Further Education*, 1951, was prepared by Barbara Price. 'What went fundamentally wrong . . .': Guy Oddie.

189. 'The biggest conflict . . .': Pat Tindale.

189. 'Their determination . . .': Guy Oddie.

189. Finmere and Great Ponton: David and Mary Medd, Edith Moorhouse. Guy Oddie, Sir William Pile, Pat Tindale; *AJ* 30 June 1960, pp. 1005–16; BB No. 3, *Village Schools*, 1961; Stuart Maclure, *Educational Development and School Building*, 1984, pp. 164–5.

190. Investigation of children's views on their schools: *AJ* 16 Jan. 1963, pp. 150–61.

191. A & B Branch after 1964: Michael Hacker, John Kay, Dan Lacey, David Medd. For Dan Lacey: *AJ* 27 Nov. 1985, p. 24.

192. Performance specifications: Michael Hacker, John Kay, David Medd. For Method's work in this field: Consortium for Method Building, Annual Report, 1973, pp. 3–13.

192. Furniture: David Medd; *AJ* 3 Nov. 1955, pp. 605–8; 12 Jan. 1956, pp. 59–63; 26 Oct. 1966, pp. 1035–40; 9 Aug. 1967, pp. 345–9. See also Medd in *BSI News*, June 1972, pp. 11–12; *Times Educational Supplement*, 23 May 1975. For the Counties Furniture Group: *Official Architecture and Planning*, vol. 29, Sep. 1966, pp. 1335–9; *Counties Furniture Group Newsletter*, 7 Oct. 1972.

194. 'Community schools and colleges' before 1964: Len Marsh, Harry Rée. Continuity with Henry Morris's ideals: Harry Rée, *Educator Extraordinary*, 1973, pp. 112–15; for the intended college of further education by A & B Branch, *ibid.*, pp. 103–5. See also Paul Widlake, 'The Origins of Community Education', paper for Community Education Development Centre, Coventry, 1981.

196. Conversion of secondary moderns into 'community' comprehensives: see e.g. Cambridge conference on 'Building for Education' reported in *AJ* 3 July

1968, pp. 8–13; *AJ* 17 Feb. 1971, pp. 362–7, 422–8; and Eric Pearson and Michael Hacker in *AR* vol. 150, July 1971, pp. 3–6, 23–34.

196. 'Society is no longer prepared . . .': *AR*, vol. 150, July 1971, p. 23.

197. A & B Branch's 'community' projects: Michael Hacker, Dan Lacey, David Medd, Graham Parker. Chaucer School, Ilkeston: *AJ* 6 June 1973, pp. 1355–7; Maclure, *op. cit.*, pp. 186–7. Maiden Erlegh: *AJ* 11 Nov. 1970, pp. 1147–53; BB No. 48, Maiden Erlegh Secondary School, 1973; Maclure, *op. cit.*, pp. 232–5. Abraham Moss Centre: BB No. 49, *The Abraham Moss Centre*, 1973: *AJ* 7 May 1975, pp. 964–7; A & B Paper No. 1, 1978. Victoria Centre, Crewe: BB No. 59, *Victoria Centre Crewe*, 1981.

199. Notts and education: Dan Lacey, Henry Swain. For the situation in 1955–6: *AJ* 3 Oct. 1957, pp. 514–21.

200–1. Tuxford, Retford Ordsall and the contribution of David Barnes: Alan Meikle, Henry Swain. Significance of Arnold Grammar School: Eric Pearson in *AR* 150, July 1971, pp. 3–6; 'to match the social accommodation . . .': *ibid.*, p. 5.

201. The Notts 'joint-use' sports halls: Alan Meikle, Henry Swain. Bingham: *AJ* 18 June 1969, pp. 1645–53. Carlton Cavendish School and Carlton Forum: *AJ* 17 Feb. 1971, pp. 359–70, 24 Feb. 1971, pp. 421–34.

202. Sutton Centre: Alan Meikle, Henry Swain: *AJ* 26 May 1976, p. 1036, 7 Sep. 1977, pp. 439–51; Colin Fletcher, *The Challenges of Community Education: A Biography of Sutton Centre 1970 to 1982*, Department of Adult Education, Nottingham University, 1984.

204. Rise and decline of the consortia: BB No. 54, *The Consortia*, 1976; Maclure, *op. cit.*, pp. 108–19; Barry Russell, *Building Systems, Industrialization and Architecture*, 1981, pp. 483–524. For a thorough assessment of the consortia at their zenith: University College [London] Environmental Research Group, Building Economics Research Unit, 'Pilot Study on Schools Consortia', First Report, Aug. 1971.

206. CLASP 'no better or no worse than other forms of construction with regard to maintenance': Scottish Development Department, Research Group Report No. 1, *Maintenance of CLASP Construction*, 1976, p. 57. For a critical view of the environmental performance of CLASP in the mid 1970s: D. J. Leighton, *A Case Study Evaluation of Environmental Performance in Educational Buildings*, [1976], pp. 87–141 (copy in RIBA Library).

206. Fires in CLASP buildings: Hugh Morris, Guy Oddie, Henry Swain; *AJ* 30 July 1975, pp. 251–2 and 1 Oct. 1975, pp. 673–4; *Building* 1 Aug. 1975, pp. 23–5; *The Surveyor* 11 Feb. 1977, pp. 8–9; Barry Russell, *op. cit.*, pp. 659–65. Later improvements to CLASP in performance and appearance: *AJ* 27 Oct. 1982, pp. 65–9, 10 Nov. 1982, pp. 85–8, 1 May 1985, pp. 63–8. For an assessment of CLASP Mark VI by Barry Russell: *AJ* 16 May 1984, pp. 52–72.

206. Effects of inflation on the consortia: John Kay, Dan Lacey. 'The use of building systems . . .': Colin Ward, *British School Buildings, Designs and Appraisals 1964–1974*, 1976, p. x.

207. MACE: Russell, *op. cit.*, pp. 561–82. See also ACID (GLC Architecture Club Magazine), Summer 1973, pp. 8–13; *Evening Standard* 19 July 1973; *AJ* 10 April 1974, pp. 774–5, 1 May 1974, p. 735, 29 May 1974, pp. 1181–2, 10 July 1974, pp. 101–14 and 24 July 1974, p. 203.

208. A & B Branch in the late 1980s: John Kay. For the most recent official enquiry into and confirmation of the branch's status and value: *Building Design* 31 Jan. 1986, p. 1.

208. 'The Impact Abroad'. I am specially grateful to Guy Oddie for extensive help in drafting this section.

208. The Herts influence abroad. For the views of one Portuguese architect who came to work at Herts and tried to dispense some of its philosophy at home, I am grateful to Vasco de Moura.

210. Ehrenkrantz and SCSD. For British views see Russell, *op. cit.*, pp. 529–49; Michael Hacker in *AJ* 22 Nov. 1967, pp. 1288–90; Building Centre Intelligence Report No. 3, Patrick Hislop and Christopher Walker, *School Community Systems Development*, 1970. See also E. Ehrenkrantz, *The Modular Number Pattern*, 1956. On the Toronto development: Russell, *op. cit.*, pp. 551–9.

210. Anglo-American exchanges: Michael Hacker, David Medd, Peter Newnham, Guy Oddie, Sir Antony Part. Part's American articles appeared in *Architectural Record*, Feb. 1956, pp. 209–17; *Architectural Forum*, Oct. 1956, pp. 133–9; *American School and University*, 1956–7, pp. 71–82. David and Mary Medd's observations of American schools were published as BB No. 18, *Schools in the USA: A Report*, 1961; Michael Hacker's as A & B Branch Design Note No. 7, *USA Visit*, 1970.

212. Exporting CLASP: Henry C. Morris, Henry Swain. For the Venezuela project: David Medd, Henry C. Morris; *Boletin Bimestral de la Fundación de Edificaciones y Dotaciones Educativas* (FEDE), No. 6, Sep.–Oct. 1982.

213. British schools and Western Europe: David Medd, Guy Oddie. See especially two OECD publications principally by Oddie: *School Buildings and their Effective Use*, 1966, and *Industrialized Building for Schools*, 1971.

## CHAPTER 8

For discussions and material on the University of York, I am grateful to Sir Andrew Derbyshire, Lord James of Rusholme, Maurice Lee, Patrick Nuttgens and John West-Taylor. Early architectural assessments appear in *AJ* 13 June 1962, pp. 1327–36, and 15 Dec. 1965, pp. 1435–58.

214. For the background to York's foundation: J. S. Purvis, *Towards a University*, n.d.; Lord James of Rusholme, *The Start of a New University*, paper given to Manchester Statistical Society, 9 Feb. 1966.
214. Sussex: David Daiches, *The Idea of a New University*, 1964, esp. pp. 201–15 (essay by Sir Basil Spence).
215. 'I had great fun . . .': John West-Taylor. Nuttgens's hope for the job: Patrick Nuttgens.
216. 'Nobody had talked . . .': Sir Andrew Derbyshire.
217. Stirrat Johnson-Marshall and University College, Oxford: Sir Andrew Derbyshire, Hugh Morris.
217. 'In the style of the Cambridge backs . . .': Sir Andrew Derbyshire. Collegiate structure: Lord James. Influence of Geddes: Sir Andrew Derbyshire. Influence of Henry Morris: John West-Taylor.
218. York Development Plan. This was published as *University of York Development Plan 1962–1972*, 1962.
218. CLASP at York: Sir Andrew Derbyshire, F. W. L. Heathcote, Lord James, Patrick Nuttgens, Henry Swain, John West-Taylor. 'We talked to the . . .': Sir Andrew Derbyshire.
219. Johnson-Marshall and Parkes on university costs: in the important *AR* number on universities, vol. 134, Oct. 1963, pp. 287–8.
219. 'Stirrat insisted . . .': Sir Andrew Derbyshire. 'We were by no means stampeded . . .': John West-Taylor.
221. '. . . a common love of Siena Cathedral': Lord James. 'We went gradually down . . .': Sir Andrew Derbyshire.
221. For a socio-architectural review of York by its architects, with discussion of maintenance etc.: Robert Matthew, Johnson-Marshall and Partners, 'Architectural Implications of the York Campus Survey', paper given by Sir Andrew Derbyshire at the RIBA Conference at York, 1984.
221. CLASP Joint Development Programme at Bath: Sir Andrew Derbyshire, John Kay, Hugh Morris.
221. 'Of the relationship between architect and client . . .': extract from a memoir by Lord James for a forthcoming publication on the history and development of York. I am grateful for permission to use this.

## CHAPTER 9

As this chapter is argumentative in tenor rather than historical, references are confined to important points of information and to quotations.

226. Schools and Housing. This comparative section draws deeply upon discussion with those involved in the post-war design of both housing and schools, especially Cleeve Barr, Kenneth Campbell and Oliver Cox. The books I have found of most value are Alison Ravetz, *Rebuilding Cities*, 1980, and P. J. Dunleavy, *The Politics of Mass Housing*, 1981. A fine early essay including comparisons between what had been done in schools and housing is Paul Thompson, *Architecture: Art or Social Service*, Young Fabian pamphlet, 1963.
229. Development groups. Basic information from Elizabeth Layton, *Building by Local Authorities*, 1961, especially Chs. 2 and 9. For the fate of the MHLG's Development Group: Cleeve Barr, Oliver Cox, Pat Tindale.

234. 'A building which poses . . .': A. R. N. Roberts, *W. R. Lethaby*, 1957, p. 80.
234. 'It was necessary to strike the eye . . .': Charles Booth, *Life and Labour of the People in London*, 1st edn., 1889–91, Series 1, p. 130, quoted in T. S. and M. B. Simey, *Charles Booth, Social Scientist*, 1960, p. 192.
234. 'We are forced to choose . . .': see Appendix II.

## APPENDIX I

Much of this account of Stirrat Johnson-Marshall depends on discussion with his relatives, friends and acquaintance. I am very grateful to Joan and Percy Johnson-Marshall for their recollections and their notes on a first draft. The fullest written assessments are: *Stirrat Johnson-Marshall, Five Commemorative Speeches given at the Royal Society of Arts, 24 March 1982* (privately printed); a memoir by David Medd in *Performance*, April/May 1982, pp. 67–70; and unpublished recollections by Percy Johnson-Marshall, Dec. 1981 (copy deposited in RIBA Library biographical files).

239. 'The most influential . . .': *AJ* 23/30 Dec. 1981, p. 1224.
240–1. 'I have memories . . .'; 'it was during this period . . .': Percy Johnson-Marshall, unpublished recollections, *ut supra*.
241. 'He was always interested . . .': Cleeve Barr.
241. 'A plump gentleman . . .': Percy Johnson-Marshall, *ut supra*.
241. Liverpool: Percy Johnson-Marshall, *ibid.*; Sir Donald Gibson; letters from F. W. B. Charles to Gill Collymore, May 1983. Stirrat Johnson-Marshall's student drawings and some other material are now at the RIBA Drawings Collection.
243. Willesden: Sir Alan Harris; Percy Johnson-Marshall. Electricity showrooms: *ABN* 29 Oct. 1937, pp. 139–41. 'We argued our way . . .': Percy Johnson-Marshall. 'At Willesden they were . . .': Sir Alan Harris.
243. Isle of Ely: Sir Donald Gibson, Percy Johnson-Marshall. 'Almost a third brother . . .': Percy Johnson-Marshall, recollections, *ut supra*.
244. Singapore. This brief account is based on letters and cuttings kindly lent by Lady Johnson-Marshall.
244. India: Percy Johnson-Marshall.
244. Camouflage: David Medd, memoir in *Performance, ut supra*; recollections written by James Gardner for Colin Boyne, 1983.
244. Application for Huddersfield: among Stirrat Johnson-Marshall's few remaining papers, with details of his career to 1945.
245. Struggle for recognition of public architects: Colin Boyne, Percy Johnson-Marshall, Henry Swain. *AJ* articles: 14 Feb. 1952, pp. 206–8; 28 Feb. 1952, pp. 269–72; 13 March 1952, pp. 327–9; 15 May 1952, pp. 597–600; 14 Aug. 1952, pp. 187–9; 9 Oct. 1952, pp. 428–9; 23 Oct, 1952, pp. 488–9; 18 Dec. 1952, pp. 724–5; 1 Jan. 1953, pp. 7–11; 8 Jan. 1953, pp. 37–8. Chain Gang 'almost rudderless without him': Colin Boyne.
246. Sir Robert Matthew. An informative account of Matthew's career is contained in the typescript of a lecture given by John Richards of RMJM at Edinburgh, 15 June 1984. I am grateful to John Richards and Hugh Morris for a sight of this. For an excellent obituary by Guy Oddie: *AR* vol. 158, July 1975, p. 54. Matthew's view of relations with Stirrat Johnson-Marshall: Lady Lorna Matthew, Patrick Nuttgens.
247. RMJM: Sir Andrew Derbyshire, Maurice Lee, Hugh Morris, Peter Newnham, Patrick Nuttgens.
247. Last years: Sir Andrew Derbyshire, Lady Johnson-Marshall, Percy Johnson-Marshall, Hugh Morris.
248. 'He would come in and say . . .': James Nisbet. 'He had the ability . . .': Dan Lacey.
249. Interview of 1971; 'I suppose a Cotswold village . . .': Hugh Morris.
249. 'We could all chip splinters . . .': Colin Boyne.

# PHOTOGRAPHIC ACKNOWLEDGEMENTS

Alan Adams 4.15, 6.22, Plates XIII, XIV; Architects Co-Partnership 6.12; Architectural Press Frontispiece, 1.2, 2.6–7, 2.10–11, 3.1–4, 3.6–9, 3.13, 3.16–18, 4.1, 4.5, 4.9, 4.12–13, 4.15, 4.22–23, 4.26–27, 4.30–32, 4.34, 4.37–39, 4.42–46, 5.1, 5.4–5, 5.14, 5.16, 5.21, 5.24–27, 5.29, 5.35, 6.10–11, 6.13–15, 6.23, 6.25–26, 7.1–2, 7.5, 7.7, 7.16, 7.20–21, 7.24–25, 7.27, 8.1, 8.7, 9.1, 10.1–2, 10.7; Consortium for Method Building 7.22–23; Sir Anthony Cox 1.3; Oliver Cox 4.18; Sir Andrew Derbyshire 8.4–6; Department of Education and Science 3.14–15, 3.20, 4.3–4, 4.10–11, 4.14–16, 4.20, 4.24, 4.29, 4.36, 5.2–4, 5.5, 5.7–8, 5.10–13, 5.15, 5.17–19, 5.20–22, 5.32–34, 5.36–7, 6.5, 6.9, 6.16, 6.23, 7.3–4, 7.6, 7.10,. 7.13, 7.26, 8.2–3; William Glare 6.6; Birkin Haward 2.1, 2.2; F. W. L. Heathcote 6.1–4, 6.7; Hertfordshire County Council 4.8, 4.19, 4.21, 4.28, 4.40; Executors of Gerald Holtom Plates VI, VII, VIII; Lady Johnson-Marshall 1.5, 2.3, 2.5, 2.8–9, 10.3–6; Maurice Lee 5.28, 5.30; David and Mary Medd 2.4, 3.11–12, 4.2, 4.33, 7.8–9, Plates II, III, IX, X; National Portrait Gallery 1.6; Nottinghamshire County Council 6.17–18, 6.20–21, 6.24, 7.14, 7.18; Pat Tindale 6.8

# INDEX